African Capitalists
in African
Development

African Capitalists in African Development

edited by
Bruce J. Berman
Colin Leys

Lynne Rienner Publishers • Boulder & London

Published in the United States of America in 1994 by
Lynne Rienner Publishers, Inc.
1800 30th Street, Boulder, Colorado 80301

and in the United Kingdom by
Lynne Rienner Publishers, Inc.
3 Henrietta Street, Covent Garden, London WC2E 8LU

Library of Congress Cataloging-in-Publication Data
African capitalists in African development / edited by Bruce J. Berman
    and Colin Leys.
    Includes bibliographical references and index.
    ISBN 1-55587-417-7 (alk. paper)
    1. Capitalism—Africa. 2. Entrepreneurship—Africa. 3. Africa—
Economic policy. 4. Capitalists and financiers—Africa.
I. Berman, Bruce (Bruce J.) II. Leys, Colin.
HC800.A5643   1993
338'.04'096—dc20   93-28585
                                                          CIP

British Cataloguing in Publication Data
A Cataloguing in Publication record for this book
is available from the British Library.

Printed and bound in the United States of America

     The paper used in this publication meets the requirements
 ∞   of the American National Standard for Permanence of
     Paper for Printed Library Materials Z39.48-1984.

Contents

Contents

Preface

This book grew out of a workshop on African bourgeoisies held at Queen's University in April 1991. Three of the contributors—David Himbara, Sheila Nicholas, and John Rapley—had just completed or nearly completed doctoral dissertations at Queen's on the origins and development of the domestic capitalist classes in Kenya, Zimbabwe, and Côte d'Ivoire, respectively, and the opportunity presented itself to bring together a number of other scholars working in the same field to compare notes and discuss directions for future work. We are extremely grateful to all those who attended and made the discussions so stimulating, and not least to a group of scholars whose work is not represented here but who made particularly valuable contributions: Bonnie Campbell, Dickson Eyoh, Linda Freeman, Tom Forrest, Paul Kennedy, and Arthur Syahuka Muhindo.

We would also like to express our appreciation for the financial support given to the workshop by the School of Graduate Studies and Research, the Faculty of Arts and Science, and the Graduate Student Society of Queen's University; and for the unfailingly efficient and sympathetic help provided by Mrs. Pauline Bettney and Mrs. Bernice Gallagher. Finally, we are grateful to Lynne Rienner for her encouragement and to an anonymous reader for helpful criticisms and suggestions.

Bruce J. Berman
Colin Leys
Kingston, Ontario

1

Introduction

Colin Leys & Bruce J. Berman

What is certain is that, as a result partly of prejudice and partly of socialist dogma, Africa's capitalists have not yet been taken seriously enough. (John Iliffe, *The Emergence of African Capitalism* [London: Macmillan, 1983], p. 87.)

The aim of this book is to report some recent research on capitalist classes in relation to the development prospects of African countries. The case for doing so is that, although virtually the entire subcontinent is, for the time being at least, committed to a capitalist path of development—all the erstwhile "socialist" regimes (except Angola, thanks to its oil) having accepted capitalist-oriented structural adjustment programs by the end of the 1980s—the literature on the class most central to capitalist accumulation is remarkably small.

There is an extensive earlier literature on African *entrepreneurship*, mainly produced by economists and sociologists interested in the emergence of Africans with the skills and attitudes appropriate to doing business.[1] In that literature, however, African entrepreneurs are almost always considered as individuals, not as collective actors, as classes. The question that prompted most of the work was, from where do African businessmen [sic] come,[2] and how far can they transcend the limitations of their origins and compete effectively with non-African businesses.

Then in the 1970s came the debate about dependency. This prompted a number of studies that did look at African capitalist classes, with a view to seeing if they were as "comprador," i.e., as dependent on foreign capital, as dependency theory maintained. This work substantially broadened the scope of the enquiry and heightened its theoretical relevance. African capitalists were considered as forming collectivities, whose strength—political as well as economic—was compared with that of foreign capital, and the result laid the foundations for all subsequent enquiry. The main thrust of this work was excellently summed up in Paul Lubeck's 1987 collection *The African Bourgeoisie: Capitalist Development in Nigeria,*

Kenya, and the Ivory Coast, a volume that in several ways served as a point of departure for the work reported in this book.[3]

The dependency-inspired literature suffered from some serious limitations, however. Its authors tended to be protagonists of one side or the other in the dependency debate. The *dependentistas* (the majority) sought to show that African capitalists as a class were weak, economically and politically—economically relative to foreign capital, and politically relative to other social forces in their respective countries—for instance, the peasant masses, the parasitic bureaucracy, the urban petty bourgeoisie, or ethnic or religious forces. The anti-*dependentistas*, in contrast, sought to show that while African capitalist classes were relatively weak, they had grown significantly and relatively fast from very small beginnings and could be expected to become stronger. The problem is that both could be right, while some of the most critical questions about the impact of African capitalists on African development remain unasked.

For instance, are "domestic," "internal," or "indigenous" capitalist classes necessary for development, and if so, in what specific ways? Is there any reason why the capital accumulation process should not be organized and led by foreign capital, for example, or by some substitute agency inside the country such as a state bureaucracy (as in Meiji Japan), or by the military (as in some Latin American countries in the era of "bureaucratic authoritarianism"), or even perhaps by a religious order (as in postrevolutionary Iran)?[4] Or are there crucial tasks that in general only an internal capitalist class can and must perform?

Both sides in the dependency-inspired literature tended to assume that if there was no strong local capitalist class there could be no "national" capitalist development and, conversely, that if such a class existed, there would be. But neither assumption is self-evidently true. Historical experience elsewhere suggests a much more complex picture. In a few well-known instances (including Canada), foreign capital has predominated throughout a period of highly successful national capitalist development, while in others (including, most notoriously, Britain) the existence of a large and once seemingly competent domestic capitalist class has not ensured lasting success. The determinants of sustained capitalist development are clearly numerous and the interactions between them far from simple. Given this, we still need to ask in what specific ways a local capital-accumulating class *matters*.

Time and bitter experience have also disposed of the underlying assumption shared by both sides of the dependency debate in Africa, namely that development was possible for most African countries if their domestic or internal or indigenous bourgeoisies were up to the job. Today it is hard to feel confident that many African countries have such a prospect, however capable their internal capitalist classes may be. As Leys argues in the conclusion to Chapter 2, the problem of raising the productivity of labor on the land and of absorbing the labor force released from agriculture if such productivity gains are achieved now seems so daunting that it requires great faith in the creative powers of both capitalists and capitalistically oriented political leaders to believe that it can be solved.

In looking at the role of African capitalists today, therefore, we need to keep this context in mind. But given that the only kind of development that appears immediately practicable is capitalist development—within the framework of world markets and, at least up till now, within the constraints of IMF/World Bank regulation of African macroeconomic policy—the key questions have still to be asked: *What are the specific problems that must be solved for such development to take place? What are the functions that local capitalists are called on to perform? And what are the most significant characteristics of African capitalist classes for achieving whatever can be achieved within this framework?*

Our aim in bringing together this collection was, then, to try to go beyond the dependency-inspired literature in search of answers to these questions, noting the wide variations produced by history in the size and characteristics of Africa's capitalist classes and emphasizing the political as much as the economic aspects of their developmental role. Our central theme is that there are functions that internal capitalist classes must perform for capitalist development to occur and that the characteristics of each internal capitalist class, and the conditions in which it operates, determine how well or badly these functions are performed. This does not mean that the approach is "functionalist" in the usual sense of that word. It means studying the internal capitalist classes of Africa as determinants of the kind of development that has occurred (or failed to occur) in particular countries. To put it another way, capitalist classes in Africa are considered here as an "explanans" as much as an "explanandum": we are interested in studying "the capacities of a given class to act in relation to others, and the forms of organisation and practice thereby developed."[5]

The long-term themes outlined above are the concern of the first part of the book, comprising chapters 2–6.

In Chapter 2, Colin Leys considers some of the theoretical and conceptual issues that are posed by this way of looking at African capitalists. To a surprising degree, few clear guidelines emerge from the general theoretical and comparative literature. However, keeping the core ideas of Marx and Weber in view, the chapter argues that recent work, notably by Paul Kennedy and John Iliffe, points the way to a more open and fertile approach. In particular, Leys argues that it is the *political* as much as—or perhaps even more than—the technical-economic capacity of a capitalist class that is crucial for capitalist development, and that this should be an important field of future political research in Africa. The chapter suggests some specific questions for further research; it concludes, however, on a note of severe caution, by drawing attention to the seemingly adverse international context that any capitalist development in Africa today confronts. If African countries are to develop under capitalism, the argument goes, it is imperative to pose the right questions about its capitalist classes. A sober look at the conditions under which they have to operate today, however, must raise serious doubts about whether any such hope is realistic for many if not most African countries.

Chapters 3–6 present case studies of the evolution of the capitalist classes in three African countries: Côte d'Ivoire, Kenya, and Zimbabwe. In Chapter 3, John Rapley traces the development of the Ivoirien bourgeoisie from its origins in a class of African planters to its present condition as an increasingly sophisticated class of industrial capitalists, firmly grounded, both socially and politically, in a dominant position in Ivoirien society and capable of holding its own in dealing with foreign capital and of effectively implementing imported technology. Rapley treats the bourgeoisie as a matter of families and firms, rather than individual entrepreneurs, and analyzes their social and family ties as well as their economic ties and the network of voluntary business and professional associations through which class cohesion and class consciousness are developed. Finally, he traces the extensive presence of Ivoirien capitalists in public office at both the national and the municipal level. In Rapley's account, this is perhaps the only African class of capitalists who have so far achieved a position from which they are able both to conceive cooptative reforms and to press a recalcitrant state to accept them.

In Chapter 4, David Himbara examines the development of the capitalist class in Kenya, another country often seen as a pacemaker of indigenous capitalist development in Africa. Himbara, however, presents data that radically challenge two prevalent myths about Kenyan development—first, that Kenya's relatively impressive growth record is due in large part to having an exceptionally well-rooted and effective indigenous African bourgeoisie and, second, that it is due also in large part to having inherited an exceptionally efficient developmental state that was originally built up to serve the Kenyan settler economy. As to the first, Himbara argues that while it is true that Kenya has had an exceptionally effective indigenous capitalist class, it is Kenya's Indian community who compose it, not Kenya's African capitalists. As to the second, he suggests that the inherited developmental state was rapidly dismantled and rendered inefficient and corrupt and has been by and large inimical to capital accumulation, and not least to capital accumulation by the most productive fraction of the indigenous bourgeoisie, the Kenyan Indians.

Himbara's thesis is even more interesting when read together with chapters 5 and 6, on another former settler economy, Zimbabwe. In Chapter 5, Sheila Nicholas shows how the settlers in the former Southern Rhodesia used their control over the state to exclude Africans from virtually all avenues of capital accumulation, whether in agriculture, services,

or manufacturing, almost until the day when the country became the independent state of Zimbabwe in 1980. Yet in spite of this massive state bias
in favor of white capital, and the terrible ravages of the armed liberation
struggle in the 1970s, Nicholas shows that Zimbabweans succeeded in accumulating capital in farming, in trade, and especially in transport, so that
they were poised to move into the mainstream of the economy at independence. For the first decade of independence, however, the new regime
looked askance at its would-be domestic black bourgeoisie, professing as
it did socialist values and goals. It was not until the growing economic crisis of the later 1980s led to acute balance of payments problems and massively rising unemployment, and thus forced a reluctant change of economic policy, that the black capitalists' demands for a state policy directed
toward their interests began to be seriously entertained.

The Zimbabwean state's ambivalent relationship toward black capitalists is further illuminated by Tom Ostergaard's analysis of the Zimbabwean textile and clothing sectors in Chapter 6. Here the apparent paradox
is that the postindependence regime favored local white capital, which had
been closely allied with the racist settler state, even more than multinational capital. Ostergaard shows how this remarkable bias, in face of all
the apparent political and ideological logic of the new governing party's
history, was nonetheless rational, in the sense that the white domestic capitalist class, while being technically quite efficient, was more dependent
on the regime politically than either foreign capital or a local black capitalist class was likely to be.

While these brief summaries of the arguments of Himbara, Nicholas,
and Ostergaard inevitably do some injustice to the balanced treatments
they offer in the chapters themselves, they do bring out a central point that
is discussed more fully in Chapter 2, namely the historically pivotal role of
"outsiders." At a certain stage, outsiders can be key initiators of the accumulation process by virtue of that status, while at another they can become
politically vulnerable and even potentially an obstacle to the continuation
of that process, if there is no way either to incorporate them into the indigenous society or to secure the transfer of their capital and know-how
to others who are not seen as outsiders. It is also noteworthy that when the
outsiders are descended from immigrant groups from outside Africa (e.g.,
from Europe, the Levant, Arabia, or Asia), the academic analysis of indigenous capitalism has often been vitiated—as Himbara especially points
out in relation to Kenya—by uncritically adopting the racial labels applied
to them in real life, however much these labels reflect the racist behavior
of these same outsiders under colonialism. They have too often been
treated as mere residues of colonial rule, to be ignored and eventually dis-
pensed with, instead of being seen as long-settled nationals (with highly
attenuated links to the countries from which their forebears came and complex ties with the local capitalists of African descent) whose successful

political integration into a genuinely national capitalist class holds the key to further capitalist advance, at least in the medium run.

The last chapter in this sequence, Chapter 7 by Deborah Brautigam, raises a question of considerable interest for the fate of African capitalism, namely, whether the continent's numerous mini-manufacturing, mostly artisanal, firms represent an early, relatively "archaic" or "primitive" form of capital accumulation destined to disappear in face of competition from larger, more sophisticated companies; or whether they are capable of spearheading a new kind of industrialization process, now widely perceived as the key to dramatic growth in such dramatic success stories as Japan, Taiwan, and Italy. For Brautigam, who compares the evidence from these countries with the data on the small-firm auto parts industry collected by Tom Forrest in Nnewi, Nigeria, this is very much an open question, which further research must tackle. If, as she suggests, such research discloses significant centers and networks of vigorous manufacturing minicapitals in other African countries, the possibility of somewhat different scenarios of potential African capitalist development from those hitherto envisaged will at least need to be contemplated.

In the next three chapters (chapters 8–10), the focus shifts from the long term to the short term, each looking at a particular aspect of the impact on Africa's capitalist classes of the continent's current economic, political, and social crisis.

In Chapter 8, Catherine Boone, using the analytic framework developed by rational choice theory, shows how the logic of political stabilization in Senegal—which in its most general features operates in so many other African countries as well—has systematically blocked every initiative on the part of the Senegalese capitalist class to open up new fields of accumulation not dependent on politically managed state monopolies. Eventually this has resulted in a comprehensive crisis of the productive economy, a crisis from which no obviously productive exit route appears to exist. Whether or not the capitalist class, or some segment of it, has the will and gains enough political power to break out of the stranglehold of the old monopolistic structure and begin a significant new process of capital accumulation—and whether the material and technical basis for such a project any longer exists in Senegal—remains, in Boone's view, radically uncertain.

In Chapter 9, Janet MacGaffey examines the "second economy" in Zaire, which now accounts for an increasingly significant proportion—in some parts of Africa, perhaps by now the largest proportion—of the "real economy."[6] This sector or sphere of economic life, outside the reach of the state and largely illegal, depends for its stability and success on personal ties of kinship, friendship, and mutual obligation. This has significant costs, severely limiting the possibilities of rationally sharing services and infrastructure, including even such basic things as water, power supplies, and roads, and driving capitalists to resort to a multitude of devious, complex, and expensive means in order to carry on their businesses. Yet, Mac-Gaffey argues, more and more people have found ways of surviving by such means, which at least have the advantage of not being liable to the arbitrary and often fatally destructive depredations of the corrupt and rapacious "neopatrimonial" state. From this perspective, can we see Africa's second economies as really being its *first* truly competitive, free-market capitalist economies, the seedbeds of a new, hardy indigenous stock of capitalism sprouting in the wastelands left by the failed postcolonial state? Or are these second economy forms of capitalism really pathological forms, burdened with all sorts of crippling, politically imposed costs and doomed to be confined within the limits of the ethnic, familial, religious, and other boundaries set by their basic dependence on personal relations? And are they, moreover, also doomed to be destroyed by the predations of the state if ever they achieve sufficient sophistication to operate on an internationally competitive scale, thereby becoming visible and vulnerable? Whatever one's tentative response to these questions, MacGaffey's analysis makes it clear that the study of African capitalism cannot now proceed further without coming to terms with the scale, complexity, and vitality of the continent's second economies.

In Chapter 10, Paul Lubeck and Michael Watts examine the impact of structural adjustment—the World Bank's response to the African crisis, which has been imposed in almost all African economies at some time or other since 1980—on the Nigerian capitalist class.[7] In Nigeria, the logic of politics demands that the northern political class, which preponderates in the state apparatus, must compensate for its economic and educational weakness (relative to the south) by means of an extensive state economic sector that it effectively controls and exploits. Lubeck and Watts show, however, that the price of this logic—the almost unimaginable scale of corruption and inefficiency in most of the state economic and parastatal sectors—has been such as to drain away the developmental potential of Nigeria's huge oil and gas resources. It is true that handling these resources would have taxed the capacities of any domestic capitalist class, however mature and technically advanced, whereas Nigeria's was still very youthful (by world standards) and often energetic rather than accomplished. But the fundamental problem was the political division already mentioned, one that structural adjustment exacerbated by calling for a drastic reduction of the state's economic role. As a result, the "alliance of oil and maize"—i.e., a political alliance between the state-dominated petroleum and gas sector and the private large-farm sector, which Lubeck and Watts see as essential to the formation of a national capitalist class—remains far from realization.

In the final chapter, Bruce Berman steps away from the standpoint of most of the previous chapters and considers how far the evidence supports the idea that capitalism, at least in the forms in which we have hitherto known it, can really be expected to establish itself in Africa—a question that includes some important subsidiary questions about the likely character and role of African capitalist classes, their relation to the state, and their relation to culture and technology.

If there is a single generalization that emerges from this book, it must be that the development of capitalism requires not only competent capitalists but also a capable enabling state, and the difficulties of capitalist development in Africa are inseparable from the acute crisis of the African state. This is not, as neoliberal theory would have it, because the African state "interferes" with markets and money supply and does not permit capital to "do its thing." This line of thought is based on an ahistorical fantasy that capital is a natural growth, whereas states are unnatural constructs that threaten the development of capitalism unless contained within the strictest bounds; in reality, the state has been essential to every significant historical advance by capital. The problem in Africa, rather, is that the state's involvement with capitalism has so often been both destructive and incompetent. On the one hand, African states have steadily sunk into a parasitic corruption of staggering proportions; on the other hand, they have lost or never developed the capacity to provide capital with the myriad of complementary services it needs in order to develop—from efficient judicial administration and cheap credit to technical services and reliable information.

The failure of the African state has been no less significant in the sphere of culture and technology. A number of the other chapters touch on this sphere: the extent to which African capitalists have proved capable of not simply accumulating capital but also of transforming the means of production by assimilating and adapting imported technology—itself a cultural question—and of securing the development and diffusion of instrumental rationality in areas other than production itself, and so facilitating further accumulation while at the same time legitimating it. Speaking generally, African capitalists have not been equal to this task, whether in seeing the need for it or in wielding sufficient influence in the state to get it undertaken.

Berman returns to these themes from a different angle. Instead of asking how these problems are to be overcome, he considers the possibility that capitalism in its Western form may not be reproducible in Africa and that continuing efforts to reproduce it will only continue to be the source of social decay, economic crisis, and political violence.

Most Westerners have difficulty entertaining this possibility, Berman argues, because of the dominance of what he calls the "Western paradigm of modernity," a stereotypical abstraction of the principal features of the secular industrial nation-state in the West. This paradigm forms the underlying basis for modernization, dependency, and Marxist theories of development alike. All of these approaches have sought universal "laws" that would identify the necessary conditions for success in projects of modernization and national development throughout the world. If, however, the paradigm of modernity is not in fact reproducible in Africa, then, Berman argues, we should be prepared to revise what we consider development to be and who might be its agents. In particular, we must conceive of cultural pluralism as an essential premise of any alternative conception of development and shift our vision of indigenous cultures from one that sees them as obstacles to development to one that sees them as essential sites and objects of development.

From this radical change of approach flow a number of related conclusions, Berman argues. First, Western technology and the structural and cultural context in which it was developed cannot be transferred and applied without modification in Africa, but must be incorporated through an indigenous process of technical innovation and choice. Second, the key agents of this process, Africa's indigenous innovators and entrepreneurs, are likely to be found within microenterprises of the informal or second economy and the growing "surplus" population marginalized by efforts to reproduce Western capitalism. Third, this very different class of African capitalists cannot grow without the strategic and active support of the state, support that existing African states cannot provide. Fourth, alternative development in Africa depends upon the possibility of making new social choices, a possibility that in turn requires reforms of existing political institutions. And fifth, alternative development in Africa ultimately depends upon reforms in the world economy and within advanced capitalist states, which must themselves begin to abandon the increasingly unviable model of development implied by the paradigm of modernity.

At first sight such a departure from established ideas may appear as utopian, reminiscent of calls for a "new international economic order" and similar idealist visions of the 1970s and 1980s. However, as writers like Stephen Marglin and Björn Hettne have recently pointed out, mainstream development theorists have used their institutional power to marginalize alternative conceptions of development and dismiss them as unscientific and impractical, while sustaining efforts to reproduce the paradigm of modernity in the face of persistent failure in country after country.[8] And their critics—both *dependentistas* and Marxists—have been so preoccupied with what divides them from the mainstream that the similarity of their underlying assumptions, and their increasing implausibility, has rarely been noticed or subjected to effective criticism. Thus, the crisis of development is not only a crisis of capitalism and the state, it is also a crisis of development theory, and Berman is not so much appealing for change as underlining the seriousness of this latter crisis and seeking to make our thinking more receptive to whatever new lines of development may be evolving out of the current impasse.

Notes

1. The leading texts include Polly Hill, *The Migrant Cocoa Farmers of Southern Ghana: A Study in Rural Capitalism* (Cambridge: Cambridge University Press, 1963); Peter Marris and Anthony Somerset, *African Businessmen: A Study of Entrepreneurship and Development in Kenya* (London: Routledge and Kegan Paul, 1971); E. Wayne Nafziger, *African Capitalism: A Case Study in Nigerian Entrepreneurship* (Stanford: Hoover Institution Press, 1977); Sayre P. Schatz, *Nigerian Capitalism* (Berkeley: University of California Press, 1977); Anthony A. Beveridge and Anthony Oberschall, *African Businessmen and Development in Zambia* (Princeton: Princeton University Press, 1979); Catherine Coquéry-Vidrovitch and Alain Forest, eds., *Actes du colloque entreprises et entrepreneurs en Afrique, XIXe et XXe siecles* (Paris: Editions l'Harmattan, 1983); Keith Marsden, *African Entrepreneurs: Pioneers of Development*, International Finance Corporation Discussion Paper No. 009 (Washington, D.C.: World Bank, 1990). Of course, the later texts in this literature tend to include some of the concerns of the literature on capitalist classes, although the general distinction between the two remains clear enough.

2. The sexist bias of this literature is especially obvious in light of the fact that so much retail (and wholesale) trade in Africa is handled by women. A recent study in Ghana, for example, reports that up to 85 percent of the 1.5 million members of the Ghana Union of Traders were women, and that 75–85 percent of those involved in international trade were also women (George K. Amponsem, "Peddlers or Queens? Analysis into the Pattern of Informal Cross-National Trade and Its Socio-economic Significance in Ghana," unpublished M.A. research paper, Institute of Social Studies, The Hague, Netherlands, October 1992).

3. Lubeck's volume was also published by Lynne Rienner Publishers. For references to the wider literature on African capitalist classes inspired by the dependency debate, see Chapter 2.

4. This kind of "substitutionism" has been taken up at different times by authors on both the right and left: e.g., on the one hand, the early literature on the military in underdeveloped countries and, on the other, the Russian Bolsheviks and their successors.

5. Goran Therborn, "Why Some Classes Are More Successful Than Others," *New Left Review* 138 (1983), p. 38.

6. Elsewhere MacGaffey reports estimates of the size of the second, unreported and substantially illegal, economy as being between 66.6 percent and over 100 percent of the reported GDP in Uganda, a third of reported GDP in Morocco, and at least 30 percent of economic activity in Tanzania (Janet MacGaffey et al., *The Real Economy of Zaire: The Contribution of Smuggling and Other Unofficial Activities to the National Wealth of an African Country* [London and Philadelphia: James Currey and University of Pennsylvania Press, 1992]). Elsewhere indirect evidence suggests that the proportion of total economic activity that takes place in the second economy is at least as high as in these cases. See also Janet MacGaffey with Gertrud Windsperger, "The Endogenous Economy," background paper for *The Long Term Perspectives Study of Sub-Saharan Africa*, Vol. 3, *Institutional and Sociopolitical Issues* (Washington, D.C.: World Bank, 1990).

7. See Table I in J. Barry Riddell, "Things Fall Apart Again: Structural Adjustment Programmes in Sub-Saharan Africa," *Journal of Modern African Studies* 30, no. 1, p. 56.

8. Stephen Marglin, "Towards the Decolonization of the Mind," in Frederique Apffel Marglin and Stephen A. Marglin, eds., *Dominating Knowledge: Development, Culture and Resistance* (Oxford: Clarendon Press, 1990); Björn Hettne, *Development Theory and the Three Worlds* (London: Longman, 1990).

2

African Capitalists and Development: Theoretical Questions

Colin Leys

However development is defined, it must involve the accumulation of capital. Only out of the surplus saved from past productive effort can more of the value of development—more health or education, or more leisure, or more output—be obtained that would not otherwise be obtainable.[1] In any developing society, therefore, someone must ensure that production is organized so as to yield the necessary surplus, and see also that this surplus is set aside from immediate consumption and invested appropriately. In capitalist societies this is done by capitalists and their managers, supported, more or less directly, by the state. The modern multinational corporation (MNC) is clearly the most highly refined and potent agency of capital accumulation the world has ever seen, but even in their "home" countries, such as the United States or Japan, the tasks of accumulation are not performed by them alone; and in most underdeveloped countries, MNCs typically operate only in a limited number of sectors, such as soft drinks, beer, and oil distribution, and perhaps construction or mining. So for capitalist development to occur, there must also be local, domestic, internal, "national" (and, perhaps, "indigenous") capitalists; and these vary greatly in their individual and collective capacities—the scale of the capital they dispose of, the technical and organizational skills they command, the social cohesiveness they exhibit, the political power they wield, the ideological influence they enjoy, and so on. In the absence of any practicable alternative to capitalist development, therefore, it becomes very important to understand what determines the relative strengths and weaknesses of each underdeveloped country's internal or domestic capitalist class.

Moreover, as soon as one looks at capitalists in terms of their overall role in development, it is their political as much as their economic and technical capacity that seems important; in other words, it is as *social classes*, acting more or less consciously in their collective interest vis-à-vis other social classes, that they enter decisively into history and critically

11

affect the prospects for their countries' development. As social classes, however, African capitalists have not been extensively studied.

There are several possible reasons for this. In the first place, fully formed African capitalist classes have been the exception rather than the rule. The formation of a politically influential and productive capitalist class, with a solid and mature bourgeois culture to support and focus its economic and political projects, has never been the work of a generation or two. Even the relatively industrialized countries of the former Soviet Union are now discovering this to their chagrin—to acquire a class of parasitic nouveaux riches is one thing, but a class of serious wealth creators is quite another; and in most parts of Africa the domestic capitalist class is still at best embryonic and weak.

Second, mainstream political science in the United States, which until recently tended to dominate African political science, has consistently rejected the idea that social classes should be central objects of study.[2] It was not until the end of the 1960s, when the intellectual initiative in development studies passed to dependency theory, that the existence and importance of social classes and class politics in Africa began to be more widely acknowledged. But this happened at a price: the work that began to be done on African capitalist classes in the 1970s was seriously limited—indeed deformed—by its origins in the debate about dependency. The chief question asked was whether African capitalist classes really existed and, if so, how independent they were from foreign capital, as opposed to being compradors—mere conduits or agents of foreign capital, with no capacity or will to enforce their own independent interests at the expense of the interests of foreign capital or to promote "national" capitalist development.

This question was largely misconceived, although the studies it stimulated and the controversies surrounding them have added a good deal to our knowledge. The question was misconceived in that it begged a prior question. It assumed that the chief cause of Africa's underdevelopment, including the weakness of its internal capitalist classes, was the power of foreign capital; whereas it would be truer to say that the weakness of African capital was simply part and parcel of Africa's underdevelopment and that foreign capital filled (however inadequately and with various attendant costs) the vacuum created by the absence of strong domestic capitalist classes in Africa.[3] The capacity of the local capitalist class varies considerably from country to country in Africa: and it is far from obvious that where its capacity is low, this is because foreign capital is particularly strong. We need instead to enquire what are the important characteristics of an internal capitalist class for the process of capital accumulation—what are the key capacities it needs for national development to go forward—and then to look at the historical conditions favoring or not favoring the acquisition of these capacities by a local class of accumulators.

But in order to do this we need to clarify our theoretical terms. There has been an understandable reaction against general theory, after the exciting but inconclusive debates about modernization and dependency in the 1970s, and in face of the seemingly relentless economic decline and political decay in sub-Saharan Africa since that time. But since "data" are never really "given," but are always defined by theoretical presuppositions, we must still try to be clear about the inherited conceptual tools we are using. The first part of this chapter, therefore, briefly reviews the main theoretical and conceptual reference points for any study of capitalist classes in Africa today.

Marx and Weber on Capitalist Classes

It is natural to suppose that Marx, who made social class the hinge concept of his theory of history—the concept linking economic development to political action—provided a framework for analyzing capitalist classes that we can apply to Africa; but in reality only limited help is to be found in his work. This is mainly because in his most systematic treatment of the topic, Marx took an almost purely structuralist view of the bourgeoisie, declaring in the preface to the first edition of *Das Kapital*, that according to his standpoint individuals were of interest only insofar as they were "the personifications of economic categories," the creatures of social relations, not their authors.[4] He took England as the "locus classicus" of the capitalist mode of production up to that time and said that less developed countries could expect to follow the same path in due course, as the "natural laws of capitalist production" (which he admittedly often also called only tendencies) "won their way through," "worked themselves out with iron necessity."

In this famous passage he seems to leave no room at all for the performance of a particular country's capitalist class to make any difference. Of course, elsewhere he frequently alluded to the difference that the course of class struggles could make, and in his political writing (especially on France in the late 1840s and early 1850s, but also on Britain and elsewhere) he analyzed the different fractions of capital, the interplay of economic and political power, the complexities of capitalist ideology, and so on. But it is hard to deny that the dominant theme in his thinking is the unfolding logic of capital accumulation and above all its impact on the workers: the prime determinant of the outcome of the class struggle is "the development of the working class itself," not that of the bourgeoisie. That a capitalist class had emerged and become economically (if not politically) dominant in Britain was obvious; that capitalist classes would become similarly dominant in Germany and France was something he assumed.[5] If a capitalist class did not achieve power, because of the resistance of precapitalist classes, this would presumably mean "the common ruin of the contending classes" (as he and Engels put it in the *Communist Manifesto*).

In Marx's account there is, then, little allowance for differences of degree or quality between the various national capitalist classes making a difference to how far they would become dominant and with what effects. Marx could be scathing about the political limitations of this or that national capitalist class,[6] but he never tackled the general question of what makes some capitalist classes more effective than others, or what makes a given capitalist class succeed at one time and fail at another. As is well known, Engels near the end of his life confronted the general question of the role of agency in history in his letters to Schmidt and Bloch, but with notoriously debatable results. And in spite of the extensive debate that has taken place about the limitations of the British capitalist class, few of the participants have taken up the issue systematically or comparatively; they have not asked what are the general theoretical implications of acknowledging the extent to which the political and technical incapacity of the manufacturing fraction of the British capitalist class has hampered the later capitalist development in Britain.[7]

Yet two aspects of Marx's concept of the capitalist class deserve to be emphasized and retained. First, its clear place in the general theory of the capitalist mode of production, so that a capitalist class is a class of people who occupy similar places in capitalist relations of production, i.e., appropriating surplus value and then having the possibility and the necessity to invest this surplus in ever more productive ways, to generate further surplus value. Second, the need of this class to "conquer" state power, to have the state serve its needs in reorganizing and regulating society. Taken together, these features make the bourgeoisie a class that makes history, as both the product of the logic of capitalist accumulation and its agent. Capitalists are driven to do what they do by the logic of the market ("accumulate, accumulate, that is Moses and the prophets"), but they also need to act collectively to defend and promote their interests against those of other classes. These two things, the one producing constant transformations in production (productivity-raising changes), and the other producing periodic transformations in social relations through state power (the bourgeois revolution that clears the way for the productivity increases to be sustained), make the capitalist class significant.

These points are worth stressing because of the serious dilution that the concept of class often suffers in the literature on Africa. Any category of people may be called a class, but unless the concept belongs to a theory with some potential explanatory power, labeling them in this way adds nothing of value. Marx did not provide a general theory of the ways in which capitalist classes perform their historic function, but he indicated the sort of theory it needed to be.

As for Weber, his thought has deeply marked U.S. scholarship on Africa, both through its general influence in U.S. social science and specifically through the influence on the "modernization" school of Tal-cott Parsons, Weber's translator and interpreter. But as Thomas Callaghy has shown, Weber offered a much richer and more sophisticated set of ideas for understanding the development of capitalism, and the role of cap-italist classes, than is to be found in Parsons's mechanical and ahistorical apparatus of "pattern variables."[8] It is not possible to recapitulate these ideas, which Callaghy succinctly outlines, in the space available here. The central point is that Weber's ideal of type of "modern capitalism" is one in which "instrumental rationality" is applied to every aspect of production and the state; and this further entails that many other spheres of life must also be subjected to the same rationality, or at least be made compatible with it. So not only must markets, the organization of work, accounting, taxation, and public administration exhibit this rationality, but also sci-ence, justice, morals, religious belief, and much else. Consequently, a key area of enquiry must be the extent to which the capitalist class is able to make these numerous spheres of life exhibit or at least not resist instru-mental rationality; and this in turn raises important questions about their political and cultural influence, the extent to which they are both dominant and hegemonic, i.e., enjoy both power and consent. And this in turn in-volves above all the capitalist class's relation to, and influence over, the state, which is generally speaking the only agency capable of reorganiz-ing or at least regulating all these spheres of life.

Unlike Marx, however, Weber does not propose a causal theory. He declares a wide range of social, economic, and political factors to be im-portant for the rise of capitalism, but does not suggest which are most im-portant or propose that they become important in any particular sequence. His view is "nondeterministic, nonevolutionary": what happens is the out-come of struggles and hence indeterminate.[9] This is considered by many scholars (including Callaghy) to be a merit on Weber's part, although Weber too seems to have imagined that in the long run, capitalism would become universal.

Marx, of course, thought that the logic of capitalist competition acted as a "revolutionizing" hidden hand, forcing capitalists into certain courses of action, both individually as capitalists trying to survive in the market and collectively as a class trying to advance its interests. This relentless ongoing pressure, he thought, tended to result in the installation of the cap-italist mode of production and the dominance and hegemony of the capi-talist class. And speaking generally, it is hard not to agree that this has been the tendency worldwide. On the other hand, whether or not any given country experiences this global tendency as "beneficial" or "progres-sive"—in the historical sense intended by Marx himself (meaning liberat-ing people from drudgery, advancing them to new levels of productivity, breaking their parochial chains, giving them access to the world's cultural and scientific heritage, and so on)—is another matter. Capitalism does not develop every region similarly. There are poles of growth and margins of decay: areas of "high mass consumption," and other areas that are mere pools of surplus labor, vegetating on the periphery or even sinking into social disintegration, famine, and anarchy. So what is needed is a theory of the role of the capitalist class in determining which kind of outcome occurs in particular kinds of case.

It is tempting, but certainly premature, to imagine that out of the work that is now being done the elements of such a theory will emerge, in a judicious blend of the ideas of Marx and Weber. For the moment, all that seems possible is to keep such a theory in view as a horizon—a sort of moving target that one knows one will not reach, but that serves to orient and inspire empirical research that may in due course contribute to building the theory we need.

Development Theory

It is to the credit of the modernization school, with its strong Weberian roots, that questions about domestic or internal capitalists were fairly central to it from the outset. The weakness of this approach is that it rejected the concept of social class in favor of that of "elite" and hence did not raise the issue of whether or how the internal capitalist class might be the means of transforming the social relations of production. Instead, the issue posed was how far there were internal candidates for the elite roles proper to a capitalist economy and polity, as though these roles merely had to be *occupied* for capitalist development to forge ahead. The general theme of the modernization literature was that business elites were essential to development and that factors characteristic of traditional society, especially "traditional values," inhibited the emergence of such elites. This was a central theme of the work of Everett Hagen and Bert Hoselitz, to name two of the most influential modernization theorists; and David McLelland, with Weber's thesis on the role of the Protestant ethic in mind, even developed the idea that the level of "achievement orientation" in any culture could be scientifically measured and that development could be accelerated by "injecting" businessmen in developing countries with some of the "achievement factor" that was missing in their cultures.[10] Fred Riggs and Daniel Lerner explored the ways in which societies in transition from precapitalist to capitalist relations of production offered resistance to the application or absorption of capitalist rationality by both the class of capital and the state, in terms that strikingly anticipated the World Bank's rediscovery of the same phenomenon in Africa in the late 1980s.[11]

Although no useful theory seems to have emerged from this literature, at least it paid attention to some real issues affecting the formation and efficacy of domestic, internal, or indigenous capitalist classes. In contrast, dependency theorists, in their attack on the modernization school, seemed at first relentlessly structuralist. The capitalist classes of the periphery were pictured as mere comprador agents of metropolitan capital, thanks to the global structures of dependency of which they were "bearers." This was particularly true of the influential early writing of Andre Gunder Frank;[12] though as Frank was later to point out (and as the subtitle of his first book indicated), his work as a whole was almost entirely based on the work of Latin American historians and was not particularly structuralist, except in its first chapter (which, however, was what made the greatest impression, with its grand schema of "three contradictions" and the rest). In his subsequent writing, Frank insisted that the "lumpenbourgeoisies" (as he called them) of Latin America were the product of conflicts in which embryonic parties or tendencies pushing for a less dependent, more nationalist development strategy had been defeated, with the help of outside (imperialist) interests.[13] In this version, the domestic capitalist classes of Latin America figure as more active agents of underdevelopment, but their "lumpen" (i.e., unprogressive, comprador) character still appears as a more or less unavoidable result of the structures of dependency, which also predetermine that this fraction of the domestic capitalist class will prevail.

Less fatalistic versions of dependency theory, such as that of Fernando Cardoso and Enzo Faletto, or the "bureaucractic authoritarianism" thesis of Guillermo O'Donnell, saw the character and role of the internal capitalist class as much more determined by the specific historical circumstances of each country.[14] In particular, these later products of the dependency school focused on critical economic transitions, such as the transition from primary commodity exports to industrial production, or from import-substitution industrialization to "deepening" the industrial sector, seeing these as involving radical realignments both within the domestic capitalist class and in its relations with other domestic classes and with foreign capital and the military. Indeed, these versions of dependency theory clearly combine themes from both Marx and Weber, in the way previously suggested, and are quite suggestive for the study of African capitalists—not so much in detail (since the historical contexts of Latin America and Africa are so different) as in the kind of theorizing they attempt.

Although Marxist critics of dependency theory, such as Geoffrey Kay and Bill Warren, attacked its structuralism, they did not put in its place any theory of the determinants of the course of peripheral development in general, or the varying roles of indigenous capitalist classes. Their tendency is always to look in Marx's analysis of the logic of capital accumulation for a sufficient explanation of the behavior of capitalists, both as individuals and as a class. This does not prevent them from offering some valuable insights into the question. For instance, Kay's theory of the shift from the dominance of foreign commercial capital to that of foreign manufacturing capital as an explanation of underdevelopment in the African colonies is an interesting set of hypotheses of a type that, like those of

O'Donnell, might usefully be brought to bear on the evolution of African capitalists; and it has some echoes in the contemporary literature on rent-seeking in Africa, and also in Gunilla Andrae and Björn Beckman's thesis about the vesting of particular capitalist interests as a barrier to further expansion based on "market-rationality," all of which seek to find rational explanations for types of capitalist behavior that tend to block further capital accumulation for the economy as a whole.[15]

The Comparative History of Capitalism

Until recently, scholars interested in nascent capitalism in the underdeveloped world have usually looked for parallels (or contrasts) at the history of capitalism in its area of birth, i.e., Western Europe, where David Landes and other historians of European industrialization have commented on the varying capacities, technical and political, of the various European bourgeoisies. Landes is particularly relevant for the study of African capitalist development because he tries to extract from comparative history the necessary and sufficient conditions for industrial capitalism to become established anywhere. He lays a good deal of stress on the high value that was placed in Europe, by the eighteenth century, on the "rational manipulation of the human and material environment," as indicated by such things as the scope for rationality afforded by Christianity (i.e., even by Catholicism) relative to other religions such as Islam. And in passing he endorses in general terms Weber's hypothesis about the effect of the Protestant ethic on the rise of capitalistic behavior. He stresses also the widespread interest in science in Europe; and for Europe in general and Britain in particular, he attaches particular importance to the way in which entrepreneurial values and practices were able to become established in various kinds of social "space" that was insulated, in one way or another, from the surrounding society. Thus, the city could be a space shielded from the surrounding rural society, with its traditional order and values; or religious discrimination could force minorities into business careers by excluding them from public life (for example, Dissenters and Jews in Britain).[16] This is a theme of some relevance in contemporary Africa, as we will see. By contrast, Alexander Gershenkron focused on the agencies and, above all, the states that played such a key role in the industrialization of backward economies in the nineteenth century (i.e., backward in relation to Britain's)—a theme also much debated today.[17]

But it is striking how little these and many other historians have tried to tie together these two aspects: the culture and special circumstances that give rise to an industrializing bourgeoisie, and what determines whether state power either complements or frustrates capitalist industrialization. In Carlo Cipolla's *Economic History of Europe*, for example, Claude Fohlen comments on the limitations of the entrepreneurial outlook of a large section of the French capitalist class in the 1870s, and Knut Borchardt comments on the monopolistic character of late eighteenth-century German industrialists, dependent for their success "too often on procuring courtly extravagance or the compulsory recruitment of labour."[18] But the treatment of the characteristics of these national capitalist classes is quite unsystematic in these texts, and no interest is expressed in their influence on the policies pursued by their governments. Important changes in state economic policy appear as "exogenous" changes to the environment in which these capitalists operated, to which they themselves are presented as having made no contribution at all. Of course, in the early stages of capitalist development, it can frequently happen that state economic policy reflects the interests and wishes of the capitalist class only indirectly, if at all; but from the first they naturally seek to influence policy, and the state can seldom ignore them altogether. Yet little or nothing is said in these texts about the ways in which different fractions of capital—financial, commercial, industrial, or agricultural, for example—conceived of their collective interests and organized to defend them, or tried to ally themselves with other social classes to get a "regime of accumulation" in which they could prosper.

The case is different, however, with the much more recent literature on capitalism outside Europe, and especially the work that has been stimulated by the dramatic rise of the newly industrializing countries (NICs) in Southeast Asia. In these cases, the role of the domestic capitalist class is absolutely central. Korea, especially, has been the focus of intense interest, and the formation of its industrial capitalist class is particularly interesting and instructive, involving as it does a complex mix of deep, long-term cultural and political traditions; the distinctive and radical socioeconomic transformations wrought by Japanese colonialism; the special role of the postwar U.S. military government and U.S. aid; and the forced transformation of the rent-seeking commercial bourgeoisie into a manufacturing class by the state under the Park regime after 1961.[19]

Merely to list these moments in the formation of the Korean capitalist class is, of course, to show how removed the Korean experience has been from that of sub-Saharan Africa. And in spite of its "newness," Korean industrialization was already far advanced in the 1930s, when in most of Africa it had not even begun. But even the sharp contrasts are instructive, particularly the Southeast Asian countries' centuries-long history of unified governments, shared languages and religions, powerful landowning classes, etc. Above all, the story that is now beginning to be told about these countries foregrounds their capitalist classes—in their evolving interaction with the state, other classes, foreign technology, corporate organization, cultural development, and the rest—in a way that marks it off from the story hitherto told about most European countries.[20] In this literature there is no mystery about the class forces behind, or in opposition to,

state economic policy; and future research in Africa should be able to benefit considerably from it.

Research on Capitalist Classes in Africa

With the exception of a few early studies by Marxists—mainly attempts to
characterize the whole spectrum of social classes in particular countries—
such as Samir Amin's work on Senegal, Mahmoud Hussein's work on
Egypt, or Mahmoud Mamdani's study of Uganda, little work on capitalist
classes as such (i.e., as opposed to studies of businessmen or business
elites) seems to have been undertaken before the advent of the debate on
dependency in Africa.[21] Some material on indigenous capitalists was, of
course, also generated by the debates—precursors of the dependency debate—about neocolonialism in Ghana and Tanzania, debates partly stimulated and strongly influenced by Frantz Fanon's reflections in *The
Wretched of the Earth* (reflections that were partly based on what he saw
happening in Ghana when he was in Accra in 1960 as ambassador for the
provisional government of Algeria).[22]

But in the 1970s, when the question was posed in a more general way
by the debate over dependency, research began to be undertaken that (to a
greater or lesser extent) focused primarily on domestic capitalist classes
qua classes—i.e., not merely on the quality of the entrepreneurship of the
individuals who composed them, but also on the extent to which they had
developed a consciousness of their collective interests and the organizational means to promote them politically. Leading examples of such studies are Rhoda Howard's historical analysis of the Ghanaian bourgeoisie,
Fatima Mahmoud's study of the Sudanese bourgeoisie, Malaak Zaalouk's
study of the Egyptian bourgeoisie, Nicola Swainson's study of Kenyan
capitalists, and Michael Schatzberg's study of the bourgeoisie in rural
Zaire.[23] Two collections of the late 1980s highlighted this whole period of
work: Irving Leonard Markovitz's *Studies in Power and Class in Africa*
and Paul Lubeck's *The African Bourgeoisie*.[24]

The main thrust of all these studies was to establish how far the local
or domestic capitalist class was "independent" of foreign capital, with the
explicit or (more often) implicit assumption that such independence was
the key to successful national capitalist development. The result is an in-
dispensable body of information, but the costs of their shared preoccupation with dependency theory—whether the evidence was seen as confirm-
ing or refuting it—were considerable.

The prodependency studies tended to focus on the relative limitations
of Africa's capitalist classes and to ignore their growth paths over time, especially their collective ability to learn (both technical and managerial
skills, and political skills). These studies were apt to understate the

accomplishments of the African capitalist classes and to set (implicitly) impossibly high standards for them, relative to the length of time it actually took the capitalist classes of today's industrialized countries to become effective social forces. They tended (like the Russian populists a hundred years earlier) to see capitalism as something occurring only in the visible, formal corner of the economy and to overlook the ongoing gradual but crucial transformation of rural relations of production into increasingly commercial and finally capitalist relations (with a market for land and wage labor employed in commodity production).[25] They also tended to overlook the corresponding expansion in urban areas of nonenumerated or informal economic activities of an increasingly capitalist nature. (It is interesting to reflect how little of the process of capitalist development in Britain, capitalism's original heartland, would have been captured by any contemporary study in, say, the early eighteenth century, that had focused only on what is today considered the formal or enumerated sector.) And there was a tendency to view the political role of the domestic capitalist class purely in terms of whether it "controlled" state power—and if so, whether it used this power to reduce the dominance of foreign capital in the economy—rather than to ask how far its politics were conducive to overcoming the real obstacles to sustained capital accumulation in the country, with or without the assistance of foreign capital.

Conversely, the opponents of dependency theory tended to assume that if a local capitalist class could be shown to exist (and better still, if it exercised a significant measure of political power vis-à-vis foreign capital), then the future of capitalist development was more or less assured—or at least could be presumed not to be hopeless.[26] They mostly did not critically examine the bases of accumulation of the domestic capitalist class (for instance, the extent to which it depended on politically acquired privileges or monopolies, rather than its own entrepreneurial, financial, and technical competence in the marketplace); the determinants of its internal cohesion and capacity for collective political action (for instance, how far it transcended ethnic boundaries); or its possession or nonpossession of a shared concern for establishing the general conditions needed for further accumulation to be possible (i.e., how far it had a class "project"). They tended to oppose to the *dependentistas'* pessimism about the prospects for capitalist development an equally ill-founded optimism.

After the Dependency Debate: Contemporary Research

With the advantage of hindsight, especially with the disastrous evolution of Africa's economies since the late 1970s (when most of the information in the above-mentioned studies was collected), it is possible to pose the issues in a more open way. Several illusions that tended to haunt the debate about dependency have been destroyed, such as the dream of an alternative socialist development path waiting to be taken (if only a "genuinely radical" African leadership would take it), or the fantasy of a smooth and socially benign alternative path of "genuinely independent" or "progressive" national capitalist development—dreams or fantasies against which researchers often implicitly contrasted the corrupt, socially dislocating, ugly, and immiserating experience of "actually existing" capitalist development.[27] All of this can now be replaced by a serious question: In any given country, what are the obstacles confronting a sustainable process of development of the forces of production under capitalist relations of production, and how do the historically given characteristics of the country's internal capitalist class bear on the possibilities of overcoming these obstacles?

This is not to say that questioning the moral and political implications of capitalist development is pointless, or that alternative paths of development are not worth seeking. On the contrary, as I will argue in the conclusion to this chapter, such questions seem more urgent than ever. But in order to raise such questions, the scope and limits of actually existing capitalist development in Africa have first to be properly understood, and for this we have to understand the past, present, and potential capacity of Africa's capitalist classes.

Two general books published in the 1980s do express the general point of view that has just been outlined: John Iliffe's *The Emergence of African Capitalism* and Paul Kennedy's *African Capitalism: The Struggle for Ascendancy*.[28] Both authors essentially relegate the dependency debate to the sidelines and take it as given that capitalism is developing in Africa, as elsewhere. For them, the interesting questions concern what factors affect the speed and character of capitalist accumulation, either in Africa generally or in particular regions or countries in Africa, and with what results.

Iliffe sees the distinguishing characteristics of Africa's experience of capitalism as arising from the combination of the distinctive features of the continent's precapitalist societies with the "very late stage in the global history of capitalism" that had been reached when capitalism penetrated Africa.[29] Indigenous African capitalism, which had existed here and there before colonialism, was overwhelmed by competition from advanced capital in the metropoles, backed up by colonial rule. Indigenous capitalism reemerged under colonialism, in agriculture (primarily through a gradual process of differentiation among smallholders engaged in export commodity production), in trade, and finally in industry. Iliffe offers a fascinating overview of the way religions, both indigenous and imported, have both helped and hindered capital accumulation by Africans; and in conclusion he explores the way African capitalists have fared at the hands of independent African states. This experience he divides into three broad types: anticapitalist regimes (such as Nkrumah's Ghana or Nyerere's Tanzania);

"parasitic capitalism," as in Zaire, where state power is used primarily to take capital from those who have organized its production; and "nurture capitalism," in which the state works, ostensibly at least, to support capital accumulation by Africans (as examples he offers Kenya and Côte d'Ivoire).

Iliffe is a historian. He concentrates on the origins of capitalist accumulation by Africans, without trying to predict success or failure for their efforts. Kennedy, on the other hand, is a social scientist with a historical approach. In his view, the dependency debate about the relative strengths of domestic and foreign capital was ahistorical; he believes that closer study of at least some African capitalist classes suggests that they are at a stage of development comparable to that of their European precursors not twenty, but 200, years ago.[30] He then notes the many respects in which the conditions for rapid accumulation in Africa are less promising than they seem to have been in England (for example) 200 years ago.[31] But he sees no reason to suppose that the incentives of wealth and status, combined with foreign capital's need for stable regimes underpinned by local collaborators, will not make it possible for African capitalists to keep moving up an entrepreneurial and political learning curve.[32]

Of course, Kennedy's book was written before the full scale of the recession and the so-called global restructuring of capitalism had become apparent, and his views may now be judged overoptimistic. But as an antidote to unfounded pessimism and a reminder of the persistent pressure and opportunity to make a profit that gives capitalism its distinctive dynamism—and its capacity for creativity as well as for destruction—it at least helps redirect attention back to the wider questions about the capacities of African capitalist classes, which both sides in the immediately preceding literature tended to ignore.

Among Kennedy's numerous suggestions that seem to invite further research, two seem especially worth emphasizing. One is that rising bourgeois classes have always had to make alliances and compromises with other classes and to share state power with them. Rarely have capitalists actually held "exclusive political sway" (the rhetoric of Marx and Engels notwithstanding), and least of all when they were still at an early state of development as a class. This means that it is almost as important to understand the extent to which other classes or social forces have congruent interests with those of the capitalists, or can be induced to support the policies advocated by the local bourgeoisie, as to understand the characteristics of the local bourgeoisie itself.[33]

Another suggestion to be pondered concerns the importance that anthropologists and others have attached to "outsider" status of various kinds in the emergence of capitalist accumulation.[34] Membership in a "traditional" group can help an individual capitalist to accumulate, but as often as not it is *not* being a member of the locally dominant traditional group (linguistic, religious, cultural, etc.) that provides the freedom from group pressure necessary for accumulation based on the exploitation of labor. That is, we are looking at African equivalents to the kinds of "space" seen by Landes (see page 18) as being so important for some of the early shoots of capitalism to take root in Europe.[35] Past a certain point, Kennedy notes, the ambient social structure eventually reasserts limits to the accumulation process on the part of "outsiders"—which is another way of saying that the conditions that permit the beginnings of accumulation may not permit its further development but become fetters on it, unless and until they are themselves changed (traditional power gives way to new forces).

In this context, another shortcoming of the literature on African capitalism prompted by the dependency debate can be more easily identified and overcome: the uncritical identification of domestic or indigenous capitalism with "African" capitalism. As the following chapters on Zimbabwe by Nicholas and Ostergaard, and the chapter on Kenya by Himbara, clearly show, this is a severely misleading elision. In Africa, as in Europe and elsewhere, it has often been domestic and strictly indigenous groups that are in one sense or another outsiders (in the African cases, "racially" defined outsiders) who have been responsible for much of the early development of capitalism—and whose separate status may then itself become a problem for continued accumulation in the postcolonial period.

So far, rather few studies of African capitalist classes have been undertaken from the point of view represented by Kennedy's work and advocated here—hence the impulse behind the present collection. A notable exception, however, is Janet MacGaffey's 1987 study of the capitalists of Kisangani, Zaire, *Entrepreneurs and Parasites*.[36] Although her fieldwork was done in the late 1970s, her perspective transcends the preoccupations of the times and offers an open-minded and detailed account of the development of a domestic bourgeoisie, in the full sense of the term—i.e., not confined to the sphere of circulation (trade) and not dependent on political patronage and state monopolies, but rather emerging—*in spite of* the destructive greed of the "parasites" in positions of state power—in the economic space opened up by the very destruction of the state's capacity to administer and regulate the economy that the parasites' corruption has brought about.

MacGaffey does not discuss the prospects for replacing the dominance of the parasites with the hegemony of the relatively productivist entrepreneurial class represented by the businessmen and -women of Kisangani; nor does she consider whether any project for national development is likely to emerge from this quarter. On the face of it, it does not appear likely. The capitalist class she describes seems to suffer from the contradiction that success on a significant scale would reattract the fatal attention of the parasites, and lead to another round of plunder, bringing accumulation once more to a standstill. On the other hand, her account reminds us of the resilience of the domestic capitalist classes in Africa and the dynamic potential of the accumulation process to restart itself, once a certain commercialization of the economy has occurred. It also suggests that in changed political circumstances, such as the regime change that was still being pursued in Zaire—however faintheartedly—by the "donor community" in 1992–1993, a new class of actually existing capitalists might acquire a measure of political influence and help set in motion a reversal of the long decay of the Zairian economy.

And at the very least, MacGaffey's work draws a long-overdue line between real *capitalists* and the politicians, civil servants, and colonels who use their political power to get rich—Fanon's "bourgeoisie of the state." For many years observers have imagined that the use—too often the abuse—of office in order to accumulate assets must be regarded as a route, however unsavory, by which African capitalists will in due course emerge. Parallels have been drawn between the plunder of gold from India and the Americas in the late eighteenth and early nineteenth centuries and the looting of the public treasuries in postcolonial Africa, as so many different kinds of "primitive capital accumulation." But while some individual capitalists may have emerged, or may yet emerge, from the families enriched by state corruption in Africa, in the medium run this possibility seems of trivial importance compared to the spectacular damage this same corruption has wrought, both to the infrastructure on which production depends and directly on the production process itself, including the production of many genuine capitalists who have been stripped of their capital by these same "kleptocrats." As Callaghy has aptly remarked, "Why call it [the so-called organizational or bureaucratic bourgeoisie] a bourgeoisie at all? The continued use of the term simply leads to conceptual confusion."[37]

Of course, even if we were to accept that in Zaire the vitality of its provincial domestic capitalist class holds out a possibility, however slight, of future capitalist developoment, we cannot generalize from Zaire, a very large and resource-rich economy by African standards. Many other African countries would not necessarily hold out much promise of accelerated capitalist development even if they proved to have internal capitalist classes with the capacities of those found by MacGaffey in Kisangani. And even in the case of Zaire, the question still has to be asked: If the internal capitalist class remains unable to prevent the state from sabotaging capitalist development (let alone make it actually support it), can the wider conditions for capitalist development identified by Weber ever really be secured? What MacGaffey's work does show, however, is the importance of looking objectively at the nature of the domestic classes that have emerged as one very important term in the development equation in each individual African country and region.

Other Perspectives

Three main new currents of thought have flowed into the theoretical "vacuum" that appeared to many people to have been produced by the petering out of the dependency debate, and which might have some bearing on the analysis of capitalist classes: rational choice, poststructuralism, and gender analysis.

Rational choice theory, pioneered in Africa by Robert Bates, has made interesting contributions that are relevant to the study of African capitalists, especially by exploring the relation between market rationality and political rationality.[38] Contrary to popular prejudice, this kind of analysis is perfectly compatible with the theses of classical Marxism;[39] to a large extent it can be seen as a means of specifying what in the Marxist "problematic" would be termed the contradiction between the capitalist forces of production and the precapitalist relations of production in Africa (or what in the Weberian discourse would be termed the opposition between the instrumental rationality of market relations and the means-ends rationality of patrimonial authority). The literature on rent-seeking is so far the most significant branch of this stream, certainly as far as the study of African capitalists is concerned. As Catherine Boone's chapter in this book shows, however, the crucial question of how the contradiction between the two rationalities will be resolved in any given case—whether it will end in the "common ruin" of all concerned, or whether market rationality will prevail—cannot be answered from within the parameters of rational choice theory. For this we have to go back to some broader, longer-term theory of historical change, of the kind that is so far represented only by historical materialism, or derivatives of it.[40]

As for the contribution of poststructuralism, authors such as Achille Mbembe and Jean-François Bayart have argued quite persuasively that the structuralist debates of the 1960s and 1970s (including the debate about dependency) neglected the ideal/ideological dimension of economic and political life.[41] Serious attention to the theatrical and imaginary aspects in political life discloses, on this view, historical forces that are not reducible to, nor readily subdued by, "market forces." As Bayart puts it, "Colonial creations were subject to multiple acts of reappropriation by indigenous social groups" so that what we must really study is "the cultural logic underlying configurations of power," "the deep history which underlies the present, the buried layers of the *longue durée*."[42]

There seems no reason to reject these arguments, *to the extent that* they offer new ways of understanding why the transition to capitalism that occurred so decisively in Western Europe between roughly 1500 and 1950, and which Marx and many others believed must eventually take place everywhere, may be particularly difficult or even improbable in particular cases, not least in Africa.

The caveat is important, however, inasmuch as most if not all practitioners of poststructuralist analysis (and especially in its convergence with postmodernism) reject all "great historical metanarratives," seeing the very idea of "the transition to capitalism," for example, as resting on an epistemological error ("foundationalism," the idea that knowledge rests on ascertainable foundations in objective reality); and as also involving a variety of practical and political errors, such as universalism (assuming that what holds for white Western males must hold for people everywhere), and so on. From that point of view, the questions posed in this book appear to a large extent misconceived; and so the idea of borrowing from poststructuralism to help in answering them would seem to such authors doubly erroneous. One may, however, politely dissent from this interdict and try to take advantage of their insights; but the task of doing so in relation to the distinctive cultural context and psychosocial characteristics of African capitalists remains to be undertaken.

Of the three new currents noted here, the literature on women in Africa is not only by far the largest and empirically richest, it is also the one most explicitly related to questions of social class. Yet because it is focused on the liberation of women, its direct contribution to the study of the prospects for African capitalism is inevitably limited. Most African women belong to the most exploited strata of the population, as well as being subordinate to men within all social strata; and the general tendency of the penetration of capitalist relations of production in Africa, and of state policy, has been to exacerbate their subordination (for instance, and most commonly, by granting individual title over what used to be communal land to men, and not to women, even though women do the bulk of the work on the land).[43]

Speaking generally, the African literature seems to hold few surprises concerning the relation between gender oppression and class domination. Men dominate women both within the capitalist class and as members of the exploited classes.[44] But whether this advances or hampers capitalist accumulation seems as problematic and complex in relation to Africa as it does in relation to the advanced capitalist countries. For instance, Parpart and Staudt, commenting on Mbilinyi's work on colonial Tanganyika (which shows how the state tried to create a brewing monopoly in Dar es Salaam for an expatriate-owned brewery at the expense of women brewers), conclude that "at some point . . . capital loses as it stifles exchange-oriented accumulation among women" (i.e., subordinating women may hinder the accumulation of capital if the women are capital accumulators). But they go on to say that "over the long haul, though, states may have an interest in maintaining gender hierarchy with the effect that subordinate classes reproduce themselves at lower cost" (i.e., women's unpaid family labor makes a bigger contribution to capital accumulation in the end).[45]

Here are two (competing) hypotheses (which, of course, echo longstanding debates in the advanced industrial countries); and other suggestive ideas on these lines abound in the studies on women and class such as those collected by Robertson and Berger.[46] A systematic exploration of these ideas as they bear on the role of African capitalist classes is clearly needed.

An Agenda for Future Research

One way to sum up what has been argued in this chapter is to distinguish betweeen two broad functions that need to be performed by capitalists: the organization of production and exchange and the organization of the political conditions for the continued accumulation of capital. Under the former we can also distinguish between the direct organization of production and exchange by individual capitals (not excluding cooperation between them, as in cartels, etc.) and the organization of infrastructural services necessary for production, usually (though not necessarily) provided by the state.

In theory, the direct organization of production could be undertaken entirely by foreign capital, but in practice much of what can be produced locally is unlikely to be profitable for foreign capital. Likewise, the provision of infrastructures need not be done by the state, but only very large-scale infrastructural projects or services are likely to be profitable for foreign capital, and others tend to prove difficult areas for efficient cooperation by smaller-scale, local capitals. So the role of the domestic capitalist class is important in relation to these functions. It makes a big difference whether it performs them, or ensures their performance by the state, well or badly.

Similarly with the political function. Circumstances may occasionally exist when external forces can assume responsibility for securing the political conditions for continued capital accumulation; and the deep involvement of aid donors in economic policymaking in Africa in the era of structural adjustment programs draws them inevitably into politics, to the point where cases of near-recolonization are increasingly numerous.[47] But in the long run, this is a function for which a domestic capitalist class is normally crucial.

But the domestic capitalist class does not necessarily perform either its productive or its political functions well, or even at all. What needs to be investigated is how far it performs them and what conditions determine this. The particular historical circumstances affecting its emergence and formation into a class need to be established, to discover the determinants of its technical, organizational, and financial competence and the scope of its activities in the direct organization of production and exchange; its technical and organizational competence with respect to the construction and expansion of the infrastructure; and its political solidarity and skills (in coalition building, establishing ideological hegemony, and neutralizing opposition).

This implies quite an extensive agenda for future research:

1. Identifying the different components of the domestic capitalist class—by economic sectors, or "fractions," or other categories into which it is divided—and examining their respective historical origins and growth paths.

2. Studying the way these origins have influenced the fields of accumulation they have entered, and their "business cultures," including their technical and organizational capacities; and assessing these capacities in relation to the requirements of further accumulation. How far does the class depend for continued accumulation on state-awarded privileges (monopolies, contracts, quotas, licenses, etc.) alone?

3. Examining the internal economic, social, political, and ideological relations of the class. How far does it depend on the internal relations within particular social subgroups (ethnic, male, etc.) for its economic security and prospects of further accumulation? Or to put it another way, how impersonal, instrumental-rational, have the class's internal relationships become? And how far has it begun to develop a collective class consciousness that transcends its component parts, and how far does this consciousness include a class political project or vision of the future for society as a whole? What institutions—political, social, cultural, etc.— manifest the stage reached in the formation of the class and its distinctive character?

4. Studying the relations between the internal capitalist class and other classes, especially the petty bourgeoisie, old and "new."[48] How far are they, or might they become, relations of bourgeois hegemony? How far has the domestic bourgeoisie acted in such a way as to induce other classes to accept, as in their interests, the requirements for continued capital accumulation? How far has such a conception become, or might it become, influential in determining state policy?

5. Studying the relations betweeen the domestic capitalist class, within the system of class relations as a whole and other systems of authority, power, and status that intersect with it, including gender relations.

6. Examining the relations between the domestic bourgeoisie and the state apparatus, with regard to the economic conditions for capital accumulation (infrastructure, fiscal policy, trade policy, management of foreign exchange and debt, etc.) and the political conditions for it (treatment of allied interests, regulation of labor, land policy, etc.). How developed, rational, and institutionalized are these relations (as opposed to personalized, subjective, and vulnerable to change)? How far is the state, actually or potentially, capable of instituting the necessary social and political preconditions for sustained capital accumulation?

7. Studying the relations between the internal bourgeoisie and foreign capital and the agencies of foreign capital (bilateral and multilateral funding

agencies, in particular). How far are these relations collaborative, rational, and mutually advantageous? How far has the domestic capitalist class become recognized by these external actors as a significant and reliable partner in the development process?

8. Studying decisive moments and events in the evolution of the internal capitalist class that have affected its subsequent economic and political capacity—i.e., the course of its class struggles. As in individual biographies, the study of "turning points" can powerfully illuminate all the important dimensions of its subsequent trajectory.

9. Studying the obstacles to further capitalist development. What are the main obstacles, on what do the prospects for overcoming them mainly depend, and how far is there a shared perception and understanding of these issues within the domestic capitalist class?

The Contemporary Context

A final consideration concerns the medium-run global context in which African capitalists must operate today. Every country, and so every domestic capitalist class, confronts not only a unique set of domestic problems, but also a partly unique external context—a specific historically given set of trading, financial, military, diplomatic, and other relationships, within which any future development must occur. An oil-exporting country such as Gabon, a Frontline State in the southern African liberation struggle such as Zambia, a country dependent on a single low value–added export crop such as Senegal—each has a different external environment on account of the distinctive features of its geography and history. Yet one aspect of the external environment is broadly common to all African countries, and in conclusion it seems important to touch briefly on this because, contrary to the received wisdom of only a decade or two ago, it makes the task confronting their internal capitalist classes so much harder. I refer to the growing productivity gap between agricultural production in all still predominantly precapitalist agrarian economies and capitalist production elsewhere.

The point here is a simple one, but it rarely seems to get the sober attention it deserves, perhaps because it is so troubling. All African countries without exception depend on being able to sell primary commodities for export. These exports must compete in international markets with the produce of other countries, in a growing number of which capitalist relations of production prevail, or are at least well established in certain sectors. This means that the value of these commodities is constantly falling, in the sense that less and less labor time is required for their production where they are produced under capitalist conditions of production. Unless demand rises, therefore, the price falls; and in countries where the labor time expended falls more slowly, or even stays constant (not to mention rises, which can happen if the infrastructure or other circumstances affecting production deteriorate), this means that the return to this labor falls, too. Eventually, the return to labor can fall below the level at which people will produce the commodity at all.

So stated, the point may seem abstract and theoretical. But something like this has actually been happening to one African agricultural commodity after another: palm oil, groundnuts, cocoa, coffee, cotton, and many other crops are now produced many times more productively by large-scale mechanized agriculture on large farms, estates, or plantations in Malaysia, the United States, Brazil, Egypt, Sudan, and elsewhere to the point at which export production by African smallholders is increasingly under threat, if not already finished (as in the case of Nigerian palm oil, for example).[49] And what capitalist farmers cannot produce more cheaply, capitalist manufacturers will naturally try to produce cheaper substitutes for and will aggressively market these as replacements (e.g., synthetic textiles).

Historically, of course, at the same time as capitalism has raised agricultural productivity, and by the same token reduced agricultural employment, it has opened up alternative employment in industry. However, it has seldom done both things in exactly the same place or at the same pace; the process has mostly involved very painful social dislocations, eased by large-scale migrations, often international (e.g., from Europe to North America) and over several generations.

The problem confronting Africa today is that on the one hand this kind of large-scale migration overseas is ruled out, while on the other industrial productivity is itself advancing so rapidly that the capacity of manufacturing to create alternative employment has drastically declined. Whereas it used to be imagined that African countries, as late industrializers, would be able to profit from the hard-won productivity gains of their predecessors embodied in the productive technology now available to them, the reverse now seems more true; it would be much easier for Africa to industrialize if average industrial productivity worldwide had remained at the level it was at 150 years ago. As a result, African populations are becoming increasingly marginal to global production.

Marx analyzed the "relative surplus population," the production of which he quite rightly saw as capitalism's most distinctive effect (what he called the "general law of capitalist accumulation"), into four categories: (1) a "floating" element, which we would perhaps today call frictional unemployment, i.e., people temporarily out of work due to shifts in supply and demand, changes in technology, new products, and so on; (2) "latent," by which he meant agricultural producers whose destiny was sooner or later to be forced off the land due to rising agricultural productivity; (3) "stagnant"—the unskilled but able-bodied urban unemployed, ex-peasants not absorbed into productive nonagrarian labor; and (4) "pauperism"—the permanently unemployed and largely unemployable urban pool of orphans, disabled, sick, etc., plus the lumpenproletariat—vagabonds, criminals, prostitutes, etc.[50] Using these categories, we may say that in Africa the first category is barely significant, the second category is unprecedentedly vast, and the condition of the third category is already so desperate that in many countries it increasingly shades off into the fourth and last category. (And Africa has, of course, produced some new forms of pauperism to add to Marx's list, such as the continent's 3.5 million refugees, the tens of thousands with missing limbs or eyes in Mozambique and Angola, the Somalis and Mozambicans and others permanently dependent on food centers operated by various foreign agencies, the villages in Uganda and other central African countries devastated by AIDS, and the marauding gangs of armed teenagers who threaten to become a permanent feature of life in large areas of Mozambique.)

What all this means is that the *political* problem confronting any African capitalist class, even if it can find solutions to the complex technical and economic problems involved in expanding capitalist production, often seems close to being insoluble. And yet, with a further twist of the screw, there is pressure, as much from donors as from Africa's populations, for *democratization*, which was introduced in most of today's industrial countries only after the violent transition from precapitalist agrarian society to capitalist industrial society had been largely completed and accepted, and when wage employment had begun to succeed in absorbing the displaced peasantry.

These somber reflections are not intended to imply that capitalist development is nowhere possible in Africa. Paul Kennedy's insistence on capitalism's dynamic potential needs to be kept in mind. But in studying the capacity of Africa's capitalist classes to play their distinctive role in African development, we must face realistically the difficulties they confront in the shape of world capitalism as it actually exists, and not as it existed fifty or a hundred years ago. In some African countries they may overcome the obstacles and succeed in making them into productive capitalist economies. In others, marginalization and social distress may lead to either recolonization (via successive forms of aid programs, including military aid, for example) or to various kinds of anticapitalist reaction—fundamentalist or nativist, perhaps, or some new forms of socialism—whose contours cannot as yet even be imagined. The only thing that seems reasonably certain is that understanding Africa's capitalist classes will remain important for understanding whatever happens next.

Notes

1. More equality can, in theory at least, be obtained from redistribution without any increase in capital or material output, as the example of Cuba shows; and

this can produce considerable increases in both individual and collective values such as education, health, etc. There is no obvious reason why this should not be seen as "development," but hitherto redistribution alone has not been thought of as development, which accounts for the definition adopted in the text.

2. For an interesting account of the ideological bias of U.S. development studies in the 1950s and 1960s, see Irene Gendzier, *Managing Political Change: Social Scientists and the Third World* (Boulder and London: Westview Press, 1985).

3. This point seems only too well confirmed by the fact that widespread disinvestment in Africa by multinational corporations in the 1980s did not lead to a notable strengthening of local capitalist classes or to an acceleration of national development.

4. Karl Marx, *Capital* (London: Penguin Books, 1976), Vol. 1, p. 92.

5. Marx originally seems to have expected the capitalist class to become dominant everywhere. But in the late 1870s he had some second thoughts, provoked by the Russian populists who wondered if Russia really had to go through capitalism to get to socialism; and in 1881, after much reflection, he said that his earlier view that capitalism was historically inevitable was restricted to the countries of Western Europe. In Russia (and by implication perhaps elsewhere) it might be prevented, and socialism might be attained on the basis of indigenous peasant institutions, if these institutions could be protected from the "harmful influences assailing [them] from all sides" (see Marx's famous letter to Vera Zasulich of March 8, 1881, and the discarded earlier drafts for it, in Teodor Shanin's highly relevant study, *Late Marx and the Russian Road: Marx and "the Peripheries of Capitalism"* [New York: Monthly Review Press, 1983]).

6. As Perry Anderson has pointed out, whereas in the *Communist Manifesto* Marx wrote that the "modern bourgeoisie" (which had to be the British) had conquered "exclusive political sway," in later life he began to see the British bourgeoisie as "self-limiting and subordinate in its [political] actions and aspirations" ("The Figures of Descent," *New Left Review* 161 [January-February 1987], p. 24).

7. Eric Hobsbawm, in his *Industry and Empire* (London: Penguin Books, 1969), followed Marx's structuralist approach as far as possible (and beyond), viewing British capitalists as following the "logic of capital" but in conditions inherited from an earlier period that led, in spite of their profit-maximizing behavior, to a general loss of international competitiveness. Harold Perkin and Martin Wiener, adopting a Weberian approach, saw British capitalists as having abandoned their original "entrepreneurial ideal" or "industrial spirit" in favor of the antimaterialist and antiscientific outlook of the old precapitalist political class—i.e., they did not see them as forced by the "logic of capitalism" to behave in any ideal way (see H. Perkin, *The Origins of Modern English Society 1870–1880* (London: Routledge, 1969) and M. Wiener, *English Culture and the Decline of the Industrial Spirit* (Cambridge: Cambridge University Press, 1981). Neither side in this debate offered a general theory of the role of capitalist classes in development.

8. Thomas M. Callaghy, "The State and the Development of Capitalism in Africa: Theoretical, Historical and Comparative Reflections," in Donald Rothchild and Naomi Chazan, eds., *The Precarious Balance: State and Society in Africa* (Boulder and London: Westview Press, 1988), pp. 67–99. Although Callaghy's own Weberian approach differs from the one adopted here, his argument shows significant parallels.

9. Callaghy, "Capitalism in Africa," p. 73.

10. Everett Hagen, *On the Theory of Social Change: How Economic Growth Begins* (Homewood, Ill.: Dorsey Press, 1962); Bert Hoselitz, *Sociological Aspects*

of Economic Growth (New York: Free Press, 1960); David McLelland, *The Achieving Society* (Princeton: Van Nostrand, 1961). The U.S. government sponsored training programs based on McLelland's ideas for Third World businessmen.

11. Fred Riggs, *Administration in Developing Countries: The Theory of Prismatic Society* (Boston: Houghton-Mifflin, 1964) and *Prismatic Society Reconsidered* (Morristown, N.J.: General Learning Press, 1973); Daniel Lerner, *The Passing of Traditional Society: Modernizing the Middle East* (New York: Free Press, 1958). It is noteworthy that in the late 1980s disappointed modernization theorists produced metaphors very similar to Riggs's prism to describe the so-called neopatrimonial state in Africa, diverted from instrumental rationality by the "economy of affection" and displaying simultaneously the features of the modern, technical-efficient "air conditioner" at the front and the traditional, personalistic "verandah" (where clients' needs are catered to) at the back. Cf. Goran Hyden, *No Shortcuts to Progress: African Development in Management Perspective* (Berkeley and Los Angeles: University of California Press, 1983); and Emmanuel Terray, "Le climatiseur et la veranda," in *Afrique plurielle, Afrique actuelle: Hommage à Georges Balandier* (Paris: Karthala, 1986), p. 38, cited in Donal B. Cruise O'Brien, "The Show of State in a Neo-Colonial Twilight: Francophone Africa," in James Manor, ed., *Rethinking Third World Politics* (London: Longman, 1991), p. 151. Scientific progress seems to have been modest in this sector. The World Bank's later thinking may be found in *Sub-Saharan Africa: From Crisis to Sustainable Growth: A Long-Term Perspective Study* (Washington: World Bank, 1989).

12. A. G. Frank, *Capitalism and Underdevelopment in Latin Ameria: Historical Studies of Chile and Brazil* (New York: Monthly Review Press, 1967).

13. A. G. Frank, *Lumpenbourgeoisie, Lumpendevelopment: Dependence, Class and Politics in Latin America* (New York: Monthly Review Press, 1972).

14. Fernando Henrique Cardoso and Enzo Faletto, *Dependency and Development in Latin America* (New York: Monthly Review Press, 1967); Guillermo O'Donnell, *Modernization and Bureaucratic Authoritarianism: Studies in South American Politics* (Berkeley: Institute of International Studies, University of California, 1979).

15. See G. B. Kay, *Development and Underdevelopment: A Marxist Analysis* (London: Macmillan, 1975), Chapter 5; and Bill Warren, *Imperialism: Pioneer of Capitalism* (London: Verso, 1980). Kay's argument was that manufacturing capital was gradually able to squeeze the profits of commercial capital, as a supplier of inputs to manufacturing from the colonies; and because for various reasons commercial capital was not able to reorganize production in the colonies so as to increase the amount of surplus value created there, it could maintain its own profit only by transmitting the pressure to the African peasantry by ultimately disastrous downward pressure on the prices it paid for their produce. On rent-seeking, see Mark Gallagher, *Rent-seeking and Economic Growth in Africa* (Boulder: Westview Press, 1991). On vesting, see Gunilla Andrae and Björn Beckman, *The Wheat Trap* (London: Zed Books, 1985).

16. David Landes, *The Unbound Prometheus: Technological Change and Industrial Development in Western Europe from 1750 to the Present* (Cambridge: Cambridge University Press, 1969), especially pp. 21–23 and 66–74.

17. Cf. Alexander Gerschenkron, *Economic Backwardness in Historical Perspective: A Book of Essays* (Cambridge: Harvard University Press, 1962).

18. Knut Borchardt, "The Industrial Revolution in Germany 1700–1914," in Carlo M. Cipolla, ed., *The Fontana Economic History of Europe: The Emergence of Industrial Societies, I* (Glasgow: Fontana-Collins, 1973), p. 87; see also Claude Fohlen, "The Industrial Revolution in France 1700–1914," ibid., pp. 7–75.

19. See especially Carter J. Eckert, *Offspring of Empire: The Koch'ang Kims and the Colonial Origins of Korean Nationalism* (Seattle and London: University of Washington Press, 1991) for an exemplary analysis of the formation of Korea's industrial capitalist class under Japanese rule; Clive Hamilton, *Capitalist Industrialization in Korea* (Boulder and London: Westview Press, 1986), especially pp. 29–50; also Alice H. Amsden, *Asia's Next Giant: South Korea and Late Industrialization* (New York: Oxford University Press, 1989).

20. No doubt this does an injustice to many writers who have studied the development of capitalism outside its European and North American homelands well before the recent fascination with the NICs. An interesting example of such earlier work is Norman Jacobs, *The Origin of Modern Capitalism and Eastern Asia* (Hong Kong: Hong Kong University Press and Oxford University Press, 1958), which seeks to explain, by means of a detailed comparison of Japan and China, why "not all societies accept capitalism, even when that capitalism 'knocks at the door,' as Weber and others allege" (p. 213).

21. Samir Amin, *Le monde des affaires sénégalais* (Paris: Editions du Minuit, 1969); Mahmoud Hussein (a pseudonym), *La lutte des classes en Egypte* (Paris: Maspero, 1968); Mahmoud Mamdani, *Politics and Class Formation in Uganda* (New York: Monthly Review Press, 1976).

22. Examples are Bob Fitch and Mary Oppenheimer, *Ghana: End of an Illusion* (New York: Monthly Review Press, 1966); Roger Genoud, *Nationalism and Economic Development in Ghana* (New York: Praeger, 1969); and Issa Shivji, *Class Struggles in Tanzania* (London: Heinemann, 1975). All these authors argued that contrary to their own self-representation, these regimes were capitalist but, given the limitations of the domestic capitalist class (or the real absence of such a class), were incapable of achieving "independent" national economic development.

23. Rhoda Howard, *Colonialism and Underdevelopment in Ghana* (New York: Africana Publishing, 1978); Fatima B. Mahmoud, *The Sudanese Bourgeoisie: Vanguard of Development?* (London: Zed Books, 1984); Malak Zaalouk, *Power, Class and Foreign Capital in Egypt: The Rise of the New Bourgeoisie* (London: Zed Books, 1989); Nicola Swainson, *The Development of Corporate Capitalism in Kenya 1918–1977* (Berkeley: University of California Press, 1980). Swainson's study was not exclusively concerned with the Kenyan African capitalists, but was conceived in the context of the dependency debate and was the basis for her strong antidependency stance in her article "The Rise of a National Bourgeoisie in Kenya," *Review of African Political Economy,* no. 8 (January-April 1977), pp. 39–55. The same issue of the *Review* carried an important early article on the same theme by Paul Kennedy, "Indigenous Capitalism in Ghana" (pp. 21–38). A working bibliography on African capitalist classes would be useful but lies beyond the scope of this chapter. Côte d'Ivoire and Kenya, the focus of much of the debate, served as a prime focus for the conference that resulted in Paul Lubeck, ed., *The African Bourgeoisie: Capitalist Development in Nigeria, Kenya, and the Ivory Coast* (Boulder: Lynne Rienner, 1987). Valuable collections of citations may also be found in Henry Bernstein and Bonnie K. Campbell, eds., *Contradictions of Accumulation in Africa* (Beverly Hills: Sage Publications, 1985), especially in the chapters by Björn Beckman, Gavin Kitching, and Bonnie Campbell. See also Jean-François Médard, "The Historical Trajectories of the Ivorian and Kenyan States," in Manor, *Rethinking Third World Politics,* pp. 185–212.

24. Markovitz was among the first to grasp the growth and significance of African capitalist classes in his 1977 book, *Power and Class in Africa* (Englewood Cliffs, N.J.: Prentice-Hall, 1977), Chapter 7. His edited volume of 1987, *Studies in Power and Class in Africa* (New York: Oxford University Press), followed up on

this work; Parts 2 and 3 are particularly relevant to our theme. Lubeck, *The African Bourgeoisie,* was a specific point of departure for the present collection.

25. On the very parallel debate between the Russian populists and Lenin, see the excellent overview by Gavin Kitching, *Development and Underdevelopment in Historical Perspective* (London: Methuen, 1982), Chapters 2 and 3.

26. As Beckman pointed out, this was roughly the case with the article I wrote that initiated the "Kenya debate": see Colin Leys, "Capital Accumulation, Class Formation and Dependency: The Significance of the Kenyan Case," *Socialist Register* (1978), pp. 241–266; and Björn Beckman, "Imperialism and Capitalist Transformation: Critique of the Kenya Debate," *Review of African Political Economy* 19 (1980), pp. 48–62. For an overview and bibliography of the Kenya debate see Gavin Kitching, "Politics, Method and Evidence in the 'Kenya Debate,'" in Bernstein and Campbell, *Contradictions of Accumulation,* pp. 115–151. For a retrospective comment on the debate see Colin Leys, "Learning from the Kenya Debate," in David A. Apter and Carl G. Rosberg, eds., *The New Realism in Africa* (Universities of Virginia Press, 1993).

27. The expression "actually existing capitalism" is intended to echo the expression "actually existing socialism" with which Rudolph Bahro sought to get the European left to confront the reality of the neo-Stalinist systems of Eastern Europe in the 1970s (Rudolph Bahro, *The Alternative in Eastern Europe* [London: New Left Books, 1978]).

28. John Iliffe, *The Emergence of African Capitalism* (London: Macmillan, 1983); Paul Kennedy, *African Capitalism: The Struggle for Ascendancy* (Cambridge: Cambridge University Press, 1988). Another book of the same vintage and with similar scope is John Sender and Sheila Smith, *The Development of Capitalism in Africa* (London: Methuen, 1986), but it is powered by an antidependency perspective that leads to external obstacles to capitalist development being minimized, and to no distinctions being drawn between the various African countries in terms of the prospects of enjoying capitalist development. Consistently, there is no discussion of the distinctions to be made between the continent's various capitalist classes.

29. Iliffe, *African Capitalism,* p. 4.

30. Kennedy, *African Capitalism,* pp. 112–134.

31. Ibid., pp. 99–102, 147–156.

32. Ibid., pp. 184–191.

33. Ibid., pp. 87–88. The concept of sharing state power is no doubt almost as unsatisfactory as that of controlling it. The rich problematic to be found in recent theory of the state has yet to be much applied to Africa.

34. The role of certain groups, some of which were "outsiders," was also a celebrated theme of Werner Sombart's writings on capitalism, especially the role of national traits, which he, however, attributed to entrepreneurial genes in the blood of the Frisians, the Jews, and the lowland Scots (*The Quintessence of Capitalism* [New York: Dutton, 1915], pp. 200–221).

35. Ibid., pp. 137–143.

36. Janet MacGaffey, *Entrepreneurs and Parasites: The Struggle for Indigenous Capitalism in Zaire* (Cambridge: Cambridge University Press, 1987). Another valuable monograph on class development in rural Zaire was published by Michael G. Schatzberg: *Politics and Class in Zaire: Bureaucracy, Business and Beer in Lisala* (New York: Africana Publishing, 1990). Schatzberg's focus, however, was on what he termed the "national politico-commercial bourgeoisie," the parasites of MacGaffey's title, which could hardly be considered a bourgeoisie at all.

37. Callaghy, "Capitalism in Africa," p. 85. Callaghy prefers the term "political aristocracy," by analogy with prerevolutionary France. This perhaps reflects an

American's ingrained republican distaste for aristocrats. I prefer the term "state kleptocracy" as being less complimentary.

38. Robert H. Bates, *Markets and States in Tropical Africa: The Political Basis of Agricultural Policies* (Berkeley: University of California Press, 1981) and *Towards a Political Economy of Development: A Rational Choice Perspective* (Berkeley: University of California Press, 1988).

39. On the general compatibility of rational choice theory and Marxism see Jon Elster, *Making Sense of Marx* (Cambridge: Cambridge University Press, 1985); and on the particular point of compatibility asserted here, see Christopher Colcough, "Structuralism Versus Neo-liberalism: An Introduction," in Christopher Colcough and James Manor, eds., *States or Markets? Neo-liberalism and the Development Policy Debate* (Oxford: Clarendon Press, 1991), p. 4.

40. For example, Karl Polanyi's *The Great Transformation* (New York and Toronto: Farrar and Rinehart, 1944).

41. Jean-François Bayart, "Finishing with the Idea of the Third World," and Achille Mbembe, "Power and Obscenity in the Post-colonial Period: The Case of Cameroon," in Manor, *Rethinking the Third World,* pp. 24–50, 166–182.

42. Bayart, "Third World," pp. 52, 59, 61.

43. Jane L. Parpart and Kathleen A. Staudt, eds., *Women and the State in Africa* (Boulder: Lynne Rienner, 1989), p. 12.

44. This is attested consistently by fieldwork in a wide variety of settings; see, for example, Janet MacGaffey, "Women and Class Formation in a Dependent Economy: Kisangani Entrepreneurs"; Christine Obbo, "Stratification and the Lives of Women in Uganda"; and Cheryl Johnson, "Class and Gender: A Consideration of Yoruba Women During the Colonial Period"; all are in Claire Robertson and Iris Berger, eds., *Women and Class in Africa* (New York: Africana Publishing, 1986). See also Claire Robertson, *Sharing the Same Bowl: A Socioeconomic Hisotry of Women and Class in Accra, Ghana* (Bloomington: Indiana University Press, 1984).

45. Parpart and Staudt, *Women and the State in Africa,* p. 6.

46. Robertson and Berger, *Women and Class in Africa.*

47. The intervention of donors (who are in this context mostly not donors but *lenders* concerned about the security of their loans) in Kenya in 1991–1993 is a classic example. Having obliged the government to hold elections, which it won, the donors then obliged it to accept a package of monetary reforms by withholding aid for a further four months. The World Bank's vice-president for Africa commented: "We have managed to reach agreement, and the government has come all the way to the bank" ("Penitence Wins Kenya Return of World Bank Aid," *Guardian,* April 22, 1993). See also the discussion by David Himbara in Chapter 4 of this book.

48. This usage is not very satisfactory, but was effectively popularized by Nicos Poulantzas. By the "old" petty bourgeoisie is meant the class of producers who own their own means of production but who use it themselves and do not rely exclusively on waged employees to produce the output—i.e., peasant farmers, artisans, traders. By the "new" petty bourgeoisie is meant the class of educated employees, mainly in state employment (especially in Africa), who have something in common ideologically with the old petty bourgeoisie.

49. For a further development of this point see Colin Leys, "The State and the Crisis of Simple Commodity Production in Africa," *IDS Bulletin* 18, no. 2 (July 1987), pp. 45–48. Of course, supply and demand do not stay constant, and here the problem is aggravated by the fact that all underdeveloped countries are being urged simultaneously by the World Bank to expand their exports of primary commodities, leading to still weaker prices. The effect is that governments find themselves trying to boost output by offering guaranteed producer prices that can only be

maintained by subsidies they have no other source of revenue to pay for. For the case of cocoa in Ghana, see Cord Jakobeit, "Reviving Cocoa: Policies and Perspectives on Structural Adjustment in Ghana's Key Agricultural Sector," in Donald S. Rothchild, ed., *Ghana: The Political Economy of Recovery* (Boulder: Lynne Rienner, 1991), pp. 221–232.

50. *Capital* (London: Penguin Books, 1976), Vol. 1, pp. 794–798.

3

The Ivoirien Bourgeoisie

John Rapley

Côte d'Ivoire was one of the few French colonies in sub-Saharan Africa in which a substantial number of Europeans settled. Their presence was to have a determining effect on both the emergence of Ivoirien capitalists and on their subsequent organization into a bourgeoisie. Contrary to what has traditionally been assumed, the Ivoirien bourgeoisie was not the precolonial dominant class in new clothes; in its membership and behavior it was a brand new class to Côte d'Ivoire, a class that expanded rapidly in both numbers and wealth. As time went by, it diversified its interests out of its original domain of plantation agriculture; today, in fact, the Ivoirien bourgeoisie is represented in virtually all sectors and subsectors of the economy and has become quite strong in the secondary sector.

Partly stimulated by a beneficent colonial regime, and partly in response to the later hostility of that regime and of the rival settler class, the Ivoirien bourgeoisie created political organizations to defend its interests. As a result, it was the class that ended up leading the independence movement in Côte d'Ivoire and taking control of the postcolonial state.

In the postcolonial period, the bourgeoisie has continually been reinforcing its control over the state. The manifestation of this control has been the policy orientation of the Ivoirien state, which has generously favored the continued development of the domestic bourgeoisie. At the same time, the organization and integration of the Ivoirien bourgeoisie has become quite sophisticated. Despite tensions and rivalries, the class seems cohesive and appears to share a unifying ideology.

The Ecomonic History of the Ivoirien Bourgeoisie

Early on, the colonial administration of Côte d'Ivoire decided to attract French settlers to develop a plantation economy based on the production of coffee and cocoa. The period of greatest expansion in the settler plantation economy was during the 1920s. By the 1930s, a class of Ivoirien planters was developing at a similarly fast pace. The two events were not merely coincidental.

Put in the simplest possible terms, Ivoirien plantations emerged because there were French plantations. Africans, many of them migrant laborers, went to work on those plantations and, having learned the new techniques of production, often created their own plantations after a number of years of labor. Other Africans made the acquaintance of French settlers in different ways. A number of historians agree that there was a clear relationship between the settlers and the African planters in this regard, and their claims are substantiated by a number of studies from different regions and among different peoples of Côte d'Ivoire.[1] However, while Africans learned many of the basic techniques and adopted the new crops of French plantation farming, they also adapted European techniques to make them more suitable to local conditions.

The planter class was a new class; it was not simply a case of the old dominant class taking on the new trappings of wealth and power. While the social backgrounds of the African planters varied, most appear—contrary to common belief—not to have come from the ranks of the traditional elites.[2] Former plantation laborers, by contrast, occupied a particularly important place among the planters. A great number of these laborers, in turn, were immigrants: each year hundreds of thousands of laborers were coming from the north—mainly Upper Volta—to work on plantations at harvest time, and some ended up staying behind and setting up their own plantations. This trend became pronounced toward the end of the 1950s. Other migrants, especially the Dioulas, were traders with capital to invest, and some were Senegalese or Ivoiriens from other parts of the colony.[3]

While the majority of plantation laborers were immigrants,[4] not all of them were, and from among the local workers as well there emerged many planters. Many Baoulé planters, one study found, were previously laborers, though some of them came from the urban working class.[5] Among the Abourés, many planters were former fishermen who found farming to be a more lucrative form of activity.[6]

Some planters were educated townspeople and former civil servants who saw planting as a means of ending their total dependence on the French. Planting "added or even replaced the income which their peers in other territories could earn only through the civil service."[7] What is interesting about Côte d'Ivoire is that after receiving an education, many Africans returned to running plantations, whereas elsewhere in French West Africa—with the exception of Senegal, where the peanut trade offered prospects—almost all educated Africans saw no future for themselves except in the civil service.[8] Unlike most African countries, where the only means of advancement open to educated Africans was the state,[9] in Côte d'Ivoire the option existed for educated young Ivoiriens to seek their advancement in the private sector. The fact that the educated class in Côte d'Ivoire was, in part, also a bourgeoisie was to have profound consequences around the time colonialism came to an end, since they were obviously the natural leaders of the independence movement.

Nonetheless, there were also chiefs who took advantage of their control over communal lands to engage in the primitive accumulation that would precede their growth as capitalists.[10] Particularly among the Abourés, it appears that a good number of the planters were individuals from the precolonial period's wealthiest classes.[11] Among the Gouros and Baoulés also, many, though not all, planters were chiefs; but among the neighboring Agni, where a large number of plantations were found, big planters did not emerge from among the chiefs.[12] In several other areas or ethnic groups, traditional chiefs occupied a rather small place among the planters.

Having been spawned by the settler class, the planters grew in numbers and wealth at a very rapid pace, and their production expanded rapidly. In 1920, when there were only a few dozen settlers in Côte d'Ivoire, there were only a half dozen big African planters.[13] The boom in the planter population began in the 1930s,[14] and while the settler population had pretty well stabilized by the onset of World War II, the Ivoirien planters continued to grow in number; by the postwar period, the planters outstripped the settlers in production.[15] By 1958, on the eve of independence, the total number of African planters was estimated at 20,000,[16] a figure that is commonly accepted. These were farmers whose prime activity was commodity farming and who typically made use of wage labor (not solely family labor).[17] The average farm size for those planters in the top half of this group was between 10 and 12 hectares, with an average wage-labor force of five workers.[18] In light of the technology of the time, therefore, this group represented a stratum of fairly large enterprise operators.

But these figures do not accurately represent the holdings of the new bourgeoisie; much of their surplus revenue was being reinvested in their farms, but much, probably most, of their profits went into new investments.[19] The tendency to have economic interests in addition to plantations was particularly strong among Dioula planters.[20] It was also quite typical of planters to diversify their agricultural production to avoid reliance on one commodity.

The nature of secondary investment varied. Abe planters in southeast Côte d'Ivoire were fond of "Western" types of investment, such as automated shelling machines, which they would then rent out to other farmers. Before long these were providing them with more revenue than their plantations.[21] Similarly, the richest Agni planters often handed over the supervision of their plantations to appointed managers in order to devote more time to other business endeavors into which they were expanding.[22] Abouré planters, again in southeast Côte d'Ivoire, tended to invest agricultural surpluses in buildings, making money by renting these buildings to the colonial administration, which used them for office space or residences for administrators.[23] During the 1930s, there was a general tendency among the wealthier African cocoa and palm oil planters to begin mechanizing their production, through the acquisition of such machinery as tractors. Moneylending also become a more common form of economic enterprise.[24]

Some of the planters' investments were in the urban secondary sector, but most were in the tertiary sector of trade and services; the purchase of trucks for transporting goods and passengers was virtually ubiquitous among the rich planters.[25] However, had the opportunities existed, Ivoirien capitalists would probably have invested from an even earlier date, and to a greater degree, in the urban manufacturing industry. Before 1939, industrialization in French West Africa tended to take place disproportionately in Dakar, about one-half of all the colony's industry being located there. There was very little secondary industry in Côte d'Ivoire until after the Second World War, and even then it was limited until the postcolonial period.[26] Given that Ivoirien farmers were at this time earning respectable surpluses,[27] they probably could have participated in joint ventures, although the high capital requirements of modern industry meant they were likely still unable to create factories on their own. Therefore, since this option was not open, they invested elsewhere. However, once industry began to become a real force in Côte d'Ivoire in the 1960s, they began to engage in large-scale joint ventures. In sum, the Ivoirien bourgeoisie was at this time only a latent industrial bourgeoisie, but it was a bourgeoisie nonetheless; its disposition, its holdings, and the way in which it spent its surpluses all reflected the extent of growth and development in the Ivoirien economy as a whole.

Subsequently, one can discern three phases in the maturation of the Ivoirien bourgeoisie, from its initial planter character to its current industrial one. The first of these three phases, which can be seen as transformations, applied to those capitalists who were primarily planters through the late colonial period, and who only later began extensive diversification into other sectors. A good example is Mathieu Ekra, a planter who began to diversify into the modern industrial sector in the 1960s when he participated in the creation of agroindustrial enterprises (see note 23). Georges Auguste Denise is a similar case.[28] There are others, some of whom were planters, most of whom were early SAA-PDCI-RDA (Syndicat Agricole Africain, Parti Démocratique de la Côte d'Ivoire, Rassemblement Démocratique Africain) militants, but virtually none of whom had begun investing in the secondary and tertiary sectors until at least the 1950s.

The second phase of transformation, which is probably more important than the first, was generational. This refers not to individual capitalists but to capitalist families in which planters' children (and other descendants) used the family wealth to invest primarily in the urban secondary and tertiary economy. Thus we have Fulgence Brou, Joseph Anoma, Félix Houphouët-Boigny, Gabriel Dadié, Gon Coulibaly, Marcel Laubhouet, and Moussa Diabaté, founding members of the SAA-PDCI-RDA who were most often famous for being rich farmers. In the second generation are businessmen like Gustave Brou; Lamine Diabaté; François, Guillaume, and Dia Houphouët-Boigny; Raphaël Dadié; Gilles Vally Laubhouet; and various members of the Anoma and Coulibaly families. These people have carried on the families' political traditions and are still leading members in the PDCI-RDA and/or the government, but today they are not farmers but urban business people.

The third phase of transformation applies neither to individual planters nor to planter families, but to the class as a whole, and refers to those who entered the ranks of the Ivoirien bourgeoisie in the postcolonial period. These people, who have assumed positions of political power, are and always have been urban capitalists; few were ever planters. But while their power is significant now, they were not present in the original SAA. People like Paul Akoto Yao, Victor Amagou, Eugène Anvo Guetat, Arsène Assouan Usher, Denis Bra Kanon, Auguste Daubrey, Zemogo Fofana, Amara Karamoko, Jean-Baptiste Améthier, Emmanuel Dioulo, Joseph and Hortense Aka Anghui, François Dacoury-Tabley, Charles Donwahi, Léon Amon, Louis Kouassi Kouadio, and Lambert Amon Tanoh were children with an average age of ten when the SAA was formed in 1944.

Thus, at the time of independence in 1960, the Ivoirien bourgeoisie very definitely appeared to be a planter class. Subsequent events have shown this to be in fact only a phase in the class's development. The dynamics of the class were clearly toward maturation into a full agricultural, commercial, and industrial bourgeoisie, and this maturation took place in two stages: a slow phase in the 1960–1970 period, during which time industrial investment was carried out largely by foreign capital; and a more rapid phase after 1970, when the Ivoirien bourgeoisie became primarily urban. Even during the economic hardships of the 1980s, the class continued to grow. Rates of expansion were remarkable. From 1971 to 1980, the Ivoirien bourgeoisie's share of total industrial capital grew from about 3 percent (for a total value of 1.12 billion CFAF[29]) to between 11 and 13 percent (for a total value of almost 15 billion CFAF).[30] Meantime, between 1960 and 1978, the secondary sector in Côte d'Ivoire had grown at an annual average rate of 15 percent.[31] Therefore, even for the Ivoirien bourgeoisie to hold its position would mean that it too was expanding at an average annual rate of 10–15 percent, but given that its proportionate role in the economy tripled in the second decade, this puts its average annual growth rate, in absolute terms, well above 15 percent.

A more specific example will illustrate this point more vividly. Between 1975 and 1980, the proportion of total industrial capital that was in Ivoirien hands fluctuated within a narrow range, for the most part at around 11 percent,[32] leading several observers to conclude that the class was scarcely expanding and was actually rather stagnant. But this was at a time of rapid growth in the economy, and in absolute terms the figures told a different story. *Total* private Ivoirien capital, measured in terms of assets in monetary terms, expanded at an average annual rate of 17.3 percent. Secondary industrial capital, taken alone, expanded at an even higher average annual rate of 28.4 percent.[33] In neither case was this expansion the result of a one- or two-year aberration brought on by some dramatic expansion; growth was essentially consistent from year to year.

Even in the midst of the economic crisis of the 1980s, during which time a number of foreign operations were closing down or divesting themselves of assets, the Ivoirien bourgeoisie maintained a respectable pace of activity. From 1980 to 1987, according to the research agency ORSTOM, 5,400 industrial (secondary and tertiary) firms were established in Côte d'Ivoire. Of these, 58 percent were created by Ivoiriens and only 4 percent by French investors.[34]

The Ivoirien bourgeoisie is not a class of small business people either. In the survey done for this study of how many large firms (capital over 100 million CFAF) had Ivoirien share ownership of at least 10 percent, no less than 110 companies fit these criteria.[35] These Ivoirien companies were frequently among the country's biggest revenue generators. In the 1974–1982 period, companies in this survey were well represented among the nation's top firms, calculated in terms of volume of business: depending on the year, between 28 and 45 percent of the country's top companies had private Ivoirien ownership in varying proportions.[36]

The class has also grown in size, adding new, young capitalists to its ranks, as mentioned above. Civil servants, already-existing businessmen, private sector wage earners, nonsalaried professionals, pharmacists, and the children of businessmen have all been important investors in the industrial economy. Interestingly, planters no longer figure very significantly among the country's industrial investors.[37] Indeed, many of the country's business people are relatively young: One study conducted in the early 1980s found that 51 percent of Ivoirien entrepreneurs were under thirty, and only 20.1 percent were over forty.[38] Today, recent university graduates figure prominently among the country's pool of young entrepreneurs.

The class has diversified its holdings to the point where it now has significant holdings in virtually all sectors of the economy. In the aforementioned survey of large Ivoirien companies with private Ivoirien share ownership, over half (52 percent) of the companies with Ivoirien participation were located in the manufacturing sector. Over half of these companies, in turn, were majority-owned by Ivoiriens. Less than half (42 percent) of the firms were in the tertiary sector. The remainder were mixed secondary-tertiary enterprises.[39] While the Ivoirien bourgeoisie has a broad base of activities in the secondary sector, since 1970 it has been particularly prominent in agroindustry. Only in high technology and capital goods production is the Ivoirien bourgeoisie weak.[40] Ivoirien-owned enterprises are also quite aggressive in terms of seeking out new markets, not content to restrict themselves to domestic sales. On average, the firms in the survey exported two-fifths of their output.[41] Equally important, other African countries are the most significant export markets of companies with Ivoirien share ownership, whereas France is not a very significant destination for their exports.[42]

Over time, the tendency has been for Ivoirien capitalists to become majority owners in the firms in which they have interests. While in the early postcolonial period Ivoirien capitalists were usually buying minority shares in foreign corporations, today they are far more likely to be majority shareholders in the corporations in which they buy interests. In the survey group in question, it was found that 46 percent of the companies were majority-owned by Ivoiriens, while another 4 percent had their assets divided evenly between Ivoirien and foreign interests. Overall, the average private Ivoirien share in the companies surveyed was 51.74 percent.[43] There has been a consistent trend toward Ivoirization. Of the companies in the survey that were established during the colonial period, only 12 percent were majority-owned by Ivoiriens. This leapt to 45 percent for the companies created during the 1960s, and by the 1980s, two-thirds of the new large firms being established with Ivoirien share ownership were in fact majority-owned by Ivoiriens.[44]

Finally, the Ivoirien bourgeoisie seems to have been quite effective at assimilating and adapting imported technology to local conditions. Lynn Mytelka's work on the Ivoirien textiles industry[45] provides an excellent example of the problems encountered when Ivoirien firms failed to adapt to local conditions. Mytelka accounts, probably correctly, for the difficulties encountered in this subsector by the fact that investment and innovation decisions are made by foreigners, who not only tend to import technology and production processes unaltered, but also raise the wage bill of the producing firm.

However, it is interesting that the textiles industry is one of those dominated by foreign capital. Of the firms in Mytelka's study, share ownership by private Ivoiriens rarely surpasses 15 percent of total capital, and all are run either by foreigners or by combined foreign-Ivoirien management. It appears that it is foreign owners and managers who are doing a poor job of altering their technology to suit local conditions. Ivoirien capitalists, on the other hand, arguably have a long history of adjusting technology and production processes to local conditions, dating back to the early plantations when they used smaller plots than the European settlers, scattered them throughout the forest as opposed to concentrating them on one plantation, did not fully clear the land they used,[46] and used land-intensive techniques of cultivation[47] in order to take advantage of the low cost of land. My survey found that as a rule, majority Ivoirien-owned firms in Côte d'Ivoire were run by Ivoiriens[48] and did not rely on foreign expertise the way the foreign-owned firms such as those in Mytelka's study did. It is quite likely then that Ivoirien-owned firms are better at technology adaptation than are foreign ones. Perhaps not surprisingly, there is evidence—albeit tentative—that suggests that Ivoirien-owned firms are more efficient than their foreign counterparts, with a higher capital:output ratio than either foreign or state firms.[49]

Nonetheless, at this stage the evidence regarding technology assimilation is still too limited to permit any firm conclusions for the economy as a whole. More industry-specific studies are needed, like those of Mytelka and Bonnie Campbell,[50] which closely examine the decisionmaking processes and technological innovations, looking not only at top-level management but also at engineers, technical advisers, and the like. (See Table 3.1.)

The Political History of the Ivoirien Bourgeoisie

The political history of the Ivoirien bourgeoisie is almost as long as its economic history. In its earliest days, the class linked itself to the political organizations of the French settlers, but this relationship was not amicable. By World War II the planters broke with the strongly pro-Vichyist settler class, who were exploiting the new political circumstances to try and drive their African rivals out of competition. In consequence, the Ivoirien bourgeoisie formed its own political groups, which were subsequently successful at taking control of the independence movement. In the postcolonial period, the Ivoirien bourgeoisie has reinforced its hold on the state and thus used its position of power to ensure its continued reproduction. It has also strengthened its position vis-à-vis the other classes in Ivoirien society through a combination of cooptation and repression. At the same time, it continues to build up its own cohesion through political and social organizations and an expanding network of kinship and professional linkages, through which the class seems to be articulating a distinctive unifying ideology.

Toward the end of World War II, the Ivoirien bourgeoisie took advantage of an alliance with the new governor, André Latrille, to begin the long process of penetrating the Ivoirien state. Latrille was a Gaullist. He needed a local support base but could not obtain one among the settlers, who as Vichyists strongly opposed his rule. His alternative was the planters, who had opposed the Vichy regime and supported de Gaulle.[51] So, with his support, the Ivoirien bourgeoisie formed its first political association in 1944, the Syndicat Agricole Africain (SAA), which was essentially a lobby group for the interests of its membership. The SAA was the forerunner of the Parti Démocratique de la Côte d'Ivoire (PDCI),

Table 3.1 Côte d'Ivoire's Leading Capitalist Families

FAMILY BUSINESS INTERESTS

Ablé	real estate, construction materials production, retail trade, clothing manufacturing, other interests
Achy-Brou	packaging production
Aka (Lambert)	agroindustry, samwills, retail trade, engineering consulting, household products manufacturing, electrical installation
Aka Anghui	manufacturing of soaps and edible oil products, packaging production, retail trade, sawmill, cosmetics production, industrial engineering, other interests
Akoto Yao	bakeries, real estate, other interests
Amagou	industrial metal production, flour milling, construction and public works, truck and bus production, other interests
Améthier	banking, fish farming, engineering consulting, other interests
Amon	tobacco production, insurance, air conditioning, industrial electrical installation
Amon Tanoh	retail trade, other interests
Anoma	fertilizer manufacturing, plantations, other interests
Anvo Guetat	transportation, sawmill, plantations, other interests
Aoussou	water provision, other interests
Assouan Usher	retail trade, sawmill
Babo Zobo	insurance
Billon	export trade, agroindustry, packaging production, other interests
Boni	real estate, plantations
Bra Kanon	diverse interests, relatives in banking and packaging production
Brou	bakeries, plantations, other interests
Cisse	transportation, other interests
Coffi Gadeau	wholesale and retail trade, public works, fish importing and freezing
Coulibaly (Gbon)	agroindustry, retail trade, banking, insurance, bakeries, shipping, transportation, other interests
Dacoury-Tabley	retail trade, import trade
Dadié	wood processing, vinyl input manufacturing, manufacturing of metal products
Daubrey	banking
Delafosse	banking, hotels, other interests
Denise	retail trade
Diabaté	agroindustry, other interests
Diallo	retail, wholesale and import-export trade
Dioulo	banking, truck and bus production, agroindustry, other interests
Djibo	textiles manufacturing, insurance, real estate, wholesale trade, other interests
Donwahi	import-export trade, retail trade, agroindustry, computer consulting, other interests

(continues)

Table 3.1 (continued)

Ekra	agroindustry, construction materials manufacturing, plantations
Fadiga	plastics manufacturing, other manufacturing, transportation, other interests
Fofana	import-export trade, computer consulting, other interests
Houphouët-Boigny	agroindustry, manufacturing of paper goods, water bottling, insurance, retail trade, restaurants, transportation, electronics and telecommunications, other interests
Kacou	manufacturing of metal and electrical goods, construction materials manufacturing, resorts, other interests
Karamoko (Amara)	wholesale trade, other interests
Kodja Konan	soap and toothpaste manufacturing, trade, plantations, other interests
Konan Kouassi	banking, manufacturing of cotton products, agroindustry, other interests
Konate	banking, other interests
Koné	import-export trade, other interests
Kouassi Kouadio	agroindustry, manufacturing of electrical goods, other interests
Laubhouet	agroindustry, other interests
Mockey	retail trade, private medical clinics
N'Guessan	various industrial interests
Quashie	metals production, other interests
Sidi	steel manufacturing, packaging production, other interests
Tchicaya	agroindustry, manufacturing of soaps and edible oils, other interests
Yacé	real estate
Zadi Kessi	construction and public works, water provision, water bottling, other interests
Zinzou	shipping, other interests

Sources: Teya, *Côte d'Ivoire*, pp. 16–20; *Marchés tropicaux et méditerranéens*, Dec. 29, 1972, p. 3871; Jacques Gautrand, "Tanti est arrivé," *Jeune Afrique Economie*, June 1982, pp. 58–59; Centre d'Affaire International, *Annuaire statistique*, pp. 24–26; Adompo Pascal Koki, Interview, Jan. 26, 1990 (Adzopé); Côte d'Ivoire, Office National des Télécommunications, *Annuaire officiel*; Basil Yapi, Interview, Jan. 30, 1990 (Abidjan); Isidore Yapi, Interview, Jan. 30, 1990 (Abidjan); PDCI-RDA, *Annuaire 1985–1990*, pp. 11–180; *Fraternité Hebdo*, 1986, p. 211; Côte d'Ivoire, Ministère du Plan et de l'Industrie, *Répertoire des industries*; Chambre d'Agriculture, Chambre de Commerce, Chambre d'Industrie, *Annuaire*; *Le Grand dictionnaire encyclopédique de la Côte d'Ivoire*; "Côte d'Ivoire: 30 hommes pour gérer la crise," pp. 46–59; Daingui, Interview, May 2, 1990.

which grew out of it and was officially constituted in 1946 with fundamentally the same leadership.[52] While the membership of both organizations was broadly based, capitalists were disproportionately represented in their leaderships. The SAA was founded by seven big planters, the families of four of whom later went on to become some of Côte d'Ivoire's leading industrialists.[53] On the PDCI's first provisional board, chosen at its formation, almost two-fiths of the members were capitalists or came from leading capitalist families.[54]

Given the relatively low level of industrial development at this time, the urban working class was not the political factor that it is today. What was at issue was the huge rural population, made up then, as now, of a mass of smallholder farmers, many of whom had not yet entered the market economy to any significant degree. The bourgeoisie was able to take advantage of its own rural roots, the patronage of its richer members, and its comparatively plentiful supply of leadership talent to outmaneuver its rivals in capturing this large bloc of support. By effectively establishing itself as a transethnic group that brought into its fold leading members (who usually happened also to be leading capitalists) of almost all the country's ethnic groups,[55] and by championing the abolition of the much hated colonial institution of forced labor, the SAA made itself the party of the rural population.[56] The bond was sealed in 1946 when one of the SAA's leading figures, Félix Houphouët-Boigny, at the time a member of the French National Assembly, managed to secure the abolition of forced labor, thereby gaining the almost unquestioning loyalty of the vast majority of the Ivoirien population.[57]

Days later, he joined in the creation of the PDCI. Active recruitment made it possible for the PDCI-RDA[58] to mobilize a considerable base of support; by 1950, its membership approached a million.[59] The PDCI also opened its doors to the urban petty bourgeoisie, giving the party some more radical "streaks," and also capturing support that might have gone to rival parties. Opposition parties, despite the sponsorship of the post-Latrille colonial administration,[60] failed to make substantial inroads into the PDCI's support base. However, despite the PDCI's success in making itself into a transclass movement, the leadership of the party never fell out of the bourgeoisie's hands. In fact, the capitalist leadership took advantage of a colonial campaign of repression against the party in 1949–1950 to purge the leadership of a number of noncapitalist elements.[61] By 1959, therefore, almost two-thirds of the PDCI politburo's membership were either themselves capitalists or came from capitalist families.[62]

Using these policies of cooptation, the PDCI managed to establish itself in an almost unrivaled position by the late 1950s.[63] Shortly before independence, the PDCI-RDA enacted a number of measures that would guarantee one-party rule in the postcolonial period and place controls on any opposition groups, and one-party rule was formally institutionalized shortly after independence.[64] At the same time, the remaining opposition was in many cases simply coming around to the cause of the PDCI-RDA, recognizing that opposition was not only increasingly futile, but also increasingly dangerous.

During all this time, the bourgeoisie retained its control in the highest places of power, having carried its strength in the PDCI-RDA over into the state. Of the nineteen ministers in the country's first cabinet, nine—almost one-half of the total—came from the country's leading capitalist families.[65] Since then, the Ivoirien bourgeoisie has reinforced its hold on the state, responding to challenges from rival classes with a mixture of cooptation and, when that failed, repression. At the head of power is President Félix Houphouët-Boigny, the patriarch of a family with extensive holdings in the industrial economy. But bourgeois control of the state does not end with the president, despite his considerable power. In the 1989 cabinet, at least five of the ministers were themselves prominent capitalists, and another three were from important capitalist families.[66] This represented over a quarter of the cabinet and did not include those ministers who were shareholders in corporations but not corporate directors.

Control over mayoralties is equally impressive. In 1980, over one-third of Côte d'Ivoire's thirty-eight mayors were members of the country's business elite, not including mayors who had business interests but were not directly involved in administering them.[67] After the 1980 reorganization, which expanded the number of mayoralties to 136, the number of noncapitalist mayors increased as smaller rural towns were now given mayoralties. In 1990, of those 136, twenty-one were prominent capitalists,[68] and another ten were from or closely tied to prominent bourgeois families.[69] This represented roughly a quarter of the country's mayors. In actual fact, the proportion was probably much higher, not only for the same reason mentioned with regard to the 1980 survey group, but also because information was not available on all the country's mayors. Similar representation of the bourgeoisie can be found within the National Assembly, the country's legislative body. In 1990, of the 174 deputies to the Assembly, twenty-nine were capitalists of note and another twelve had family members who were, for a total of about one-quarter of the seats.[70] Once again, the total number was certainly much higher, but even proportions of around 25 percent of the ministerships, mayoralties, and National Assembly seats are quite remarkable when one takes into account the fact that in a predominantly agricultural country, the Ivoirien bourgeoisie may account for little more than 1 percent of the population.

This relationship is reflected on the "other side of the coin." In the survey of 110 of Côte d'Ivoire's largest industrial corporations (secondary and tertiary sectors) done in 1989–1990, it was found that forty-three had direct representation in the state's apparatus of power. That is to say, in forty-three of the companies, there were owners/administrators who occupied some position(s) in the state's political elite. This represents a remarkable 39 percent of the survey group,[71] a very strong presence in the state on the part of the Ivoirien owners of capital. Undoubtedly these corporations are able to find sympathetic ears in the corridors of political power.

However, beginning in 1989, the rulers of Côte d'Ivoire faced their biggest political challenges since the country was formed in 1960. Economic austerity brought about a tremendous amount of discontent within the country, while at the same time, the events of 1989 in Eastern Europe provided considerable impetus to dissidents who had been agitating for multiparty democracy. In the past, when confronted with such challenges, the government had responded with repression, as in the Bété uprising of 1970 and in the exiling of the chief opposition leader, Laurent Gbagbo. But by early 1990, things were different. Opposition parties, especially Gbagbo's Front Populaire Ivoirien (FPI), were bolder. SYNARES, the union of university professors and also the country's only autonomous union, which has been a long-time opponent of the regime, managed to infiltrate some of the other unions in Abidjan and pull off some startlingly well-organized—and in some cases completely unexpected—strikes.[72] Meantime, student groups had organized demonstrations that quickly turned into riots when the armed forces were sent to put them down. In some places, the riots became pitched battles causing extensive damage. Finally, in May 1990, the PDCI-RDA caved in and "asked" the government to legalize the opposition and open the upcoming elections to all parties.

However, this did not represent a defeat for the ruling bourgeoisie. To use military jargon, the ruling class made a tactical retreat, regrouped, then went back into battle, at which point it won. In the elections held at the end of 1990 and the beginning of 1991, the PDCI-RDA captured almost all of the 175 seats in the National Assembly (although the FPI won nine, including Gbagbo's) and virtually swept the mayoralties. There is no doubt that the opposition was harassed, but this was not the main reason for its weakness.

With decades of experience, the advantages of office (such as privileged access to communications media), and a lot of wealthy patrons, the PDCI-RDA is far and away the richest, best organized, most cohesive party in the country. It is able to communicate its message to Ivoiriens more effectively than its rivals, and can draw upon established networks of clients to mobilize support at election time. Although in the early stages of the campaign some prominent capitalists defected to the opposition, by election time most had returned to the party fold. The opposition, by contrast, is splintered into a dozen and a half small parties (some of which are said to be sponsored by the regime as part of an effort to further opposition disunity). In the context of a first-past-the-post electoral system, all these factors became positive liabilities for the opposition. Their poor showing in the elections was thus hardly surprising.[73]

In the end, the prodemocracy agitation appears to have been almost as much a squabble within the Ivoirien bourgeoisie as it has been a struggle between the bourgeoisie and rival classes. A number of prominent capitalists and politicians patronized the new parties, in particular the FPI, a fact that indicates that they considered the party fairly receptive to their interests. The younger generation do not approve of the old guard's tactics and have pushed for reform in the PDCI-RDA.[74] Looking at these changes of outlook within the class, one realizes that the Ivoirien prodemocracy movement has not been an assault on bourgeois power; instead, the changing nature of the capitalist class is leading to demands for—or at least a willingness to accommodate—new political structures. Satisfied with the direction of reforms, many of the discontented capitalists have returned to the PDCI-RDA fold, whereas the opposition continues to suffer from its divisions.

The Ivoirien Bourgeoisie and Postcolonial State Policy

Thus, the bourgeoisie has retained its hold on the postcolonial state, as reflected in the policies it has produced to advance its own interests. One can discern two different general policy approaches that prevailed at different times. The first policy, during the 1960s, was to rely heavily on foreign capital, French in particular, to invest in the economy to spur domestic growth. Despite some appearances, there was in this no opposition to the Ivoirien bourgeoisie, but the rapid industrialization sought at that time required resources beyond the means of the class, which was anxious to reap the benefits of a fast-growing economy. Activity on the part of the Ivoirien bourgeoisie continued, but its pace was somewhat sluggish and the class tended to behave rather conservatively, preferring to invest in its traditional domains, namely, real estate, agriculture, and the tertiary sector. As for development policy, the government relied on import substitution industrialization (ISI) to build up the economy's industrial base. Only two institutions of note, the Fonds National d'Investissements and the Société Nationale de Financement (SONAFI), were created in the early 1960s to assist the development of local enterprises.[75]

However, as the 1970s approached, a policy shift began to occur. To begin with, there was a move away from ISI and toward industrialization for export. Alongside this was a growing focus on assistance to the Ivoirien bourgeoisie, with less emphasis on foreign capital (though once again there was no turn against it). In particular, there were many attempts to stimulate domestic capital to invest more in the secondary sector of the economy, in which it had until then maintained only a modest presence. In consequence, one notices that the list of policy measures to stimulate the growth of the Ivoirien bourgeoisie is considerably longer for the 1970s than it was for the 1960s. State agencies created in the second decade of independence to assist the development of and provide credit to private Ivoirien capital included the Fonds de Garantie des Crédits Accordés aux Entreprises Ivoiriennes (FGCEI) (1968), the Fonds Spécial pour les Petites et Moyennes Entreprises (FSPME) (1970), the policy change involved in the Réforme de la politique du crédit, the Banque Centrale des Etats de l'Afrique de l'Ouest (1973), and the Office de Promotion de l'Entreprise Ivoirienne (OPEI) (1980).[76] This shift in the policy orientation of the Ivoirien government is a reflection of the rise of the industrial faction of the Ivoirien boureoisie at this time, as seen in its greater activism in private interest groups and the Chamber of Industry.

Throughout the entire postcolonial period, though, the Ivoirien state preserved an environment of political stability and a liberal investment climate, along with a tax system that has been quite beneficial to capitalists. With substantial World Bank assistance, Côte d'Ivoire has built up one of the most extensive transportation infrastructures in sub-Saharan Africa. Even in the late 1980s, in spite of economic austerity, the government planned to build an additional 1,000 kilometers of roads.[77] It has benefited from its membership in the CFA zone to preserve currency stability. Through the use of its cocoa and coffee marketing board, CAISTAB, it mobilized relatively large amounts of capital for investment subsidies in the industrial sector during the 1960s and 1970s.[78] At the same time, it was not plundering the agricultural economy in order to do this; from 1960 to 1975, the state oversaw a fourfold increase in the value of primary production by creating a number of state corporations whose task was to stimulate increased agricultural output.[79]

The Organization of the Ivoirien Bourgeoisie

Another noteworthy aspect of the Ivoirien bourgeoisie is the extent of its integration in terms of its kinship and professional relationships. In much the same way as studies of corporate elites in advanced capitalist countries have revealed high degrees of intermarriage or joint directorships, a survey of the Ivoirien bourgeoisie reveals that many, perhaps most, of the owners and directors of the country's largest corporations are closely tied to one another through marriages or joint directorships. This does not, however, result from common ethnic origin. Although some of the country's sixty ethnic groups are slightly underrepresented in the bourgeoisie, none is so strongly represented as to approach anything nearing dominance. Moreover, capitalists do not restrict their associations to members of their ethnic group. On the contrary, capitalists intermix freely with one another with little apparent regard to ethnicity, and business families very often are married into one or more other ethnic groups. For instance, the Coulibaly family network of professional and kinship linkages includes, among others, Senoufos, Malinkés, Dioulas, Sanwis, Baoulés, Abourés, and a Mauritanian. This incomplete list represents groups from three of the four major ethnic groupings of the country (Mandé, Voltaic, and Akan), as well as at least one foreign family, so the network is not regional but quite national in scope. The Coulibaly family network is not exceptional, save perhaps for its size. The Houphouët-Boigny network is actually more extensive, although its base is somewhat more southern, being composed to a greater extent of families of two of the country's major groupings, namely, Akan and Krou. Nonetheless, it is indirectly linked to the Coulibaly network, and Félix Houphouët-Boigny was himself personally close to the original patriarch of the Coulibaly clan, Gbon Coulibaly.

The network of interrelationships is a complex web. Families are tied to other families, which are in turn tied to other families, in a seemingly endless chain that ultimately connects most of them. Nonetheless, the end result is not amorphous. Certain families, which have built up extensive networks of linkages, have made themselves particularly powerful. Perhaps the country's two most powerful in this regard are the Houphouët-Boignys, the president's family, and the aforementioned Coulibalys, descendants of the great northern chief Gbon Coulibaly.

In an informal way, one can observe the activities of this "high society" of capitalist families by reading the weekly Abidjan entertainment review *Le Guido*. In a society section reminiscent of Britain's *Tattler*, there are photo essays from art exhibitions, official receptions, grand openings, and cocktail parties held by large firms to commemorate such things as company anniversaries. There we find the same familiar faces of the Ivoirien bourgeoisie and political elite rubbing shoulders with one another. In much the same way as business deals in advanced capitalist countries are often set over lunches at exclusive restaurants, the Ivoirien bourgeoisie has its own meeting places and social gatherings.

But these are by no means the Ivoirien bourgeoisie's only forms of contact. There is also quite an extensive network of professional organizations and interest groups. A few operate under state patronage, in which case one of their functions is to provide a *conduit* between business and the state; in addition, some, though formally subordinate to the state, are in fact essentially autonomous. Others enjoy complete autonomy. Some are several decades old, others are very recent creations, and still others have come and gone. Some are designed specifically for Ivoirien business people, some for "African" business people, and others for business people of all nationalities. Some are general groups to which all business people may belong; others are sector or industry specific.

The Chambers of Industry and of Commerce, which are among the most important of these groups, operate under state patronage, though that does not impede them from articulating an independent voice for Ivoirien business. In fact, the Chamber of Industry is one of the institutions that first served as a mouthpiece specifically for Ivoirien capital. Family members of the Ivoirien political-economic elite (that is, leading capitalist families that also occupy prominent positions in the state) are strongly represented on the executives of both chambers.[80] Corporate directors place a great deal of value on these institutions as sources of information.[81] In addition to these two official institutions, there are small chambers of commerce situated in cities and towns throughout the country. These, in turn, are supplemented by the Jeunes Chambres Economiques.

An example of an autonomous group is the APPMECI (an association for the promotion of small and medium-sized Ivoirien businesses), created in 1967 by a group of Ivoirien businessmen in order to pressure the government into giving more support and assistance to emerging Ivoirien capitalists. The APPMECI's first president was Lambert Konan, one of the early leaders of the industrial faction of the Ivoirien bourgeoisie and a member of the country's political-economic elite. Other autonomous business interest groups include the Syndicat des Entrepreneurs et des Industriels de Côte d'Ivoire, which was formed in 1934 by French businessmen but which has in the postcolonial period been increasingly occupied by Ivoiriens,[82] and the Union Patronale de Côte d'Ivoire, which is the country's main employers' group; it is headed by an Ivoirien businessman.[83]

Then there is a host of industry-specific interest groups, including the Fédération Maritime de la Côte d'Ivoire (actually a federation of four interest groups), the Syndicat des Agents de Voyages et de Tourisme en Côte d'Ivoire, the Association Professionnelle des Banques et Etablissements Financiers de Côte d'Ivoire, the Comité des Assureurs de Côte d'Ivoire, the Fédération Ivoirienne des Industries du Textile et de l'Habillement, the Syndicat des Importateurs de Bétails et de Volailles de Côte d'Ivoire, the Groupement Interprofessionnel de l'Automobile, the Syndicat des Commerçants Importateurs et Exportateurs, the Syndicat des Exportateurs et Négociants en Bois de Côte d'Ivoire, the Syndicat des Petites et Moyennes Entreprises, the Syndicat des Producteurs Industriels de Bois, and the Syndicat National des Transports de Marchandises et Voyageurs. Relations between these groups and the government can at times be conflictual, although cooperation is also frequent, and corporate executives sometimes name their industry's interest group as their most useful source for business information.[84]

There are also organizations that serve as meeting places between Ivoirien capitalists and their foreign counterparts, such as the Club des Hommes d'Affaires Franco-Ivoiriens, run jointly by the Ivoirien government and the French embassy; the World Trade Centre Club, administered by government officials; and the American Chamber of Commerce. A similar international group is the Round Table of African Businessmen, established in 1990 by the African Development Bank; it has directors from a number of African countries, one of whom is an Ivoirien businessman, Charles Donwahi.

Finally, there are what one might call informal business associations, clubs, or groups. Interestingly, though perhaps not surprisingly, these may well be the most important class organizations for the Ivoirien bourgeoisie. Especially significant are service clubs, such as the Lions and Rotary clubs. It is said that virtually all PDGs (*président et directeur-général*, the equivalent of a chief executive officer) belong to one or other of these organizations, so that they become one of the most common forums for intraclass communication. Business matters always arise, and personal contacts are made, at the meetings of these associations.[85] There are also investment clubs, which are essentially mutual funds with a membership of 200. Investment clubs serve as interest groups in that the members are frequently corporate executives from different firms who join to create new ventures, thereby uniting their companies.[86]

Through all these formal and informal institutions of class organization and integration, the Ivoirien bourgeoisie appears to articulate a coherent ideology that unites its members. This seems especially so among younger capitalists, who seem to share a particularly strong common consciousness, based on a sense of business superiority vis-à-vis their older counterparts. In interviews, I found that younger capitalists often spoke of the fact that older business people were merely investors, whereas they comprised a generation of genuine entrepreneurs and "idea men." Younger capitalists almost always offered the same reason for having chosen business as a career: lucrative public sector positions were no longer available to university graduates.

Not surprisingly, therefore, the Ivoirien bourgeoisie is a comparatively well-educated class.[87] This manifests itself in a degree of intellectual sophistication that appears superior to that of the expatriate business community. An apparent outcome of this education is that nationalism seems to occupy a central position in the ideology of the Ivoirien bourgeoisie. While stressing their cosmopolitan nature, and therefore soliciting contracts and joint ventures with foreign investors, younger Ivoirien capitalists nonetheless appear to see themselves as forming a generation that is retaking control of the country's economy.[88] And so, for example, the recent creation of companies like SIALIM (Nestlé's rival in the production of sweetened condensed milk) or PRIMA (a modern supermarket) evoked pride, because both cases represented the breaking of foreign domination or monopoly of a given subsector. Blaise K. Tanoh, the founder of SIALIM, said in a recent interview: *"Les Africains deviennent de plus en plus nationalistes. Nous avons tous les mêmes intérêts économiques"* ("Africans are becoming more and more nationalist. We all have the same economic interests").[89] In fact, Tanoh's quotation goes beyond nationalism to another element of the class's ideology—a budding pan-Africanism. There is an obvious awareness on the part of Ivoirien business people that the collapse of Communism in Eastern Europe will cause a loss of interest in African ventures on the part of First World investors. The response has been to initiate joint ventures and broaden contacts with business leaders in other African countries in order to lessen dependence on Western capital.[90]

In sum, one sees that Ivoirien business culture resembles those of advanced capitalist countries to a considerable extent. This is reflected in the general conservatism of African businessmen and their penchant for such things as expensive European suits. On the other hand, there are distinctively African characteristics that figure importantly in their culture. Perhaps most important of all is the continuing overriding importance of personal relationships; incoming expatriate business people often fail to appreciate the essential requirement of an introduction by a mutual friend to cultivating a business relationship with an Ivoirien capitalist. There also lingers the practice of ostentation, not for its own sake but for the sake of the business. Ivoirien businessmen sometimes go out of their way to impress their success upon others by such things as chauffeured Mercedes-Benzes; it is also a way of earning the confidence of others that they are good business managers. This may be a holdover of the ostentation of traditional chiefs anxious to earn the respect of their people. It is worth noting, though, that one finds this behavior less frequently among younger Ivoirien entrepreneurs, who sometimes consider it a wasteful use of resources.

The Ivoirien Bourgeoisie and Foreign Capital

Although the Ivoirien bourgeoisie's relationship with foreign capital is primarily a relationship with French capital, there has been a continuous diversification in the postcolonial period. Business people and the government have been trying to attract investors and entrepreneurs of other nationalities, showing a particular interest in Americans, and this policy has attained a certain degree of success, even though foreign capital in Côte d'Ivoire is still overwhelmingly French.

However, the relationship between the Ivoirien bourgeoisie and French capital is not as simple as it might appear. The foreign business people with whom Ivoirien capitalists do business are divided at the outset into two groups: on the one hand, there are foreigners whose base of operation is abroad and who maintain branch offices/plants in Côte d'Ivoire; on the other, there are people of foreign nationality whose families nonetheless reside in Côte d'Ivoire and in many cases have done so for many generations.

The latter constitute what can be called the "French Ivoiriens," and their behavior is significantly different from that of their other foreign, mainly French, counterparts in a number of ways. Simply speaking, they are Ivoirien oriented in their behavior. While French-owned businesses typically import just over half of their inputs, and foreign businesses of other nationalities have even higher import:output ratios, French Ivoiriens import much less than half of their inputs and use very little foreign staff; only Ivoirien capitalists have lower import:output ratios.[91] When they do import inputs, French businesses tend rather strongly to buy them from France; however, there is no such tendency on the part of French Ivoiriens.[92] Moreover, these investors are not as likely to repatriate profits to France as are ordinary French investors.[93] All in all, the French Ivoiriens are oriented toward the local economy, not toward that of France.

Therefore, it is telling that Ivoirien capitalists are more likely to do business with the French Ivoiriens than they are with other foreign capitalists.[94] This particular relationship appears to have been a beneficial one to the Ivoirien bourgeoisie in that it has contributed to the growth and maturing of the class. The history of the Blohorn family provides a good illustration of this point. The first of the Blohorns came to Côte d'Ivoire over six decades ago to build a refinery that would produce soap from the plentiful local supply of palm oil. Early on he made the acquaintance of some Ivoiriens who would go on to be among the country's leading capitalists and politicians. Later, members of the Blohorn family would be instrumental in establishing Ivoirien business organizations like the Syndicat des Industriels et Entrepreneurs de Côte d'Ivoire (the AICI) and the Chamber of Industry. In the postcolonial period, the company began to Ivoirize first its administration, then its capital.[95] In sum, some Ivoirien business families, particularly the Aka Anghui family,[96] grew alongside the Blohorn family, in a relationship of apparent mutual gain.

The ties between the Ivoirien bourgeoisie and the rest of foreign capital are not quite as strong. To begin with, foreign holdings are typically wholly owned subsidiaries. In addition, foreign-based investors tend to be involved in the tertiary sector (trade and services): 41 percent of total French capital stock, for instance, is currently located in trade.[97] Both of these facts signify a lesser degree of involvement in the local economy, a lesser degree of linkage to the Ivoirien bourgeoisie, and a consequent higher degree of higher capital mobility. Thus, as foreign capital is in relative decline in its share of the economy's total capital,[98] it can be surmised that this is more likely to be foreign subsidiaries withdrawing their operations than it is French Ivoiriens disinvesting.

The official stance with regard to the relationship with foreign capital has always been that the latter benefited the Ivoirien economy by making up for the shortfall in investment capital that could be mobilized locally, especially in the early postcolonial period. This may be so, although it is likely that French Ivoirien capital played a more helpful role than foreign capital as such. The interests of foreign capital and of French Ivoirien capital clearly diverge, and the former does not have the same vested interest in the well-being of the Ivoirien economy as does the latter. Some foreign companies, Nestlé being a case in point, have proved to be very hostile to the success of local entrepreneurs who are seen to be a threat. Foreign banks also have been less than forthcoming with investment loans for Ivoirien businesses, preferring safe investments in large, established multinationals. One sees the sort of cleavage between foreign capital and "settler" capital of which Arghiri Emmanuel spoke in reference to the colonial period.[99] The ability of the Ivoirien bourgeoisie to respond to these challenges through the medium of the state has varied. In times of economic hardship, the bourgeoisie is placed in a position of greater vulnerability, particularly with regard to foreign lending agencies; at other times, it has more leeway to assert itself vis-à-vis foreign capital. Overall, one might call the relationship conflictual but amicable. However, the relationship of mutual benefit has been that with French Ivoirien capital.

Discussion

Côte d'Ivoire's record of growth and development has been well documented elsewhere. From a comparatively ordinary base at the time of independence, the country has attained one of the highest per capita incomes in sub-Saharan Africa.[100] All sectors of the economy have grown, though manufacturing has grown fastest.[101] As a proportion of total exports, manufactured exports have doubled in the postcolonial period, and today the country records the highest value of manufactured exports in all of sub-Saharan Africa.[102]

Côte d'Ivoire's postcolonial economic achievements have resulted in no small part from the fact that this development has been spearheaded by an Ivoirien bourgeoisie. To begin with, the class's control of the state exercised a determining influence on the type of development policy chosen and the effectiveness with which it would be implemented. When the Ivoirien bourgeoisie came to power, it already had vested interests in the private sector. Political power thus became a means to promote and secure private accumulation, the means to an end; it did not become the end in itself, namely, the primary avenue for accumulation and upward mobility, as has been said to have been the case elsewhere in Africa.[103] This permitted the fluidity in the ruling elite that is necessary to political stability, because individual capitalists could afford to relinquish power provided their class interests were still represented. It also entailed the encouragement of general economic growth, rather than the promotion of particular interests, because the bourgeoisie needed an expanded domestic market as well as increased supplies for its factories; the state was therefore expected to preside over a widespread economic expansion and not simply the enrichment of one group at the expense of others.

In addition, in its economic activities the Ivoirien bourgeoisie has had a more beneficial impact on the economy than has its foreign counterpart. Ivoirien capital's close integration into the economy—relative to foreign firms, Ivoirien firms use more local inputs, hire more Ivoirien managers, establish more joint ventures with African businesses from neighboring countries, export more of their goods to other African countries, and reinvest more of their profits locally[104]—has meant the Ivoirien bourgeoisie's growth has produced more spin-off benefits in the national (and regional) economy than has the growth of foreign capital. The expansion of Ivoirien capital has thus "dragged" the economy, or parts thereof, behind it.

However, the most pressing question concerns the future of the Ivoirien bourgeoisie. In the course of the 1980s and early 1990s, Côte d'Ivoire has been weathering a severe recession. Growth slowed to the point that by the late 1980s, the economy actually began to contract in real terms; per capita incomes have declined; bankruptcies have risen; inflation is said to be reaching record levels.[105] Many observers have concluded either that the Ivoirien miracle has run its course, or that there never was an Ivoirien miracle and that the predictions of underdevelopment theorists foreseeing structural limits to the country's growth have been fulfilled. Added to this is the political challenge faced by the ruling class now that a legal opposition exists.

It is too early to say what the eventual outcome of the present economic crisis will be. It is not obvious that the crisis arose from structural blockages (usually attributed to the shortcomings of an extensive development model). Moreover, current data may overstate the depth of the recession, reflecting the wide-scale dissolution of the public sector and the contraction in export revenue due to plummeting world coffee and cocoa prices, but obscuring the records in other sectors. In this regard it is telling to note that Ivoirien capital continued to prosper during the 1980s, if at a more modest pace than in the 1970s. In fact, Ivoirien capital has been the most dynamic component of the economy, growing more quickly than the economy, any of its subsectors, and both the foreign and state components of capital. Therefore, while conventional wisdom has always held agriculture to be Côte d'Ivoire's engine of growth, the crisis in agriculture reflecting the slowing of the engine, it can be argued that the real engine has been the Ivoirien bourgeoisie, and agriculture its fuel. This does not mean that there is no crisis, for deprived of fuel the engine will eventually cease to operate. But what it does mean is that the engine is still operating; it may have slowed, but not to the same degree as has been assumed. As for the Ivoirien bourgeoisie's hold on political power, this will in large measure be determined by medium-term economic developments. For the time being, though, it appears secure in office.

Yet even if the Ivoirien bourgeoisie emerges from this current crisis, leaner but robust and with its hold on political power relatively intact, challenges remain. In particular, the apparent regionalization of world trade into a few blocs and the reduced interest of the developed industrial countries in their developing counterparts may pose severe threats to the Ivoirien bourgeoisie's access to export markets and investment capital. The debt crisis in both Côte d'Ivoire and its African trading partners and the continuing slump in world commodity prices show no sign of easing in the near future. Finally, there remains the environmental challenge and the limits to growth placed thereby on a class using a classical development model, a threat that has already manifested itself in Côte d'Ivoire in, for example, the problems of deforestation and the apparent exhaustion of farmland supplies.

The Ivoirien bourgeoisie has been anticipating these challenges with varying degrees of effectiveness, although it has shown little sensitivity or imagination in preparing for the environmental challenge; responding to it may be its most daunting task. How the class, and the state that represents it, will meet these challenges remains to be seen. But the Ivoirien bourgeoisie is at least as well positioned as any other ruling class in sub-Saharan Africa to overcome these obstacles to its future development.

Notes

1. See Ruth Schachter Morgenthau, *Political Parties in French-Speaking West Africa* (Oxford: Clarendon Press, 1964), p. 168; Hubert Deschamps, "France in Black Africa and Madagascar Between 1920 and 1945," in Peter Duignan and L. H. Gann, eds., *Colonialism in Africa 1870–1960*, Vol. 2 (Cambridge: Cambridge University Press, 1970), p. 238; Hubert Fréchou, *Les planteurs européens en Côte d'Ivoire* (Dakar: Institut des Hautes Etudes de Dakar, 1955 [Travaux du Département de Géographie no. 3]), p. 23; M. Dupire, "Planteurs autochtones et étrangers en Basse-Côte d'Ivoire orientale," *Etudes éburnéennes* 8 (1960), pp. 48–49; Dotou Janvier Segla, *Immigration étrangère et économie de plantation dans la région d'Agboville à l'époque coloniale* (Abidjan: ORSTOM, Centre de Petit Bassam, 1978), pp. 15–30; P. du Prey, *L'histoire des ivoiriens* (Abidjan, 1962), p. 172. The case of Gabriel Dadié, who was an employee of the colonial regime, provides an excellent case of an African who learned his techniques directly from Europeans, in this case from two French colleagues who had left their administrative positions to take up plantation farming with great success. Dadié went on to be not only one of Côte d'Ivoire's richest planters, but also a founding member of the colony's independence movement. See *Mémorial de la Côte d'Ivoire*, Vol. 2 (Abidjan: Editions Ami, 1987), p. 190.
2. See, for example, David Groff's case study of Assikasso: David H. Groff, "The Development of Capitalism in the Ivory Coast: The Case of Assikasso, 1880–1940," Ph.D. diss., Stanford University, 1980, pp. 394–395.
3. Morgenthau, *Political Parties*, p. 173; Anyang' Nyong'o, "The Articulation of Modes of Production: The Political Economy of Coffee in the Ivory Coast, 1840–1975," Ph.D. diss., University of Chicago, 1977, pp. 82, 176; Peter Lionel Wickins, *Africa 1880–1980: An Economic History* (Cape Town: Oxford University Press, 1986), p. 78; Prey, *L'histoire des ivoiriens*, p. 172; Dupire, "Planteurs autochtones et étrangers," pp. 102–104.
4. On the Eglin plantation, for instance, out of 2,358 workers, 72 were Malian, 152 were Ivoirien, and the remainder came from Upper Volta (Segla, *Immigration étrangère*, pp. 22–23).
5. Dupire, "Planteurs autochtones et étrangers," pp. 102–104.

6. Albert de Surgy, *Les pêcheurs de Côte d'Ivoire*, Vol. 2, *Les pêcheurs lagunaires* (Paris: Centre Nationale de Recherche Scientifique; Abidjan: Centre National de Documentation de Côte d'Ivoire, 1964), p. 114.

7. Morgenthau, *Political Parties*, p. 171; *Mémorial de la Côte d'Ivoire*, Vol. 2, p. 243.

8. Morgenthau, *Political Parties*, p. 12.

9. E. A. Brett, "State Power and Economic Inefficiency: Explaining Political Failure in Africa" (Manchester: Political Science Association Conference, 1985).

10. See Morgenthau, *Political Parties*, pp. 171–172.

11. See l'Abbé Jean-Albert Ablé, *Histoire et tradition politique du pays Abouré* (Abidjan: Imprimerie Nationale, 1978).

12. Y.-A. Fauré and J.-F. Médard, "Classe dominante ou classe dirigeante," in Fauré and Medard, eds., *Etat et bourgeoisie en Côte d'Ivoire* (Paris: Editions Karthala, 1982), p. 133.

13. *Mémorial de la Côte d'Ivoire*, Vol. 2, p. 243.

14. Ibid., p. 224; 1934–1935 were years of particularly rapid growth.

15. Morgenthau, *Political Parties*, p. 169.

16. Ibid., p. 175.

17. In the 1930s, wage labor was used mainly during the busy seasons. The use of wage labor began to spread particularly after World War II. See Wickins, *Africa 1880–1980*, pp. 168–169, and Nyong'o, "The Articulation of Modes of Production," p. 175.

18. Henrik Secher Marcussen and Jens Erik Torp, *The Internationalization of Capital: Prospects for the Third World* (London: Zed Books, 1982), p. 128.

19. Morgenthau, *Political Parties*, p. 215. For a detailed example of the diversification of interests by an African planter, see the case of Kwasi bi Yuza, a Gouro planter, in Claude Meillassoux, *Anthropologie économique des Gouro de Côte d'Ivoire* (Paris: Mouton, 1964), pp. 328–330.

20. A. Köbben, "Le planteur noir," *Etudes éburnéennes* 5 (1956), pp. 102–103.

21. Dupire, "Planteurs autochtones et étrangers," pp. 100–101.

22. Köbben, "Le planteur noir," pp. 82–86.

23. Ablé, *Histoire et tradition politique*, pp. 105–107. Some particularly prominent capitalists emerged from among the Abourés, among them Mathieu Ekra, whose family had taken up coffee cultivation in 1920, the first to do so in Bonoua. Ekra himself was a planter—the first in Bonoua to cultivate pineapples—who later diversified his interests into the secondary sphere of production (ibid., p. 108n). He now has interests in Nouvelle SIACA, which cans and exports pineapple slices and juice, and Nouvelle SERIA, which produces construction materials.

24. Wickins, *Africa 1880–1980*, pp. 168–169.

25. See Dupire, "Planteurs autochtones et étrangers," pp. 100–101; Jean Suret-Canale, *Afrique noire occidentale et centrale,* Vol. 3 (Paris: Editions Sociales, 1972), p. 186.

26. D. K. Fieldhouse, *Colonialism 1870–1945* (New York: St. Martin's Press, 1981), p. 100. See Guy Cangah and Simon-Pierre Ekanza, *La Côte d'Ivoire par les textes* (Les Nouvelles Editions Africaines, 1978), pp. 134–136, for a detailed, and short, inventory of the secondary industry in Côte d'Ivoire in 1931.

27. The Ivoirien planters certainly had the disposable income necessary for sizable capital accumulation. Given that Ivoirien farmers at this time had a much higher average income than did other French West African farmers (see Virginia Thompson and Richard Adloff, "French Economic Policy in Tropical Africa," in Peter Duignan and L. H. Gann, eds., *Colonialism in Africa 1870–1960,* Vol. 4 [Cambridge: Cambridge University Press, 1975], p. 143), it is virtually certain that the top Ivoirien planters formed the richest African agrarian class in French West

Africa. Given that the richest Europeans in Côte d'Ivoire were the settlers (Alain Tirefort, "Le bon temps: Approche de la société coloniale: Etude de cas: La communauté française en Basse Côte d'Ivoire pendant l'Entre-Deux-Guerres [1920–1940]," thèse de 3e cycle, EHESS, Paris, 1979, pp. 289–290), not the traders or colonial officials, it is probably reasonable to conclude that the richest Ivoiriens were similarly the planters, not traders, civil servants, or teachers. They were perhaps even the richest African class in all of French West Africa.

28. The Denise family now has interests in pharmaceuticals.

29. Jean Chevassu and Alain Valette, *Les industriels de la Côte d'Ivoire: Qui et pourquoi?* (Abidjan: ORSTOM, Centre de Petit Bassam, 1975 [Série sciences humaines]), p. 15.

30. Marcussen and Torp, *The Internationalization of Capital*, p. 101; Chevassu and Valette, *Les industriels de la Côte d'Ivoire*, p. 5, Table 1; *L'économie ivoirienne* (Paris: La Documentation Africaine [EDIAFRIC], 1982), 10th ed., pp. 190–191.

31. Pierre Biarnès, *L'Afrique aux africains* (Paris: Armand Colin, 1980), p. 190. See also the World Bank's annual development reports.

32. *L'économie ivoirienne* (p. 57) provides the following statistics:

Year	Proportion
1975	9%
1976	11.3%
1977	11.9%
1978	11.6%
1979	13.2%
1980	11%

33. The actual figures for the expansion in capital assets (in millions of CFAF) were as follows (ibid., pp. 57, 117):

	Total Industrial Capital	Secondary Capital
1975	12,944	4,400
1976	—	6,900
1977	18,185	10,400
1978	22,910	11,000
1979	30,550	14,900
1980	33,678	19,700

It would be difficult, if not impossible, to construct an adequate deflator for these figures, due to uncertain data on price indexes for the industrial sector. However, it is clear that most of this expansion resulted from new investment, not accrued value (data on investment and changes in companies' registered capital can be obtained in *Marchés tropicaux et méditerranéens*, published by Moreux). Therefore, it is reasonable to conclude that most of this expansion did not stem from inflationary pressures.

34. *Marchés tropicaux et méditerranéens*, May 5, 1989, p. 1215.

35. See John Rapley, *Ivoirien Capitalism: African Entrepreneurs in Côte d'Ivoire* (Boulder; Lynne Rienner, 1993), Appendix 1. In fact, there were probably another 200 companies this large that had Ivoirien share ownership but were left out of the survey due to insufficient data.

36. Ibid., Table 5.5. The wide range results from the small size of the survey groups used.

37. Chevassu and Valette, *Les industriels de la Côte d'Ivoire*, pp. 15–16; Claude de Miras, *La formation de capital productif privé ivoirien: Le secteur menuiserie à Abidjan* (Abidjan: ORSTOM, Centre de Petit Bassam, 1975 [Série

sciences humaines]), pp. 65–71; Claude de Miras, *La formation de capital productif privé ivoirien: Le secteur boulangerie* (Abidjan: ORSTOM, Centre de Petit Bassam, 1976 [Série sciences humaines]), pp. 46, 47, 53, 55; Andrea Calamanti, *The Securities Market and Underdevelopment* (Finafrica-Cariplo-Milan: Giuffre, 1983), pp. 121–123; Jean-Marc Gastellu and Affou Yapi, "Où situer les grands planteurs villageois?" *Cahiers ivoiriens de recherche économique et sociale* 30 (September 1981), p. 45.

38. Didier Kouadio Koffi, *La création des entreprises privées par les nationaux en Côte d'Ivoire* (Abidjan: CEDA, 1983), pp. 55–57.

39. See Rapley, *Ivoirien Capitalism*, Appendix 1. The survey did not include firms that were restricted to the primary sector.

40. Ibid., Chapter 5.

41. Ibid., Appendix 1.

42. Ibid.

43. Ibid.

44. Ibid., Table 5.3.

45. Lynn Krieger Mytelka, "The Limits of Export-Led Development: The Ivory Coast's Experience with Manufactures," in John Gerard Ruggie, ed., *The Antinomies of Interdependence* (New York: Columbia University Press, 1983); see also "Investissement étranger direct et choix technologique dans les industries ivoiriennes du textile et du bois," *Revue canadienne d'études du développement* 4, no. 1 (1983); pp. 95–123. Another valuable study is Bonnie Campbell, "Neocolonialism, Economic Dependence and Political Change: A Case Study of Cotton and Textile Production in the Ivory Coast 1960 to 1970," *Review of African Political Economy* 2 (1975), pp. 36–53.

46. Morgenthau, *Political Parties*, p. 168.

47. That is to say, they minimized the use of labor and capital inputs, which were expensive relative to the cost of land, thereby reducing cost per output.

48. Three-quarters of the corporations that were majority-owned by Ivoiriens were found to be administered by Ivoiriens. Anecdotal evidence did not reveal any tendency to rely on foreign technical expertise. See Rapley, *Ivoirien Capitalism*, Appendix 1.

49. See Rapley, *Ivoirien Capitalism*, Chapter 5, especially notes 16 and 49.

50. See note 45.

51. See *Mémorial de la Côte d'Ivoire*, Vol. 2, p. 291, and Tirefort, "Le bon temps," pp. 188–252. A number of the planters had also been supporters of the earlier Popular Front government.

52. Aristide Zolberg has documented the close ties between the SAA and the PDCI; see *One-Party Government in the Ivory Coast* (Princeton, N.J.: Princeton University Press, 1964), pp. 152–154.

53. The seven planters were Georges Kassi, Joseph Anoma, Amadou Lamine Touré, Djibril Diaby, Gabriel Dadié, Félix Houphouët-Boigny, and Fulgence Brou; see Laurent Gbagbo, *La Côte d'Ivoire: Economie et société à la veille de l'indépendance (1940–1960)* (Paris: Editions l'Harmattan, 1982), p. 29. The official list adds two names to these: Kouamé Adingra and Kouamé N'Guessan, (*1946–1986, il y a 40 ans naissait le PDCI* [Abidjan: Editions Fraternité Hebdo, 1986], p. 211), but it is the other seven whose families have since gone on to take up prominent positions among the Ivoirien ruling class. The four whose families went on to become prominent capitalist ones were Anoma, Dadié, Houphouët-Boigny, and Brou; for details of their business holdings see Table 3.1.

54. These were Houphouët-Boigny, Jean Delafosse, Germain Coffi Gadeau, Gabriel Dadié, Joseph Anoma, Antoine Konan Kanga, Georges Auguste Denise,

and Denis Coffi Bilé. See PDCI-RDA, *Annuaire 1985–1990* (Abidjan: Editions Fraternité-Hebdo, 1987), p. 389; for details of the business holdings of the most prominent of these see Table 3.1.

55. The Agni were the only notable exception (Fauré and Médard, "Classe dominante ou classe dirigeante," p. 128); Zolberg (*One-Party Government*, p. 67) also says that "the Agni remained outside the mainstream of African organizational life" in the 1940s.

56. In fact, the abolition of forced labor was in the Ivoirien bourgeoisie's interests; since only French farmers had access to this resource, it constituted an unfair subsidy from the point of view of the Ivoirien planters.

57. Indeed, Houphouët-Boigny became a hero all over French West Africa.

58. "RDA" refers to the *Rassemblement Démocratique Africain*, an umbrella organization of French West African parties whose formation was spearheaded by the PDCI. To this day, PDCI-RDA remains the official name of the party.

59. Jon Woronoff, *West African Wager* (Metuchen, N.J.: Scarecrow Press, 1972), p. 37.

60. See Morgenthau, *Political Parties*, pp. 189–202, for a chronology of these attempts on the part of the colonial administration to weaken the PDCI-RDA. The governors after Latrille tried to remake their alliance with the settlers, though by this time the planters were too well established as a political force to be eliminated.

61. See Gbagbo, *La Côte d'Ivoire*, pp. 91–102. One should note, however, that Gbagbo himself does not consider the bourgeoisie to have been anything but a comprador one.

62. These men were Houphouët-Boigny, Philippe Yacé, Georges Auguste Denise, Germain Coffi Gadeau, Koffi Aoussou, Antoine Konan Kanga, Denis Coffi Bilé, Mathieu Ekra, and Alcide Kacou (PDCI-RDA, *Annuaire 1985–1990*, pp. 401–402). For details of the business holdings of the more prominent among these see Table 3.1.

63. See Zolberg, *One-Party Government*, pp. 188–215.

64. Brigitte Masquet, "Côte d'Ivoire: Pouvoir présidentiel, palabre et démocratie" *Afrique contemporaine* 114 (March-April 1981), pp. 10–22, 17; Zolberg, *One-Party Government*, pp. 255–268.

65. These were Houphouët-Boigny, Jean-Baptiste Mockey, Georges Auguste Denise, Jean Delafosse, Alphonse Boni, Alcide Kacou, Antoine Konan Kanga, Koffi Aoussou, and Charles Donwahi (PDCI-RDA, *Annuaire 1985–1990*). For details of the business holdings of the most prominent among these see Table 3.1.

66. The prominent capitalists were Félix Houphouët-Boigny, Auguste Denise, Mathieu Ekra, Hortense Aka Anghui, and Jean-Claude Delafosse. Those whose family members were prominent capitalists were Alain Gauze (family of Denis Bra Kanon), Vincent Tioko Djédjé (family network of Etienne Affot Lattier, which includes the Houphouët-Boigny, Yacé, Coffie Gadeau, Daubrey, and Assouan Usher families), and Balla Keita (Coulibaly family). Most of the related families have in the past had members who were ministers. See Table 3.1 for details of these individuals' or families' business holdings.

67. These mayors were Victor Amagou (Marcory), Léon Amon (Dimbokro), E. Desnoces Anvo Guetat (Abengourou), Félicien Kodja Konan (Divo), Emmanuel Dioulo (Abidjan), Arsène Assouan Usher (Cocody), Jean-Baptiste Mockey (Grand-Bassam), Jean-Baptiste Améthier (Bonoua), Denis Bra Kanon (Daloa), Léon Amon (Dimbokro), Philippe Yacé (Jacqueville), Ouattara Thomas d'Aquin (Katiola), Lanciné Gon Coulibaly (Korhogo); PDCI-RDA, *Annuaire 1985–1990*. See Table 3.1 for details of their business holdings. Ouattara Thomas d'Aquin was an army general with business interests; he died in early 1990.

68. These were Antoine Adou Kouao (Bétié), Hortense Aka Anghui (Port-Bouët), Victor Amagou (Marcory), Jean-Baptiste Améthier (Bonoua), Thomas Assi Kaudhis (Adzopé), Arsène Assouan Usher (Cocody), Pierre Billon (Dabakala), Joseph Bombo (Grand-Lahou), Edmond Bouazo Zegbehi (Issia), Denis Bra Kanon (Daloa), François Dacoury-Tabley (Gagnoa), Auguste Daubrey (Sassandra), Charles Donwahi (Soubre), Lamine Fadiga (Touba), Ossey Denis Gnansou (Agboville), Amara Karamoko (Mankono), Félicien Kodja Konan (Divo), Sourou Kone (Kolia), Moussa Konet (Kani), Pierre Koffi N'Guessan (San Pedro), and Philippe Yacé (Jacqueville). For details on the business holdings of the most prominent of these, see Table 3.1.

69. These were (with family members in parentheses, after mayoralties): Noël N'goran Koffi (Didiévi; Aoussou Koffi), Berthe Sawadogo (Fresco; Etienne Affot Lattier family network), Marthe Achy-Brou (Grand-Bassam; Achy-Brou family), mayor of Akoupé (also from the Achy-Brou family), Daouda Coulibaly (Korhogo; Coulibaly family), Lenissogui Coulibaly (Boundiali; Coulibaly family), Philippe Kouassi Cowppli Bony (Bouaké; Cowppli Bony family), Gervais Kadio Morokro (Niablé; Kadio Morokro family), Dembélé Yaya (Kouto; Kone family), Ernest Mobio N'Koumo (Abidjan; Mobio N'Koumo family). For details of the business holdings of the most prominent among these, see Table 3.1.

70. See Rapley, *Ivoirien Capitalism*, Table 3.2 for details.

71. See Rapley, *Ivoirien Capitalism*, Appendix 1.

72. Workers in financial institutions, bus drivers, doctors and nurses, students, and even soldiers were among those who joined the strikes.

73. For a summary of the election see Gerald Bourke, "A New Broom," *Africa Report* (January-February 1991), pp. 13–16; for an interpretation of the PDCI-RDA's victory see Y.-A. Fauré, "L'économie politique d'une démocratisation: Eléments d'analyse à propos de l'expérience récente de la Côte d'Ivoire," *Politique africaine* 43 (October 1991), pp. 31–49.

74. Bourke, "A New Broom," p. 15; Fauré, "L'économie politique d'une démocratisation," p. 39.

75. Bonnie Campbell, "Etat et développement du capitalisme en Côte-d'Ivoire," in Catherine Coquery-Vidrovitch and Alain Forest, eds., *Entreprises et entrepreneurs en Afrique*, Vol. 2 (Paris: Editions l'Harmattan, 1983), pp. 306–307.

76. Claude de Miras, "De la bourgeoisie d'état à l'avènement d'un milieu d'entrepreneurs ivoiriens?" in Coquery-Vidrovitch and Forest, *Entreprises et entrepreneurs en Afrique*, p. 198.

77. *African Business,* November 1985, p. 80.

78. During much of the postcolonial period, about one-third of Côte d'Ivoire's cocoa and coffee (the country's main export revenue commodities) earnings were appropriated by the state, primarily through the agency of CAISTAB: Eddy Lee, "Export-Led Rural Development: The Ivory Coast," *Development and Change* 11 (October 1980), p. 637. In the 1977 boom year, the amount came to US$1 billion: Robert Hecht, "The Ivory Coast Economic 'Miracle': What Benefits the Peasant Farmers?" *Journal of Modern African Studies* 21, no. 1 (March 1983) p. 30.

79. Bastiaan A. den Tuinder, *Ivory Coast: The Challenge of Success* (Baltimore: Johns Hopkins University Press, for the World Bank, 1978), Table SA8, Statistical Appendix. This network of parastatals has since been wound down, due to economic austerity.

80. In the case of the Chamber of Commerce, these names include Lamine Fadiga (president) and Joachim Richmond (vice-president). Other prominent Ivoirien capitalists on the board of directors are Madeleine Tchicaya and Georges Kassy. In the case of the Chamber of Industry, these names include Joseph Aka Anghui, Edmond Anoma, Frédéric Ablé, Jean-Baptiste Améthier, Gustave Brou, Kouadio Kouassi, and Maxime Ekra.

81. Nidgin Aoussi, interview, March 22, 1990 (Abidjan).

82. During the 1970s, representatives of Ivoirien-owned companies occupied an average of about one-third of the positions on the board of directors, making the class overrepresented in proportionate terms. See *Hommes et organisations d'Afrique noire* (Abidjan: Ediafric), 1972–1978; June 8, 1984, p. 1518; *Marchés tropicaux et méditerranéens*, 1970–1985.

83. It was created in 1965 as the *Association Interprofessionelle de la Côte d'Ivoire*, and 600 companies belong to it today (*Fraternité Matin*, February 28, 1990, p. 8).

84. Jacques Huot, interview, January 23, 1990; Aoussi, interview.

85. Guy Camara, interview, March 15, 1990 (Abidjan); *Fraternité Matin*, April 25, 1990, p. 2.

86. The example of *La financière*, the original investment club, is representative of this; Diagne Loum, interview, February 19, 1990 (Abidjan).

87. In a survey of a number of leading businessmen for whom biographical data were available, it was found that over half were graduates of institutions of higher learning (universities, teacher's colleges, and, in the colonial period, the École Ponty in Dakar). Of this educated group, over half in turn had attended foreign universities. The survey was of the business community as a whole, and it is likely that younger businessmen had an even higher level of education as a group. See John Rapley, "Class Formation in French West Africa: The Rise of an Ivoirien Bourgeoisie," Ph.D. diss., Queen's University at Kingston, 1991, Appendix 3. Such a proclivity toward higher education has always been the norm among the Ivoirien bourgeoisie; even in the early days of the Ivoirien planter bourgeoisie, not only did leading planters often attend French universities, but they were also more likely to send their children to school than were, for example, most traditional chiefs. See Immanuel Wallerstein, *The Road to Independence* (Paris: Mouton, 1964), pp. 138–139; Marcussen and Torp, *The Internationalization of Capital*, p. 128; Nyong'o, "The Articulation of Modes of Production," p. 188; Masquet, "Côte d'Ivoire," p. 10.

88. One Ivoirien corporate executive, educated in France, even used the terminology of dependency theory to describe the country's previous colonial relationship to France and the consequent actions of a national bourgeoisie to achieve national development rather than metropolitan exploitation (Aoussi, interview).

89. Gwénola Possémé, "Le Patron de SIALIM a confiance" (interview with Blaise Kouadio Tanoh, founder and president of SIALIM), *Jeune Afrique economie* (February 1990), p. 38.

90. Examples of such joint ventures are the sister companies of La Financière and the multinational retail sales and distribution network being put in place by PRIMA. See Diaby Aboubakar, "La compétition: La règle d'or," *Fraternité Matin*, March 6, 1990, p. 6, for an interview with Bemba Saloma, president and director-general of PRIMA, in which this pan-Africanist ideology is stated succinctly.

91. Jean Chevassu and Alain Valette, *Les relations intermédiaires dans le secteur industriel ivoirien* (Abidjan: ORSTOM, Centre de Petit Bassam, 1975 [Série études industrielles]), Table 6. It also appears that these ratios have since come down for French Ivoirien and Ivoirien businesses.

92. Ibid., Table 7.

93. Chevassu and Valette, *Les industriels de la Côte d'Ivoire*, p. 16.

94. Ibid., p. 17.

95. Blohorn, *Blohorn: Un demi siècle, 1929–79* (Abidjan: Blohorn, 1979).

96. Hortense Aka Anghui is also one of the country's leading political figures.

97. Christine Kerdellant, "Pourquoi les français s'en vont," *Jeune Afrique plus*, January-February 1990, p. 91.

98. See ibid. for a good exposé on this topic.

99. Arghiri Emmanuel, "White Settler Colonialism and the Myth of Investment Imperialism," *New Left Review* 85 (1974).

100. In 1990, only six countries (Cameroun, Congo, Botswana, Mauritius, South Africa, and Gabon) had higher per capita incomes (World Bank, *World Development Report*, 1992).

101. See annual World Bank development reports for details.

102. Roger C. Riddell, "Côte d'Ivoire," in Roger C. Riddell, ed., *Manufacturing Africa: Performance and Prospects of Seven Countries in Sub-Saharan Africa* (London: James Currey; Portsmouth, N.H.: Heinemann, 1990), p. 152; World Bank, *World Development Report*, 1992, p. 248.

103. See Brett, "State Power and Economic Inefficiency."

104. For a discussion of this latter point, see Rapley, *Ivoirien Capitalism*, Chapter 6.

105. See *African Business*, October 1992, pp. 21–22.

4

Domestic Capitalists and
the State in Kenya

David Himbara

Kenya's relatively successful development record has been widely attributed
to its efficient state and to the productive capacity of its African capitalist
class. This chapter critically assesses this conventional wisdom and offers an
alternative interpretation of Kenyan realities. First, it suggests that most accounts of Kenya's success are problematic. Beginning with the tendency to
assess its performance by "African standards," such a comparative framework is bound to overstate Kenya's case, given the generally impoverished
social and economic conditions of the region. Second, it demonstrates that
the conception of the Kenyan state as efficient is misguided in view of the decline and even collapse of some key elements in the country's national and
East Africa's supranational institutional apparatus since the mid-1960s, a factor that led to a sustained intervention by some international development institutions (IDIs) in an attempt to limit the damage. Third, it shows that the
analysis of the Kenyan capitalist class is off the mark. The African segment
that occupies center stage in most writing on the question remains, at best, a
bourgeoisie-in-formation, with the informal sector, or *jua kali*, serving as the
real training ground for potential African industrialists. The Kenyan and East
African Indians, who spearheaded the formation of the money economy in
the region from the 1800s onward, and led the conversion from merchant to
industrial capital after the 1950s, were misconstrued as "foreign," or "Asian"
capital and largely ignored. It is this segment, which constitutes the most
technically competent and largest-scale homegrown fraction of capital, that
largely accounts for Kenya's relative success, as far as domestic accumulation is concerned. However, a coherent state apparatus able to marshal development by utilizing their entrepreneurial skills is still lacking.

Scholarly Interpretations
of Kenya's Postcolonial Performance

Kenya's relative success, as compared to other sub-Saharan African countries, is easily confirmed by macrostatistics in various reports by IDIs and

69

the Kenyan government. The World Bank's data, for example, show that Kenya's growth rates in manufacturing, agriculture, and the service sector were consistently higher than those of almost all other sub-Saharan African countries from the mid-1960s to 1980. During the "lost decade" of the 1980s, when they all performed poorly, Kenya's decline was less dramatic.[1] In its survey of 1988, the United Nations Industrial Development Organisation (UNIDO) stated that "Kenya has had an impressive record growth over the last two decades"; this was demonstrated by the fact that its per capita GNP grew at a net annual rate of 2 percent during the period 1965–1985. Comparatively, average per capita income remained stagnant in Zimbabwe, Tanzania, and Sudan and became negative in Uganda, Somalia, and Zambia during the same period. UNIDO concluded that not only was Kenya "the most dynamic and thriving national economy of East Africa," but also that the country possessed "one of the highest levels in sub-Saharan Africa" of gross capital formation.[2] More recently, the United Nations' *World Economic Survey 1990* highlighted Kenya's progress in diversifying its economy and in deepening its industrialization process, as manifested in the successful import substitution program that has led to "the availability of domestically manufactured goods on the local market."[3] Kenya's own surveys drew similar conclusions; for example, the *Economic Survey 1989* indicated that the country's manufacturing sector experienced "an impressive growth" rate of 6.0 percent in the previous year, a factor that was accounted for by "adequate supplies of raw materials for the agro-based industries" and by "rising domestic demand" of locally made products.[4] More recently, the Kenyan government accounted for its postindependence success by placing an emphasis on its political orientation and on the character of its overall development strategy: "While much of Africa veered towards socialism Kenya's pragmatic economic policies established a dynamic mixed economy."[5]

Most scholars interpreted such, or similar, macrostatistics as signaling the efficiency of the postcolonial state and the productive capacity of Kenya's African capitalists.[6] For example, Arthur Hazlewood and Gerald Holtham maintained that the Kenyan government's effectiveness was proven by, among other things, its implementation of development plans that, on the one hand, attracted foreign capital to modernize the country's economy and, on the other hand, successfully fostered an African entrepreneurial class. In the authors' view, accomplishments in the latter task were most remarkable: "Kenyanisation of existing businesses owned by non-citizens has been pursued, almost to completion."[7] For Colin Leys, the effectiveness of the state was demonstrated by its ability to successfully displace "monopolies enjoyed by foreign capital and substitute monopolies for African capital, and . . . to enable them to occupy the space created for them in the newly accessible economic sectors."[8] Nicola Swainson maintained that an African national bourgeoisie had emerged in Kenya and were now in control of the state, which they successfully used to assert themselves in some important economic niches that were previously an exclusive terrain of multinational corporations (MNCs). According to Swainson, the sophistication of African capitalists was marked by their setting up manufacturing firms "in direct competition to powerful foreign corporations" to the extent that "in some instances, foreign capital has been threatened," an inconceivable undertaking without a supportive and highly competent state.[9] More recently, Jean-François Médard (agreeing with Richard Crook) upheld the thesis that Kenya's (and Côte d'Ivoire's) superior performance was due to "a higher level of state capacity," a factor established by "the level of efficiency of administration and parastatals," which was higher "than in the rest of Africa."[10]

As previously noted, these interpretations of Kenya's performance and the sources of its relative success are problematic, beginning with the tendency to measure its accomplishments by the standards of the "rest of Africa." Not only is this comparative framework uncomplimentary, it exaggerates the Kenyan case, as J. B. Wanjui has aptly remarked:

> When outsiders wish to praise Kenyans for their economic and social achievements, they most often do so by noting that Kenya is considerably more advanced than other African countries. Since we all know that the economic and political performance of most African states has been dismal, this compliment sharply qualifies the accolade as, at best, faint praise and avoids the greater question of how Kenyans would measure up to the optimum standards applied to non-African societies. . . . Until we dare compare our performance with successful nations of the world, instead of with failures, we have no . . . cause for self-congratulation. By world standards no economy in Africa is performing as it should.[11]

The Kenyan State After 1963:
Decline, Disintegration, and Reconstruction

The conception of the Kenyan postcolonial state as efficient proves false on closer investigation. The rapid "Africanization" of the Kenyan and East African administrative apparatus signaled the unraveling of the Kenyan state's capacity, by its own admission. It was stated in 1965 that "we must employ . . . large numbers of foreign experts both to assist in planning and carrying out the work that needs to be done."[12] Six years later the report of the Ndegwa Commission on the Civil Service restated that Kenya's administrative needs "can be met with the help of overseas donors and the international aid agencies but even that help, welcome though it is, does not match the problem."[13] The Ndegwa Commission caused more harm, however; its recommendation, implemented in the 1970s, held that there ought to be "no objection to the ownership of property or involvement in business by members of the public services to the point where their wealth is augmented perhaps substantially by such activities."[14] That this quickened the tempo of the disintegration of the state apparatus was confirmed by the *Waruhiu Report* of 1980, which stated that the Ndegwa Commission had been "misinterpreted," and this led to "gross neglect of public duty and misuse of official positions and official information in furtherance of civil servants' interests."[15]

The "gross neglect of public duties" meant the decline and even collapse of some key elements of Kenya's administrative apparatus, including national ministries, and the organizations responsible for infrastructure and development issues. In the case of ministries, the former principal policy and developmental apparatus of the state, the Ministries of Commerce and Industry (then and now separated to form two ministries) and of Finance and Economic Development, became largely counterproductive. The Ministry of Commerce and Industry was so incompetent that, as the Kenya government conceded in the mid-1980s, it required as many as thirty approvals within and outside that ministry to start an enterprise in Kenya, a process that took as long as three years.[16] The extent of the degeneration of the ministry was further shown by the fact that, by 1991, according to the controller and auditor general, it was no longer "possible to ascertain the financial position of the Ministry," especially as it had no reliable records relating to its responsibilities since 1979.[17] Commerce and Industry was no longer an effective arm of the state for implementing industrial and commercial plans. It is, therefore, not surprising that Kenya ceased to be an attractive destination for foreign investments, notwithstanding the fact that that was supposed to be the basis of the country's development strategy. On the contrary, in response to the decline of the various administrative and infrastructural facilities in Kenya, substantial divestment occurred in the 1980s, especially by large U.S. manufacturing companies, such as Firestone and Eveready, which were acquired by local Indians (more about this below).

In light of the near collapse of the Ministry of Commerce and Industry, a number of IDIs sought to limit the damage by reconstructing some of its key elements. The World Bank took the lead, particularly in efforts to reintroduce and implement policies aimed at encouraging foreign investments in Kenya and expanding the country's manufacturing and export capacity. Among the schemes revived by the World Bank was the concept of export processing zones (EPZs), which had been featured in Kenya's development plans since the 1970s, but had not been implemented until a number of Kenyan Indian capitalists successfully undertook their own EPZs in the late 1980s and early 1990s (as indicated below). With the Bank's financing and direct monitoring, construction of industrial sheds and other facilities for EPZs at Athi River outside Nairobi was well advanced by 1993, with Mombasa targeted next. Among other programs sustained by the

World Bank was the Kenya Exporter Assistance Scheme (KEAS), whose objective was to help exporters use Kenya's Lomé Convention status and exploit access to the European Community and South African markets.[18] An even larger scheme was USAID's Kenya Export Development Support (KEDS) aimed at creating employment and foreign exchange earnings through exports.[19] The United Nations Development Programme (UNDP) was one of the IDIs attempting to reconstruct the Kenya External Trade Authority (KETA), which became moribund during the 1970s.[20]

In the case of the Ministry of Finance and Economic Development (currently separated to form two ministries and with Finance no longer attached to the Office of the Vice-President), while its development plans impressed most scholars, hardly any of them were ever successfully implemented. Part of the problem was a lack of skilled personnel, which led to a weak relationship between planning and implementation from the mid-1960s. For instance, the first postcolonial development plan of 1964–1970 was judged mediocre because, as the International Monetary Fund (IMF) reported, "the time spent on its preparation was too short to cover sufficient details to permit firm conclusions on the set targets."[21] The director of a twenty-five person Canadian team stationed in the ministry throughout most of the 1970s, which prepared the 1974–1978 and the 1979–1984 plans, recalled that not only was there little or no integration of planning and operations in Kenya, but also "there was a shortage of trained planning and management staff at all levels and, if not a lack of commitment to the idea of planning itself, at least a not uncommon unwillingness in practice to accept the restraints it imposed."[22]

Other failings in the ministry included a near-total breakdown of its capacity to collect duty, sales, and income tax. Worse still, the ministry's ability to generally supervise the country's revenues deteriorated, and it was itself consistently among the most corrupt state agencies. Indeed, the ministry engaged in widespread "unauthorized expenditures" and other illegal practices, such as unapproved duty refunds, which, as the controller and auditor general stated in 1991, "in effect resulted in Government paying duty and sales tax on behalf of individuals."[23] The level of unauthorized expenditures by Finance and other Kenyan ministries steadily increased from the mid-1960s; the latest data available show that these expenditures cost the Kenyan people and aid donors some Shs24,345,043,120 in 1990, a figure that represented an increase of over 55 percent from the previous year.[24] Attempts by the IDIs to reconstruct the Ministry of Finance and the associated tax-collecting departments are discussed below.

The circumstances of the East African supranational state agencies and common market (largely established from the late 1940s) are also indicative of the essentially negative role of the post-1964 Kenyan state. Since Kenya, the most commercially and industrially advanced member of the East African partnership with Uganda and Tanzania, stood to be affected most negatively if the market was lost, it was expected to play the leading role in preserving it. This was the hope of the East African manufacturers and foreign investors, most of whom resided in Kenya, who reminded the government that

> as the most advanced of the three partners, Kenya should take the lead in indicating ways and means . . . of strengthen[ing] the Community and effectively demonstrate to not only the present partners but also potential partners and other countries of Africa, that the East African Community is a live and vital body.[25]

Unfortunately, such advice was not taken seriously, as indicated, for example, by the anti–common market rhetoric and economic nationalism in Kenya's National Assembly. The speaker of the house, Humphrey Slade, constantly had to warn members of parliament not to make allegations against Kenya's East African Community partners:

> You know the Rule to which I refer so often, and it is particularly important for all of us that we preserve the best possible relations with our neighbours. Therefore hon. Members must avoid any allegations that, operating the Treaty within the bounds of the Treaty, our partner States are doing something wrong or unfair.[26]

The East African common market with all its associated services collapsed in 1977, with Kenya taking the lead in ending the life of those elements that might have been saved:

> In January 1977, Kenya took a bold step in breaking up the East African Airways. Tanzania had earlier pleaded with the members of the East African General Assembly to save the airline, and later retaliated by closing all its borders with Kenya. . . . Tanzania explained her action: "If Kenya did not want air, railway and sea links with her neighbours, there should be no reason why she should want a road link with her neighbours." Kenya was thus mistaken in thinking that Tanzania could not block her access to the southern Africa market.[27]

The effect of the collapse of the common market and joint services was devastating for Kenya in several critical ways. First, most Kenyan manufacturing firms began to operate at half or less of their capacity, since they lost the larger East African market; further, Kenya was rendered unattractive to large-scale foreign investments whose interest in the area was the larger and unrestricted East African common market. In effect, the last major MNC investment in Kenya was the General Motors automobile assembly plant outside Nairobi, established before the collapse of the common market in 1977. Second, and perhaps most damaging, was the demise of the formerly East Africa–wide supranational organizations, particularly those responsible for duty and tax collection, such as the East African Customs and Excise and the East African Income Tax Department. The fragments of these departments, which were inherited by the Kenyan government (operating under the Ministry of Finance, itself in dire straits, as shown above), barely functioned at all, as indicated by escalating amounts of uncollected taxes of all types.[28] In an effort to avert a total breakdown of these departments and the parent ministry, the UNDP, the World Bank, and USAID established in 1989 a program to help modernize the tax system in Kenya. These aid agencies began to provide technical, administrative, and operational assistance to the Ministry of Finance and to the Income Tax Department. The project was expected to lead to more efficient revenue collection, increased taxpayer compliance, and more reliable internal auditing systems. Besides providing training and formulating new tax policies, the agencies installed computers to help generate and preserve more reliable data.[29] Harvard University's Institute for International Development (HIID) had also had a team of experts in Kenya since 1985 providing "technical assistance to the Ministry of Finance in Kenya in the preparation of tax policy options and possible administrative improvements in their tax systems."[30]

The story of the East African organizations and facilities responsible for transport and communication infrastructure that were taken over by Kenya is similar. In the case of the oldest and undoubtedly the most critical parastatal, the East African Railways Corporation (EARC), its replacement became known more for its corruption than for its services. The Kenyan Railways Corporation (KR) was consistently found to be among the most notoriously incompetent of the parastatals and could hardly be relied upon to play a meaningful role in transporting either goods or people. The Parliamentary Public Investments Committee reported in 1991 that KR had run a "cumulative deficit" of Shs841,055,075, with the government writing off most of this and infusing even more capital to revive the corporation. Meanwhile, KR was involved in various scandalous schemes, including attempts to export its own rails as scrap metal.[31] The British government, through the Overseas Development Administration (ODA), became the main benefactor of the KR and the Harbours Corporation, aiming at making them commercially viable by providing personnel to give training and to reorganize record-keeping and purchasing policies;[32] the International Development Association (IDA) also "sought to bolster their management and financial operations."[33] The East African Posts and Telecommunications (EAPT), now Kenya Posts and Telecommunications (KPT), not only became unable to provide effective services and meet its loan obligations (including those to the World Bank), it accumulated billions of shillings in bad debts. Its losses stood at Shs3,332,248,666 in 1988, with 20 percent of this figure representing the unpaid bills of government ministries and departments.[34]

In the case of Kenyan domestic institutions (as opposed to East African Common Services Organisations) formerly responsible for maintaining national infrastructures, namely, the Ministry of Local Government and the municipal and county councils that it oversaw, as early as 1969 it was reported that "every county council is on the verge of collapse," and they did so later in the same year.[35] Mombasa, the second largest municipality, containing key national and East African infrastructures, especially port facilities, collapsed and was taken over by the Ministry of Local Government in Nairobi in 1976. The City of Nairobi itself, the administrative, commercial, and industrial center of Kenya, managed to survive the 1970s before crumbling in 1983. It was replaced by a commission appointed by President Moi, a development that worsened the situation, until 1993 when an elected administration took office as a result of the multiparty elections late in the previous year. The implication of the deterioration of these administrative units under the aegis of the Ministry of Local Government is that key economic infrastructures were not being maintained. By the late 1980s, the state's capacity had diminished to the extent that private sector companies began to build and maintain their own roads and provide their own water supplies and their own generators for electricity, in view of the frequent disruptions, since neither the municipalities nor the national ministries were able to deal with these problems. In connection with the country's main industrial area in Nairobi, the Kenyan Association of Manufacturers (KAM) wrote to its membership saying that industrialists had

> agreed to pay . . . towards the construction of the alternative route to Outer Ring Road to reduce volume of traffic during peak hours on Likoni and Enterprise Roads. . . . We are writing to appeal to you to make your contribution.[36]

The record of Kenya's development institutions created after 1964 to implement localization-Africanization-Kenyanization-indigenization programs is probably the most pitiful; in fact, most of these institutions and the schemes they sought to implement never got off the ground, contrary to the expectations of earlier studies. The institutions in question became instead an additional problem, as they merely consumed state and international aid funds through corruption, with a pathetic record with regard to their mandates. As early as 1979, the presidential Committee of Review of Statutory Boards Report had warned that the Industrial and Commercial Development Corporation (ICDC), the principal government development agency, was "an extreme though not exceptional example of poor investment." The committee reprimanded Kenya's parastatal sector by noting that it had become personalized for private profit or aggrandizement. "The economic and social costs of delay of taking action to remedy these serious problems are simply too unacceptable."[37] The impaired condition of

Kenya's development institutions led to yet another presidential commission in 1982, which recommended that "it is a matter of high priority for the Government to divest" itself of most of these parastatals.[38] Almost a decade later, the Kenyan government conceded in 1990 that "these entities are inefficient, poorly managed, unprofitable and a burden on the taxpayers on account of heavy budgetary subsidies made to them year after year."[39] However, little or no action was taken, for, yet again, the 1991 Parliamentary Public Investments Committee found "with deep concern" that the chief executive officers of most state corporations "were directly involved . . . in corrupt practices which adversely affected the financial operations of the corporations."[40] By 1993, Kenya's parastatal sector was responsible for the greater part of the country's $6 billion debt.[41] It is, therefore, not surprising that Kenya's development institutions failed to achieve even modest success in their principal goal of fostering an African capitalist class, as becomes clear below.

As the capacity of the Kenyan state apparatus deteriorated, and some of its elements collapsed altogether, the IDIs and donor countries increasingly provided personnel and larger amounts of aid and grants to stabilize the situation. Not only did the scale of aid to Kenya expand steadily during the 1970s and 1980s, it was pledged ahead of the intended fiscal period to enable the government to incorporate aid and grant funds into its budgetary projections and plans and to counter its balance of payments problems.[42] However, the donor community, led by the IMF and the World Bank, suspended this practice in 1991 and instead imposed on Kenya a comprehensive structural adjustment program (SAP). SAP called for, among other things, liquidation and/or privatization of most of Kenya's parastatal sector, reduction of the size of the regular civil service, devaluation of the Kenyan shilling, and relaxation of the rules regarding repatriation of earnings by foreign investors. Further, undertaking multiparty general elections, curbing high-level corruption, and improving human rights were made part of the conditions for resuming aid to Kenya.[43] It should be noted, however, that project aid valued at $850 million to $1 billion a year was not affected; what was suspended was mostly budgetary and balance of payments support facilities.[44]

The influence of the donor community in Kenya was by now so decisive that the Kenyan government not only succumbed and provided a detailed privatization plan at the November 1991 donor consultative meeting held in Paris,[45] but, most remarkably, grudgingly yielded to multiparty general elections subsequently held in December 1992. With regard to privatization, eighteen parastatals that were to be sold or liquidated, including the Tiger Shoe Company (formerly a state-assisted venture by African capitalists, which collapsed and was taken over by the ICDC, its main financier), East African Fine Spinners, Uplands Bacon Factory, and Kenya Taitex Mills. The parastatals considered unprofitable but worth saving

were obliged to sign "performance agreements" in which external consultants had to take over their effective management in order to rehabilitate
them in preparation for future privatization (e.g., Kenya Airways entered
into a management contract with Swissair to raise its performance to acceptable standards before it could be privatized). Each performance agreement included such measures as the reduction of the number of employees and the appointment of a new board of directors to counter past corrupt
tendencies, especially political patronage. Local parastatal managerial personnel were no longer to be appointed on political criteria but on executive
qualities, with the blessing of the IDIs and foreign consultants. All Kenya's
leading parastatals, including the ICDC, Industrial Development Bank
(IDB), National Cereals and Produce Board (NCPB), Agricultural Finance
Corporation (AFC), Coffee Board of Kenya (CBK), and Kenya Tea Development Authority (KTDA), were obliged to sign such contracts.[46]

It was generally assumed that most aid programs to Kenya would re-
sume after the 1992 multiparty general elections, since it was one of the key
conditions the government had to meet. This was not the case, however, especially as the same party, Kenya African National Union (KANU), and the
same president, Daniel arap Moi, won the elections, assisted significantly by
an ethnically fragmented opposition.[47] Instead, the IMF and World Bank insisted that the implementation of SAP had not gone far enough in such areas
as contracting the civil service; privatization, or liquidation of parastatals;
and devaluation of the Kenyan shilling. A cumulative aid fund of about $400
million was consequently withheld. The European Community (EC) followed their lead by insisting on conditionality before releasing some ECU
163.5 million worth of aid under the Fourth Lomé Convention.[48] Principal
donor countries, such as the United States, adopted the same position.[49] In
reaction to the unyielding position of the IDIs and donor countries, a de-
spondent Moi regime hurriedly submitted in February 1993 to some of the
measures called for by SAP: the Kenyan shilling was floated and fell by 37
percent; the powers of the Kenyan central bank were eclipsed by ending its
monopoly in trading and allocating foreign currency; regulations on repatri-
ating earnings in foreign exchange were eased.[50] The Kenyan government
was by now literally on its knees. As the Kenyan minister for finance,
Musalia Mudavadi, put it, "We have gone a long way in meeting the demands of the IMF, World Bank and Western Donors. We anticipate that our
discussions with [them] . . . will lead to new aid programs."[51]

It was hoped that these measures would persuade the IMF and the
World Bank, whose mission to determine the release of the badly needed
aid and grant funds took place in March 1993. Nevertheless, the Moi
regime initially rejected the IMF–World Bank structural adjustment demands. Barely a month after adopting a go-it-alone stance, however, the
regime reversed course after it became effectively isolated from both domestic and external actors in the Kenyan drama. Opposition party FORD-

Kenya demanded that the IMF–World Bank reforms continue, for "if pressure is not kept up, mismanagement and corruption will continue."[52] Elements of the agrarian bourgeoisie (especially export producers) saw the government's rejection of reforms as killing their trade, because the country lacked sources of foreign exchange to support export trade. Without balance of payment support from donors, in the view of this element of the domestic bourgeoisie, "there may not be any Kenyan flowers reaching Europe or indeed elsewhere."[53]

The reverse side of this problem soon became clear when Kenya failed to meet the conditions of foreign investors, especially the international airlines; they could not repatriate their earnings as the central bank of Kenya did not have the required hard currency. This led some of the airlines to threaten to close down their operations and withdraw from Kenya.[54] By mid-April 1993, lack of foreign currency and poor maintenance of government-owned petroleum refinery facilities were forcing European airlines to cut back or reroute their flights into Kenya. Principal carriers of Kenya-bound tourists (including KLM, British Airways, and Lufthansa German Airlines), now the main source of income for Kenya, suspended direct flights into Kenya and introduced stopovers in Cairo or in neighboring Uganda and Tanzania. Some airlines were said to be importing their own fuel.[55]

In the aftermath of these developments, the Moi government had second thoughts about its go-it-alone policy; it caved in and unexpectedly devalued Kenyan currency by a further 23 percent, following earlier devaluations. In an even more revealing turn of events, the government addressed one of the leading issues that had soured its relationship with its international backers: corruption and mismanagement. It closed twelve "political banks" that were politically well connected but financially insolvent and dependent on deposits from corrupt parastatals and similar institutions. The state had lent these banks over Shs11 billion ($234 million) against "the assets that the government's own analysts say do not exist."[56]

Devaluation and closure of the political banks led to the release by the World Bank of some $85 million in frozen aid in April 1993.[57] The European Community was also said to be about to release some of its frozen aid in response to these developments. The World Bank and the IMF were once again discussing with the Kenyan government further implementation of reforms necessary for the release of accumulated aid amounting to over $400 million.

Kenya's Domestic Capitalists:
The Issue of African Accumulation

The Kenyan capitalist class has been largely equated with black Africans, with various hypotheses advanced with regard to their origins, scale of operation, and performance. What is clear, however, is that they began their first widespread attempts at business after World War II. In this phase, African businessmen began to participate not only in a wider variety of microbusiness activities, but also in more complex enterprises. The main source of investment were the relatively large amounts of money—by prewar African standards—available from the earnings and gratuities of ex-soldiers who had participated in the war. The pooling of some of these earnings resulted in a boom in trade and the formation of many companies. It was reported, for example, that while trading by Africans was inconsequential prior to World War II, by 1946 there was "a steady pressure from a large number of Africans for facilities to engage in trade."[58] With regard to the formation of limited liability and shareholding enterprises, seventeen African "public companies" with a nominal capital of Shs4,270,000 were incorporated, while fifty-three African "private companies" with a nominal capital of Shs2,706,000 had been established by 1949.[59] However, no sooner were most of these companies formed than they ran into management problems and disintegrated. A 1945 report of the Registrar of Companies had already cautioned that African managers and promoters of companies were essentially "defrauding shareholders of the funds of companies which they are running."[60] Five years later, the performance of African companies had worsened, as a 1950 assessment by the Registrar of Companies reported:

> I have looked into the files of all these Companies and do not think there is a single one whose affairs I can honestly describe as satisfactory. . . . I cannot help feeling that legislation is necessary to control the formation of Companies by Africans. I fully realise the political dangers in that the cry of discrimination would at once be raised, but the fact remains that the Companies already incorporated by Africans during the last five years have collected from a vast number of African individuals a sum certainly in excess of 1 1/4 million shillings, of which by far the greater part is now hopelessly lost.[61]

Far from hindering the rise of African enterprise as is often claimed,[62] the colonial state provided a remarkable network of infrastructural support aimed at engendering a business "spirit" in the "African" in the aftermath of the collapse of most of their companies. This began, interestingly enough, with quit notices to some Indian traders in the early 1940s. A report by the office of the district commissioner in 1944 stated:

> There are 28 Indian lessees of stalls in the Nairobi Municipal Market. In addition Indians rent 15 stalls as stores. Their premises were built as stalls . . . but were let as stores before the war since they were lying unused. . . . The Town Clerk is therefore serving notices on a number of these store lessees to quit within a reasonable period. Court action will be taken if they do not comply. These premises will be made available for African occupation.[63]

The selective highlighting of the limit of credit to Africans in the existing literature omits the fact that the state sought to facilitate the rise of competent African businessmen who could utilize specialized state credit productively. Thus, to check loss of monies and high indebtedness among African businesses, the Credit to Africans (Control) Ordinance was amended (August 31, 1948) not only to limit credit given to an African by a non-African to Shs200, but to enable more competent traders to borrow larger sums of money "where application for such credit is made in writing and approved by an Attesting Officer."[64]

Next was the drive to create mechanisms through which aspiring African businessmen could acquire more knowledge of trade in such subjects as bookkeeping, marketing, and other matters deemed necessary by state agencies. The Department of Trade and Supplies in the Ministry of Commerce and Industry began to sponsor African traders to attend the Jeanes School courses created for that purpose.[65] Subsequently, the Credit to Africans (Control) Ordinance of 1948 was amended in 1957, raising the credit ceiling from Shs200 to Shs2,000, and in some selected cases more than this, when it was deemed that a large pool of competent African businessmen existed.[66]

Perhaps the most ambitious program was the Loans to African Industrialists, Artisans and Businessmen Scheme that became operational in 1956. The scheme was designed to provide working capital and credit to purchase other requirements to the more able Africans in the commercial and industrial sectors (but not agriculture). The loan ceiling was raised to Shs10,000; applications in excess of that amount had to be processed by the Ministry of Commerce and Industry instead of local boards or loan committees. The main policy objective was that "Africans should be trained and possibly be given financial assistance so as to operate their own commercial projects or small industrial concerns."[67] The applicant had to be an African who had "established himself in a trade, business or industry" and who had "indicated through his own efforts that he has the necessary ability to operate his business with a reasonable measure of success," or had "a suitable qualification granted by a recognised technical school."[68] The security for loans included "a simple agreement" at the discretion of the board or loan committee. The scheme remained operative up to 1965–1966 when the ICDC took over responsibility for financing small businesses.[69]

Finally, the Ministry of Commerce and Industry helped establish African chambers of commerce. The correspondence between the Ministry of Commerce and Industry and the district commissioner of Kiambu indicates the role of both levels of the state. The former's view and objective was that "we regard it as most important that these African chambers should be established on a proper basis." Perhaps in view of past mismanagement problems of most African companies, the ministry stated that "as regards auditing, we should put in something rather firmer than would be necessary for ordinary chambers of commerce."[70] The Kiambu African Chamber of Commerce was one of the first ones to be established, with D. W. Waruhiu as its president and James Njenga Karume as its secretary.[71] With these roots in the 1950s, Karume remained one of the most successful African businessmen in the postcolonial period.

The above schemes did not, however, engender a successful class of African commercial or industrial capitalists. With regard to the progress of the African Industrialists, Artisans and Businessmen Scheme, it was stated in 1959 that

> we seem to be faced with too many traders and a marked reluctance to repay loans. . . . [A] great deal of work will be required before we can adjust the attitude of mind which is clearly holding up the implementation of the scheme . . . though both Mr. Parkin and myself believe that there is considerable need for it to enable the better African traders to compete . . . with the Asians.[72]

The postcolonial achievements of African businessmen have not differed greatly from those of the colonial era. We have established that the development institutions created to support them after 1964 rarely functioned. It has now been officially acknowledged that the poor condition of most state agencies coupled with the lack of African entrepreneurs meant that Africanization was "not very successful in the private sector owing to the fact that managerial expertise required to run commercially viable industrial and commercial enterprises was in short supply."[73] Moreover, "businesses transferred in this process from nonindigenous to indigenous businessmen reverted to the former through 'back door'" transactions.[74]

The African commercial and industrial groups such as Gikuyu Embu Meru Association (GEMA), which Swainson saw as spearheading "the move of indigenous capital into production,"[75] and which Leys conceived as the signaling of the emergence of "mass investment companies,"[76] did not differ from the general picture. The source of GEMA's success had more to do with its special relationship with the Kenyatta state than its business acumen. GEMA's executives were all Kikuyu associates of President Kenyatta, who dominated almost all key state positions. Examples included Duncan Ndegwa (governor of the Central Bank of Kenya), Matau Wamae (executive director of the ICDC), Mwai Kibaki (minister for finance), Julius Kiano (minister for commerce and industry), John Muchuki (executive chairman of Kenya Commercial Bank), Kihika Kimani (chairman of KANU's Nakuru branch), Margaret Kenyatta (Kenyatta's daughter and the mayor of Nairobi), and Njenga Karume (a nominated member of parliament). The loss of their positions in the state after Kenyatta's death saw GEMA collapse, with its membership fighting for control of the various ranches, farms, and companies and with the Moi government facilitating the collapse by banning all "tribal organizations."[77] President Moi had his own reasons to end GEMA and to "save" the "redeemable" elements in it (for example, Karume and Kibaki until 1988). GEMA was at the center of the change-the-constitution conspiracy of 1976, in which leading Kikuyu politicians, businessmen, and senior civil servants sought to prevent the then vice-president, Daniel arap Moi, a non-Kikuyu, from becoming president as the Kenyan constitution required.[78]

By the late 1980s and early 1990s, the potential source for African entrepreneurship was not state-sponsored schemes or government officials who used their position in the state to become rich, but the informal, or *jua kali,* sector, where small operators acquired considerable technical skills and linked up with larger manufacturing firms for their mutual benefit. According to studies done by the Kenya Management Assistance Programme (K-Map), this was occurring in a number of subsectors such as the furniture, garment, and construction industries, where large firms, in order to cut costs, began to subcontract to smaller *jua kali* ones. This development was widespread by the 1980s, leading K-Map to conclude that "sub-contracting seems to have taken root in Kenya."[79] Efforts to promote this segment of African entrepreneurship have been under way, with the UNDP and International Labour Organisation (ILO), among others, playing a leading role. A major policy document, *A Strategy for Small Enterprise Development in Kenya: Towards the Year 2000,* was issued by them in 1988. These agencies were also instrumental in organizing the 1990 Seminar on Industrial Subcontracting to further foster an environment in which small enterprises could be assisted by linking them to larger manufacturing firms as suppliers of certain inputs.[80] It is interesting to note that, at this conference, "there was general consensus that if the [proposed] subcontracting exchange is to be established, it should be situated in the offices of a private sector body," and not those of the state.[81] Hence the establishment of the Kenyan Subcontracting and Partnership Exchange (KSPE), whose task was to facilitate and deepen the process; funded by the UNDP and UNIDO, the KSPE was already operational in 1993.[82]

The Kenyan state itself has been forced to turn to this strategy in the aftermath of its failure to create African enterprise through the so-called Africanization of existing commercial and industrial firms. The *Development Plan 1989–1993* conceded that "a serious omission has been the neglect in exploiting the full potential of the small-scale and *jua kali* sector enterprises. This potential can no longer be ignored."[83] It is rather ironic that this strategy had been implemented from 1945 to 1964 with the adoption of the Stirton report. In strikingly similar terms, the report argued that

production of building materials, building construction, blacksmithing and repairing, tailoring, spinning, weaving, bicycle repairing, lorry and car repairing, cart making, soap making, furniture making . . . in a small

way may not be regarded as fully fledged industries, but . . . these form
the only basis upon which can be built a standard of industry that will
cater to African markets, and ultimately absorb large numbers of persons
in employment not directly concerned with land. *Hence the reason for
the suggested concentration of activity on minor works already established, in preference to frantic efforts to introduce something that is
likely to fade out with the first signs of failing enthusiasm.*[84]

Kenya's Domestic Capitalists:
The Role of the Kenyan-Indian Bourgeoisie

The most remarkable aspect of the post-1963 development literature on
Kenya is that it is largely silent on the role of East African Indians. The
few scholars who understood their role as a homegrown accumulating
class (as opposed to foreign or Asian capital) included Indu Chandaria,[85]
Robin Murray,[86] and Colin Leys. Leys aptly remarked that they had "produced a merchant capitalist class which was poised by the 1950s to become an indigenous industrial bourgeoisie of the classical type."[87] Nicola
Swainson, however, the main author of reference on the development of
corporate capitalism in Kenya, conceptualized them as "Asian capital" and
did not consider them particularly important except "a few large conglom-
erates."[88] Likewise, in his 1989 study of the glass manufacturing industry
in Kenya, Peter Coughlin asserts that "Kenya Glass Ltd. was started in
Mombasa in 1946 by the Madhvani Group out of India."[89] Since the Madhvani family are not black, but East Africans of Indian descent, their enterprises are transferred to the foreign category by sheer force of ideology.

To transcend this misconception it is necessary to trace the rise of
commerce and industry in East Africa, beginning with the coastal areas
where Indian immigrants settled for several centuries. It was from within
this community that a merchant class evolved who "quickly established
themselves as the bankers and money-lenders."[90] Almost the entire trade
of Zanzibar and the mainland, "which was estimated to exceed £1,500,000
a year, passed through Indian hands."[91] Even when European participation
in East African commerce increased toward the end of the nineteenth century, "the Indians' dominant position was still maintained. No imports
could be distributed to native customers in the interior without [Indian]
agency."[92] The capacity achieved by these merchants before and during
the early colonial days is demonstrated by the legacy of such pioneers as
Alidina Visram and A. M. Jeevanjee. Beginning in Zanzibar and Bag-
amoyo in 1877, Visram's chain of businesses soon spread all over East
Africa, developing local trade by buying sugar, cotton, simsim, and
beeswax. Visram was probably the first significant industrialist in Uganda,
Kenya, and Tanganyika, opening a soap factory in Mombasa in the late

1900s, cotton ginneries in Kampala and Mombasa in the early 1910s, oil mills at Kisumu and the coast, and a sawmill near Nyeri in this period. Errol Trzebinski rightly accords him a place among Kenya's pioneers.[93] Jeevanjee's achievements were almost equally spectacular; he operated trading ships between East Africa and the Indian subcontinent, construction firms, and a real estate empire in Nairobi. He also founded the *East African Standard* in 1902.[94] On a much smaller but nonetheless important scale, other early traders made a mark in creating the money economy, conducting hinterland trade, and extending the internal market. Pioneers such as M. D. Puri and Adamjee Aliboy "were well established at Machakos before the time of the railway, and many others used rail transport to press further inland."[95] The Uganda-Kenya Railway was thus to pave the way for coastal merchants and financiers to move into the East African hinterland.

The European domination of politics and agriculture in Kenya from the 1900s did not alter the strategic position that Indian traders occupied in relation to the internal market, as W. MacGregor Ross noted in 1927: "Undeniably the Indian traders managed practically the whole of the internal trade."[96] More than twenty years later, the East African Royal Commission came to the conclusion that they were largely responsible for creating the region's internal trade.[97] Trzebinski also observed that whenever government posts were set up in Kenya, Indian traders "soon followed and opened one or two dukas. Before long they multiplied to become flourishing trading centres until all the African trade for miles around was in their hands."[98]

Some of the merchants began to convert their retail and wholesale empires into industrial capital from the late 1920s. Examples of industrial groups that began in petty trade before moving into the wholesale trade and eventually into manufacturing abound.[99] These include Kenya Aluminium Works (now Comcraft), specializing in aluminum and steel (formed in 1929 by the Chandaria family); the Madhvani Group, in sugar, steel, and plastics (since the 1920s); the Kenya Glass Works (since the 1940s); the House of Manji (since the 1940s); the Mehta Group, with various industrial projects all over East Africa (since the 1930s) producing sugar, steel, and plastic products; the Nalin Group, operated by the Khimasia family (since the 1940s), presently running a number of steel factories, including Special Steel Mills at Ruiru; the Chandaria Group (not related to Comcraft Group) in paper-packaging industries (since the 1950s); Elephant Soap Factory (since the 1930s); and Sunflag Textile Mills (since the 1950s).

The tempo of industrialization quickened considerably from the 1940s to the early 1960s, reflecting the creation of key national ministries, supranational state agencies, and a number of specialized regulatory bodies that became responsible for development. Among the key ministries was the

Ministry of Commerce and Industry, which was created by breaking up the Ministry of Agriculture and Natural Resources.[100] It was also in this period that the role of the Indian bourgeoisie increased substantially due to their successful entry into large-scale industrial production. The Kenya Aluminium Works (Kaluworks) was described by the officials in the Ministry of Commerce as "undoubtedly enterprising and has started and got quite a number of different enterprises going, and they appear to have very considerable financial resources."[101] Groups such as Madhvani were so effective that incoming foreign capital found it difficult to compete. Such was the case when East African Industries, Uniliver's subsidiary, began manufacturing cooking oil, margarine, and vegetable ghee. When East Africa Industries applied for a duty refund so it could reduce costs and become more competitive, the Kenyan government (which had shares in it), rejected the request, noting that it was competition from Madhvani "that East Africa Industries is unable to face and not competition from overseas" and that "East Africa Industries had no case."[102]

A good measure of the increasing influence by the Indian bourgeoisie due to their role in the East African economy was the fact that they began to head key private sector organizations as well as consultative state bodies that included government officials and members of the domestic bourgeoisie. For example, the leading business association, the Association of the Chambers of Commerce and Industry of Eastern Africa, was headed by the Ugandan Indian industrialist, R. J. Mehta.[103] D. P. Chandaria (of Kaluworks), B. S. Mohandra, and E. W. Mathu represented the business community on the Board of Industrial Development, an important arm of the Ministry of Commerce that advised the government on industrial matters. The board was responsible for one of the principal policy documents that guided the industrialization process through the 1950s.[104]

An entirely different environment emerged after independence in 1963. In place of the successfully mediated environment created to encourage and support local segments and foreign capital, a ferocious and protracted struggle between the state, now controlled by Kenyan Africans, and the commercial and industrial bourgeoisie ensued. The main point of contention was the desire to empower a black Kenyan business class to play a leading role in commerce and industry. The Indian shopkeepers (*dukawallahs*) were seen as the stumbling block and subjected to quit notices (as in the 1940s). The alternatives facing local Indians in the 1960s and 1970s were in effect either to leave Kenya or move from trade into another sector. As was stated by the minister for commerce and industry, "The government expects that the majority of the affected non-citizens will either leave Kenya or move into other sectors where their contribution is required such as the manufacturing industries."[105] That is what in fact happened; the Indian entrepreneurs forced out of their businesses were either lost to Kenya as they emigrated to other countries, or moved into more complex sectors of the economy, such as manufacturing, finance and banking, insurance, tourism, and construction.

Meanwhile, the collapse of the East African common market, the attempted coup d'état in 1982, and the disintegration of the national infrastructures saw some foreign manufacturing companies selling their subsidiaries to local industrialists in the mid-1980s. The largest of these included Firestone (EA), Eveready Batteries, Marshalls, the Commercial Bank of Africa, and Twentieth Century Fox Cinema in 1986. Due to their size, managerial requirements, capital, and international sophistication with regard to credit transactions and technical agreements and arrangements, these companies were all acquired by local Indian capitalists.[106] Besides being the only category of local social forces capable of taking over large foreign industries (since state parastatals were also collapsing in the late 1970s and 1980s, and African companies faced the same fate), local Indians continued to create new enterprises, indicating that they were either more committed to Kenya than foreign capital or less free to invest anywhere else.

It is in this period that some of the Kenyan Indian merchant groups that had converted themselves into industrial capital in previous decades took larger corporate form, as exemplified by the Comcraft Group, the House of Manji, the Madhvani Group, the Mehta Group, the Sunflag Group, and the Nalin Group. Besides internationalizing their activities, some of these industrial groups started some of the largest and most sophisticated enterprises in Kenya, particularly in the steel sector, as exemplified by Comcraft's Mabati Rolling Mills and Kaluwork's Rolling Mills (established in 1988 at Mariakani). Successful conversion to more challenging industrial activity was by no means limited to older groups. In the late 1960s, 1970s, and 1980s, groups such as the East African Foundry Works, Specialised Engineering, and Marshall Fowler began to manufacture more complex industrial goods and components such as lathe machines and industrial plants. Steel Structures was manufacturing industrial and milling plants, concrete mixers, ploughs, and block making machines. Orbitsports was exporting sporting balls to European countries, including Germany, France, and Britain. Firms such as Victoria Furniture manufactured office and industrial furniture for the domestic and export markets. In the pharmaceutical field, Cosmos emerged as one of the most promising companies active in both local and export markets. Companies such as Ken-Knit (textiles with a subsidiary in steel and wheat farming), Orbit Chemicals (detergents and chemicals), and Doshi (steel tubes), like most of the other firms mentioned, moved on to the manufacturing sector from wholesale or retail trade. By 1993, some Kenyan industrialists were operating industrial parks that specialized in exports. The most successful of these was the first export zone (EPZ) to come on-stream in Kenya, the Sameer Industrial Park, associated with industrialist Naushad Merali.[107]

The industrialist, promoter, and coffee farmer Mohan Galot, with his industrial park in Athi River, was also making a mark during the late 1980s
and early 1990s, with a business empire that included textiles, liquor, and
glass manufacturing.

Conclusion

The Kenyan development experience is thus more complex than previous
research suggests. The state remains largely a counterproductive factor, incapable of implementing a coherent development plan. Its international
backers appear to be reassessing their role in the reconstruction of the
Kenyan state apparatus. The Kenyan bourgeoisie clearly requires a more
informed and expert state to mediate the divergent needs of its different
segments. The African segment, especially those businessmen that began
in the state by "colonizing" its elements, have been largely discredited by
their inability to sustain themselves in the marketplace. It is the *jua kali*
operators that have proved to be the exception and the most promising
African entrepreneurs. Some small-scale accumulators in this sector have
acquired considerable technical capacity, a factor that escaped the attention of the Kenyan state, but not that of large-scale manufacturing enterprises, which began to subcontract to them in a number of subsectors, or
the international aid agencies, which began to support them. The segment
of the Kenyan bourgeoisie with an established history of accumulation, the
Kenyan Indians, which has proved itself in the realm of production, has
been hindered from deepening its operations by lack of a conducive set of
state policies, markets, and national infrastructures. They have expanded
largely for negative reasons of defense against Africanization, yet it is to
this fraction of the local bourgeoisie that Kenya owes its "good" economic
performance, such as it is. To its credit, the Kenyan state did not squander
the skills of this segment (as did its more reckless Tanzanian and Ugandan
counterparts); however, the Kenyatta and Moi governments have not provided an environment in which this fraction, together with foreign capital
and the *jua kali* sector, could deepen Kenya's industrial base to the extent
their technical capacity would have allowed.

Notes

1. See World Bank, *Sub-Saharan Africa: From Crisis to Sustainable Growth*
(Washington, D.C.: World Bank, 1989); *World Development Report* (Washington,
D.C.: World Bank, 1990.)
2. UNIDO, *Kenya: Sustaining Industrial Development Through Restructuring and Integration* (New York: United Nations, 1988), pp. 3, 55.
3. United Nations, *World Economic Survey 1990* (New York: United Nations,
1990), p. 29.

4. Republic of Kenya, *Economic Survey 1989* (Nairobi: Government Printer, 1989), p. 118.

5. Republic of Kenya, *Kenya: Export Processing Zones* (Nairobi: Government Printer, 1993), p. 1.

6. For a fuller critical analysis of the Kenyan literature, especially the "Kenya debate," see David Himbara, "Myths and Realities of Kenyan Capitalism," *Journal of Modern African Studies* (March 1993).

7. Gerald Holtham and Arthur Hazlewood, *Aid and Inequality in Kenya* (London: Overseas Development Institute, 1976), pp. 24–27.

8. Colin Leys, "Accumulation, Class Formation and Dependency: Kenya," in Martin Fransman, ed., *Industry and Accumulation* (London: Heinemann, 1982), p. 180.

9. Nicola Swainson, "The Rise of a National Bourgeoisie in Kenya," *Review of African Political Economy* no. 8 (1977), p. 49; Nicola Swainson, *The Development of Corporate Capitalism in Kenya 1918–77* (Nairobi: Heinemann, 1980), p. 18.

10. Jean-François Médard, "The Historical Trajectories of the Ivorian and Kenyan States," in James Manor, ed., *Rethinking Third World Politics* (London: Longman, 1991), p. 194.

11. J. B. Wanjui, *From Where I Sit: Views of an African Executive* (Nairobi: East African Publishing House, 1986), pp. ix, 32.

12. Republic of Kenya, *Sessional Paper No. 1, 1965, African Socialism and Its Application to Planning in Kenya* (Nairobi: Government Printer, 1965), p. 20.

13. Republic of Kenya, *Ndegwa Commission Report,* 1971, as cited in Republic of Kenya, *Waruhiu Report,* 1980 (Nairobi: Government Printer, 1980), p. 83.

14. Republic of Kenya, *Ndegwa Commission (Inquiry in Public Service and Remuneration Commission)* (Nairobi: Government Printer, 1971), pp. 13–14.

15. Republic of Kenya, *Report of the Civil Service Review* (or *Waruhiu Report*) (Nairobi: Government Printer, 1980), pp. 37–39.

16. Republic of Kenya, *Sessional Paper No. 1 on Economic Management for Renewed Growth* (Nairobi: Government Printer, 1986), p. 99.

17. Republic of Kenya, *The Appropriation Accounts, Other Public Accounts and the Accounts of the Funds for the Year 1989/1990 Together with the Report Thereon by the Controller and Auditor General* (Nairobi: Government Printer, 1991), p. 68.

18. *Economic Review*, Nairobi, January 4, 1993.

19. Ibid.

20. UNDP, "Project Document: Export Development, Diversification and Promotion," 1986. *KEN/86/107, MCI.*

21. International Monetary Fund, *Surveys of African Economies: Kenya, Tanzania, Uganda, and Somalia* (Washington, D.C.: IMF, 1969), p. 170.

22. John Saywell, "York University Kenya Project," in Tim Pinfold and Glen Norcliffe, eds., *Development Planning in Kenya,* Geography Monograph No. 9 Toronto: York University, 1980), pp. 1–5.

23. Republic of Kenya, *The Appropriation Accounts, Other Public Accounts and the Accounts of the Funds for the Year 1989/90, Together with the Report Therein by the Controller and Auditor General,* Vol. 1 (Nairobi: Government Printer, 1991), p. 7.

24. Ibid., p. 2. For a fuller account of this problem since the mid-1960s and the role of the Kenyatta government in actually encouraging it, see David Himbara, *Kenyan Capitalists, the State, and Development* (Boulder: Lynne Rienner, 1994).

25. T. W. Tyrrell, executive officer, Kenyan Association of Manufacturers, to J. Kibe, permanent secretary, Ministry of Commerce and Industry, May 5, 1969 (KAM files).

26. Republic of Kenya, *The National Assembly Official Report*, Vol. 17 (Part 2), June 28, 1969, August 19, 1969, p. 3221.

27. Katete Orwa, "Foreign Policy, 1963–1986," in W. R. Ochieng, ed., *A Modern History of Kenya 1895–1980*, (London: Evans Brothers, 1989), p. 235.

28. For example, Kenya's Customs and Excise Department was reported to have failed to collect some Shs2.3 billion in 1989. *Daily Nation*, November 3, 1989; see also *Kenya Times*, November 9, 1989.

29. See *Daily Nation* and *Standard*, November 23, 1989.

30. Harvard Institute for International Development (HIID), *1987–1989 Biennial Report* (Cambridge: HIID, 1989), p. 78.

31. Republic of Kenya, *Third Report of the Public Investments Committee on the Accounts of State Corporations* (Nairobi: Government Printer, 1991), pp. 2, 10.

32. Overseas Development Administration, *Britain and Kenya: Partners in Development* (London: ODA, 1989).

33. *Financial Review*, Nairobi, July 20, 1987.

34. Republic of Kenya, *Public Investments Committee on the Accounts of State Corporations*, 1991, pp. 19–20.

35. Minister for Local Government, Republic of Kenya, *The National Assembly Official Report*, Vol. 17, September 30, 1969, to November 5, 1969, pp. 367–370.

36. KAM to all members, "Lunga Lunga—Outer Ring Roads Project," October 5, 1988 (KAM files).

37. Republic of Kenya, *Committee of Review of Statutory Boards Report*, 1979, p. 22.

38. Republic of Kenya, *Report and Recommendations of the Working Party on Government Expenditures* (Nairobi: Government Printer, 1982), p. 43.

39. Republic of Kenya, *Development Plan 1989–1993* (Nairobi: Government Printer, 1990), pp. 152–153.

40. Republic of Kenya, *Third Report of the Public Investments Committee Report on the Accounts of State Corporations*, 1991, p. v.

41. Inter Press Service, "Kenya: Opposition Party Urges Government to Speed Reform," February 25, 1993.

42. On this point and other aid-related programs in Kenya, especially the involvement of the international development agencies in administering it, see David Himbara, *Kenyan Capitalists, the State, and Development* (Boulder: Lynne Rienner 1994), Chapter 5.

43. See *New York Times* and *Financial Times*, November 27 and December 1, 1991.

44. *Reuter European Business Report*, "Kenya Announces Economic Reforms," February 19, 1993.

45. SRI International, *Parastatals in Kenya: Assessment of Their Impact and an Action Plan for Reform*, final report prepared for the Kenyan Association of Manufacturers (Nairobi: SRI International, 1992), p. 16.

46. Ibid., pp. 14–16.

47. Principal of these parties are FORD (Forum for the Restoration of Democracy) Asili of Kenneth Matiba, FORD Kenya of Oginga Odinga, and the Democratic Party of Mwai Kibaki. FORD Asili and the Democratic Party effectively confirmed the division betweem the Kikuyu of Murang'a and the Kikuyu of Nyeri. Matiba's party took almost all seats in Murang'a, Kiambu, and Nairobi, while Kibaki won in his home area of Nyeri and neighboring areas. Oginga Odinga and his FORD Kenya could win only in Luoland. President Moi, who failed to win a single seat in the above areas, could carry only Kalenjin regions and those of other

smaller ethnic groups around the country. The 1992 multiparty general elections, vote rigging notwithstanding, suggest that a coherent national political elite does not exist in Kenya.

48. European Information Service, "EC/Kenya: Foreign Minister to Urge Renewal of International Aid," February 27, 1993.

49. See, for example, the interview with the U.S. ambassador, Smith Hemptstone, in *Economic Review*, Nairobi, January 11, 1993.

50. *Reuter Library Report*, "Kenya Shilling Nosedives as Flotation Takes Hold," February 24, 1993.

51. Horace Awori, "Kenya: Reforms Unlikely to Hoodwink IMF, World Bank," Inter Press Service, February 22, 1993.

52. Paul Muite, vice-chairman of FORD Kenya, cited in "Kenya's Economic Prospects Bleak," *Agence France Press*, March 25, 1993.

53. Kasanga Mulwa, chairman of the Fresh Produce Exporters Association of Kenya (FPEAK), cited in "Kenya: Horticulture Farmers Want IMT Reforms Back," *Reuter European Business Report*, March 30, 1993.

54. Horace Awori, "Kenya: Airlines Threaten to Pull Out," Inter Press Service, March 31, 1993.

55. Manoah Esipisu, "Fuel Shortage in Kenya Forces Airlines to Divert Flights," *Reuter Library Report*, April 15, 1993.

56. *Financial Times*, March 24, 1993; see also the editorial comments in the same issue.

57. *Economist*, April 24, 1993.

58. Provincial commissioner, Central Province, to chief secretary, "Trading Licences," November 15, 1946. Ministry of Commerce and Industry *MCI/6/782*, Kenyan National Archives (KNA).

59. Department of the Registrar General, Law Courts, "African Companies," June 23, 1949. *MCI/6/788*, KNA.

60. Ibid.

61. Registrar of Companies, "African Companies," October 12, 1950. *MCI/6/789*, KNA.

62. On the myth that the colonial state and the immigrant communities prevented Africans from participating in commerce and industry, see E. A. Brett, *Colonialism and Underdevelopment in East Africa* (New York: NOK Publishers, 1973), p. 294; Nicola Swainson, "Indigenous Capitalism in Postcolonial Kenya," in Paul Lubeck, ed., *The African Bourgeoisie: Capitalist Development in Nigeria, Kenya, and the Ivory Coast* (Boulder: Lynne Rienner, 1987), p. 140; Peter Marris and Anthony Somerset, *African Businessmen* (London: Routledge and Kegan Paul, 1971), p. 228.

63. Secret: Office of the District Commissioner, Nairobi, to the chief secretary, December 29, 1944. *MCI/6/782*, KNA.

64. Board of Commerce and Industry, Working Party on Assistance to African Traders, May 22, 1955. *MCI/6/821*, KNA.

65. Commissioner for local government to all town clerks, clerks to county councils, presidents of African District Councils, August 15, 1955. Prominent local industrialists that were used as models for the would-be African businessmen included M. Manji of the House of Manji. See *Ministry of Local Government/3/144*. KNA.

66. J. G. Courtenay-Bishop, Department of Trade and Supplies, to M. Paterson, secretary for Commerce and Industry, February 28, 1957. *MCI/6/782*, KNA.

67. Department of Local Government to all town clerks, all clerks of county councils, presidents of African District Councils, August 15, 1955. *MLG/3/144*.

68. Ministry of Commerce and Industry, "Manual of Instructions for Boards and Committees Established to Make Loans to African Traders, Artisans and Industrialists." *MCI/6/1275*, KNA.

69. See *Report of Controller and Auditor General, 1965/1966*, p. v.

70. V. A. Maddison to G. D. Parkin, September 2, 1959. *MCI/6/750*, KNA.

71. See A. J. F. Simmance, district commissioner, Kiambu, to the Registrar of Societies, April 22, 1959. *MCI/6/750*, KNA.

72. V. A. Maddison, PS, Ministry of Commerce and Industry, June 29, 1959, Minutes on C/TRDS/Central/Vol D/. *MCI/6/1275*.

73. Republic of Kenya, *Development Plan 1989–93* (Nairobi: Government Printer, 1989), p. 224.

74. Ibid., p. 161.

75. Swainson, "The Rise of a National Bourgeoisie in Kenya," pp. 50–51.

76. Leys, "Accumulation, Class Formation and Dependency," p. 183.

77. See *Daily Nation*, January 9, 1979; October 10, 1980; November 22, 1981; December 17, 1984. See also *Standard*, February 2, 1979, and *Weekly Review*, January 1, 1982.

78. See *Weekly Review*, March 24, 1989.

79. A. N. Morara, "Linking Industry for Faster Development," paper presented at the Industrial Subcontracting Seminar by UNDP in Collaboration with UNIDO, ILO, and the Ministry of Industry, Nyeri, March 4–9, 1990.

80. Seminar cited in note 79.

81. Kenyan Association of Manufacturers, *Report on Industrial Subcontracting Seminar by UNDP in Collaboration with UNIDO, ILO and the Ministry of Industry* (Nairobi: KAM, 1990).

82. Interview with Emma Muchene-Kolaas, manager, Kenya Subcontracting and Partnership Exchange, January 1993.

83. Republic of Kenya, *Development Plan 1989–1993*, p. 164.

84. J. S. Stirton, "Report on Rural Industries," June 15, 1945. See also the Secretariat Circular Letter No. 4 and correspondence, January 25, 1945. *MCI/6/1833*, KNA. (Emphasis added.)

85. Indu Chandaria, "The Development of Entrepreneurship in Kenya," B.A. thesis, Department of Economics, Harvard College, 1963.

86. Robin Murray, "The Chandarias: The Development of a Kenyan Multinational," in Raphael Kaplinsky, ed., *Readings on the Multinational Corporation in Kenya* (Nairobi: Oxford University Press, 1978).

87. Colin Leys, *Underdevelopment in Kenya* (Los Angeles: University of California Press, 1975), p. 38.

88. Swainson, *Development of Corporate Capitalism in Kenya*, pp. 125–130.

89. Peter Coughlin, "What's Going On in the Glass Manufacturing Industry," *Industrial Review*, Nairobi, February 1989.

90. Lawrence Hollingsworth, *The Asians of East Africa*, (London: Macmillan, 1960), p. 12.

91. M. H. Hill, *The Permanent Way: The Story of Kenya and Uganda Railway* (Nairobi: East African Literature Bureau, 1949), p. 255.

92. Ibid., p. 28.

93. Errol Trzebinski, *The Kenya Pioneers* (London: Heinemann, 1985), p. 42.

94. Ibid.

95. Marjorie Macgoye, *The Story of Kenya* (Nairobi: Oxford University Press, 1986), p. 16.

96. W. McGregor Ross, *Kenya from Within* (London: George Allen and Unwin, London, 1927), pp. 415–416.

97. East African Royal Commission 1953–1955, *Report (O.H.M.S., Cmd 9475)* (London: HMSO, 1956), pp. 65–194.

98. Trzebinski, *The Kenya Pioneers*, p. 77.

99. For a fuller account of the transition from merchant to industrial capital, see Himbara, *Kenyan Capitalists, State and Development*, Chapter 3.

100. See "Notes of a Meeting Held in the Secretariat on the 17th March to Discuss the Division of Responsibility for Various Matters Between the Member for Agriculture and Natural Resources and the Member for Commerce and Industry." *MCI/4/5*, KNA.

101. Ministry of Commerce and Industry memo, January 31, 1949. *MCI/6/20*, KNA.

102. P. C. Harris (A.S.C.I [1]), June 10, 1960. *MCI/6/696*, KNA.

103. See the correspondence between the British secretary of state for the colonies, A. T. Lennox-Boyd, and R. J. Mehta in *CS/1/16/35*, KNA.

104. See Colony and Protectorate of Kenya, *The Report of the Committee to Examine the Need for Economic Assistance for Primary and Secondary Industries, Excluding Agriculture in the Colony* (Nairobi: Government Printer, 1955).

105. Mwai Kibaki, cited in *Daily Nation*, January 1, 1969.

106. See *Weekly Review*, "Magnate Merali Increases Empire," July 15, 1988. See also *Financial Review*, "Who Is Buying the Town" and "The House Alibhai Rebuilt," December 5, 1988.

107. Republic of Kenya, *Kenya: Export Processing Zones*, p. 7.

5

The State and the Development of African Capitalism in Zimbabwe

Sheila M. Nicholas

The role of Africa's internal or domestic capitalist classes has hitherto not been assigned an important place in explanations of the weaknesses of Africa's economies. Insofar as they have been considered, the tendency in the literature has been to focus upon the ability of foreign capital to make the political and economic elites of developing countries into its clients. Much less consideration has been given to the role of internal social forces, or government ideology, in creating conditions conducive to sustained capital accumulation and growth of output. Yet it is becoming increasingly evident that the kind of domestic bourgeoisie a country has makes a difference, and that the role of the colonial state in Africa, and in many cases also the postcolonial state, has been a key factor in determining the relative strength—or more often weakness—of Africa's domestic bourgeoisies.

The case of Rhodesia/Zimbabwe is interesting in that it throws this dimension into particularly sharp relief. The history of preindependence Rhodesia illustrates the importance of government policies favoring the development of a national, albeit settler, bourgeoisie; and the history of independent Zimbabwe illustrates what happens when these policies no longer operate. In practice, the independent government continued to support the settler bourgeoisie, but with declining enthusiasm on account of its racist past; however, it resisted policies needed to foster the emergence of a black capitalist class, partly on ideological grounds and partly from a reluctance to share political power with a new indigenous class of capitalists. Eventually, however, the demands of an economy resting on the logic of the market led to a crisis in which their reluctance to assist the expansion of an internal class of black capitalists had to be, and was, overcome.

From the 1890s to World War II:
Opposition to African Capitalism

Initially the British South Africa Company (BSAC) and its white settlers were interested only in the exploitation of a Second Rand, which was

believed to lie below the soil of Rhodesia. The settlers turned to the indigenous population to produce the food required for themselves and their
mine workers; and for the time being the emerging African peasantry was
not seen as a threat to white settlers, who found it more profitable to buy
and trade in African commodities than to be involved in agricultural production themselves.[1] On the other hand, the development of African artisans was halted almost as soon as it began. The European artisans who
came to help build the new colony petitioned to have African artisans excluded from their trades, arguing that such competition would be a disin-
centive to the immigration of new settlers whom the BSAC dearly wanted.
In a similar manner, Africans wishing to enter commerce were severely restricted in order to protect European commercial interests.[2]

When, around the time of World War I, it was finally conceded that
there were no extensive gold deposits in Rhodesia, Europeans who decided
to stay turned to agriculture to support themselves; consequently their preoccupation with economic competition from African artisans was extended
to include African farmers. However, despite their confinement to lands
with poor soil and unreliable rainfall, some African farmers continued to
prosper. There is evidence that by 1922 a stratum of African peasant farmers was poised for transformation into a class of capitalist farmers. This
process was halted, however, by settler interests, which gained more
power after Rhodesia became a self-governing colony in 1923.[3] Following
the 1921–1923 slump in cattle and maize prices, which emphasized the
precariousness of settler prosperity, settlers lobbied the government to implement policies that would remove Africans from direct economic competition.

The idea of racially separated development was most clearly embodied in the Land Apportionment Act (LAA) of 1930. The LAA demarcated
separate areas where black business people and farmers were obliged to
pursue their economic activities separate from the European segments of
the economy. In addition to the "Native reserves," one component of the
LAA was the designation of Native Purchase Areas (NPAs), where
Africans who proved that they had the capacity both to pay for the land
and to develop it could purchase plots. The terms under which Africans
bought their plots placed a considerably greater burden on them than the
terms offered to European settlers; but despite these obstacles, Africans
had purchased 548 NPA farms by 1936 (a total of some 188,186 acres at
an average plot size of 250 acres).[4] Most of the farms were acquired by the
elite—teachers, religious ministers, chiefs' families, successful business
people, retired policemen, and court messenger-interpreters—many of
whom were from South Africa. Many of these farms were not developed
because the government refused to give Africans title to the land, so that
they could not use it as security for loans. On the other hand, attempts to
raise capital from selling firewood or opening stores were considered by

the Land Board to detract from the efforts called for by good farming techniques, and so they too were discouraged.[5]

The implementation of the LAA required moving Africans off European-designated lands onto already overcrowded reserves, forcing the government to implement a program to rationalize land use. The policy of centralization, as it was called, reallocated land to farmers in the reserves according to the ability of each region to sustain the population at subsistence level. In addition to these land policies, there were also pricing policies that discriminated against African farmers in favor of the settlers. The Maize Control Act of 1931 set up a two-tier pricing system that in effect taxed the profits of African producers, who produced maize largely for home consumption, to subsidize the production costs of European farmers, who grew grain largely for the lower-priced export market.[6] The Cattle Levy Act of 1931 similarly transferred African surpluses to the European sector of the economy. As a direct result of these policies, peasant agricultural production was largely eliminated as a path of capitalist accumulation for the African petty bourgeoisie, and the process of differentiation among this class was stalled.

African business people found even greater opposition to their existence in the urban centers. In the African areas around the European towns, African entrepreneurs established businesses despite municipal governments' reluctance to grant them legal status. African enterprises were highly regulated by the municipal councils, which determined such aspects as the types of business the African communities needed and the kinds of goods African consumers desired. Regulations were imposed upon African business owners with regard to the location and hours of business, the number of employees they could have, and the race of the customers they could serve.[7] In spite of these encumbrances, government records show a steady, though very slow, expansion of African commerce in the urban areas.

Less fortunate were African artisans, who had continued to grow in numbers throughout the 1920s and 1930s but were dealt a serious blow by the 1934 Industrial Conciliation Act (ICA). The ICA excluded Africans from the term "employee," thus disqualifying them for apprenticeships. This prevented many from acquiring skills that could eventually have contributed to the development of a stratum of African manufacturers.

From World War II to the 1970s: A Narrow Channel for African Capitalism

The outbreak of World War II disrupted world trade patterns and affected the path of capitalist development in Southern Rhodesia in two ways. In the first place, wartime Britain consumed more tobacco products, and a

dollar shortage forced tobacco companies to meet the increased demand
from countries within the sterling area. The result was that many Rhodesian farmers switched from maize to tobacco production, which brought
about a boom in capitalist agricultural production at the same time that it
undermined the country's self-sufficiency in food. In the second place,
secondary and tertiary industries grew rapidly, sparked by a wartime strategy of import substitution,[8] and required the encouragement of an urban
African workforce. It appeared that the settler state would have to reconsider the role it had previously laid out for Africans in the colony.

During the early 1940s, the government commissioned a study to find
ways to encourage the absorption of rural Africans into the market economy by stimulating the expansion of African capitalism, but without en-
croaching upon the dominance of the settler-owned sectors of the economy. Briefly, the findings of the Native Production and Trade Commission
(1944) recognized that without the encouragement of the government
(which certainly would not be forthcoming), settler economic dominance
would prevail because Africans were not at that time able to invest in large
enterprises in any sector of the economy, with the exception of a few
African traders and a number of African concerns in the milling industry.[9]

However, the settler state also recognized that, if the trend of declining food production was to be reversed, it would be necessary to take active steps to reorganize and encourage peasant agricultural production;
thus began a rationalization program for the Native reserves aimed at improving productivity. First, the government pursued a program of forced
destocking, which—given the low prices paid for the stock—was really a
forced decapitalization of the African rural petty bourgeoisie. Second, it
attempted to implement the Native Land Husbandry Act (NLHA), which
aimed at increasing productivity in the reserves by giving productive farmers security of tenure. The government envisioned that owners of noneco-
nomic units would dispose of their land and move to the cities, creating an
urban working class for the growing industrial sector, while productive
farmers would be able to consolidate their landholdings. Perhaps the
Rhodesian government expected a stable rural middle class to emerge from
this program (which was the strategic aim of Kenya's Swynnerton Plan,
upon which the NLHA was modeled). However, the farm sizes were too
small to be the basis for substantial accumulation, especially given the
continuation of discriminatory prices for maize. Even the NPA farms were
too small to be a substantial source of capital accumulation. The NLHA
was thus a way for the state to encourage the development of peasant output at the same time that it prevented African farmers from threatening settler agricultural predominance.[10]

One of the important consequences of the destocking program mentioned above was the liquidation, but also the partial monetization, of large
amounts of African capital that had been held in cattle stocks. Those

affected looked for alternative ways to employ their money, and this created a surge in the demand for trading sites throughout the rural areas. By 1950, Africans had leased 1,800 rural trading sites, mostly as general dealers, and the number slowly climbed to 2,238 by 1956.[11] Throughout the 1960s and 1970s, business activities were pursued in a growing variety of artisanal and service activities, but a general dealer's license remained the easiest to obtain and thus the most sought-after way to enter business. By 1961, there were 2,798 licensed general dealers among the great variety of millers, builders, carpenters, brickmakers, and other trades people who made up the list of 17,046 Africans who were licensed by the government to carry on independent businesses.[12] By 1975, it was claimed that the number of commercial enterprises had risen to 15,000,[13] with an annual gross turnover of $110 million.[14]

These numbers need to be interpreted with caution in light of the fact that many members of the comparatively small new African petty bourgeoisie were barely able to make a living from their businesses. Most commercial businesses were established on specific sites in the African areas around the European towns. For the most part, African business owners owned only one (usually modest) business each, although there are some indications of differentiation to be found among the government reports of applications to enlarge the size of stores or build department stores.[15]

Throughout the 1960 and 1970s, African business people expanded into other service areas as the needs of the growing urban population changed. In this period, the most lucrative sector for Africans was transport. Most owners of cars or taxis purchased their vehicles as a result of savings in the higher-paying African jobs in the formal sector. Usually the owner also worked as driver and mechanic, but a few made the leap into owning fleets of taxis or buses, and it was these men who formed the nucleus of the preindependence embryonic African bourgeoisie.

This African petty bourgeoisie, a bourgeoisie-in-the-making, faced many obstacles in this phase of its development. Many of the new ventures were undercapitalized due to the fact that their lack of freehold land titles prevented most African business owners from obtaining bank loans. After erecting their business premises, many were left with insufficient capital to buy an adequate, let alone comprehensive, stock.[16] In addition, many new business owners lacked managerial experience and basic bookkeeping skills and this also disadvantaged them, especially in their dealings with wholesalers, who were primarily Europeans and Asians. Moreover, in response to the growing numbers of African entrepreneurs, the government imposed a variety of regulations determining such aspects as the location of businesses and the distances between stores owned by the same trader,[17] which further hampered the expansion of those who were most successful.

All that has been said thus far underlines the important role a state can play in shaping economic forces. Initially it was the African farmers who, by virtue of their farming experience, held the advantage in the colonial economy. This advantage, however, was systematically eliminated by a settler government committed to European-led development. The channeling of all resources, both government and private, into the European-owned areas of the economy resulted in one of the most advanced economies on the African continent. The severe control of the expansion of African capitalism and the redirection of African rural surpluses into the European agricultural sector helped to create a strong European bourgeoisie and a small and very weak indigenous capitalist class. From the beginning, the settler state and the European capitalist class were mutually supportive; this became especially clear during the period of Rhodesia's unilateral declaration of independence, when the strength of the European-owned sectors of the economy permitted some decisive political battles to take place.

The inherent contradictions of a development strategy that was not based upon the logic of the market, however, were inevitably to bring about its collapse. The "winds of change" that swept across Africa in the 1950s and 1960s encouraged Africans, peasants and business owners alike, to struggle for political and economic equality. The systematic restrictions on the expansion of African capitalism had created a numerically small and economically weak class of African petty capitalists that could serve as a powerful ally neither for the Europeans endeavoring to defend the capitalist system, nor for the African nationalists struggling to remove the racist settler government from power. Most important, at independence the indigenous capitalist class was too weak to assert its political interests under the new African government.

From 1980 to the Present: The African Bourgeoisie

After the repeal of the Land Tenure Act in 1979, African business people were able to rent and own properties in any business district, and in the first three years following independence, the flood of settler capital out of Zimbabwe lowered urban land and rental prices, making way for the movement of African entrepreneurs into the commercial centers of the cities.[18] Here Africans entered a highly competitive market dominated by large settler commercial capital. The Africans' smaller stocks and turnovers were a disadvantage, although price controls went some way toward minimizing this. In the formerly African urban areas, African small business remained dominant, although there was some expansion by larger retailers and—in the late 1980s—also by large-scale settler commercial capital.

As regards manufacturing, the number of African manufacturers that have emerged since independence is still very small. According to unofficial estimates from informed observers in the Central Statistical Office and the Ministry of Trade and Commerce, in 1988 much less than 5 percent (and perhaps even less than 3 percent) of the manufacturing sector was owned by incorporated African enterprises. Africans responded to the opportunity to invest in manufacturing by investing in the production of consumer products such as furniture, electrical appliance assembly, cosmetics, clothing, food processing, and printing and paper products. The largest obstacle facing new industrial entrepreneurs was that goods produced by simple processes were already being manufactured by local firms—the result of the import substitution strategy pursued during Rhodesia's period of unilateral independence from Britain. And a critical condition of success for any new firm is technical expertise, which most African business owners lack due to the previous bias in the education and apprenticeship systems.[19] Most entrepreneurs interviewed in 1988–1989 had established businesses related to their previous work history; during their employment in a European-owned firm they had acquired skills—technical and managerial—and accumulated savings that then allowed them to establish their own manufacturing concerns.

African expansion into large-scale capitalist farming also proceeded very slowly. Despite the opening up of rural land outside the communal areas to ownership by all races, by 1986 it was estimated that only some 300 Africans had invested in large capitalist farms.[20] By 1991 it was calculated that African capitalist farmers, mostly members of the political elite, owned 8 percent of the commercial farming land.[21]

The State and African Capitalists

It has often been noted that, unlike many postcolonial regimes, the Zimbabwe African National Union–Patriotic Front (ZANU-PF) inherited a sophisticated economy with an extensive infrastructure. What is less frequently recognized is that the economic development of Rhodesia had occurred under specific conditions: (1) a motivated and sophisticated group of white settlers; (2) an ample supply of cheap labor; (3) the protection of local industrial development against the onslaught of cheaper imports during the Unilateral Declaration of Independence (UDI) period of sanctions; (4) a white working class whose high incomes and protected positions afforded a ready market for the consumer goods many local firms began to manufacture during UDI; and (5) a government highly motivated to maintain its economic control by supporting local white entrepreneurs, and its political control by excluding Africans from political participation. It is rarely recognized that any government that did not follow the previous path would be kicking away the props that had supported Rhodesia's economy. It was the absence of the last factor, a strong state commitment to support local capitalists, that proved to be an obstacle to the expansion of the African capitalist classes after independence.

One major reason the new regime did not begin to promote the interests of African capitalists was that, for purposes of racial reconciliation, it abandoned a racial perspective. Another reason was the political orientation of the Mugabe government. The Marxist ideology used to express and explain the exploitation of the African masses and their alienation from the land was a powerful tool for mobilizing support for the guerrilla struggle during the 1970s. There were committed socialists among the members of the Mugabe government and the higher civil service, and it appears they believed that their development objectives could be actualized only if the government maintained firm control of the economy. Thus, there was little room for the encouragement of an internal African bourgeoisie in the policies the government pursued.[22]

In the period immediately following independence, the Mugabe government's emphasis was on controlling the economy and investment so that it could engineer a major redistribution of wealth from the rich whites to poor Africans, especially in the rural areas, where a political commitment was made during the liberation struggle.[23] The Mugabe government also pursued a broader policy of increasing the government's control over the direction of development and ownership of the economy. In seeking extensive control of the economic processes in Zimbabwe, the government saw itself as the primary indigenous "entrepreneur." As a result of these factors, the ZANU-PF government, unlike most postcolonial African regimes, did not support the African business sector against settler or Asian capital, although the government's regulation of foreign investment went some way to protecting local investment in general. Privileged access to credit, licenses, and markets was not granted to African nationals.

This is not to say that the government neglected indigenous business entirely. In 1983, the government created a Small Enterprises Development Corporation (SEDCO), a parastatal that combined previous government lending institutions aimed at encouraging the development of small-scale African enterprises. SEDCO's objective was to help the emergent businessman or businesswoman with fewer than fifty employees and no more than Z$500,000 net assets. While any small business was eligible for loans and help from SEDCO, the main thrust of SEDCO's policy was to promote the development of commercial and industrial enterprises in the rural areas to help redistribute wealth away from the urban centers. There was also a mandate to promote cooperative ownership of these enterprises, as opposed to individual ownership.

Larger African firms were forced to apply to the white-owned financial institutions for loans or to the Zimbabwe Development Bank (ZDB). The goal of the ZDB was to promote economic development by providing capital for expansion, modernization, and new investments. Money for these loans was provided by the Reserve Bank of Zimbabwe in partnership with a number of foreign (national and multinational) financial institutions.

The ZDB was to provide long-term loans to medium- and large-scale enterprises in manufacturing, mining, and agroindustrial projects and, particularly important in Zimbabwe's economy, to provide foreign currency as well. From the sketchy data that are available, it appears that the major recipients of loans from the ZDB were in fact subsidiaries of multinationals. For example, of the ten projects supported by the ZDB in 1985/86, only one was granted to an indigenous manufacturer.[24] Similarly, of the seventeen projects approved for financing in 1986/87, only two were indigenous enterprises: a commercial poultry farm with a beer garden, and a printing company. On the other hand, Johnson and Johnson (Pvt.), Zimbabwe Bata Shoe Company, and Blue Ribbons Foods—all well-known multinationals—received financing.[25] Since loans from the ZDB were granted according to the same eligibility criteria as those used by the commercial banking sector, many African entrepreneurs were evaluated as being too risky for loans. Many criticized the Zimbabwean government for not creating a separate source of venture capital for African entrepreneurs as was done in Kenya and Nigeria. The consequences of the structural obstacles to African development continued to inhibit the expansion of African capitalism.

On the one hand, the state's relationship with the African capitalist classes may be explained by its "socialist" orientation, which promoted state ownership against private ownership. But the government's actions in other areas[26] indicate that there was also a strong desire not to reduce the state's freedom of action. The Mugabe government used the highly regulated economy it had inherited from the Smith regime to pursue its goal of gaining control of the path of economic development. So long as the economy was largely owned by settlers, the government had an obvious justification for its commanding role in it. It is very likely that the state's dominance in the economy would be challenged should a strong African capitalist class emerge that also could justify its expansion in terms of the "national interest." Moreover, an indigenous capitalist class might well make political claims upon the state in return for its political support.

Thus, in the first ten years of independence, the indigenous bourgeoisie, while not hindered, was not encouraged. Any development it achieved was accomplished in spite of its weak and peripheral position vis-à-vis the government and the settler bourgeoisie. This state of affairs began to change slowly after 1989, however.

The Relationship Between Settler and African Capitalists

The importance of having a model for entrepreneurial success cannot be overstressed, since the transmission of capitalist rationality and a capitalist work ethic is required if capital is to be accumulated locally. Yet since

independence, there has been little interchange between the settler bourgeoisie and African capitalists. The large-scale settler capitalists were
highly organized prior to independence and had a close working relationship with the government, especially under the difficult conditions of UDI.
UDI was, in fact, a period of high integration between the government and
the business community and between different sectors of business as they
fought international sanctions and the internal guerrilla war together. At
independence the settlers consequently faced a hostile new government,
and moreover one that professed a wish to dismantle capitalism as well as
promote the interests of Africans. Open hostility was alleviated by the
government's recognition that it needed the skills and capital of the settler community if it was to maintain the Zimbabwean economy during the
period of transition following independence. But there was a constant battle between the government's policies of trying to control the nature and
pace of investments according to its own political priorities and what the
business community considered was necessary for the continuation and
prosperity of capitalism.

Apart from agriculture, settler capitalist interests were represented by
the Confederation of Industries (representing manufacturing interests), the
chambers of commerce, and the Chamber of Mines. Prior to independence,
these groups, divided by their sectoral interests and competition for limited
foreign exchange, were united in their general opposition to the development of African capitalism in urban areas. In the late 1970s, however, the
chambers of commerce began to encourage the development of African
entrepreneurs in recognition of their power as a potential ally should the
"Marxists" form the government, and after independence in 1980, the
commercial sector of the settler bourgeoisie continued to make the greatest efforts to include the African "business community" in its political representations. African businessmen and businesswomen interviewed in all
sectors had the highest praise for the help extended to them by the racially
integrated Zimbabwean National Chamber of Commerce (ZNCC). The
ZNCC actively recruited Africans and provided them with seminars relating to business management and support services for their businesses. In
contrast, African owners of industrial enterprises reported that the Confederation of Zimbabwean Industries (CZI) offered them no support and
did not seem interested in them, and some CZI officials who were interviewed did indeed see the recruitment of African members only as a way
of appeasing the government. Because the great majority of new businesses were in the commercial sector, the CZI had yet to feel the need to
actually consider and represent the interests of African industrialists.

The government demanded that African and settler groups representing the interests of different sectors of the economy should integrate with
each other.[27] The most notable aspect of this directive was that the government saw no difference between the interests of African capitalists and

settler capitalists; it did not encourage the formation of a business association to articulate and promote the particular interests of African capitalists. As a result, the CZI continued to fight to preserve existing industrial enterprises rather than lobby the government to encourage new African investment. And while the ZNCC did press the government on a few issues faced by African business alone, such as title deeds for land in the communal areas, without which rural business owners are unable to qualify for loans, these representations offered solutions largely within a preindependence framework.

The Struggle over
Venture Capital for African Entrepreneurs

In general, one of the greatest obstacles facing African entrepreneurs in Zimbabwe is a lack of capital. In part this is the result of the lack of collateral for rural business owners who own enterprises in the communal areas and have no title deed to the premises and/or land. This formerly applied to most of the urban areas as well, but has changed since the repeal of the LAA. In general, new entrepreneurs are seen as high risks by banks, and consequently the banking community has failed to support entrepreneurial initiatives among African business people. In 1988–1989, bank development officers stated that few African individuals were making applications for loans for investment.

Recognition of this fundamental obstacle to expansion led to an initiative by African businessmen in Salisbury in late 1978 to form their own bank. The impetus came from the African Business Promotion Association (ABPA), which was formed in September 1977 by leading African businessmen who were interested in helping indigenous Africans to "dedicate themselves to the maintenance of the free enterprise system."[28] The Banking Act of Rhodesia required a new bank to have a minimum of R$1,000,000, and the 1,664 members of the ABPA agreed to pay at least $50 each to establish the new bank. It was also backed by eight companies.[29]

In February 1979, before independence, the Registrar of Banks refused to approve the ABPA's application on the grounds that approval for the probably short-lived institution would be against the public interest, since it would further weaken an already shaky money market.[30] P. Mpofu, spokesman for the ABPA, commented that the registrar's decision would perpetuate "white privilege and control of vital economic interests in Zimbabwe."[31] When a second application was turned down on the same grounds, the ABPA responded by denouncing the United African National Congress government of the day as "incapable of sweeping away both the political and economic anomalies of the Rhodesian Front for the benefit of the Africans."[32]

It appears that the ABPA was defeated. However, in March 1980, following the election of ZANU-PF, the president of the Rhodesian African Chamber of Commerce, Ben Mucheche, met with the new prime minister, Robert Mugabe, to discuss the establishment of a development bank for African capitalists. This meeting appeared to reestablish the initiative among African businesses for an African-owned bank. The Zimbabwe Consortium Bank, to be opened in May 1980, was to be established with an initial Z$10 million put up by African businessmen. While overseas investors would own 48 percent of the shares in the Bank, African Zimbabweans would maintain a controlling interest of 52 percent. The main purpose of the bank was to provide venture capital to African businesses.[33]

The March application for certification of the Zimbabwe Consortium Bank was still under review in May 1980. Unfortunately, the public record of the efforts of the ABPA to establish an African-owned bank ends here. It is evident that the reason for the white-owned financial sector's refusal to approve the application was to maintain its monopoly of financial control. Less clear is the reason for the Mugabe government's lack of support for these efforts by African businesses. However, the Mugabe government's announcement in October 1980 that it had taken a majority stake in a new bank in partnership with the Bank of Commerce and Credit International goes some way to explaining the absence of government support.[34] It was a widely held opinion among those involved in the development of investment projects that state approval of this new project was due to the fact that it offered the government equal partnership in the venture, an offer not made by the African business community. With the establishment of the Bank of Commerce and Credit of Zimbabwe (BCCZ)[35] in early 1981, the Mugabe government was able to expand its own presence in another sector of the economy, a much higher priority than creating conditions conducive to the expansion of African capitalism.

To illustrate the importance of a new financial institution in Zimbabwe that could provide loan capital to African entrepreneurs, we may look at a case study of an African manufacturer of paper products. Mr. B got a job working for a South African–owned packaging company in 1965, where he was trained as a print finisher and converter. Three years later he joined a local settler-owned printing firm, where he climbed to the position of assistant printer, which was two steps below a journeyman—a job reserved for whites. In 1971, he was promoted to the position of journeyman because the general manager recognized his expertise. His promotion to senior supervisor in 1976 was met with opposition, but he held the position until 1980 when, he claims, he was fired for hiring ex-combatants. After working as an administrative assistant to a printing union for two years, he decided to set up his own printing shop. He waited one and a half years for project approval from the Ministry of Commerce and Industry, a delay largely due, he felt, to a lack of sympathy on the part of the white civil servants. The application for a Z$800,000 loan in foreign currency was approved when a multinational pulp and paper mill agreed to be the guarantor in exchange for a 39 percent share in the venture. This agreement was dissolved, however, when the new partner refused to purchase new equipment from France and Switzerland and instead wanted to use second-hand equipment from its plant in South Africa.

In 1983, Mr. B entered an agreement with another corporation to be guarantor of the loan in exchange for a 49 percent share of the project—which the corporation unilaterally changed to 51 percent following a board meeting, with the promise that upon repayment its share would be lowered to 49 percent. The local corporation provided the rental property as well as the management system, including accounting and financing, while Mr. B's company was in charge of merchandising. The corporation charged Mr. B's company a 23 percent administration fee as well as an additional interest charge to cover administration of the loan from Grindlay's Bank.

In 1985, the corporation argued that the venture was not profitable and pressed Mr. B to sell his interest. He hired an independent auditor who concluded that the business was profitable but that the administration fee of 23 percent should be renegotiated. The corporation refused to reconsider its fees and applied to separate the manufacturing aspect of the business from the merchandising side. A court challenge to this application was decided in favor of Mr. B, who did not wish to separate the production from the merchandising side of his business. Following this, he began to negotiate with the corporation for controlling shares of both the manufacturing and merchandising interests. Almost Z$2 million was required to purchase the equipment and the building and no bank was willing to finance his business, because they all believed that he was experienced only in production and would be unable to manage the business. He did not qualify for a loan from the Zimbabwe Development Bank since his business was not a new project, nor was the financing required for capital improvement. In the end, the Bank of Credit and Commerce (Zimbabwe) agreed to take the equipment as collateral and provided a loan for all but Z$300,000, which was raised through private means. Mr. B believes that it was because BCCZ was new in the financial market and was more willing to back new entrepreneurs that he was able to get a loan. Mr. B's case underlines how important the availability of venture capital is to the development of indigenous ownership. Without access to capital, the status quo can be easily maintained through tight moneylending practices. That the settler bourgeoisie was well aware of this is evident in the struggle that developed around an apparently new commitment on the part of the Zimbabwean state to promote indigenous ownership of the economy.

New Government Initiatives for African Business

Unemployment was the major crisis confronting the government by the end of the decade. This crisis was created by settler capitalists' refusal to invest in an economy they believed to be unprofitable, and an accessible educational system that fostered hopes of employment in relatively well-paying jobs. In 1989, it was estimated that there were 1 million job seekers compared with 1.1 million workers in formal sector employment. From 1990, there would be approximately 200,000 new school leavers each year seeking jobs in a formal sector that barely invested enough to maintain its capital stock.

There were also external pressures. The government's eligibility for foreign aid loans was made conditional upon the adoption of an International Monetary Fund structural adjustment program. In keeping with its concern to be seen by the electorate as defiant in the face of international pressures, as well as to retain some degree of control over development priorities, the Zimbabwean government, in 1986, began a process of consultation with CZI, ZNCC, and industry-specific associations to create a liberalization program that would promote industrialization and employment without threatening local industries. These deliberations culminated in a shift in Zimbabwe's macroeconomic policies toward trade liberalization, the end of price controls and subsidies, a decrease in the deficit, a decrease in the number of public sector employees, the privatization of parastatals, more attractive foreign investment conditions, a separation of the state and party, and multiparty democracy. In spite of the "home-grown" origin of this structural adjustment program, it was later approved by the IMF.

These economic changes were accompanied by an announcement by Mugabe that the government would now actively support indigenous capitalism. In December 1990, the government opened the Indigenous Business Development Centre (IBDC), the aim of which was to promote African capitalists. News reports suggested that the IBDC was an initiative taken by eighteen African entrepreneurs[36] who wanted to provide African business owners with management training and business counseling services. A meeting held in December between these entrepreneurs and President Mugabe and four cabinet ministers resulted in government backing. With government support the IBDC was transformed from a consulting firm to a source of venture capital, to "shift ownership of the economy through the promotion of black enterprises."[37] It was promised that the government would quickly pass an indemnity bill that would set aside Z$500 million as a guarantee against which local African entrepreneurs could borrow to finance their projects. This eventually resulted in the establishment of the Venture Capital Company (VCC), which would offer African entrepreneurs interest-free loans for new projects. A total of

Z\$100 million (as compared with the original promise of \$500 million) was made available, financed by a consortium of international development finance interests (40 percent), the Reserve Bank of Zimbabwe (20 percent), and local commercial and merchant banks (40 percent). African entrepreneurs would be expected to raise 20 percent of their capital and the VCC would act as a partner. The ultimate goal was to allow indigenous business borrowers to buy out the VCC's share within six years of establishing their businesses.

The response from the settler bourgeoisie was sharply against this development. They reminded the government that racial discrimination was against the constitution of Zimbabwe and that some whites were, in fact, indigenous. The government, it said, had abandoned its policy of reconciliation in favor of reverse discrimination. One article in the *Financial Gazette* tried to discredit African businessmen as small-minded traders whose profits, acquired through "price-cheating" and failing to observe price and wage controls, were used for self-aggrandizement rather than reinvested in productive enterprises.[38] The article ended by reminding the government that many black businessmen were now managing directors of subsidiaries of multinationals, and declared that to support these men was to support the multinationals.

The struggle over control of the financial sector heated up following Barclay Bank's announcement that it would sell 25 percent of its shares to the public. The director of the IBDC, Mercy Zinyama, argued that the government should buy the shares and eventually turn them over to the IBDC, to allow indigenous business people greater control over the financial sector. The response from the CZI was that this was an "outrageous" proposal and out of step with government policy to reduce state involvement in the economy. The real issue was that African ownership of a portion of the financial sector threatened settler access to finance capital.

This could, then, be the beginning of the emergence of a significant African capitalist class in Zimbabwe. The general economic conditions, however, were not conducive. The government switched to supporting the African capitalists at a time when the economy was undergoing a process of liberalization, thus submitting new enterprises to international competition, whereas protectionist policies have generally been needed to nurture the development of infant domestic industries.

Conclusion

The history of Zimbabwe's capitalist and protocapitalist classes underlines the importance of a supportive political relationship between the state and the local bourgeoisie. Prior to independence, the settler state directed its efforts toward expanding and strengthening the settler bourgeoisie. As a result the settler bourgeoisie developed into a technically competent, financially strong, and politically influential class allied firmly with the settler state—an alliance that proved particularly useful during UDI.

The converse side of this was the antagonistic relationship between the settler state and African capitalists, large and small. With their profits redirected to settler-owned parts of the economy and their access to the market hindered by the lack of infrastructural developments and numerous state laws to inhibit their expansion, the indigenous capitalist classes emerged slowly and were technically and financially very weak. While the removal of racist legal obstructions to the expansion of African capitalists might seem to be all that is required for indigenous capitalism to grow, this study indicates that a supportive state is essential to its expansion. In the postindependence period, the Zimbabwean state directed its efforts at reducing, or at the very least limiting, settler control of the economy by expanding the presence of the state in the economy rather than by encouraging the expansion of African capitalism. The African capitalist classes remained economically weak and consequently politically weak and, until 1990, were unable to convince the government to establish conditions for their expansion.

For its part, the Zimbabwean government failed to see the importance of nurturing a strong political relationship with the indigenous capitalist classes. Encouraging the development of an indigenous capitalist class is one way for the state to counteract negative reactions to economic policies that bolster capitalist accumulation, rather than redistributing wealth. This was particularly important at the end of the 1980s in Zimbabwe, as the implementation of the structural adjustment program forced the government to implement policies that were supposed to foster capital accumulation but that reduced the poorer classes' access to education and health care as well as their overall economic position. The government could argue that its new policies would encourage the development of an indigenous capitalist class that not only would keep its profits in the country and thus benefit everyone, but that also shared the history of exploitation with the general population and thus could be said to have the true "national interest" at heart. Moreover, other classes were likely to accept a close relationship between the state and an indigenous capitalist class more easily than between the state and settler or foreign capital. And, at a time when the government was being forced to reduce its presence in the economy, it might be able to retain some influence over the direction of investment by supporting indigenous capitalists.

Notes

1. See Robin Palmer, *Land and Racial Domination in Rhodesia* (Berkeley: University of California Press, 1977) and I. Phimister, *An Economic and Social*

History of Zimbabwe, 1890–1948 (London: Longman, 1988) for in-depth studies of this period of Zimbabwe's history.

2. See, for example, Stephen Thornton, "The Struggle for Profit and Participation by an Emerging African Petty-Bourgeoisie in Bulawayo, 1893–1933," in *The Societies of Southern Africa in the 19th and 20th Centuries,* Vol. 9 (London: Institute of Commonwealth Studies, 1978), pp. 63–85. For a more detailed discussion of the early political economy of the petty bourgeoisie see Chapter 2 of Sheila M. Nicholas, "The Development of African Capitalism in Zimbabwe," Ph.D. diss., Queen's University at Kingston, Canada, 1992.

3. Phimister, *An Economic and Social History of Zimbabwe,* p. 76.

4. A. C. Jennings, *Native Affairs Department Annual* (Salisbury: Government of Rhodesia, 1932), p. 74.

5. B. Davis and W. Dopcke, "Survival and Accumulation in Gutu: Class Formation and the Rise of the State in Colonial Zimbabwe," *Journal of Southern African Studies* 14 (October 1987), p. 68.

6. This interpretation is found in C. F. Keyter, *Maize Control in Southern Rhodesia, 1931–1941: The African Contribution to White Survival* (Salisbury: Central Africa Historical Association, 1978).

7. For details of the kinds of restrictions placed upon African businesses see data taken from reports of the chief native commissioner in Nicholas, "Capitalism in Zimbabwe," Chapter 2.

8. See the discussion of this development in Phimister, *An Economic and Social History of Zimbabwe,* pp. 222–230. Most of the capital invested, however, came from foreign sources. In 1951, a peak year for investment in the immediate postwar period, £50,700,000 was invested by foreigners, accounting for 90 percent of all investment in that year. See D. G. Clarke, *Foreign Companies and International Investment in Zimbabwe* (Gwelo, Rhodesia: Mambo Press, 1980), p. 26.

9. For more details of the findings of the commission, refer to Nicholas, "Capitalism in Zimbabwe," Chapter 3, especially pp. 89–98.

10. For differing points of view on the effects of the Native Land Husbandry Act see the following: Palmer, *Land and Racial Domination in Rhodesia;* William R. Duggan, "The Native Land Husbandry Act of 1951 and the Rural African Middle Class of Southern Rhodesia," *African Affairs* 79 (1980), pp. 227–239; Terence Ranger, *Peasant Consciousness and Guerrilla War in Zimbabwe* (Harare: Zimbabwe Publishing House, 1985).

11. These data are found in the reports of the secretary for native affairs, chief native commissioner, and director of native development for the years cited. For further discussion and details see Nicholas, "Capitalism in Zimbabwe," Chapter 3.

12. City of Bulawayo, *Report of the Director of African Administration for the Year Ending June 30, 1961* (1961), p. 100.

13. C. G. Msipa, "The African Retail Market Opportunities and Difficulties," *Rhodesian Journal of Economics* 9, no. 1 (1975), p. 15.

14. Ibid., p. 16.

15. The data on the growth of the urban petty bourgeoisie are to be found in the municipal reports of the directors of native administration. The reports of Hugh Ashton, director of native administration for the municipality of Bulawayo, commented frequently on the development and struggles of the African trader in the townships. For a detailed examination see Nicholas, "Capitalism in Zimbabwe," Chapter 4.

16. Southern Rhodesia, *Report of the Secretary for Native Affairs, Chief Native Commissioner and Director for Native Development for 1951* (1952), p. 27.

17. Ibid., p. 94.

18. Data on the development of African enterprises since independence are very difficult to collect since, in its efforts to create a nonthreatening environment

for white capital, the present government has declined to keep racially specific data. Most of the quantitative data also are estimates provided by informed observers and participants. Some of the data presented here are based on interviews conducted between January 1988 and June 1989. The names of potential interviewees were gathered from officials in the government, financial institutions, business associations, and personal contacts. Those who agreed to be interviewed were asked questions about the history of their businesses, the problems they faced at various stages in their business activities, organization of their businesses, association with and opinions about business associations, their political and community involvement, suggestions for economic reforms, and personal data regarding education and formal sector employment.

19. Tafirenyika Moyana, "Creating an African Middle Class: The Political Economy of Education and Exploitation in Zimbabwe," *Journal of Southern African Affairs* 4 (July 1979).

20. S. Moyo, "The Land Question," in *Zimbabwe: The Political Economy of Transition, 1980–1986* (Dakar: CODESRIA Books, 1986), p. 188. According to government statistics, there were 5,481 large-scale farms in Zimbabwe. See Republic of Zimbabwe, *Statistical Yearbook* (Harare: Government Printer, 1987), p. 142.

21. Carole Pearce, "Right Way, Wrong Sign-Post," *Southern African Economist* (August-September 1991), as reproduced in the *Zimbabwe Press Mirror* 10, no. 9 (September 23, 1991), p. 6.

22. Some commentators on "socialism" in Zimbabwe have noted that the reforms promoted by the Mugabe government are no more than those pursued by any liberal government. But having said that, they have already recognized an interesting aspect of ZANU-PF's policies that deserves further consideration.

23. As the 1989 elections showed, the rural areas remain the political basis of ZANU-PF.

24. See Zimbabwe Development Bank, *Annual Report*, 1985–1986.

25. See Zimbabwe Development Bank, *Annual Report*, 1986–1987.

26. In the same way, the government did not encourage the entrepreneurial spirit found in the informal sector, which flourishes everywhere in Zimbabwe. Rather, the informal sector has been the object of systematic government efforts to control it and prevent its expansion. For example, the Mugabe government fought against pirate taxis in a country where there is an acute transportation shortage, which the pirate taxis help to overcome. In addition, in 1988, the government cracked down on people running small businesses from their homes. Such part-time services as were offered by home renovators, furniture makers and repairers, and seamstresses disappeared quickly from public view. This action stemmed in part from the government's position that the informal sector did not provide meaningful jobs and that all efforts at job creation should be directed toward the formal sector.

27. For more details about African business groups and their integration with settler groups see Nicholas, "Capitalism in Zimbabwe," Chapter 8, especially pp. 281–286.

28. *Rhodesia Herald*, January 1, 1979.

29. *Rhodesia Herald*, November 27, 1988.

30. *Rhodesia Herald*, March 9. 1979.

31. *Rhodesia Herald*, March 17, 1979.

32. *Rhodesia Herald*, August 6, 1989.

33. *Sunday Mail*, March 30, 1980.

34. The major shareholders were members of the ruling families of Saudi Arabia, Kuwait, Bahrain, and Abu Dabi. *Rhodesia Herald*, October 9, 1980.

35. In 1991, the Bank of Commerce and Credit had its banking rights suspended in Britain due to suspicions of fraudulent practices. Subsequently the Zimbabwean government took control of BCCZ.

36. The *Financial Gazette* reported that it was eight on February 1, 1991.

37. *Financial Gazette*, January 11, 1991.

38. *Financial Gazette*, February 1, 1991.

6

The Role of the "National" Bourgeoisie in National Development: The Case of the Textile and Clothing Industries in Zimbabwe

Tom Ostergaard

On the basis of an empirical case study of the textile and clothing industries in Zimbabwe, I attempt in this chapter to make a contribution to the debate about the role of the national bourgeoisie and its relationship to the state.[1]

Several factors make the textile and clothing industries particularly interesting. They were among the first industries to develop in the then Rhodesia. Since Zimbabwe's independence in 1980, these industries have exhibited considerable dynamism. Their growth rates in terms of output, exports, investments, and employment creation have all been remarkably above those of the manufacturing sector as a whole. Moreover, the textile and clothing industries are dominated by a group of white settlers, many of whom were born in the country. The involvement of foreign capital in these industries is minimal.[2]

The basic objective of the research was to see how the self-proclaimed socialist government of Zimbabwe had treated the mainly settler-owned textile and clothing industries. It turned out that despite the history of ninety years of apartheid-like racial discrimination prior to independence and the ideology of the new government, the relationship between the new state and the settler fraction of the internal bourgeoisie was not contradictory. On the contrary, during the 1980s the Mugabe government, like the Smith regime before independence, favored the settler fraction over the interests of both indigenous (black) and foreign capital.

This chapter first examines the reasons behind the state's favorable treatment of the settler fraction. It goes on to suggest why the apparent favoritism shown toward the oppressors of the past did not create a crisis for the government. It then outlines the relationship of the state to settler capital in more detail, and concludes with a discussion of the wider theoretical significance of this case for African development.

Determinants of State Policy

What determines whether state power complements or frustrates capitalist industrialization? How can existing theory help us to understand why the self-proclaimed Marxist-Leninist government of Zimbabwe continued to favor the settler fraction of the bourgeoisie?

The simple instrumentalist approach involves the claim that the state is an instrument of the ruling class. A series of criticisms have rightly been leveled against this crude argument. Bob Jessop[3] maintains that if the state is a simple instrument of class rule, it is necessary to explain how the dominant mode of production is successfully reproduced when the economically dominant class does not actually occupy the key positions in the state system. This is very pertinent to the Zimbabwean case. During the UDI period, the state was to some extent an instrument of the ruling class. The close relationship—and overlap—between the private sector and the state during this period even made some observers talk about a corporate state. With the advent of independence, however, the economically dominant white settler class was virtually excluded from the state apparatus, which was quickly Africanized. The white settlers could no longer directly utilize the powers of the state to further their private economic interests.

Joachim Hirsch also makes some observations pertinent to the present study.[4] He refers both to the basic structural constraints that shape the policymaking process and to the situational logic that predisposes the governing groups to discriminate in favor of capital. Among the basic structural constraints, he emphasizes (a) the general exclusion of the state from the essentially "private" productive core of the capitalist economy; (b) the dependence of state expenditure on revenues withdrawn from the total surplus created within the capitalist economy; and (c) the "governing groups" in charge of the political system (notably officials and politicians), who have a vested interest in securing capital accumulation as a basic precondition of their own reproduction as people living off politics. Owing to the first constraint, Hirsch also argues that state intervention is essentially reactive, inasmuch as it responds to particular economic events and their political repercussions rather than trying to control fully every movement in the circuit of capital.

Hirsch's discussion provides a good starting point for our analysis. Owing to the state's near exclusion from the productive core of the textile and clothing industries, it can withdraw revenues from them only as long as private industrialists are allowed to operate efficiently. The industries' large and growing contribution to Zimbabwe's foreign exchange earnings was also a major explanatory factor. In other words, the state perceived the textile and clothing industries as a hen that laid golden eggs.[5] The textile and clothing industries also provided jobs. The industries accounted for nearly one-quarter of total manufacturing employment, and the rate of employment creation in the textile and clothing industries far exceeded that of the manufacturing sector as a whole. Moreover, this labor force resided predominantly in the two largest cities, Harare (the capital) and Bulawayo. Keeping these individuals in employment was obviously important.

Nicos Poulantzas's argument that incoherence in state policies is attributable to administrative inertia, "muddling through," and bureaucratic ponderousness also applies particularly well to the Zimbabwean economy, which was extensively controlled by the bureaucracy.[6] He argues that the state reflects and condenses all the contradictions in a class-divided social formation and that state power is always the power of a definite class to whose interests the state corresponds. This should not be taken to mean that the state serves as an instrument of the dominant class. Rather, it implies that, to the extent that the state successfully performs its general function in managing class contradictions and thereby securing cohesion, it maintains the political conditions necessary for the reproduction of the (dominant) mode of production.[7] This is in line with the argument that the agents of the state see it as being in their own interest to maintain the dynamic branches of industry, be they white- or black-owned.

Most important to the present analysis, Poulantzas argues that the capitalist state must prevent any political organization of the dominated classes that would threaten to end their economic isolation (i.e., the competitive individuation of producers that prevents them from experiencing production relations as class relations). If we extend this proposition and apply it to the Zimbabwean case, it might be argued that the "governing groups" feared a challenge from the rise of a black industrial bourgeoisie.[8] Although the governing group depended on the continued success of the industrial sector, its political position within the state apparatus was virtually insulated from the settler bourgeoisie. Had an indigenous black bourgeoisie arisen, however, it might have been able to penetrate the state apparatus and contest the protected position of the governing group.[9] Thus, owing to the history of racial discrimination and the demographic composition of the electorate, white industrialists were practically excluded from political power due to their skin color; a black industrialist was not.

We may conclude from the above that there was a coincidence of interests between the dominant class (which, for historical reasons, happened to be a largely white bourgeoisie) and the agents of the state (the governing group), who were predominantly black. Both had an interest in keeping the established, settler-owned industry running. In this case, the agents of the state functioned as if they were a social class. Policy determination was thus a two-way street—or, one is tempted to argue, the product of an alliance—between the dominant class and the agents of the state, but it was the needs of the dominant class that took primacy in the last analysis.

At a less abstract level, John Saul's prediction at the time of Zimbabwe's independence seems to have been valid.[10] He speculated that there was a very real possibility that Zimbabwe would become trapped on the terrain of short-run calculation; "circumstances" would never be quite "ripe for socialist change."[11] With powerful forces acting quite self-consciously to reinforce pragmatism and caution, the long-term goals of transformation appear to have withered on the vine.

Having attempted to explain theoretically why the postindependence government of Zimbabwe should have continued to favor the white-owned companies within the textile and clothing industries, we now ask why this apparent favoritism toward the oppressors of the past did not create a crisis for the independent government.

The Art of Government

President Mugabe spoke quite explicitly of the difficulties he faced in striking a balance "between maintaining white confidence and also satisfying the expectations which our people have."[12] It is obvious that the legacy of ninety years of racial oppression led to a "revolution of rising expectations" among the black population at independence. And after 1980, the government indeed made major strides in providing health, education, and social services to the masses. This undoubtedly contributed to the public impression that the government looked after the general interest of the population.

On the other hand, we must take into account the interests of those who occupied positions within the state apparatus. The legacy of a publicly controlled economy was ideal for the new political and bureaucratic elite; when the former white occupants departed, there was a multitude of vacant slots to be filled by Africans. As one government official put it: "At independence there were many politicians to be accommodated." The size of the bureaucracy mushroomed, growing from 62,000 in 1980 to 181,000 in 1989.[13] In 1989, almost a fifth of GDP—more than double the sub-Saharan average—was devoted to public sector pay,[14] and Zimbabwe had no less than twenty-one ministries.[15] The many civil servants, and their families, had reasons to be content with overall government policies.

Within the textile and clothing industries, moreover, the absence of labor unrest during the greater part of the 1980s indicated that the government may have been perceived as neutral in the capital-labor relationship. This is even more remarkable when one considers that the government's labor policies were reminiscent of the UDI period. As the new minister of labor, Frederick Shava, told a works council seminar at David Whitehead Textiles in March 1984:

> It is our firm belief that the regulated system of labour relations which we have in Zimbabwe is more beneficial for the community as a whole, rather than the dog-eat-dog philosophy of the so-called free labour movement which operates in some other countries more developed than our own.[16]

The minister may not have known that except for the substitution of "Zimbabwe" for "Rhodesia" he was using word for word a speech delivered by the former Rhodesian minister for labor, Ian McLean, in 1970.[17]

Nevertheless, the new government was perhaps *seen* to be on the side of labor. Soon after independence, it took emergency measures to establish a national minimum wage. Nominally, wages for industrial and commercial workers almost tripled during the 1980s. However, after 1983, inflation increased at a higher rate than nominal wages. Thus, in real terms, by the late 1980s many of Zimbabwe's workers earned less than they had in 1980.[18] But whereas nominal wage increases may have been judged by workers to be a direct result of government support, inflation was probably seen as being beyond its control.

Moreover, in spite of the technological upgrading in the 1980s, Zimbabwe's textile and clothing industries managed to increase employment substantially. After independence, working conditions and benefits within the industries also saw some slight improvement. With regard to labor, we might conclude that government and labor tacitly agreed not to derail the established, settler-owned companies.

The textile and clothing industries also had important links to the agricultural sector. A very large number of peasant families grew cotton and depended on it as their only source of cash income. The number of registered cotton growers increased in the 1980s to more than 150,000, over five times the number at independence.[19] Small-scale and communal farmers also increased their share to 55 percent of the crop deliveries to the Cotton Marketing Board. Jeffrey Herbst has argued that the Commercial Cotton Growers Association skillfully used its shared interest with the peasant growers in its public relations campaign and price negotiations with government.[20] Moreover, it is clear that the peasant growers, who were an important part of the electorate, had a vested interest in keeping the textile industry healthy in order to secure a market for their cotton.

Irrespective of the government's degree of commitment to socialism and the actual possibilities of implementing a transition to socialism in Zimbabwe, the official socialist ideology undoubtedly played a major role. If concrete steps toward the implementation of a socialist order were lacking, the barrage of socialist rhetoric emanating from the state-controlled newspaper, radio, and television served as a smokescreen, diverting attention away from the implications of the business-as-usual policies of the government. As Gorm Rye Olsen[21] argues with regard to the least developed peripheral countries, the political-ideological interventions of the state are overdeveloped vis-à-vis their economic and social basis.

The governing group also exploited public sentiments against foreign, especially South African, capital. Arnold Sibanda argued that imperialism became a scapegoat for the failure of socialist rhetoric to deliver anything to the discontented masses.[22] Sibanda maintained that government takeovers of foreign capital were justified in terms of resistance to imperialism.

Having elaborated on the reasons for the rather surprising acceptance of the policies favoring settler-owned companies, it should be added that the days of silent approval may have ended. In the course of 1990, a wave of corruption scandals shook the country. There was growing dissatisfaction with the government, and a large portion of the population was visibly disgusted with the politicians—the "chefs"—as they were sarcastically called in public parlance.

To conclude this section, during the 1980s, the agents of the state were relatively successful in maintaining a balance compatible with both social cohesion and the interests of the bourgeoisie. In essence, the Zimbabwean state was running basically a capitalist project with socialist rhetoric and a careful set of policies to keep the population with it.

The Development of the Textile and Clothing Industries

We turn now to the empirical evidence on which this study is based. Background information on the textile and clothing industries is followed by an analysis of state policy toward the white and black fractions of the national bourgeoisie as well as foreign capital.

The roots of Zimbabwe's modern textile and clothing industries go back to the colonization of the country in 1890. When they actually began is partially a question of defining the term "industry." We know that the Ndebele grew cotton and made durable garments before 1870.[23] It is reasonable to assume, however, that modern technology was not employed until it was introduced by settler immigrants.

The vast majority of the early settlers were either South African born or had spent some time "down south."[24] Many of the early settlers were Jews, who had emigrated from Russia to settle in South Africa. When the Jewish immigration quota in South Africa was filled, these Russian emigrants went on to Southern Rhodesia. In old Russia, a large proportion of the Jewish population were either moneylenders or tailors. These skills they brought to Southern Rhodesia. As a result, in 1990, Zimbabwe's more than 200 registered clothing companies were largely in Jewish hands.

The outbreak of World War II ushered in a new epoch in the development of the Rhodesian economy. As imports from Europe were slashed, government realized that drastic action would be needed to overcome the anticipated supply bottlenecks. A particular stimulus to the textile and clothing industries was provided by the British decision to place the Imperial Air Training Scheme in Southern Rhodesia. The scheme massively expanded the domestic market for cotton goods, which were already in short supply. However, it required the personal lobbying activity of a representative of the Empire Cotton Growing Corporation before the government was ready to move.[25]

The government acted as a thorough midwife in the birth of the textile industry. It provided loans, and plant and equipment were ordered from England. In 1942, the Cotton Research and Industry Board, a statutory body, commenced production at the new spinning mill. At this time, the production of cotton was limited to a few hundred bales per year. Therefore, "to induce the natives to grow cotton in the reserves," the government decided to guarantee the price of cotton.[26] In the mid-1940s, when prospective entrepreneurs felt assured that sufficient yarn would be available from the government mill, a large number of people applied to start production in the textile and clothing industries.[27] Government held the view that cotton should be developed into one of the main industries of the colony; moreover, it wanted the industry to grow from local (i.e., settler) capital. The government made this clear when it turned down a request from Consolidated Textiles Mills of Natal to establish a textile factory near the spinning mill in Gatooma. The minister of finance stated that "government was not prepared to allow any outside interests to be associated with the spinning industry."[28]

Most of the expansion of the textile industry occurred after 1948 in the special circumstances created by a new customs agreement with South Africa.[29] Between 1948 and 1953, Southern Rhodesia's exports of apparel to South Africa increased fortyfold; and yarns, textiles, and apparel in 1953 accounted for well over half of all of Southern Rhodesia's exports to South Africa.[30]

Southern Rhodesia got the lion's share of the benefits of the Central African Federation (1953–1963) between the present states of Zimbabwe, Zambia, and Malawi. To ensure a market for the cotton growers, in 1954 the Federation passed the Cotton Industries Act, which prescribed that all cotton grown in the region must be offered for sale to the Cotton Industries Board and that the board must buy it at a fixed price. Seventy-five percent of the cotton produced within the Federation was grown in Malawi, but the only cotton-spinning mill was in Southern Rhodesia.[31]

When the mill experienced financial losses in 1955, it was taken over and expanded by David Whitehead, a British company, which a few years earlier had established a weaving factory near the mill. By 1954/55 David Whitehead accounted for a quarter of the total yarn consumption in the Federation. The company therefore had a vital interest in securing control of the yarn supply.

Rhodesia's historical ties to South Africa were intensified during the UDI period (1965–1980). When UN sanctions were imposed, South Africa was the only "legal" trading partner. As a result, overall exports to South Africa quadrupled between 1965 and 1973.[32] Furthermore, due to preferential treatment, South African investments grew to about a quarter of the total capital stock in Rhodesia.[33] Parallel with this, many non–South African foreign enterprises went through a "Rhodesianization" process. That is, when foreign subsidiaries were effectively cut off from their parent companies, the local executives (who were nearly all white Rhodesians) were free to make their own decisions and to reinvest locally made profits that would otherwise have been repatriated.[34]

Furthermore, the myriad of regulatory mechanisms, introduced to protect the balance of payments, functioned both as channels for passing government resources to the different white constituencies and as channels for participation by the white community.[35] In many senses, therefore, the UDI period increased the "corporatist" character of the state, providing a structured place for a set of white interests.[36] Because of the international isolation, the UDI period also enhanced the sense of unity and solidarity within the settler community.

Between 1966 and 1974, the textile sector registered an average annual growth rate of 11 percent, 2 percent higher than the growth rate for the manufacturing sector as a whole.[37] Its share of the gross output of the manufacturing sector rose from 7.5 percent in 1965 to 10.4 percent in 1975. Colin Stoneman[38] maintains that the increase in importance of the textile sector was the result of state intervention. There was substantial investment in textiles, and clothing manufacturers were required to buy a yard of local cloth for every yard imported.

In the mid-1970s, the Zimbabwe liberation movement escalated its guerrilla warfare against the white colonial settler state. In 1979, the Lancaster House Conference was called because the guerrilla war had produced a strategic stalemate and had shifted the balance of forces in favor of the liberation movement.[39] Owing to pressure from Britain, the United States, and some of the Frontline States, the guerrillas' political organization, the Patriotic Front, was forced to accept a constitution of unprecedented constraints, in effect guaranteeing white minority or foreign ownership of all the country's main economic resources for ten years.[40]

Thus, Zimbabwe inherited modern textile and clothing industries that owed much of their existence to a long-standing and close cooperation between the state and the settler bourgeoisie. South Africa's important role as an export market was also made possible by a series of government-negotiated trade agreements with that country. We turn now to a brief survey of the successful performance of the textile and clothing industries in the 1980s.

The Present Status of the Textile and Clothing Industries

The following statistics demonstrate that the textile and clothing industries stand out within the manufacturing sector as a whole.

Output

Between 1980 and 1989, the output of the textile industry (including cotton ginning) more than doubled. Whereas the manufacturing sector as a whole expanded at only 3 percent annually, the textile industry achieved an average growth rate of 11 percent per year. The performance of the clothing industry was less spectacular; it followed the average trend of the manufacturing sector as a whole.

In 1987, the combined output of the textile and clothing industries (Z$967 million) was almost equivalent to the contribution from the iron and steel, metals, and machinery sectors together. Textiles and clothing accounted for 14 percent of the value of total manufacturing output in 1987.[41]

Exports

The exports of both textiles and clothing have expanded significantly. After the depressed export years of 1982/83, textiles and clothing have become increasingly important export commodities. Their share of total manufactured exports increased steadily from 6 percent in 1982/83 to 19 percent in 1987, when exports amounted to ECU 52 million.[42] Textile and clothing exports now exceed those of any other manufacturing subsector. Measured in ECUs, total manufactured exports have declined since 1984, and the value of exports in the late 1980s fell below the 1980 level. Textile exports have increased, albeit at fluctuating rates, since 1982; the average value of exports for the 1984–1988 period was 30 percent above the 1980 level. Clothing exports have grown both steadily and rapidly since 1983; exports more than quadrupled between 1983 and 1988. Despite the significant decline in exports in the early postindependence years, exports in 1988 were 65 percent higher than in 1980.

Investment

Overall investments in the manufacturing sector declined each year from 1981 to 1985.[43] Investments increased in 1986 and 1987, but were still below the level of investments in 1982. In textiles and clothing, the decline in investment ended in 1983. Since then, investments in the textile sector have increased considerably but at irregular growth rates. The clothing sector, on the other hand, experienced sustained growth in investments, averaging 20 percent per year between 1983 and 1987.

The textile subsector has attracted by far the largest amount of investment in the manufacturing sector. It accounted for more than one-fifth of total manufacturing investments over the 1984–1986 period. This proportion (equivalent to ECU 66 million) was about twice as large as the textile sector's share of the total manufacturing output.

If we examine investment in relation to the gross output of particular branches of the manufacturing sector, we get a different indicator of investment activity. Over the 1984–1986 period, the amount invested in the manufacturing sector as a whole corresponded to only 3 percent of its gross output. This is extremely low by international standards. Over the same period, investments in the textile sector amounted to 5.4 percent of output, considerably higher than the investment ratio of the metals and iron and steel sectors. Investments in the clothing sector, however, lagged far behind. They averaged only 1.5 percent over the period, although preliminary evidence for the period 1986–1990 indicated a strong resurgence in clothing sector investments.

Employment

In 1987, the textile (including cotton ginning) and clothing industries employed almost 40,000, nearly one-quarter of all those employed in the manufacturing sector. Between 1980 and 1987, employment in these industries expanded by 23 percent, as opposed to 7 percent growth in overall employment in the manufacturing sector.

In conclusion, the textile and clothing industries have performed far above average in terms of output, exports, investment, and employment. The next section examines how the black-ruled government of Zimbabwe treated these industries in the 1980s.

Industrial Policy and Its Effects

Policy Toward the Settler-owned Companies

Beating competition from Botswana. Toward the end of 1982, projections were made that imports of clothing from Botswana would amount to $7 million,[44] almost three times as much as in 1981.[45] Having invested heavily in new productive capacity and facing sluggish demand on the drought-affected domestic market, particular sections of the clothing industry in Zimbabwe were hard hit by competitive imports from Botswana. On behalf of its constituent companies, the Zimbabwe Clothing Council (ZCC) lobbied government to take action to protect the local clothing industry. The ZCC argued, undoubtedly correctly, that a large portion of the imports from Botswana actually originated in South Africa: front companies were set up in Botswana to take advantage of Botswana's open general import license (OGIL) agreement with Zimbabwe. The government acted swiftly and deleted from the OGIL all clothing of Botswanan origin.[46] The government's decision to take steps against the imports from Botswana won the praise of the ZCC.[47]

The South African factor no doubt had a major impact on the decision to curb clothing imports from Botswana. But $7 million worth of imports from Botswana could not have posed a serious threat to Zimbabwe's clothing industry as a whole. The imports from Botswana represented only 5 percent of the gross output value of Zimbabwe's clothing industry. It is clear, therefore, that the government put itself out to accommodate the interests of a handful of Zimbabwean companies threatened by competitive imports from Botswana.

Although the suspension of the OGIL lasted only one month, the trade rift with Botswana had not been solved. In 1983, the Zimbabwean minister of industry, Simba Makoni, recognized that the textile and clothing industries had been the worst affected by the economic downturn in 1982 and 1983. Also recognizing the importance of those industries, he said that government "had adopted several measures to support and maintain the production level in the industry. One of these was to wage 'an ongoing battle' against the importation of clothing."[48] The quota for imports of Botswana clothing was reduced in 1983 to $5.5 million and again in 1984 to $3.3 million. Also in 1984, a 20 percent surcharge was imposed against clothing imports from Botswana.

Botswana regarded these quota impositions as a cruel blow to its clothing industry. Zimbabwe's argument was that most of the Botswanan companies were merely fronts for South African concerns wishing to break into the regional market.[49] But as the director of the Botswana Employers' Federation rightly commented: "One wonders why Zimbabwe introduced these measures against Botswana when Zimbabwe had a trade surplus with Botswana of $50 million in 1984."[50]

Subsidizing inputs. During the 1982–1983 crisis, the government also came to the assistance of the textile industry. Until August 1983, the local selling price of cotton lint had been linked to international market prices. Facing steeply rising lint prices, the textile industry's interest group, the Central African Textile Manufacturers Association (CATMA), proposed a cost-based pricing formula.[51] From CATMA's perspective, the result was even better than a cost-based pricing formula: the government fixed the price at $1.65/kg and it remained there until 1990!

In Zimbabwe, all cotton purchases and sales are handled by the Cotton Marketing Board (CMB), a parastatal. The freeze on the domestic selling price of lint obviously affects the profitability of the CMB. During the first five years after independence, the CMB registered a deficit on its trading account only once (in 1982), but after the price freeze it was permanently in the red. The CMB's accumulated trading deficit between the price freeze (1983) and 1988 amounted to $94 million, of which $74 million was accounted for by subsidies to the local spinners, to whom the CMB had been selling cotton lint at 25 percent below cost price (and half of the lint export price).[52]

Curbing labor demands. Like successive white regimes before it, the independent government made it effectively impossible for unions to use strikes as a weapon.[53] In 1981, 550 workers at the Rhodian [sic] Clothing Factory in Bulawayo went on strike in a dispute over a proposed bonus scheme. When the company sacked all the workers, the minister of labor was called in to resolve the matter.[54] The dispute ended only a few days later as a result of a meeting between the factory's management and the industrial council of the clothing industry.[55] The assurance given to the factory management by the industrial council chairman epitomizes the relationship between workers and employers in the textile and clothing industries:

> We would teach the workers the proper channels for airing their griev-
> ances. The workers had no right to strike. For that reason we accepted
> that the workers would forfeit payment for the four days they had not
> worked.[56]

Moreover, during the 1982–1983 crisis, government sided with indus-try in its wage negotiations with the labor unions. Ever since the mid-1970s, the National Union of the Clothing Industry (NUCI) had called for, and obtained, annual wage increases of around 25 percent. In 1982, how-ever, the employers refused NUCI's proposal for wage increases around 20 percent. After three industrial council meetings failed to reach a com-promise, the minister of labor was called in to mediate.[57] As the wage dis-pute was still unsettled seven months later, it was referred to an industrial tribunal.[58] After another five months, NUCI handed the matter over to the ombudsman because the minister of industry had failed to appoint an in-dustrial tribunal to look into the dispute. The minister responded, "There is no basis for that union to take any court action against the government. Also, that union does not know that there has been a recession and drought which has affected their industry."[59]

By March 1984, a newly appointed minister of labor said that he hoped trade unions would soon change from unions of protest to unions of development. In reference to the wage dispute in the clothing industry he made the following remarks: "The Zimbabwe textiles industry is under extreme economic pressure. . . . It is clear, therefore, that workers' wage demands must not be excessive."[60]

After more than two years of battle, NUCI obtained a "small wage in-crease" for its workers. Thanks to the sympathy of government, the em-ployers had won; said Mr. Pasipanodya, general secretary of NUCI, "We also realize that the clothing industry has been going through hard times."[61]

The weakness of NUCI was primarily a reflection of the debilitating legislation governing its scope of action. In view of the above, it was hardly surprising that the ZCC reported that labor was not a problem during the second half of the 1980s. Moreover, the episode supports Hirsch's theory about "structural selectivity" and my own argument, derived from this, that the government perceived the textile and clothing industries as a hen that laid golden eggs. Had the government been determined to implement a transition to socialism, it would not have continued—almost unchanged —the labor practices of the past regime.

Rescuing ailing companies. Government participation in industry tended to be undertaken not out of any ideological commitment to socialism, but rather from the classical capitalist state motive of rescuing lame ducks.[62]

In 1983, during the crisis, Zimbabwe Spinners anticipated a trading loss of around $1 million, following a similar loss in 1982. It was rescued by a $500,000 subscription of shares from the Industrial Development Corporation (IDC).[63]

When David Whitehead also faced hard times, the IDC provided a vital capital injection and in 1990 still retained about 9 percent of the shares in this large company. The government also took a major share in Delswa, a leading clothing company, out of concern over the high degree of foreign ownership in that company (the desire to dissociate itself from South African involvement was a major motive).

The government's assistance to these established, large-scale, and white-owned companies stood in stark contrast to the treatment of indigenous (black) entrepreneurs.

Policy Toward Indigenous (Black-owned) Enterprises

Government policy toward emergent enterprises, i.e., predominantly, but not exclusively, black entrepreneurs, suggests continuity rather than transformation. Did the government actually wish to promote the development of a class of black industrialists?

Structural barriers. As Nicholas shows in Chapter 5, for decades racial discrimination barred black entrepreneurs from establishing industrial enterprises outside the informal sector. The small-scale sector in Zimbabwe was, therefore, far less developed than in many other African countries. Yet according to Roger Riddell, "Perhaps the most striking feature of the post-independence period has been the *continuity* in policy towards the manufacturing sector with the UDI-period."[64] The government actually expanded the regulatory powers it had inherited in several areas, but the operational environment of black industrialists was not improved. In 1990, the import allocation system, for example, was still based on a quota system from 1966 that divided the available foreign exchange among the companies existing at that time. The system rewarded conservatism and penalized new entrants, including innovative black entrepreneurs.[65] Heavy government regulation, however, did provide opportunities for patronage and "extra income" for the public office holders and administrators.

In addition to this, small-scale enterprises were up against a series of government regulations biased in favor of large enterprises, they lacked access to capital, and they had insufficient marketing and management skills—to mention but a few constraints.

The Small Enterprise Development Corporation (SEDCO). According to the National Development Plan of 1988 (p. 22):

> Government will support the development of small-scale industries particularly in rural areas and at growth points as a strategy for creating additional employment opportunities. This will be done through provision of infrastructure as well as provision of credit facilities and technical facilities through SEDCO.

SEDCO, the Small Enterprise Development Corporation, was a parastatal launched in 1984 to encourage and assist in the establishment of small-scale enterprises in the areas of commerce, manufacturing, services, and construction. In view of the structural barriers facing emergent industrialists, government support via SEDCO was lukewarm.

This was most evident in the government's meager financial commitment to SEDCO. When SEDCO was launched, it was envisaged that a capitalization of $37 million was required to run the program. Over the first three years, however, government disbursed only $5 million to SEDCO. This was slightly improved upon in the 1990 government budget, which included a $7 million equity provision for SEDCO, but the government's commitment to SEDCO remained feeble.

SEDCO's inadequate capital base was a severely limiting factor. Every year the corporation was not fully staffed; in 1990, SEDCO was operating with half its actual staff requirement.[66] Staff shortage meant that SEDCO was able to process less than half of the 1,200 applications during the year 1988/89. The chairman of SEDCO also complained that its salary structure was below that of other parastatals and that this had led to fifteen staff resignations in 1988/89.[67] Worse still, not all applications that were approved could be financed, due to lack of funds.

By February 1990, SEDCO had financed a total of 121 manufacturing projects. About 30 percent of these were clothing manufacturers. One of the largest, which employed around twenty people, specialized in making cloths for shoe polishing at the Harare Sheraton. Another of the larger ones, with fifteen employees, concentrated on making money bags for the Reserve Bank of Zimbabwe; several made school uniforms. The SEDCO-promoted clothing manufacturers typically employed three to five people, and most of them sold their goods on the local farms or to Indian dealers in the towns.[68]

SEDCO's loan terms were hard for most people to meet. The interest rate charged was 16 percent for rural and 18 percent for urban projects; by comparison, the commercial banks' prime rate was only 13 percent. The repayment rate for working capital was three years and for machinery only four to five years. It might be argued that SEDCO had to apply such loan terms in order to avoid losses. On the other hand, for a government dedicated to encouraging black industrialists, it would seem reasonable to have charged no more than the prime rate. The limited scope of SEDCO's activities, and its severe loan terms, support the assertion that government was not interested in promoting black industrialists. As the government's commitment to socialism was largely rhetorical, the most plausible explanation of this was that the "governing groups" were not enthusiastic about the prospect of the development of a strong black bourgeoisie.

Misguided support to emergent black entrepreneurs. According to a senior official of the Ministry of Industry and Commerce, the government held the view that emergent black businessmen would quickly graduate from traders into true manufacturers. Either the official had this wrong or the government was blatantly naive. Herbst stated that the government was "trying to create a new class of Black businessmen by giving them preferential access to import licenses."[69] While government evidently promoted African commerce, it did not seriously endeavor to foster the much needed development of black industrialists in the textile and clothing branches.[70]

As is common throughout the industrial sector, clothing companies had their foreign exchange allocations reduced, some of them quite dramatically. To illustrate: the managing director of one of the larger clothing companies in Bulawayo informed me that his foreign exchange allocation had been cut from $580,000 in 1980/81 to $60,000 in 1990. In addition, over the same period the value of the Zimbabwe dollar plunged from DM3.25 per dollar, to DM0.63 per dollar.[71] The net effect of this double punch was that the company could import only enough cloth to keep the factory running for two weeks a year. The situation of this company was not unique. The World Bank[72] found that the allocation to some companies in the textile sector represented only 7 percent of their foreign exchange expenditure for 1982. My analysis of the textile and clothing industries indicated that nominal foreign exchange allocations to companies were cut by an average of 40 percent.

In view of the drastic reductions in foreign exchange allocations, how did the clothing companies manage to import large quantities of cloth?[73] The largest exporters generally obtained sufficient foreign exchange for the required importation of industrial materials through the Export Revolving Fund.[74] Many others, however, had to resort to expensive middlemen who, somehow, managed to secure an import license for materials.

One black official of the Ministry of Industry and Commerce, who was directly involved in the allocation of import licenses, stated that most of the import licenses for industrial materials were given to emergent black businessmen. He even acknowledged that the criteria were not followed to the letter when emergent businessmen submitted applications. Unfortunately, it became common practice for some of these businessmen to sell illegally their import license to established clothing companies.[75] Import licenses were sold at face value, or more; i.e., the permission to import say $100,000 worth of cloth was sold for at least $100,000. In an interview, an official of one of the larger clothing companies in Bulawayo reported that 60 percent of its cloth was obtained through these so-called briefcase businessmen, and several middle-sized exporters indicated that this proportion was fairly typical for the industry as a whole.[76]

One could say that it takes two to commit a crime like this: the seller and the buyer. One could also argue that the established companies were forced to get supplies by whatever means available, and that the briefcase businessmen resorted to their trade in order to survive in the hostile business environment facing emergent black entrepreneurs. In the final analysis, the fault lay with the government for allowing this to occur.

Apart from raising the cost of imported inputs used by the established companies, the government's practice of favoring emergent black businessmen in the allocation of import licenses had counterproductive side effects. It bred distrust, instead of cooperation, between the black and white sectors of the industry; it fostered poor business ethics and it did not promote the establishment and success of genuine black industrialists. It needs emphasizing that the phenomenon of the briefcase businessmen must not be interpreted as indicative of the behavior of the black fraction of the national bourgeoisie as a whole. As we have seen, briefcase businessmen were essentially parasites, not industrialists, who owed their existence to patronage.

Enough has been said to argue that the government could not seriously have desired to promote black industrialists within the textile and clothing industries. This was both unfortunate and surprising. It becomes even more extraordinary, however, when we discover that government also favored settler-owned companies vis-à-vis foreign-owned companies in the country.

Policy Toward Foreign Capital

Unlike the manufacturing sector in general, the textile and clothing industries were not dominated by foreign capital. According to UNIDO,[77] 83 percent of the capital assets in the clothing sector was held by local owners; in textiles the share was 76 percent. This compared with 52 percent for the manufacturing sector as a whole.[78] As the textile industry in Zimbabwe consisted of only a handful of large companies, it is possible to explore whether government favored local over foreign capital in that subsector.

Discrimination against foreign capital. The textile industry had only six spinning mills. The largest companies included David Whitehead Textiles (a subsidiary of the British transnational Lonrho), Spinweave and Cone Textiles (both locally owned), and Merlin (locally incorporated but with South African capital). As far as I know, foreign capital of any consequence was represented only by David Whitehead and Merlin.

The clothing industry comprised more than 200 registered companies and around 600 informal operators. Of all of these, only about seven companies counted as nonresident. However, these companies were considered nonresident simply because the former settler owners had left the country. No foreign company had actually come to invest in the clothing industry in Zimbabwe. For this reason, this section deals only with the textile industry, in which foreign capital was represented.

The locally owned textile companies generally felt that government was supportive of their industry. For example, commenting on a new investment project, the managing director of Cone Textiles stated publicly: "We are very pleased with the way the Ministry of Industry and Technology has responded to our projects."[79] Similarly, on behalf of the textile industry as a whole, the chairman of CATMA said: "We feel government has greatly assisted us."[80] In view of the extent of its approved investment projects, Spinweave undoubtedly would also have considered government to be supportive.

But for foreign capital in the textile industry, it is quite a different story. There is no doubt that there was general discrimination against foreign capital in Zimbabwe. The twelve-page form on which applications to import plant and/or raw materials for a manufacturing project had to be made began with questions on possible foreign ownership.[81] Nonresident companies were restricted from borrowing on equal terms with local companies. Foreign companies could borrow only an amount up to the equivalent of 25 percent of their share capital and resources owned; yet for resident companies, the sky was the limit.

It seems that David Whitehead, the leading representative of foreign capital in the textile industry, had to put up with slower than average treatment of its investment applications. For example, it was almost impossible for David Whitehead to replace outdated machinery. In 1988, the company applied for an import allocation to import splicers for its winding machines, but two years later government still had not replied.[82]

Between 1985 and 1990, David Whitehead invested only $15 million.[83] Compared with the amounts invested by locally owned companies, this was not much. David Whitehead's investments were equivalent to only 2.7 percent of the company's turnover during the period. By comparison, the textile industry as a whole invested an average of 5.4 percent of turnover in the period 1984–1986. When asked to characterize how much of its plant was outdated, the managing director of David Whitehead said "at least 50%."

David Whitehead obtained most of its foreign exchange for investments through the government but, owing to its foreign ownership, had to pursue every possible avenue. The Swiss government, for example, provided a $14 million mixed credit (25 percent grant) tied to purchase of machinery in Switzerland.[84] The Danish Department of International Development Cooperation (DANIDA) was also approached by David Whitehead for investment funds. DANIDA agreed to provide a loan to David Whitehead, but in 1988 the government of Zimbabwe turned down the proposal.[85] The situation was so bad that when Spinweave, a Zimbabwe-owned company, sold its old equipment to buy new machinery, David Whitehead bought it. Yet the two companies were competing in the same lines of production.

David Whitehead also struggled when it came to the availability of foreign exchange for spare parts and raw materials. In 1988, several manufacturers had to accept cuts in their foreign exchange allocations for the first half of the year. Quotas in the textile industry were reduced by an average of 42 percent, but David Whitehead's was sliced by 54 percent—the single largest reduction.[86] According to David Whitehead's 1988 annual report, its standard foreign exchange allocation was only enough to cover 15 percent of what was needed for maintenance.

Conclusion

In this chapter I have used an empirical case study of Zimbabwe's textile and clothing industries to try to throw light on the relationship between the state and the national bourgeoisie. In these important industries it has been demonstrated that in spite of the history of racist discrimination and the new regime's socialist ideology, the government has continued to favor the settler fraction of the internal bourgeoisie. Moreover, while doing this, the Mugabe government has neglected—if not directly opposed—the development of a class of indigenous, black industrialists. The government has even discriminated against foreign capital in order to promote the interests of the settler fraction of the bourgeoisie.

In the first two sections of this chapter, I advanced various theoretical propositions to explain why the independent government of Zimbabwe supported settler-owned textile and clothing capital and why this did not give rise to popular protest. But the fact that the Zimbabwean state favored settler capital more than foreign capital raises a wider theoretical question. In Kenya it seems rather to have been the other way round: i.e., there was a tendency to favor foreign transnationals over local (Indian) capital. What explains this apparent difference in the relationship between the independent states of Zimbabwe and Kenya and their respective fractions of settler capital? In other words, what are the general conditions that affect the way different kinds of capitalist classes in different circumstances relate to state power?

As regards Zimbabwe, one might speculate that local white capitalists were somehow "easier" for the Mugabe government to accept than local black capitalists would have been—i.e., that some sort of internalization of the hierarchy of prejudice on the part of the black elite had occurred. While there might have been an element of this, it is probably more important that the agents of the state, or the "governing groups," saw it as being in their own interest to maintain the inherited dynamic branches of industry, be they white- or black-owned. At independence the settler textile and clothing capitalists had technical expertise and management and finance experience, which made their sector relatively efficient and productive. After independence, moreover, the existing governing groups feared that if Africans developed into a capitalist class they might well represent a rival power base.

On the other hand, during the 1980s it seems as if settler-owned textile and clothing capital did not need anything from the state that would have entailed substantial political costs. Settler-owned companies had matured to such a point that further political favors were not needed. Thus, the symbiosis of the state and settler capital in postindependence Zimbabwe rested on some fairly special conditions.

It follows that the color, or race, of the capitalists is not, in itself, necessarily a variable of great interest. In a wider theoretical context it is more relevant to ask: What are the things that a domestic bourgeoisie, as opposed to foreign capital, does or may do in relation to capital accumulation? Although this question has not been directly addressed in the present case study, it is reasonable to assume that the settler textile and clothing capitalists in Zimbabwe have had a tendency to reinvest a higher proportion of their net earnings than foreign-owned companies, that profit repatriation was less significant, and that they identified their interests more with that of the national economy as a whole.

We can then ask: What difference does it make to this if such domestic capitalists are not of the same color, religion, language group, or whatever as the dominant elements in control of the state? The Zimbabwe case tends to support the argument that being "outsiders" has some positive advantages for capitalists at a certain stage of development:[87] (1) outsiders *must* make money, not being eligible for power by ascriptive routes, (2) they may do so efficiently, being free from the precapitalist obligations to others in society that detract from capitalist efficiency, and (3) their external links may confer technical-economic advantages on them as capitalists—a productive culture, for instance, plus know-how (technical, financial, organizational, etc.) and perhaps network links useful for obtaining credit, inputs, market outlets, etc. On the negative side, outsiders may be politically vulnerable because they are not able to build a popular base to exercise hegemomy. In the case of Zimbabwe's settler textile and clothing capitalists, this vulnerability was compensated for in the 1980s by their centrality to the politics of power being pursued by the Mugabe regime. Whether it would continue to be compensated for in the 1990s and beyond was another question.

Notes

1. I would like to acknowledge the generous assistance I have received in particular from Roger Leys. Several others deserve recognition, among them Knud Erik Svendsen, Colin Leys, Ruzvidzo Maya, Gorm Rye Olsen, Manfred Bienefeld, and all the participants in the April 1991 Queen's University workshop on African bourgeoisies.
2. The research for this study was carried out in Zimbabwe from June to September 1990 while I was a visiting research associate with the Zimbabwe Institute of Development Studies in Harare.
3. Bob Jessop, *The Capitalist State* (Oxford: Basil Blackwell, 1982).
4. Hirsch's ideas are summarized, with extensive references, in Jessop, ibid., pp. 97–99, 105.
5. Flatow and Huisken focus on the state in its mediating role between particular and general interests of capital. They argue that the general interest becomes a particular interest of the state apparatus, but as the state has no privileged knowledge of the general interest, it responds instead to the specific demands of particular interests. See Sybille von Flatow and Freerk Huisken, "Zum Problem der Ableitung des bürgerlichen Staates: Die Oberfläche der bürgerlichen Gesellschaft, der Staat, und die allgemeinen Rahmembedingungen der Produktion," in *Prokla* 7 (1973).
6. Nicos Poulantzas, *Political Power and Social Class* (Paris: Maspero, 1968). (Cited from the English translation [London: New Left Books, 1974].)
7. Jessop, *The Capitalist State*, pp. 159–160.
8. My usage of the term "governing group" is equivalent to the term "bureaucratic bourgeoisie" preferred by many. The latter has unfortunate class connotations, and I view the governing group as a social category, not a social class. See Gorm Rye Olsen, "Økonomi og Politik i den Arabiske Verden," Ph.D. diss., Akademisk Forlag, Aarhus, Denmark, 1988.
9. Sverrisson also points to the conflict of interest between the bureaucracy and indigenous black entrepreneurs. See Arni Sverrisson, *Entrepreneurship and Industrialization: A Case Study of Carpenters in Mutare, Zimbabwe*, Discussion Paper No. 186 (Lund, Sweden: Research Policy Institute, 1990).
10. John Saul, "Zimbabwe: The Next Round," *Monthly Review* 32, no. 4 (1980).
11. ZANU's electoral manifesto stated that "one of the existing practical realities is the capitalist system which cannot be transformed overnight. . . . Private enterprise will have to continue until circumstances are ripe for socialist change." See John Saul, *Socialist Ideology and the Struggle for Southern Africa* (Trenton: Africa World Press, 1990), p. 116.

12. Cited in Saul, *Socialist Ideology*, p. 126.

13. Government of Zimbabwe, "Economic Policy Statement: Macro-economic Adjustment and Trade Liberalization," July 1990, p. 10.

14. *Financial Times*, August 21, 1989.

15. Zimconsult, *Zimbabwe Country Study and Norwegian Aid Review* (Harare: Zimconsult, 1989).

16. Zimbabwe Information Service, press statement, 137/84/SN, March 6, 1984.

17. Stoneman and Cliffe made a similar observation. They pointed out that in May 1980, Shava's predecessor, Kumbirai Kangai, also used this very speech. See Colin Stoneman and Lionel Cliffe, *Zimbabwe: Politics, Economics and Society*, Marxist Regimes Series (London: Macmillan, 1989), p. 106.

18. Jeffrey Herbst, *State Politics in Zimbabwe* (Harare: University of Zimbabwe Publications, 1990), pp. 193–205.

19. *Financial Gazette*, April 4, 1986.

20. Herbst, *State Politics in Zimbabwe*, pp. 94–96.

21. Olsen, "Økonomi og Politik i den Arabiske Verden."

22. Arnold Sibanda, "The Political Situation," in Colin Stoneman, ed., *Zimbabwe's Prospects: Issues of Race, Class, State, and Capital in Southern Africa* (London: Heinemann, 1988).

23. Robin Palmer and Neil Parsons, *The Roots of Rural Poverty in Central and Southern Africa* (London: Heinemann, 1977), p. 225.

24. Ibid.

25. Industrial Development Advisory Committee (IDAC), minutes, in the National Archives of Zimbabwe.

26. IDAC, minutes (ninth meeting), National Archives of Zimbabwe.

27. IDAC, *Third Report*, National Archives of Zimbabwe.

28. IDAC, minutes (eighteenth meeting), National Archives of Zimbabwe.

29. Ian Phimister, *An Economic and Social History of Zimbabwe, 1890–1948* (London: Longman, 1988), p. 255.

30. C. H. Thompson and H. W. Woodruff, *Economic Development in Rhodesia and Nyasaland* (London: Dennis Dobson, 1953), pp. 90, 170.

31. Federal Government of Rhodesia and Nyasaland, Cotton Industry Working Party Report, June 19, 1956, National Archives of Zimbabwe.

32. Roger Riddell, "Industrialization in Sub-Saharan Africa, Phase 1: Zimbabwe," Overseas Development Institute, London (1987, mimeo), p. 91.

33. Duncan Clarke, *Foreign Companies and International Investment in Zimbabwe* (Salisbury: Mambo Press, 1980), pp. 15–33.

34. Herbst, *State Politics in Zimbabwe*, p. 112.

35. Stoneman and Cliffe, *Zimbabwe: Politics, Economics and Society*, p. 16.

36. D. J. Murray, *The Governmental System in Southern Rhodesia* (Oxford: Clarendon Press, 1970).

37. Daniel Ndlela, "The Manufacturing Sector in the East and Southern African Subregion, with Emphasis on the SADCC," in Samir Amin, D. Chitala, and I. Mandaza, eds., *SADCC: Prospects for Disengagement and Development in Southern Africa* (London: Zed Books, 1987), p. 143.

38. Colin Stoneman, "Industrialization and Self-Reliance in Zimbabwe," in Martin Fransman, ed., *Industry and Accumulation in Africa* (London: Heinemann, 1982), pp. 281–282.

39. Ibbo Mandaza, ed., *Zimbabwe: The Political Economy of Transition, 1980–1986* (Harare: Jongwe Press, 1987), p. 2.

40. Colin Stoneman, *Zimbabwe's Inheritance* (London: Macmillan, 1981), p. 5.

41. Census of Production 1986/87, unpublished data for 1987 provided by Central Statistical Office, Harare.

42. Ferro-alloys are deducted from manufactured exports because they are considered mineral products. See Roger Riddell, *ACP Export Diversification: The Case of Zimbabwe*, Working Paper No. 38 (London: Overseas Development Institute, 1990).

43. The analysis of investments is based on ECU values of net capital expenditure on plant and machinery. Source: *Quarterly Digest of Statistics* and unpublished CSO data, Harare.

44. Unless otherwise indicated, dollar signs denotes current Zimbabwe dollars.

45. *Herald* (Harare), October 28, 1982.

46. Zimbabwe Information Service, press statement, 805/82/DC, September 9, 1982.

47. See the *Sunday Mail* (Harare), September 12, 1982, and the *Chronicle* (Bulawayo), September 15, 1982.

48. *Herald*, November 7, 1983.

49. *Herald*, March 29, 1985.

50. *Chronicle*, May 31, 1985. In 1984, Zimbabwe obtained 19 percent of its imports from South Africa, its largest trading partner. Moreover, at the height of Zimbabwe's rhetorical warfare against South Africa, Mugabe in 1986 simultaneously threatened to impose sanctions and renewed Zimbabwe's then twenty-four-year-old trade accord with South Africa.

51. Zimbabwe Information Service, press statement, 490/83/JM, July 14, 1983.

52. *Financial Gazette* (Harare), June 10, 1988. Cotton lint constituted about half the cost of making yarn. The lint price was therefore crucial to the spinners. Cotton Marketing Board, annual reports, various years.

53. See Herbst, *State Politics in Zimbabwe*, for a good discussion of government policy toward labor.

54. *Herald*, September 23, 1981.

55. Each industrial branch has an industrial council; that of the clothing industry consists of five employers' representatives and five trade union representatives.

56. *Herald*, October 24, 1983. The Labor Relations Act (1984), in which government institutionalized its approach to strikes, gradually lost importance in the late 1980s as the liberalization of the economy was initiated. Collective bargaining was introduced in 1990.

57. *Sunday Mail*, October 27, 1982.

58. *Herald*, May 23, 1983.

59. *Herald*, October 24, 1983.

60. Zimbabwe Information Service, press statement, March 6, 1984.

61. *Sunday Mail*, December 30, 1984.

62. During an interview in 1989, a high-ranking official of the Industrial Development Corporation, a parastatal, informed the author that the IDC never buys into a well-operating company. The IDC takes shares in an existing company only when it is dying, or in trouble, and when it is deemed strategic to the economy.

63. *Herald*, October 20, 1983. Later, the company, to be known as Spinweave, became one of Zimbabwe's most successful textile companies.

64. Riddell, "Industrialization in Sub-Saharan Africa," p. 33.

65. Stoneman and Cliffe, *Zimbabwe: Politics, Economics and Society*, p. 156.

66. The information in this section is drawn from SEDCO's 1989 annual report, as well as SEDCO's quarterly statistical report to the management (fourth quarter 1989/90), provided in draft form to the author.

67. SEDCO annual report, 1989, p. 7.

68. The information on SEDCO is based on personal interviews in September 1990.

69. Herbst, *State Politics in Zimbabwe*, p. 120.

70. On December 27, 1990, the state-controlled newspaper, the *Herald*, again expressed the hope that black businessmen would soon graduate from small-time retail stores to serious big-time manufacturing business. It stressed, however, that "the one thing that the vast majority of black businessmen are guilty of is that business for them means flashy cars and big houses. They want their profits tomorrow, and seem to lack the concept of building businesses for posterity."

71. Deutsche marks are quoted here because the company purchased most of its materials in West Germany.

72. World Bank, "Zimbabwe: An Industrial Sector Memorandum," World Bank, Washington, D.C., 1987.

73. In 1987, total fabric imports (mostly synthetic) amounted to $44 million. Total fabric imports thus exceeded total fabric exports by $14 million (unpublished CSO statistics compiled by author).

74. Since 1983, all companies whose export product contains no more than 60 percent of imported inputs are eligible to receive foreign exchange for the required inputs through the Export Revolving Fund.

75. See *Africa South*, June 1991, p. 10.

76. At a trade liberalization conference in Harare on August 30–31, 1990, I had the opportunity to discuss "briefcase businessmen" with the 200 black and white business and government delegates. The phenomenon appeared also to be common in other branches of industry.

77. UNIDO, "Industrial Development Review Series: Zimbabwe" (Vienna: UNIDO, 1987).

78. Of the eleven branches of manufacturing industry, clothing and textiles rank one and two, respectively, in shares of local ownership.

79. *Herald*, April 5, 1984.

80. *Financial Gazette*, June 13, 1986.

81. Form issued by Ministry of Industry and Commerce, April 24, 1990.

82. *Financial Gazette*, June 15, 1990.

83. Unless otherwise stated, the information on David Whitehead is based on two personal interviews with the managing director in 1988 and 1990.

84. *Sunday Mail*, February 18, 1990.

85. Interview with the head of the DANIDA mission in Harare, August 1990.

86. *Financial Gazette*, January 29, 1988.

87. See Paul Kennedy, *African Capitalism* (Cambridge: Cambridge University Press, 1988).

7

African Industrialization in Comparative Perspective: The Question of Scale

Deborah Brautigam

Marxists and neoclassicalists alike picture the capitalist class in developing countries in similar terms. For Marx, "the industrially more developed country presents to the less developed country a picture of the latter's future."[1] Similarly, neoclassical convergence theory suggests that indigenous industries in particular sectors will, over time, come to resemble those in other countries, and that this is true whether one looks at Dar es Salaam or Detroit. They will increase in scale and size, use similar technologies, and be organized in similar ways. These structural characteristics of industry in turn ensure that those who finance, manage, and own these industries will, over time, come to resemble one another as members of a class with common interests.

The scale of industrial development has a political side. The debate over the formation of the indigenous bourgeoisie in Africa has usually centered on its dependence on or independence from foreign capital, and more recently over its relationship with the state: patrimonial, prebendal, or "nurturing." Yet internal characteristics such as enterprise size and scale are also important characteristics of indigenous capitalist development. When the state stifles smaller-scale indigenous industry by offering subsidies only to foreign investors, to firms of a certain (large) size, or to state-owned enterprises, it shapes the formation of the business class and provides incentives for its political activity. A small class of large-scale producers is likely to spend considerable energy trying to achieve or preserve its particularistic access to special state resources or protection, pressuring the state to maintain or erect barriers to entry and exit, establish or protect monopoly rents, or create structural rigidities. In contrast, a large class of small-scale producers may be less likely (or able) to organize or to exercise "lobbying and cartelistic power" for redistribution on behalf of their special interests.[2]

Thus, industrial scale and enterprise size can affect the political as well as the economic role of an indigenous bourgeoisie. Further, when

variables of scale and size figure into government decisions on the allocation of resources such as credit, information, or input subsidies, or into
taxation and resource extraction policies, the shape of this class and its future economic—and political—strength can change. Capital accumulation,
technological learning, and other characteristics of capitalist development
are in theory bound up with questions of scale and size.

The question of the scale of industry is particularly relevant in Africa
in the 1990s. As Alexander Gerschenkron noticed when he examined late
industrializers in Europe, states in countries lacking a sizable indigenous
capitalist class often try to accelerate the development of large-scale modern industry by investing directly in large-scale factories and state-owned
enterprises, or by providing support to encourage this type of large-scale
production in enclaves of modern industry.[3] Africa has been no exception
to this tendency.

At present, accelerated industrialization on the basis of large-scale,
enclave, or state-owned enterprises seems to have failed in Africa.[4] Efforts
to privatize much of this investment have found troublingly few takers.[5] At
this point, few members of the indigenous bourgeoisie have the skills or
the capital to manage or finance many of these auction block assets. Recently, observers both in and outside the World Bank and other international agencies have argued that African countries need at this point to
back away from previous industrial strategies and return for a time to commodity and natural resource exports. On the other hand, the radical restructuring over the past decade has offered possibilities for a new beginning for industry, with competitive, dynamic, small-scale firms owned and
managed by Africans.[6] Given the small size of many African markets and
the extremely low capacity utilization rates of factories built to capture
economies of scale, small-scale firms may appear more appropriate. Can
these small-scale firms serve as a viable engine of industrial growth and,
perhaps, as an alternative path to industrialization?

This chapter examines the potential for the emergence of a dynamic
African bourgeoisie based on relatively small-scale industrial enterprises.[7] The chapter has several aims. First, it attempts to add a historical
dimension to the question of the role of small firms in industrial development. Second, it adds a comparative dimension by examining three
cases where a substantial amount of industrial activity takes place via
small-scale firms: Japan, Taiwan, and north-central Italy. Although different from each other and from Africa, these three cases are linked by a
common thread: the role of the state was instrumental in providing the
foundation upon which small firms became an engine of broad-based
growth. Finally, the chapter introduces a case from Nigeria to compare
and contrast small firm capitalism there with that present in the other
three countries.

Small in Historical Perspective

Historically, most industrialized countries have passed through stages when their bourgeois class was composed predominantly of small-scale enterprises. Evidence from both cross-country and time series data suggests that in developing countries, small enterprises perform at the very least an important transitional role as national income increases and production shifts from agriculture into manufacturing.[8] However, in most views, this role is temporary and confined to the middle phases of industrialization; large firms will ultimately prevail.[9] In part, the rise of large firms is said to be supported by changes in consumer preferences. As incomes in an economy rise, consumer preference for the quality of goods produced by small firms using traditional technologies drops, and preference for higher-quality goods rises. Economies of scale lower costs for large producers, strengthening them in competition with small producers. Efforts by later industrializing countries have added to these scale advantages the special state assistance enjoyed by large firms: tariff protection, subsidized credit, investment incentives, and state-financed access roads, electrical connections, and water supply. Ian Little, in an extensive comparative study on small manufacturing enterprises, pronounced their fate thus: "[They] are destined to near extinction unless they become a protected species."[10]

Others stress the continuing importance of a large sector of small firms in modernizing economies. Small-scale, family-based production may ease the changes associated with large-scale industrialization, allowing for the accumulation of surpluses in a socially less painful manner. Initial investment costs are lower, enabling broad participation and allowing capital to be accumulated and reinvested, avoiding the necessity of incurring substantial debts. Likewise, management and technical skills may be honed over time, strengthening local capacity to adopt, maintain, and ultimately reshape foreign technology. Politically, avoiding the concentration of industry in the hands of a small number of large firms reduces the scope for concentration of political power. Finally, a new group of analysts argue that small firms have the potential to produce more flexibly, to specialize in short runs for specialized markets, and to allow more worker participation in "crafting" industrial products.[11]

In an unregulated, market-based economy, scale and enterprise size would be a function of the stage of industrialization and the products produced, the skill of available managers, the amount of finance available for investment, the degree of competition, and other factors that shape the decisions of entrepreneurs. When small industries are dominant at a later stage of industrialization, it is generally in response to a favorable policy or regulatory environment, perhaps one in which protection for small enterprises inadvertently creates a "growth trap" by making it unattractive for small enterprises to grow out of their protected size. In other cases, small indigenous businesses may represent a frustrated response by the majority of domestic capitalists to incentives and regulations that protect a small number of large domestic and foreign enterprises and force most indigenous firms to stay small. Frequently, countries with high degrees of corruption and unstable policy environments stimulate a preference for diversification of business concerns. Rather than reinvesting and growing with one enterprise, entrepreneurs reinvest profits in a number of businesses, spreading risk. Encouragement of contractual forms such as subcontracting can also encourage the entry of small industries into certain sectors.

During the 1980s, when economic crisis flooded the urban informal sector with new entrants and their predominantly survival-oriented activities, renewed attention to the role of small industries came from nontraditional places: Europe and Northeast Asia. Japan had long been regarded as an exception, with an abundance of small firms thought by many analysts to be low-productivity victims of dualistic labor markets, kept in existence by subcontract linkages because they enabled the larger firms to shed labor when necessary while avoiding the necessity to break employment guarantees to their own employees. Later, evidence from Japan as to the actual efficiency of small firms joined cases from West Germany, Hong Kong, north-central Italy, and Taiwan to suggest that perhaps alternatives to large-scale convergence existed. In the most optimistic scenarios, areas with small but dynamic enterprises were labeled "informal economies of growth," characterized by small but highly flexible independent firms that produced intermediate inputs for a number of clients, had a marked "export orientation," and demonstrated high levels of innovation and an ability to adapt imported technology.[12] In the next section, we look more closely at these distinctive cases. Do they challenge the model of linear progression and convergence on a single, large-scale industrial model? Do they provide lessons for Africa in developing strategies of industrialization? And what do they imply about the political economy of small-scale industries?

Cases of Small-Scale Capitalism: Japan, Taiwan, Italy

These case studies focus on four key factors in examining the experience of small, dynamic enterprise development in three countries. First, they focus on the origins of small-scale entrepreneurs and of their original capital. Second, they look at the articulation (when it occurs) of small enterprises with other enterprises: small firms with large firms, small firms with foreign firms, and small firms with other small firms. Third, they consider the importance of networks, of ethnic and family ties, and of community in creating an "enabling environment" in which a bourgeoisie of small, dynamic firms can flourish. Finally, they highlight the role of government. In particular, they ask: Do these small, dynamic firms thrive only through special protection, as Little argued?

Japan

Japan, according to David Friedman, is a "misunderstood miracle," and much of the misunderstanding concerns the role of small-scale producers in the Japanese economy. Countering the stereotype of small firms as a dying species, Friedman argues that in Japan there has been a "dramatic expansion of smaller producers throughout the nation's economy."[13] Japan provides potent evidence that convergence theory—the idea that industrialization moves firms, industries, and economies toward similar structures over time—may not be universally valid. Small firms not only survived in Japan's rapid modernization and growth, Friedman argues, they actually thrived: "The widespread perception of Japan's smaller firms as technically inferior, using cheap labor, and subject to cyclical shocks to the benefit of large factories—the so-called dual structure argument—is substantially mistaken."[14]

Clearly dynamic, many of these Japanese enterprises are also *very* small. In his case study of Sakaki township in rural Japan, Friedman describes a highly industrialized village, where the bulk of firms have one to three employees (42 percent) or four to nine employees (36 percent): "The town's industrial activity is concealed in small, often shabby, corrugated metal structures that look like storage sheds or garages. Inside these imposing buildings, however, are . . . high tech factories of the first order."[15] Microenterprises with one to nine employees account for some 75 percent of all manufacturing firms in Japan.[16]

Small industries in Japan operate predominantly through their linkages with other enterprises, producing not the finished output of traditional crafts, which were largely sold directly to the final consumer, but intermediate goods, which other enterprises use to assemble their own products. Subcontractors make up some 65 percent of small and medium-sized enterprises in manufacturing.[17] Entrepreneurs frequently work for another firm for five to ten years before leaving to start their own businesses. As the owner of a successful small business, an entrepreneur has the chance to make much more money than is possible in employment with large firms, even given the high rate of failure.[18]

Like Europe, Japan entered its industrial period with a combination of free labor and a traditional apprenticeship (*deshi*) system. Apprentices received low wages but stayed the course because they expected to gain skills and then set up their own enterprises. During the Meiji period in the last quarter of the nineteenth century, the government pushed the establishment of large enterprises, which were eventually privatized. Over the course of industrialization, large *zaibatsu* received attention; small enterprises were left to fend for themselves. The bulk of financing arrangements for small firms in the 1920s resembled African *susus* and *tontines*. In Japan, these revolving loan societies (*mujin* companies) required members to contribute to a central fund; loans were allocated by turn or by lot.[19]

From the Meiji period until the mid-1930s, large and small firms were primarily linked indirectly through market ties. Large firms sold raw and processed materials to small firms, which transformed the products into final goods for local or export sales. Small firms depended on informal sources of credit, primarily from the *tonya*, or coordinating contractors. World War II influenced regional industrial development through the military-directed decentralization of military factories to rural areas. By the postwar era, the Liberal Democratic Party, which relied for political support on both small farmers and small firms, had created an institutional framework to support small producers. Small-firm banks were considerably strengthened, and the state established nearly 180 subsidized research centers. As Michael Piore and Charles Sabel describe it, "These research centers collaborated with nearby universities and national technical institutes to develop new products and processes and to facilitate their diffusion among small firms. One of these centers might, for example, demonstrate the use of a new machine and plan its introduction into a particular firm; or it might sponsor research on promising new industrial techniques."[20]

The institutional shift that injected the most energy into small-firm vitality, however, was the rise of subcontracting. Even before the Second World War, small firms had developed a network of flexible contract arrangements with large firms and with each other. The craft base of traditional Japanese production adapted well to many of the new organizational forms brought in from the industrialized West.[21] Aided by the pressures of a large domestic market, Japanese firms were highly competitive, forcing small and medium-sized firms into strategies of rapid and responsive innovation. Many failed, but low barriers to entry and exit allowed continual recycling of investment capital. Larger companies subcontracted for many production inputs, although the percentage varied by industry. Smaller firms relied heavily on contracts. In 1982, 80 percent of firms with four to forty-nine employees relied on subcontracting for 60 percent or more of their sales.[22] The high rate of subcontracting did not put the firms in a position of dependency, however: even the smallest family firms normally produced for an average of three separate clients. Small firms, Friedman concludes, were riskier than the large firms. They had high rates of entry and of exit, but those that survived actually surpassed larger firms' profit ratios, and this profitability was largely a function of their flexibility and ability to innovate.

In Africa, the correlation between being small, operating outside of legal boundaries, and using traditional craft techniques is high, but not complete. In Japan, it is low. In addition, the contemporary Japanese experience sheds little light on the question of upgrading and graduation of traditional "microenterprises," yet it does say something about the cultural contexts supportive of a substantial sector of small-sized industries and about the evolution of institutions that benefited small firms. For example, while the small firms that exist today are divorced from past apprenticeship systems, they seem to have evolved a new variant on an old model. In Sakaki, Friedman found that 80 percent of the small local firms were begun by entrepreneurs who had received their training in other local enterprises, both small and large. In another, Japanwide, study, Tadao discovered that the proprietors of nearly 70 percent of all small and medium-sized firms were former blue-collar employees of small firms.[23]

Japan seems to provide strong evidence for the notion that small firms there have been a "seedbed" of entrepreneurial development, but with an important proviso. In high-technology industries, gaining technical skills is critically important. These entrepreneurs did not come simply from small firms; they came from small, specialized industrial enterprises that trained them in the specific skills they would need to start their own firms and to win production contracts. Regionalism is another motif running through the Japanese story. The rapid evolution of Sakaki township is but one example of the construction of a complementary cluster of businesses with family ties—competing but also cooperating, and displaying high mobility, and high flexibility. Social networks, family, and personal contacts are also critical cultural factors facilitating trust and lowering the cost of transactions. Finally, the role of the state has been critical in establishing the conditions under which small enterprises could thrive in Japan. In Sakaki, although some firms received financing from the firms that purchased their intermediate goods, many relied on financing by the state's small-firm capital assistance arm; smaller firms also had disproportionately more state assistance in obtaining initial investment capital, and Japan provides some twenty times as much finance to small business as does the United States.[24] In addition, Japanese culture and values shaped institutional differences in semiformal finance mechanisms. While countries like the United States and Britain were developing local savings and loans and building societies to finance housing, the Japanese set up small finance outlets such as the Small Business Finance Corporation, established in 1953 to provide mortgage-like financing for small-scale, independent factories. Finally, government institutions such as the Japan Small Business Corporation, the Subsidy System for Managerial Strengthening of Small and Medium Enterprises, and government-owned equipment leasing foundations offer advice, training, and assistance to small and medium-sized enterprises in

Japan, a reflection in part of the political power enjoyed by small enterprises as a group.

Japan's successful evolution of small enterprises depended on state intervention, and microenterprises in Japan are far from being struggling establishments on the edge of extinction. Little argued that countries that protect small enterprise per se are "trying to swim against the tide of history."[25] How atypical is Japan's experience? While the sectoral stages of growth were followed in Japan, the size shift was not; indeed, employment in small-scale manufacturing has grown disproportionately. Evidence from South Korea, sometimes called the "new Japan," indicates a shift there in the relative size of the small and medium-sized industry sector. Scale increased from the 1960s to the mid-1970s, whereupon a burst of activity from new, technology-oriented small and medium-sized industries in the 1980s reversed the size trend in Korea.[26] The Japanese evidence and new information from South Korea indicate that small may thrive, but it may be a very different kind of small than the enterprises that currently make up Africa's informal sector.

Taiwan

While Japan has been an industrialized nation since the early twentieth century, Taiwan's industrialization sprang from a much more recently established base. In 1952, agricultural and processed agricultural products made up 92 percent of the island's exports. Twenty years later, industrial products made up 84 percent of exports, and national income (among the most evenly distributed in the world) had risen faster than in almost any other industrializing nation.[27] Observers attribute Taiwan's success story to many variables: heavy doses of U.S. aid; a base of industry left behind by the Japanese; an extensive land reform; strong state institutions; Confucian values; and the threat of communist China across the Taiwan Strait. Some attribute its success as well to the country's enormous number of small firms.

More than any other industrialized country, Taiwan may represent a case of industrialization via large numbers of small firms. The evolution of this process began rather traditionally. Samuel Ho's study of small enterprises in Taiwan charts what appear to be fairly usual changes, with a high number of traditional small firms declining over time. In 1930, 75 percent of manufacturing employment was located in firms with one to nine employees; over time, the bottom third of this sector (one to three employees) became concentrated in tailoring and repair enterprises. By 1980, Ho comments, these very small enterprises were "insignificant," but small and medium-sized enterprises continued to be established, and in many cases, to grow. Figures from 1983 indicated that 85 percent of all Taiwanese factories had from one to forty-nine workers (down from 94 percent in 1966), and that the fixed assets of 89 percent were below US$250,000.[28] Samuel Ho traces this slightly upward size shift to the changing composition of Taiwan's industrial base, from agroindustries with few important economies of scale to industries such as electronics, synthetic fibers, and petrochemicals, which do have important scale economies and do not have easily separable components that might lend themselves to subcontracting.[29]

Like the small factory owners in Japan, Taiwanese entrepreneurs normally gained skills working in modern sector manufacturing and then established their own small firms, perhaps responding to the values reflected in the well-worn Taiwanese saying: "It is better to be the head of a chicken than the tail of an ox." The legal obstacles to "formalization" in Taiwan are not complex, yet even so, many enterprises producing nontraded goods choose to remain unregistered; one example located half of the country's furniture producers in the unregistered "informal sector."[30] Furthermore, regulations such as the Factory Law, which requires firms of a certain level of capitalization and employee size to offer vacation, insurance, and other benefits, exempt most small manufacturing firms.

Unlike the Japanese example, Taiwan does not appear to be a case of strong state support for small firms. Formal credit for small enterprises appears to have been as difficult in Taiwan as in many other areas of the developing world; small enterprises traditionally relied on rotating credit societies, *minqing*, the Taiwanese version of African *susus*. More recently, however, a highly developed informal market has attracted funds from the formal banking system for on-lending to small enterprises at higher interest rates. Much of this latter lending occurs between larger firms and the small firms they subcontract to and know well, reducing transaction costs banks would face in lending to the same firms.

Whether the small enterprise sector in Taiwan will evolve further along the lines of "flexible specialization" as is true in Japan, or whether it will decline in importance, is not yet clear. While Donald DeGlopper argued in 1979 that "the large number of small manufacturing enterprises we see now are the consequence of economic growth and prosperity, not of the lingering hand of tradition,"[31] Alice Amsden noted in the same volume that "the existence of a large number of very small firms which do not appear to be upgrading their technology is the Achilles' heel of industrialization in Taiwan. The problem takes the form of the small firm's failure to merge or grow amid the scarcities created by fast industrialization economy-wide." Puzzling over the fact that these firms not only failed to merge or to grow, but also appeared stubbornly resistant to "disappear[ing] quickly and obligingly," Amsden nonetheless predicted that "the future of this class of petty producers is pointed in the direction of paid employment."[32]

Changes in the structure of small enterprise development in Taiwan happened sometimes with great rapidity and against the grain of conventional wisdom. Factory employment in rural Taiwan (outside the five main cities), for example, rose over the five years 1966 to 1971 from 30 percent to 48 percent of total factory employment, assisted by an excellent and well-distributed rural infrastructure.[33] And although Ho's 1980 study argued that subcontracting and cooperative arrangements with large firms appeared to be less important in explaining the survival of small factories in Taiwan than in Japan, Tyler Biggs and Brian Levy in 1988 noted a "proliferation" of subcontracting between independent producers of intermediate goods and final assemblers, suggesting rapid change in this area as well.[34] Biggs and Levy explain successful small firm development as partly a function of clustering, of the "increased social and physical proximity among larger factories and subcontractors and among traders and sellers," which reduced the costs of search, negotiation, and monitoring of contracts.[35]

As in Japan, government policy made it possible for small firms to enter new markets with relative ease. While the government did not provide much in the way of credit for small firms in Taiwan, it facilitated the curbside markets in which they obtained finance through mechanisms such as penalties for nonobservance of postdated checks, a common financing device. In addition, the government encouraged the entry of specific multinational corporations with incentives targeted selectively at firms, not for the employment possibilities they offered, but for the extent of their potential backward linkages: i.e., the percentage of input components supplied by local contractors. Government encouragement of demand for local products facilitated increases in technological capacity among small firms, many of whom quickly developed specialized market niches. But if, as Biggs and Levy argue, the key to the success of niche specialization lies partly in the simultaneous development of highly sophisticated traders who could reduce market transaction costs and target specific markets quickly, then one might expect that some areas in Africa, with preexisting networks of experienced and entrepreneurial traders, may have special advantages if the next round of industrialization there experiments with a flexible specialization model.

Japan and Taiwan are, perhaps, sui generis. Both are Asian cultures, both had extensive land reforms, and both have histories of support for smallholder agricultural production, an important base for modernizing economies that has been neglected in Africa. The last case, however, draws on a European experience, in a less developed region of a country that remained somewhat backward compared with the first industrializers. Although, again, historically and institutionally quite different from Africa, the Italian case at least demonstrates that the success of small enterprises in modern industrial development can be realized outside the Asian environment.

Italy

> The third Italy . . . occupies the middle ground of the central-northeastern regions and is noted for its booming economy of specialist workshops and mini factories, most of which has mushroomed since the end of the war. Here traditionally rural regions—typically, the Veneto, Emilia Romagna, Tuscany and the Marche—have been transformed into centres of sophisticated cottage industry whose job creation, industrial exports, income and value added have increased at a rate well above the national average.[36]

Italy provides the third example of a thriving small business environment. Firms with fewer than 100 employees dominate Italian industry; a 1980 study estimated that nearly 50 percent of industrial workers were employed by plants of fewer than twenty employees.[37] These small artisanal firms, dubbed "microcapitalists" by Linda Weiss, produce not simply the Benneton garments for which they have received attention, but also textiles, motorcycles, farm machinery, ceramic building materials, shoes, and even minimill steel.

The "third Italy" phenomenon has its origins in the Depression era garment industry. Industrial retrenchment led to the shedding of some operations by larger industries, with the subsequent sale or lease of capital equipment to workers. But it was not until the 1950s and 1960s that the industrial response to union action led to another wave of industrial decentralization, with skilled workers establishing small industrial firms under contracts with their former employers. The rapid growth that resulted surprised most observers: in 1963, in the Modena region, almost 5,000 artisanal enterprises existed, while in 1975, the region boasted nearly 21,500.[38] The Emilio-Romagna area dropped from 52 percent agricultural employment in 1952 to 20 percent in 1971. In both instances, the workforce moved overwhelmingly into small, local, industrial, and related service enterprises.[39]

At the beginning, not much differentiated these small firms from sweatshops. As Piore and Sabel describe it, skilled workers put their families and relatives to work in these small shops, ignoring labor regulations, tax payments, safety standards, and social security requirements. Yet this "underground economy" emerged into the light within a decade, with substantially higher productivity, higher wages, and higher regional incomes per capita than the national average.[40] The development and innovative capacity of these small firms were heightened by the formation of autonomous federations that provided information on technology, markets, and inputs, so as to link subcontractors with assemblers and to coordinate production.

During the decade of the 1950s, the Italian government shaped the conditions under which small enterprises could thrive. Several specific acts provided a nurturing environment, including the 1947 establishment of Artigiancassa to support artisans and its upgrading to include a well-funded low-interest loan and grant program in 1952; Law 860 of 1956, which offered special privileges to registered artisan firms; the 1957 act, which gave ten-year tax exemptions for newly established artisan firms; the decision of the state to pay social insurance premiums for apprentices; and government-sponsored training for the production of garments and building materials, and general engineering.[41]

Clearly, Italian firms receive substantial financial incentives to stay small. Weiss found that, in contrast to the common portrait of interest subsidies for large firms, in Italy small industry received 80 percent of subsidized loans, with the region now known as the "third Italy" receiving half of them.[42] The Italian government is also noted for a "high tolerance" for nonregistered activity.[43] Some might characterize this combination of factors as a "growth trap" where the benefits of expansion are outweighed by its opportunity costs; however, it is difficult to see how these regions of Italy would have developed in the absence of these incentives.

Again, the relevance to Africa may seem problematic. The third Italy developed out of an economy that was already partially industrialized, where technical institutes had been founded late in the nineteenth century and factories had existed since the 1920s. Yet the Italian experience does have relevance for those concerned with the shape and prospects of African capitalism. As in Japan and Taiwan, the development of small industries was based on artisanal traditions underpinning a culture supportive of small, family-run firms. Two other factors are relevant: ties of commerce and trade had long linked these Italian provinces with foreign countries; and much of the government support these enterprises received came from regional and municipal, not federal, levels.[44]

It is important to emphasize that the boom in small enterprises did not represent an upgrading or graduation of traditional artisans per se; most of the original microentrepreneurs were trained in the factories established before 1950, leaving to set up their own firms—at first out of a lack of alternatives, later out of a growing culture of independent entrepreneurship. The Italian government intervened actively in support of small enterprises in particular industries: light engineering and building materials received disproportionate amounts of support. Over the first twenty years of the small firm support policy, low- to medium-technology "modern" industries received two-thirds of loans and grants and expanded employment from 25 to 42 percent of the workforce; "traditional" industries, with less than a third of funding assistance, dropped from 67 to 40 percent.[45] The Italian government's view of small industry was clearly strategic, not as a mechanism to preserve jobs in the traditional cottage sector, but as a plan to promote a viable alternative to industrial concentration.

Lessons from the Italian case show that the advantages of small-scale industry—innovativeness, flexibility, avoidance of industrial concentration—

are not necessarily linked to supporting the traditional artisanal structure. It shows as well that family organization of production can go hand in hand with innovation, productivity, and efficiency. The third Italy's microcapitalists, however, received their training in other modern industries and in formal technical schools, suggesting that Africa's weak supply of both may be a critical bottleneck in engendering any similar dynamic response.

Lessons of the Japanese, Taiwanese, and Italian Experience

What are the lessons of these three cases? Small firms in countries with dynamic small-scale production sectors seem not to fit the image of primarily independent, traditional artisans and cottage industries with upgraded skills, but rather reflect strong links to modern industry. Many small entrepreneurs began as workers in modern small, medium, and large enterprises, gaining skills and expertise before leaving to start their own firms. Contacts with modern firms continued to be important in these cases —subcontracting to larger firms or other small firms, in particular, but also in industry associations and cooperative ventures with similar firms.

Similarities existed in other key areas. Early in the course of small-scale industrial development, entrepreneurs in two of these countries (Japan and Taiwan) relied on small, revolving credit and mutual loan societies for their capital; later, the government often stepped in with special, targeted programs (Japan and Italy). The microcapitalism of these cases is based on strong artisan and craft cultures, where family serves as a help rather than a hindrance in the business and where communities provide opportunities for cooperation in industry clusters and networks of producers at similar levels. Finally, in all cases, but primarily in Italy and Japan, governments have played crucial roles. But this has not always been the national government; sometimes regional and local governments have created the necessary "enabling environment."

At first glance, many factors distinguish these stories from Africa's current realities. In Japan, by 1920 almost 100 percent of the population was literate.[46] Taiwan and Italy have had high literacy rates as well, bearing out one statement that "high educational achievement turns out not to be merely characteristic of Japan but typical of all rapidly-growing countries."[47] Across the African continent, basic skill and education levels are extremely low, not to mention more advanced skills in science, engineering, and other technical areas. Some exceptions exist: Mauritius, with almost 100 percent literacy, for example. Yet the contrast should not be with Japan, Taiwan, and Italy today, but with their situation as they embarked on the industrial path. Taiwan, for example, had only a 45 percent adult literacy rate in the early 1950s, comparable to that of many of sub-Saharan Africa's more developed regions: for example, Côte d'Ivoire (43 percent in 1989) or Nigeria (42 percent in 1989).[48] It is thus possible to speculate that the combination of an expanded scientific and technical knowledge base, combined with newly rational-legal political institutions, may emerge to shape the evolution of small, modern capitalists in some of these areas. What would be necessary for this to occur?

Africa: Possibilities for Microcapitalism

Looking at the long road ahead for industry in Africa, it might be argued that the base for industrialization hardly exists in most African countries, that the moment is not at hand for a substantial role for an industrial bourgeoisie, and that development strategies should return instead to commodity production, mining, and the multitude of microenterprises that form the low-productivity survival activities of the "informal sector." These cases, however, allow for a more positive view of the possibilities for a leading role played by an indigenous class of small-scale, but modern, industrialists.

Aside from several excellent in-depth case studies[49] and a host of somewhat dated surveys, we know very little about the structure of the small enterprise sector in Africa, the market and institutional environments they operate in, and the factors that determine the scale of industrial enterprises. However, recent African case studies suggest that in some countries, indigenous capitalism is, in fact, responding to the new environment established by structural adjustment programs. In Ghana, where a structural adjustment program has perhaps come furthest in providing a positive incentive environment for investment and production, a recent study found that "contrary to some observers' perceptions, investment *is* taking place, at least among SSEs (small scale enterprises, with 10–49 workers)."[50] Although many of the owners of the 672 small firms surveyed complained about the increased prices, working capital shortages, and depressed demand associated with the economic crisis and the subsequent reform program, a number of entrepreneurs had established small enterprises in the post-1984 period. The researchers noted strong signs of a shift toward capitalist relations of production, especially in the shift of labor from family to paid workers, and of a dramatic "leap forward" in the technological sophistication of small firms compared with studies one of the researchers had undertaken in the mid-1970s.[51]

Surveys such as this Ghanaian study can provide only glimpses into the changes currently under way in African socioeconomies. Much more fieldwork is needed, translated into African case studies that can capture more of the details of the rapid transitions "from peasant to artisan," and from trader to industrialist. However, it makes a critical difference which small businesses become the subject of these case studies. Many small enterprises in Africa *are* members of a "dying species" struggling to survive amidst economic crisis and overwhelming competition. Others may in fact have the potential to form the nucleus of a sustainable indigenous capitalism, composed at least for the foreseeable future of dynamic and modern small-scale firms. The Nigerian cases of Ile Ifé and Nnewi provide two contrasting examples of small-scale industrial development.

Small-scale Capitalism in Nigeria

Sara Berry's study of motor mechanics in Ile Ifé examines the transition to capitalism as it is happening in many places in Africa, from a family-based mode of agricultural production linked to a precapitalist artisan system (in the sense of an absence of a general system of production based on freely emerged wage labor). Berry's study showed, much as one by DeGlopper did for furniture artisans in 1968 Taiwan, that the apprenticeship system was under strain, with competition from wage labor sapping the incentive to undergo a long period of poorly remunerated training. Berry argues that local artisans'

> strategies for gaining access to markets and resources seem to come into conflict with their ability to manage the production process, especially as their firms prosper and expand. . . . The potential for small firms to contribute to aggregate growth through reinvestment of their own profits is determined, not only by their efficiency in using available resources, but also by the conditions under which they obtain them.[52]

Both the Ile Ifé mechanics and the Taiwanese artisans preferred diversification into related activities, sometimes into real estate, and often investment in their children's education, to continuing to reinvest profits into their furniture or motor repair businesses. Furniture makers continue to craft wooden furniture in Taiwan, but the economic growth that has brought prosperity does not rest on such graduated artisans. It rests instead on their children, who were educated in the sciences and technology and are now working overtime to adapt innovations to Taiwan's island conditions.

The problems described by DeGlopper in a medium-sized town in Taiwan, and the analysis advanced by Berry for a medium-sized town in Nigeria, point to fundamentally the same strategies and constraints. Berry argues that "the conditions for doing business in western Nigeria favor strategies of investment and productive organization which restrict increased productivity. Hence the very process of building up a firm fosters constraints on business expansion and helps to perpetuate social relations that often divide people in similar economic circumstances. . . . Accumulation and differentiation are so closely linked to access to the state."[53] DeGlopper's 1968 research in LuGang described a similar phenomenon for Taiwan's furniture artisans, noting their tendency to diversify into real estate and land, to stay small, and to obtain resources from and retain obligations to the extended family. His artisans, who relied on manual labor and traditional hand tools, were perched on the edge of a mechanical revolution. They watched with interest, and not a little trepidation, the one shop that had embarked on a division of labor based on electric power tools, with hired labor paid by the day rather than, in the traditional craft mode, by the piece. DeGlopper found that artisans and furniture entrepreneurs were investing in education for their sons, with the aim of government or corporate employment. Capital accumulation strategies among this group of fairly informal producers thus failed to increase productivity or expand their enterprises.[54] The apprenticeship system was crumbling, with young men opting for modern sector jobs with immediate wages; the remaining apprentices came from rural farm families, not from the town.

DeGlopper and Berry both concentrated on groups in the painful throes of the passage from one system to the next—and quite possibly, to paraphrase Barrington Moore's vivid expression, on a "class over whom the wave of history is about to roll." Yet while they observed the struggle of these small-scale artisan-industrialists, the stage was being set for the rapid emergence of other clusters of small entrepreneurs—often with a commercial and not an artisanal background—as "microcapitalists." Looking at the LuGang artisans with their hand tools and apprentices, who would have guessed that on the same island, modern small-scale industry was gearing up for a sustained burst of output that would help propel average per capita income from US$170 in 1962, when Taiwan ranked with Zaire and the Congo, to over US$10,000 in 1991?[55] Similarly, Berry's penetrating analysis, which deepens our understanding of western Nigeria's movement "from peasant to artisan," gives no indication that in another part of Nigeria—Nnewi township—a lineage-based, spare parts trade and distribution system was about to transform itself into a thriving cluster of small modern factories, established, interestingly enough, under contracted management and technical advice from Taiwanese technicians.

The Case of Nnewi

The town of Nnewi in Anambra state in eastern Nigeria has long been the home of a widely spread network of Igbo transport magnates, who have largely controlled the transport and spare parts trade in Nigeria. Stella Silverstein describes how at the turn of the century Nnewi entrepreneurs entered the palm oil market, collecting and transporting palm oil and later investing in vehicles for general transport.[56] The national network of spare parts distribution and sales was established along lineage lines, with relatives clustered at the center of each web of distribution and nonrelatives at the borders. After the civil war, many Igbo entrepreneurs returned to Imo and Anambra states, reestablishing their transport and imported spare parts businesses. Beginning in 1979, when the government instituted import licenses, making it difficult for those without political connections to gain access to foreign exchange, many traders began to think about going into production themselves.

During the decade of the 1980s, Nnewi township developed a significant cluster of dynamic small and medium-sized industrial firms producing consumer products as well as intermediate inputs for other industries. The range is broad: from automobile spare parts to mineral processing equipment and industrial molds.[57] Because the factories described here fit the portrait of the "missing middle" of dynamic, small- and medium-scale modern industries thought to be underrepresented in Africa,[58] understanding the origin and prospects for this cluster of factories is of particular importance.

Tom Forrest describes a pattern of entry into production for some of these local manufacturers:

> After elementary education and a period of apprenticeship usually lasting four or five years with an established motor parts trader, the dealer creates his own company buying and selling locally. Later there is a shift to direct importation and the establishment of overseas contacts usually in the Far East (Japan, Korea, Taiwan, Singapore, Hong Kong). A manufacturing venture is then started after visits to the Far East. Existing market channels can be used to promote the new product. This pattern can be highly compressed. In one case, there was only six years between the start of training in the motor parts trade and the start up of manufacture at the age of 27.[59]

Many of these enterprises started quite small. A survey conducted in late 1991 found that of twenty-two factories, 43 percent had twenty workers or fewer at start-up.[60] Within a few years, almost half of these small firms had increased the scale of employment above twenty workers. Unlike most "informal enterprises," these factories almost always began formally, registering their businesses sometimes several years before beginning production. In addition, they generally used imported machinery (sometimes second-hand) one step down the product cycle, at the technical level now being outgrown in the East Asian NICs.

The factories in this part of Nigeria were all established by men, generally of similar backgrounds, who had followed a fairly common pattern. More than half (55 percent) of the entrepreneurs were sons of farmers; only five had fathers who had been traders—even petty traders. Yet these sons of farmers themselves became traders, and it is their origins in trade that sets this group of entrepreneurs off from those who have entered industry with capital gained through access to political resources, through capital accumulated in agriculture, or with capital amassed during a civil service career. Of the twenty-two manufacturers interviewed, only three do not currently maintain an active trading business.

Most of these entrepreneurs would like to rely on formal sector financing. Although only 27 percent of entrepreneurs received loans to start their factories, an additional 23 percent received loans from Nigerian banks after factory start-up. Half have so far relied entirely on their own (or family) savings and reinvested earnings, although close to half of this number, 18 percent of total entrepreneurs, have loan applications pending. In other words, almost three-quarters of these industrialists either have received or have applied for bank loans.

Unlike the small-scale producers of Japan, Italy, and Taiwan, these industries are not characterized by extensive subcontracting, although the firms are generally quite interested in the potential that exists to produce inputs for larger Nigerian companies. One company does produce small aluminum parts for a large, state-owned automobile assembly plant; another produces industrial molds under contract, but such relations are currently the exception rather than the rule.

Many of the entrepreneurs in this study have relatives involved in business. The impact of these family "networks" is mixed. According to one entrepreneur: "Brothers in business don't last." However, the trading networks in this area have engendered a particular form of cooperative competition. Traders, for example, often share facilities and offer credit on easy terms. They might share goods with a competitor, offering one out of twenty loads to a competitor to sell. Some of this culture appears to have been transferred to manufacturing. Manufacturers commonly share equipment (generally forklifts), or lend technicians and engineers to other factories when needed. The kind of cooperative subcontracting common in areas like north-central Italy, however, does not seem to exist in this region of Nigeria.

In general, these members of Nigeria's indigenous bourgeoisie fit Schumpeter's description of early capitalist development. They have tremendous personal energy, remain very involved in their businesses, and project a very optimistic vision of their future. More than half of these firms have grown significantly since being established, and many of the industrialists described additional product lines they planned to expand into, pointing to formal feasibility studies or the ongoing construction of a new factory site.

Dynamic small-scale industry has not arisen in eastern Nigeria as a response to specific government industry programs. "The government does a lot—but it all adds up to nothing," commented one of the most successful Nnewi entrepreneurs, adding: "I think they should cut down on all these special programs for industry and just build *roads* and provide water." On the other hand, several of these industrialists have been reached by special government loan programs, such as the National Economic Reconstruction Fund (NERFUND) and the World Bank–supported Small and Medium Enterprises Credit Program; and several mentioned the assistance they had received from government-supported research and development institutes, notably the Onitsha Metallurgical Institute of Technology and PRODA, the government-sponsored technology institute in Enugu.

Conclusion

In the Nigeria we know from Sara Berry and a host of other researchers, we expect to see the auto mechanics of Ile Ifé, but we do not expect this thriving cluster of specialized small- and medium-scale industrial capitalists. What explains the case of Nnewi? Is it a reflection of the models developed in Asia and Italy? And where in Africa might other clusters of apparently sustainable industrial capitalism be located?

Small-scale capitalism in eastern Nigeria both resembles and differs from the Japanese, Taiwanese, and Italian cases described earlier. Like the other cases, family ties are clearly important in these firms, and the commercial networks created by trading families now serve to transmit, at lower transaction cost, the goods produced by new industrialists. Subcontracting and the articulation of large firms with small ones do not yet characterize this African cluster, although the potential is clearly there. In Taiwan, the government required larger firms and foreign firms to obtain a certain percentage of components locally; this target was continually revised upward on a regular basis. Nigeria also has targets like this, but in the case of the automobile industry, for example, the targets for local sourcing have been ignored by the industry year after year with no visible consequences.

Must the state be supportive of capitalists for capitalism to thrive? The cases of Japan, Taiwan, and Italy argue that, in contrast to much of the current rhetoric about the magic of the marketplace, government, sometimes national and often local, plays a key role by providing the right environment for the group of dynamic enterprises with the potential to create well-paid jobs with prospects of greatly increased productivity. Yet the multitude of products produced by small industrialists means that government-supported research and extension cannot easily substitute for critical entrepreneurial functions: taking risks, developing new products, finding a market niche. But as a minimum, governments in Japan, Taiwan, and Italy provided the broad base of a largely literate population; upon that base, they also established research institutes, training facilities, and, frequently, targeted credit. Observers of the Nigerian state have variously claimed that it is parasitical, practices "pirate capitalism," or operates by "prebendal" norms and values.[61] Nnewi manufacturers tend to agree. Quite likely, if the small-scale industrialists of Nnewi are thriving, it is not due to nurturing by the Nigerian state. In addition, these industrialists are members of the Igbo ethnic group, against which the other areas of Nigeria fought a protracted civil war in the late 1960s. They are not generally able to gain political access to state resources, as other ethnic groups may be able to do. Eastern Nigeria's capitalists are thriving not due to the protection of the state, but due to their superior technical, managerial, and entrepreneurial competence.[62]

Small-scale, indigenous, industrial capitalism like that in Nnewi is one possible future for African industry. But it would be a serious misinterpretation of the historical evidence to conclude from the experience of Italy, Japan, and Taiwan that the African informal sector itself, and the multitude of urban microenterprises that have sprung up to provide needed income for the urban unemployed, may be the seedbed of an alternative industrial future for Africa. To better understand the growth trends, characteristics, and role of these smaller-scale firms, research needs to point not to these informal sector microenterprises, but rather to the areas in Africa where regional clusters of indigenous firms already operate on capitalist principles, despite the absence of generalized capitalism in the country as a whole. In this way, from the bottom, they can affect the evolution of the cultural and economic institutions that will underpin modern capitalism in Africa, and may determine whether it becomes a capitalism of small firms or one of large—one based on cooperative networks and family firms or on anonymous production relations.

Research and thinking about industrialization in Africa might consider searching for more areas like Nnewi township, areas where local networks of dynamic small and medium-sized industries are already forming. Linkages created through neighborhood and lineage ties have economic advantages: they can heighten trust and complementarity and reduce information and search costs—the kinds of transaction costs that distort developing markets. They reduce the costs of learning to industrialize. It will be important to map the networks within which small industries operate; to look for instances of linkages between firms, whether large or small; and to concentrate on areas where people *are* "building the means of production," where an indigenous small-scale capitalism is being formed. Many of the successful cases in Japan, Taiwan, and Italy are regionally based: Sakaki township in Japan, Taichung in Taiwan, Emilio in north-central Italy. Industries like those established at the Suame Magazine in Kumasi, Ghana, or the integrated coffee production and processing operations of the Bamiléké in Cameroon are good possibilities for further research.[63]

Africa's industrial bourgeoisie may not resemble those of Japan, Taiwan, or Italy, and it is clear that African countries must still pass through many transitions before building a solid institutional base for capitalism. Alexander Gerschenkron argued that "only when industrial development could commence on a large scale did the tension between the preindustrialization conditions and the benefits expected from industrialization become sufficiently strong to overcome the existing obstacles and to liberate the forces that made for industrial progress."[64] The case of Nnewi shows that it is possible for substantial industrial progress to begin in a particular region, with small-scale, indigenous industrialists who can comfortably use foreign technology, but whose firms are rooted in indigenous institutions, customs, and values. In Africa, the large-scale capitalism of Gerschenkron's prediction may yet translate into a multitude of progressive small and medium-sized firms.

Notes

1. Karl Marx, *Das Kapital*, 1st ed., Preface, cited in Alexander Gerschenkron, *Economic Backwardness in Historical Perspective: A Book of Essays* (Cambridge: Cambridge Belknap Press of Harvard University Press, 1962), p. 6.

2. See Mancur Olson, *The Rise and Decline of Nations: Economic Growth, Stagflation, and Social Rigidities* (New Haven: Yale University Press, 1982), p. 62.

3. Gerschenkron, *Economic Backwardness*, p. 10.

4. See, for example, Thandika Mkandawire, "The Road to Crisis, Adjustment and De-Industrialization: The African Case," *Africa Development* 13, no. 1 (1988); Sanjaya Lall, "Structural Problems of Industry in Sub-Saharan Africa," background papers, *The Long-Term Perspective Study of Sub-Saharan Africa*, Vol. 2, *Economic and Sectoral Policy Issues* (Washington, D.C.: World Bank, 1990); Lynn Mytelka, "The Unfulfilled Promise of African Industrialization," *African Studies Review* 32, no. 3 (1989), pp. 77–137.

5. See Peter Lewis, "The Political Economy of Public Enterprises in Nigeria," Ph.D. diss., Princeton University, 1991, pp. 551–560.

6. See, for example, Deborah Brautigam, "Regional Industrialization in Eastern Nigeria," report prepared for the Western Africa Department, Country Operations Division, World Bank, Washington, D.C., 1992; Tom Forrest, "The Advance of African Capital: The Growth of Nigerian Private Enterprises," in Frances Stewart, Sanjaya Lall, and Samuel Wangwe, eds., *Alternative Development Strategies in Africa* (London: St. Martin's Press, 1992); William F. Steel and Leila M. Webster, "Small Enterprises in Ghana; Responses to Adjustment," Industry and Energy Department Working Paper Industry Series No. 33 (Washington, D.C.: World Bank, 1990).

7. Earlier versions of this chapter were discussed at a conference, "Identity, Rationality and the Post-Colonial Subject: African Perspectives on Contemporary Social Theory," February 28, 1991, at Columbia University, and at the Workshop on African Bourgeoisies organized by Queen's University, Ontario, Canada, April 12–13, 1991. Participants in both conferences offered numerous helpful suggestions. I would especially like to thank Bruce Berman, Sara Berry, Theodore Bestor, Tyler Biggs, Bonnie Campbell, Tom Forrest, Colin Leys, Paul Kennedy, and William Steel for helpful suggestions. They are not to blame for the errors that remain. This paper was originally written while I was a visiting fellow at the World Bank, under an International Affairs Fellowship from the Council on Foreign Relations; however, I am solely responsible for the views and opinions expressed in this chapter.

8. Tyler Biggs and Jeremy Oppenheim, "What Drives the Size Distribution of Firms in Developing Countries?" E.E.P.A. Discussion Paper No. 6 (Cambridge: Harvard Institute for International Development, 1986).

160 *Deborah Brautigam*

9. Dennis Anderson, "Small Industry in Developing Countries: A Discussion of Issues," *World Development* 10, no. 11 (1982), p. 921.

10. I. M. Little, D. Mazumdar, and J. M. Page, Jr., *Small Manufacturing Enterprises: A Comparative Analysis of India and Other Economies* (New York: Oxford University Press, 1987), pp. 9, 17.

11. Michael J. Piore and Charles F. Sabel, *The Second Industrial Divide: Possibilities for Prosperity* (New York: Basic Books, 1984).

12. Alejandro Portes, Manuel Castells, and Lauren A. Benton, eds., *The Informal Economy: Studies in Advanced and Less Developed Countries* (Baltimore: Johns Hopkins University Press, 1989).

13. David Friedman, *The Misunderstood Miracle: Industrial Development and Political Change in Japan* (Ithaca: Cornell University Press, 1988), p. 2.

14. Ibid., p. 127.

15. Ibid., p. 182.

16. Statistics Bureau, *Japan Statistical Yearbook*, 1984.

17. Momtaz Uddin Ahmed, *The Financing of Small-Scale Industries: A Study of Bangladesh and Japan* (Dhaka: University of Dhaka, 1987), p. 93.

18. "The startups for new manufacturing firms are so high in Japan that in any given year the number of new, small-scale startup factories is equal to more than half the *total* number of manufacturing factories" (Friedman, *Misunderstood Miracle*, p. 144).

19. Ibid., pp. 162–163.

20. Piore and Sabel, *Second Industrial Divide*, pp. 223–224.

21. Gustav Ranis, "Factor Proportions in Japanese Economic Development," *American Economic Review* (1957), pp. 598–602.

22. Friedman, *Misunderstood Miracle*, p. 148.

23. Ibid., p. 143, citing Kiyonari Tadao.

24. Hugh Patrick and Thomas Rohlen, "Japan's Small-Scale Family Enterprises," Working Paper No. 3, Center on Japanese Economy and Business, Columbia University, 1986, p. 9.

25. Little et al., *Small Manufacturing Enterprises*, p. 17.

26. Yeo-Gyeong Yun, "Promoting Small and Medium Industries: The Korean Experience," *Asian Development Review* 6, no. 2 (1988).

27. Deborah Brautigam, "The State as Agent: Industrialization in Taiwan 1952–1972: Lessons for Sub-Saharan Africa," in Howard Stein, ed., *Asian Industrialization and Africa: Policy Alternatives to Structural Adjustment* (London: Macmillan, 1993).

28. See Donald DeGlopper, "Artisan Work and Life in Taiwan," *Modern China* 5, no. 3 (1979), p. 285; Laurids Lauridsen, "Smallness No Longer Appropriate: State and Industrial Adjustment in Taiwan," in Meine Pieter van Dijk and Henrik Secher Marcussen, eds., *Industrialization in the Third World*, EADI Book Series (London: Frank Cass, 1990), p. 74.

29. T. Biggs and K. Lorch, "Small Enterprise and Market Transactions in Taiwan: The Role of Government Policy," paper presented at the 41st annual meeting of the Association for Asian Studies, Washington, D.C., March 17–18, 1989; Samuel Ho, "Small-Scale Enterprises in Korea and Taiwan," World Bank Staff Working Paper No. 384, April 1980, p. 26.

30. Biggs and Lorch, "Small Enterprise," p. 14; also see note 39.

31. DeGlopper, "Artisan Work," p. 286.

32. Alice Amsden, "Taiwan's Economic History: A Case of 'Etatism' and a Challenge to Dependency Theory," *Modern China* 5 (1979), pp. 371, 375.

33. Ho, "Small-Scale Enterprises," p. 23.

34. Tyler Biggs and Brian Levy, "Strategic Interventions and the Political Economy of Industrial Policy in Developing Countries," E.E.P.A. Discussion Paper No. 23 (Cambridge: Harvard Institute for International Development, 1988), p. 24.

35. Ibid., p. 26.

36. Linda Weiss, *Creating Capitalism: The State and Small Business Since 1945* (New York: Basil Blackwell, 1988), p. 20.

37. In 1951, 99.4 percent of industrial firms were "small" (100 or fewer employees) and provided 52 percent of employment; this had hardly changed at all by 1971, with 99.5 percent of firms qualifying as small, and providing 53 percent of employment. Weiss, *Creating Capitalism*, pp. 14–15; C. Barberis, *L'artigianato in Italia e nella Comunitá economica europea* (Milan: F. Angeli, 1980), p. 53, cited in Weiss, *Creating Capitalism*, p. 15.

38. Manuel Castells and Alejandro Portes, "World Underneath: The Origins, Dynamics and Effects of the Informal Economy," in Portes, Castells, and Benton, *Informal Economy*, p. 23.

39. Vittorio Capecchi, "The Informal Economy and the Development of Flexible Specialization in Emilia-Romagna," in Portes, Castells, and Benton, *Informal Economy*, p. 198.

40. Piore and Sabel, *Second Industrial Divide*, pp. 226–228, passim.

41. Weiss, *Creating Capitalism*, pp. 55–80.

42. Ibid., pp. 69–70.

43. Louis A. Ferman, Stuart Henry, and Michele Hoyman, eds., "The Informal Economy," special edition of the *Annals of the American Academy of Political and Social Science* 493 (1987), p. 165.

44. Piore and Sabel, *Second Industrial Divide*, pp. 226–227.

45. Weiss, *Creating Capitalism*, p. 98.

46. Toshio Toyoka, ed., *Vocational Education in the Industrialization of Japan* (Tokyo: United Nations University, 1987).

47. Ryokichi Hirono, "Japan: Model for East Asian Industrialization?" in Helen Hughes, ed., *Achieving Industrialization in East Asia* (Cambridge: Cambridge University Press, 1988), p. 246.

48. Brautigam, "State as Agent."

49. Among them, Sara Berry, *Fathers Work for Their Sons: Accumulation, Mobility, and Class Formation in an Extended Yorùbá Community* (Berkeley: University of California Press, 1985); Janet MacGaffey, *Entrepreneurs and Parasites: The Struggle for Indigenous Capitalism in Zaire* (New York: Cambridge University Press, 1987).

50. Steel and Webster, "Small Enterprises in Ghana," pp. ii, 26.

51. Ibid., p. 45.

52. Berry, *Fathers Work for Their Sons*, p. 139.

53. Ibid., p. 165.

54. DeGlopper, "Artisan Work," p. 306.

55. Robert Wade, *Governing the Market: Economic Theory and the Role of Government in East Asian Industrialization* (Princeton: Princeton University Press, 1990), p. 38; Nicholas D. Kristof, "A Dictatorship That Grew Up," *New York Times Magazine*, February 16, 1992.

56. Stella Silverstein, "Socio-Cultural Organisation and Locational Strategies of Transport Enterprise: An Ethno-Economic History of Nnewi Igbo of Nigeria," Ph.D. diss., Boston University, 1983; Stella Silverstein, "Igbo Kinship and Modern Entrepreneurial Organization: The Transport and Spare Parts Business," *Studies in Third World Societies*, no. 28 (June 1984).

57. Eight of the industrialists surveyed by the author in October and November 1992 concentrated primarily on automobile and motorcycle spare parts (brake pads, brake linings, brake fluid, rubber fan belts, car batteries, Peugeot front grills, hubcaps, rearview mirrors, plastic motorcycle fenders, automotive oil filters, wheel block sleeves, bolts and coupling pins, automotive cables, and assorted clear and colored plastic auto parts). The others produced primarily nonautomotive items (synthetic marble, electrical wires and cables, switchgears and electrical fittings, plastic electrical accessories, toilet paper, refined palm kernel oil, aluminum pots, tableware, dies, cleaning and personal care products, rolled steel filing cabinets, cement, industrial molds, milled maize and rice, and mineral processing and road construction equipment). Brautigam, "Regional Industrialization."

58. See Lall, "Structural Problems."

59. Forrest, "Advance of African Capital."

60. Brautigam, "Regional Industrialization."

61. See Richard Joseph, *Democracy and Prebendalism in Nigeria* (Cambridge: Cambridge University Press, 1987); Sayer Schatz, *Nigerian Capitalism* (Berkeley: University of California Press, 1977).

62. See the introduction in Colin Leys, "Interpreting African Underdevelopment: Reflections on the ILO Report on Employment, Incomes and Equality in Kenya," *African Affairs* (October 1973), pp. 425–428.

63. For the Ghanaian case, see Ian Smillie, *Mastering the Machine: Poverty, Aid and Technology* (London: Intermediate Technology Publications, 1991).

64. Gerschenkron, *Economic Backwardness*, p. 11.

8

Accumulating Wealth, Consolidating Power: Rentierism in Senegal

Catherine Boone

This chapter makes a case for more systematic and theoretical treatments of the political sphere—that is, of the production and reproduction of state power—in studies of African capitalism.[1] It does so by showing how gathering and reproducing state power shaped the character and capitalist potential of Senegal's accumulating class. In Senegal, a mode of domination based upon cooptation and clientelism emerged, underpinning a ruling alliance composed of a fissiparous "political class" and a rural Islamic "aristocracy." Import-export trading circuits created by colonial merchant capital remained the prime site of accumulation in the postcolonial economy. These same commercial circuits became prime avenues for extending state power into the rural areas, channeling the flow of resources that linked rural "indirect rulers" to the state, and absorbing the nascent Senegalese business class into the patron-client structures of the regime. Structures of political control and of accumulation merged and intertwined, creating forms of politicized accumulation in the commercial sector that helped to consolidate political power and to expand the ruling alliance.

The regime used trade controls to canalize, structure, and even constrain possibilities for accumulation in an effort to broaden the ruling alliance while simultaneously stifling deep conflicts of interest within it. Private ambitions were reduced to the goal of tapping opportunities for state patronage, including commercial rentier activities, compromising the willingness and ability of factions within the ruling alliance to pursue collective action aimed at broad political or economic reform. Senegal's political stability, and the durability of the original ruling coalition of politicians and the saintly Islamic aristocracy, bears testimony to the success of these efforts. So does the enduring weakness of local capital. The regime succeeded in coopting the indigenous business stratum, dissipating its coherence as a distinctive force in national politics.

In the 1960s, these strategies were complemented by neocolonial interests vested in Senegalese light industry and the import trade. Foreign monopolies in these areas were protected and preserved, helping Senegal to remain in the good graces of the ex–colonial power. Senegal received a substantial inflow of external grants and loans, a detachment of French troops to aid the regime in times of crisis, and a corps of French "technical assistants" that helped to insulate sensitive domains of domestic policy-making from the pressures of factional in-fighting and patronage politics. Over time, however, the political logic guiding the use of state controls over commerce began to diverge from the economic logic of neocolonialism. As the regime tapped resources from the commercial sector to generate an ever larger pool of patronage resources, and as trade controls were manipulated to insert a widening array of the regime's clients into the import-export trade, the hierarchical and centralized structure of domestic trading circuits began to crumble. Clientelism within the regime fragmented private interests and facilitated political control, but it eroded the capacity of the state to direct economic activity. This was manifest in the growing inability of the regime to sustain the old monopolies underpinning neo-colonial interests in trade and light industry, or even to defend its own claim to a share of the export crop. Rentiers clustered around and within an increasingly incoherent state apparatus. Even if there were a social agent to promote a "nurture capitalism" project, by the 1980s state power did not exist in the form and measure needed for such an undertaking.

The case of Senegal contributes to other analyses of indigenous accumulation in three ways. First, it shows how the political circumstances structuring the acquisition of wealth affect the political coherence, economic ambitions, and business strategies of the accumulating class. In particular, it focuses attention on ways in which clientelism and rentierism can inhibit the emergence of indigenous capitalist classes. Second, it underscores the importance of rural class relations in shaping possibilities for capitalist transformation. The political authority of Senegal's postcolonial regime was rooted in the old structures of rural "indirect rule" that allowed the state to both govern and exploit an impoverished, export crop–producing peasantry. These arrangements limited opportunities for private accumulation in agriculture and in activities ancillary to the export trade. Third, Senegal is a stark reminder of the enduring legacies of colonial merchant capital in West Africa. The postcolonial state took root in the *économie de traite* that was the hallmark of French colonialism in the Sahel. The regime strove to reproduce the conditions that sustained this economy and its own power: indirect rule, a groundnut-producing peasantry that was both shored up and "squeezed" in the face of declines in productivity, and market monopolies that allowed both traders and the state to collect groundnut profits that were generated by buying cheap and selling dear. The regime's dependence upon the old order helps to explain the weakness of capital—both local and foreign—as a force structuring social relations of power and production in Senegal.

Rentierism and Clientelism

I define rent-seeking as activities aimed at collecting price premiums created by noncompetitive market conditions (scarcities, monopolies, barriers to market entry imposed by nonmarket forces, etc.).[2] Premiums exist in the sense that profit margins collected by buyers or sellers are higher than they would be under competitive conditions. The analysis here is concerned with markets that are not governed by competitive price-setting because governments restrict buyers' or sellers' entry into the market, restrict supplies of commodities to the market, and/or ration scarce commodities. In these situations, rent-seeking is politically mediated. State agents mete out opportunities for collecting rents, or they collect rents themselves (on their own account or in the name of the state).

Rents can constitute a form of primitive accumulation, as can inherited wealth or any other form of windfall profit. For the emergence of African capitalism, the key question is: Will wealth collected in the form of rents be transformed into capital through productive investment?[3] There is no a priori answer to this question. Nicola Swainson described how Kenyans used resources accumulated through nonproductive activities in commerce or in the political sphere to invest in industry.[4] Yet productive investment is not necessarily the outcome, in Africa or elsewhere. As Brenner has observed, "Historically, the build up of wealth in the hands of 'potential' investors has occurred time and time again without discernible effect."[5]

To describe a situation wherein rent-seeking becomes a dominant and enduring end in itself, I use the term "rentierism." Rentiers channel their wealth into consumption, place acquired rents in new or bigger rent-collecting activities, make political investments that enhance their ability to collect rents in the future, buy real estate, or send their money to foreign bank accounts. They do not turn their wealth into capital by combining it with wage labor to create relative surplus value, which would be embodied in new commodities or services. When does rent-seeking turn into rentierism?

How rents will be deployed depends in very large part upon social, economic, and political conditions that structure incentives and opportunities and risks. Basic as it seems, it remains important to underline the fact that capitalist production cannot occur without wage labor, private property, and markets. Conditions as general as these are important in shaping the scope of investment possibilities in agriculture in much of sub-Saharan Africa. In addition, the explicitly political conditions under which rents are created and collected shape the likelihood of investment. The emergence of segments of the accumulating class that are interested in, able to, and finally obliged to promote the process of investment and reinvestment in production remains an event of great political contingency.

It is contingent upon how state power is used to structure the array of other possibilities for deploying wealth. (Are there more lucrative and less risky options?) The development of a stratum of indigenous capitalists is also contingent upon the existence of states and regimes with the institutional capacities and political drive that are required to promote and protect capitalists' interests in the face of competing demands and political needs. Questions about state capacities, social agency, class consciousness, and wider domestic struggles over wealth and power are brought to center stage.

This is how political clientelism becomes relevant to prospects for capitalist development. Writers such as Peter Flynn and Robert Fatton show that patronage politics is one means by which dominant social groups can work to subordinate and disorganize subaltern classes.[6] Patron-client networks regulate and narrow access to the state and state resources. They are mechanisms that distribute state-controlled resources strategically, working either to marginalize key individuals and groups or to win their political support (or acquiescence). Clientelist systems are distinctive in that benefits and sanctions are distributed to individuals rather than social groups. Flynn maintains that the most striking feature of clientelistic systems of political control is "the degree to which vertical clientelistic chains and the dyadic links of personal interdependence cut through and weaken efforts toward class and other category group organization."[7] The logic of this argument can be extended to power relations *within* the ruling strata of postcolonial Africa. State agents are themselves tied into a clientelist system of political control when they secure access to jobs and opportunities for private accumulation through patronage networks. Big men, rural notables, and Africa's old aristocracies are tied to the state when possibilities for reproducing existing power become dependent upon access to resources distributed by the regime. This was the logic underlying colonial indirect rule.

Members of ruling alliances and their counterparts within state bureaucracies are targets as well as the prime beneficiaries of clientelist systems of political consolidation and control, and rent-collecting opportunities can be the patronage resource that is used to make them into clients. Under such conditions, rentierism is not unstructured or guided solely by particularistic interests in private gain. Rents provide resources for building hierarchical relations of clientelism between the wielders of state prerogative and those dependent upon their services. Patronage networks can emerge as the informal and fluid institutional structures organizing power within the state apparatus and binding together the disparate elements of a ruling alliance. Retaining privileged access to state resources can be the lowest common denominator that unites a coalition composed of factions that have different, even contradictory, long-term interests and political needs.

How do these political arrangements affect possibilities for indigenous capitalism? To use the language of Nicos Mouzelis, a mode of political domination that works through clientelistic hierarchies has particular reproduction requirements or conditions of existence.[8] Unlike a mode of domination enforced through the "dull compulsion of economic necessity," the form of political subordination inherent in patron-client relations is enforced by clients' continuing dependence upon resources under the discretionary control of patrons. When regimes facilitate the investment of wealth in self-expanding, self-reproducing capitalist enterprises, they are eroding conditions that make patronage and clientelism effective mechanisms for organizing and consolidating power. Capitalists acquire, through private ownership of means of production, a self-renewing base of accumulation that is not directly dependent upon handouts from the regime. They gain a measure of autonomy. This is why, I argue, regimes that rely heavily on clientelism to enforce cohesion within the ruling stratum tend not to facilitate or encourage the transformation of wealth acquired through rent-seeking activities into capital. Rentiers remain clients, coopted, controlled, and ever dependent on the discretionary exercise of state power from above.

Clientelism also fosters relations among members of the accumulating class that cut through and weaken efforts to mobilize corporate demands for a "nurture capitalism" project. Strategies of advancement tend to be oriented toward manipulating patterns of policy implementation and climbing the ladder to move closer to the centers of state power, rather than toward mobilizing groups to bring pressures to bear on the policymaking process. Indeed, the success of a clientelistic system of political control can be measured against this standard. Members of the accumulating class risk all when they rock the boat—they can easily be marginalized and excluded from the patrimonial flow of resources that constitutes the basis of their wealth and privilege. Within the ranks of the accumulating class, clientelism militates against the emergence of a distinctive corporate identity (class consciousness) or a "bourgeois" agenda defined in "nurture capitalism" terms.

Finally, where discretionary use of state prerogatives and patronage-based controls over resource flows are pervasive, general economic conditions become unpropitious for fixed investments that are inherently risky and that do not yield immediate profits. Investments are particularly risky when profitability depends on markets, tax regimes, bureaucratic transaction costs, etc., that are subject to the control of potentially arbitrary, hostile, or rapacious state agents. Local investment of funds that are accumulated illegally is also a high-risk strategy (better to send the funds abroad in this case). If these considerations affect the calculations of foreign investors, then domestic entrepreneurs are even more vulnerable and sensitive to them. Those able to amass important sums of wealth tend to be clients of some patron; they are vulnerable to changes in their own (or their patron's) political fortunes. The structure of incentives thus favors continued rent-seeking.[9]

Senegal's Ruling Alliance

Decolonization brought to power a factious ruling coalition between the Senghor-led Union Progressiste Sénégalaise (UPS) and Senegal's Islamic leaders. The Islamic leaders' power was rooted in their spiritual authority, in a mode of groundnut production forged under colonialism, and in the commercial and political structures that tied peasants to the colonial order. Saintly marabouts allocated land to small producers, shaped patterns of production, appropriated part of the agricultural surplus, and commanded the religious and political loyalties of much of the population in Senegal's export crop–producing region. UPS party leaders and cadres were drawn largely from the administrative, professional, and political strata created under colonialism, strata that arose as profitable trading opportunities open to Senegalese narrowed and family wealth was invested in education and municipal politics.

Senegal's colonial economy was dominated by merchant capital, and it was largely through trading structures created by merchant capital that the ruling coalition would extract its share of the economic surplus. Under these conditions, the economic interests and political needs of the ruling coalition as a whole were not staked on accelerating the emergence of capitalist social relations within the social formation at large, and in the rural sector in particular. This is not to deny that the economy and the ruling class were "dependent" upon forces that linked Senegal's market-oriented agriculture to the international capitalist economy—forces that lay in large part beyond the control of the regime. Nor is it to deny that the survival of the regime depended in large part on the inflow of cash and investment capital that the ex–colonial power and, later, institutions such as the World Bank would provide. But when confronted with forces that tended to promote the rise of productive capital at the expense of merchant capital and precapitalist systems of agricultural production, the stance of the ruling coalition would be highly ambivalent, even contradictory.

In the postcolonial version of indirect rule in Senegal, economic links between the regime and the Islamic marabouts were institutionalized in vertically integrated rural marketing structures. Agricultural cooperatives, the rural outposts of the state apparatus, distributed inputs (seeds, credit, fertilizers) to producers; the same institutions held a legal monopoly over the purchase of the export crop, groundnuts. In Senegal's groundnut basin, cooperatives came under the control of marabouts who used their influence to strengthen their hold over their clients and followers and to increase their personal wealth. The Dakar elite, for its part, relied on the marabouts to ensure rural peace and order, mobilize votes, and sanction the mechanisms that allowed the regime to buy groundnuts cheap.

Within the Dakar-based political class, President Senghor used the pact with the rural leaders as the bedrock of his own authority over a regime built through the politically enforced fusion of the old "assimilated" political elite of Senegal's Quatre Communes, a newer and younger stratum of left-leaning and reform-oriented intellectuals and nationalists, the heads of ethnic associations that emerged after World War II to represent regional interests, and the former colonial Senegalese civil service.

Progressive urban groups that were incorporated into the Senghoriste political parties of the 1950s represented the prime source of tension within the regime. Incorporation of these elements into the dominant party helped to build winning electoral coalitions, but it introduced deep contradictions into the party's policy agenda.

Animation rurale, Senegal's version of grassroots socialism, was the most conspicuous sign of a cleavage within the political elite that was potentially fatal to the ruling coalition as a whole. As conceived by French planners and progressive elements within the Senghor regime in the late 1950s and early 1960s, *animation rurale* was a program aimed at restructuring rural social relations to free peasants from what was defined as the exploitative and oppressive grip of rural notables, including the marabouts. Truly democratic and participatory rural cooperatives were to be the motor of change; by bypassing the old patrons, brokers, big men, and other rural intermediaries, peasants could be incorporated into democratic state structures directly. Cooperatives could support innovation in production, promote food crop production, and offer technical training. Planners believed that these initiatives would increase agricultural output and productivity, reduce peasants' dependence on imported rice, and enhance rural well-being. That the regime pursued this reform agenda for some five years, between 1958 and 1962, indicates the weight of the reformist current within the political elite. That *animation rurale* was eviscerated when its leading proponents were purged from the regime in 1963 is a sign of the unwillingness of Senghor to jeopardize and weaken the alliance between the regime and the rural notables.

Senegal's constitutional crisis of 1962–1963 accelerated the centralization of executive power in the hands of Senghor, the rise of a de facto one-party state, and the merging of party structures with those of the government administration. This process was accompanied by a wave of repressive measures that drove organized political opposition parties and leaders underground, into jail, or into the smothering embrace of the ruling party.

Strong-arm tactics were used to consolidate Senegal's political class along the lines of what Donal Cruise O'Brien called spoils-oriented factions.[10] Cooptation and clientelism served as mechanisms for dissipating tensions within the ruling alliance and splintering coalitions that had been mobilized around reform and the rivals of Senghor. Struggles over ideology and reform gave way to factional struggles for the control of resources flowing through the state apparatus. The political class that emerged was held together by an "organic unity" based upon members' interests in capturing the jobs, subsidies, contracts, rents, sinecures, loans, payoffs, and favors.[11] Party patrons distributed government resources to their electoral clienteles, much as marabouts distributed government resources to their followers. Clientelism and cooptation became pervasive mechanisms of rule and political domination.

The financial resources that built and sustained this political machine came in large part from the old commercial circuits created by merchant capital. Sixty percent of the government's fiscal receipts in the 1960s were drawn from the import-export circuit.[12] A substantial share of the government's resources also flowed in from abroad, mostly in the form of grants and concessionary loans.

The Rise of Rentierism and a Rentier Class

The weakness of the indigenous business class at the time of Senegal's political independence in 1960 was, in part, a reflection of the weaknesses of capital itself in structuring the social relations and forces of production. Peasant households were poor, did not employ wage labor, invested little, and accumulated little wealth in comparison to their coffee- and cocoa-cultivating counterparts in Ghana, Côte d'Ivoire, and western Nigeria. These peasants were responsible for producing Senegal's marketed agricultural surplus. Industry barely existed before World War II. The profitability of the European trading houses that dominated the colonial economy rested upon monopolistic forms of control over exchange, enforced by the state. Trading monopolies, oligopolies, and cartels generated rents for colonial merchant capital. At the same time, they worked to circumscribe possibilities for the development of Senegalese capitalism.

The postcolonial state reproduced the monopolistic trading structures that were built during the colonial period. The sphere of circulation, rather than the sphere of production, remained the locus of accumulation in the national economy. A barrage of administrative mechanisms (including legal monopolies, licensing, import controls, and price-setting) allowed the regime to regulate access to the commercial circuit, especially the import-export trade. Administrative controls not only raised commercial margins by restricting competition (thereby creating rents), but also helped to define the share that traders at various levels of the commercial hierarchy would collect. Regulating commerce was a powerful instrument for structuring private accumulation. The regime used this instrument to enhance its own power and to focus private ambitions on commercial rent-seeking opportunities that were mediated by the state. A rentier class emerged, composed of Dakar-based politicians and functionaries, the rural elite, and Senegal's indigenous business strata. This class became a powerful force shaping the course of postcolonial economic development.

The rise of rentierism and an indigenous rentier class involved two processes. First, the most dynamic elements of the Senegalese business stratum were coopted into the patronage machine. Second, members of the political class moved into state-mediated rentier activities, again in the commercial sector.

The 1960s: The Africanization of Trade

At the time of independence in 1960, French firms owned over 95 percent of Senegal's modest industrial sector, which consisted of groundnut processing firms and light manufacturing firms serving the local market. French corporations owned all the banks, and French commercial houses monopolized the import-export trade at the wholesale level. Immigrant French and Lebanese businessmen dominated retail trade in the urban and rural areas. They also invested in a broad array of competitive activities in the service sector (laundries, hotels, restaurants, travel agencies, movie theaters, real estate agencies, etc.). Within the formal economy, the Senegalese private sector comprised about 300 "medium-scale" *commerçants* in semiwholesale trade and perhaps several thousand small-scale transporters and traders.[13] Most were connected to the groundnut trade as subcontractors, agents, or middlemen in circuits dominated by French trading houses.

In the mid- to late 1950s, French trading companies operating in Senegal responded to rising overhead costs and the slump in world commodity prices by moving out of retail trade. As they began to consolidate their operations at the wholesale level in Dakar, Senegalese traders and transporters expanded their operations in the rural areas. Indigenous traders were an important part of the rural electoral coalition that brought Senghor to power.

The streamlining of the French merchant houses accelerated in 1960 when the government placed the export of groundnuts under state monopoly. European commercial houses withdrew abruptly from the rural areas. From the perspective of Senegalese transporters and traders, this process cleared the way for expansion. Businessmen aspired, first and foremost, to take over middleman positions between groundnut producers and the Port of Dakar.[14] Access to importation, the most profitable segment of the commercial sector, was also a priority. Most of them, however, needed capital.

The government moved at this juncture. It defined the rural economy as a "commercial vacuum" and laid out a strategy to ensure that the "Africanization" of commerce would be carried out in an "organized and orderly" way.[15] The government created new bureaucratic structures to oversee, manage, and finance "the insertion" of local *commerçants* into trading niches vacated by the French companies.

In 1960, the newly created Office de la Commercialization Agricole (OCA) assumed control over the purchase of the groundnut crop from producers. The decision to place the commercialization of groundnuts under state control would prove to be a decisive constraint on possibilities for strengthening the Senegalese commercial class. State control ultimately closed off an avenue of accumulation that began to open in the 1950s. For the regime, however, this move was critical, for state-controlled groundnut circuits were the veins through which government influence and patronage flowed into the rural areas. Competition in groundnut purchasing would short-circuit the emerging postcolonial hierarchy of power and influence, jeopardizing a structure of indirect rule in the countryside that was shored up by credit, groundnut purchasing, and input distribution systems set in place and financed by the state. The groundnut marketing board became the single largest patronage combine in postcolonial Senegal.

While the regime took away from Senegalese traders with one hand, it could still give with the other. Because the bureaucratic structures for crop collection and purchase were not fully in place until 1968, between 1960 and 1967 the OCA licensed about 1,000 individuals each year to handle this activity. Senegalese traders thus reaped the first fruits of political independence in a way that consolidated their ties to the regime. Many of those who obtained licenses were political influentials and "*bons militants*" at local levels of the ruling party.[16] Commercial margins set by the marketing board allowed the most favored individuals to accumulate millions of CFA francs in gross profits during the transition period.

Senegalese businessmen were also "inserted selectively" into the wholesale and retail trade, downstream from the European commercial houses. Wholesale and semiwholesale trading licenses were distributed through the party bureaucratic machine in a process that drew even more Senegalese traders into the orbit of the regime. At the same time, those in strategic political positions were able to tap profits generated through trading activities, either directly or as *prête-noms* (front men) for Lebanese and Senegalese merchants. The Dakar Chamber of Commerce, still under the unchallenged control of French trading interests, railed against the practice of political patronage that permeated the licensing process.

The government also responded to the ambitions of Senegalese traders by making "space" for them in the distribution of imported consumer goods. State planners sponsored the creation of two retail consortia that positioned Senegalese traders downstream from the largest European wholesalers. Officials then selected about 1,000 individuals who received state loans to buy into these ventures. Forty or fifty individuals were offered particularly large loans for this purpose. Some of the beneficiaries of the consortia initiative were established traders; others were members of what the minister in charge called "a new class of *techniciens-commerçants*." Under terms negotiated by the government, the large French trading companies allowed consortium members to purchase imported consumer goods on credit. These arrangements provided businessmen who were selected by the regime with access to working funds and imported consumer goods.

The consortia fell apart in the early 1960s. Undeterred, the government devised a new formula that increased its control over the distribution circuit and the Senegalese traders who operated within it. The consortia were restructured into one state-run company, the Société Nationale de Distribution (SONADIS).[17] The government itself purchased manufactured goods and food staples from the French importers. Goods were sold either by the government itself (through SONADIS stores) or on credit to Senegalese businessmen operating independent outlets. As SONADIS became the largest retail distributor of consumer goods in the rural areas in the 1960s, hundreds of Senegalese traders became either SONADIS employees or indebted to it.

For a better-placed stratum of Senegalese traders and would-be traders, more attractive opportunities opened up in the 1960s. The state-controlled commodities trade generated immediate profits for individuals who obtained contracts to operate in this domain.

In addition to overseeing the commercialization of the export crop, the OCA controlled the importation of Senegal's staple food, rice. In the 1960s, rice imported to Senegal by the state was sold, on credit, to twenty leading Dakar businessmen and other bigwigs, fifty "large-scale traders," and 200 "medium-scale" traders chosen by the regime.[18] These individuals distributed about 120,000 tons in the mid-1960s at profit margins fixed by the government. Rice quotas generated substantial profits for the individuals who obtained them. This business was a tremendous boost to the development of a wealthy stratum of politicians and local businessmen with political connections.

The Narrow Scope of Senegalese Business

Investment in Senegal's manufacturing sector grew at a rate of 14 percent per annum between 1962 and 1967. The overwhelming majority of this was French capital, and ex–colonial commercial houses—led by SCOA, the CFAO, and the CNF—were among the largest investors. Senegal's investment code offered extremely favorable terms to foreign firms. The free flow of capital within the Franc Zone reduced risks. More decisive in attracting new investment, however, was the regime's commitment to very high levels of protection against imports. To help ensure the profitability of new manufacturing ventures, the government subjected foreign goods likely to compete with local industrial output to import licensing and granted these licenses to the trading houses that owned local industry. This made local industries and their commercial partners the biggest rent-collectors in Senegal. The easy availability of rents and the small size of Senegal's domestic market tempered their enthusiasm for deepening their industrial investments.

Lebanese traders emerged as the dominant importers of goods not governed by the import licensing regime, the main clients of the European trading houses, and the leading urban and rural semiwholesalers/retailers. Some Lebanese-owned firms were counted among Senegal's thirty largest commercial enterprises in the 1960s, on a par with some of the smaller, family-run French trading companies. And some Lebanese invested in light industry (baked goods, packaging, paper products, etc.) in the 1960s. They represented the first line of competition that Senegalese businessmen confronted.

The political status of the Lebanese segment of the private sector remained ambiguous and insecure. They were perceived universally as foreigners by the Senegalese, even though many were born in Senegal and held dual citizenship. The Lebanese community had invested shrewdly in politics since the 1950s (if not before), shoring up their political status as they extended their sphere of business operations. But insecurity of political status militated against the productive investment of capital accumulated by the Lebanese business community in Senegal. "Most of them . . . feeling themselves to be insecure as a group anyway, . . . took the conservative option of remaining in their existing business, even with declining profits."[19] Many chose to send their wealth abroad, diversify into a wide range of commercial activities (including transport), or invest in urban real estate, rather than to make fixed investments in productive activities. The insecurity of the Lebanese was exploited by state agents interested in tapping a share of their trading profits in the form of *prête-nom* commissions, payoffs, gifts, etc. Rita Cruise O'Brien drew this conclusion about the process: "Following independence, national politicians seemed by design to be more interested in letting the Lebanese operate their system of [political payoffs for] protection rather than support the rise of a local bourgeoisie which might have been politically more outspoken and more of a challenge."[20]

Below the Lebanese in what remained a hierarchical structure of control over trade were Mauritanian retailers and microretailers. Through

Lebanese intermediaries for the most part, they purchased imported and locally manufactured goods on credit. Male members of Mauritanian families and their servants rotated in and out of Senegal, working as immigrant shopkeepers until a relative arrived to take their place. They lived in and ran the corner shops that urban dwellers visited daily. Mauritanians were well integrated into Senegalese life: they offered credit to households and safeguarded their clients' cash deposits. By the 1980s, Mauritanian business groups controlled networks of boutiques, and some were important wholesale buyers of consumer goods. Senegalese merchants did not fare particularly well in urban retail and microretail trade. Extremely small commercial margins and lack of access to credit militated against their success in this sector.

Lack of access to bank credit represented a formidable obstacle to the development of Senegalese businesses in all sectors of activity. The national development bank concentrated on financing the groundnut campaign, and the commercial banks in Dakar remained French-owned in the 1960s. The conservatism of the private financial institutions, their long-standing links with European trading houses, and their unwillingness to place confidence in African borrowers made it almost impossible for Senegalese to obtain commercial bank financing. In 1970, only three Senegalese-owned private trading firms were borrowers at Dakar's private banks.[21] As a result, indigenous business interests were pressured to look to politicized government channels to secure cash and credit.

Conditions prevailing in the rural sector also worked to canalize Senegalese businesses toward state-mediated commercial opportunities. Groundnuts were not very lucrative commodities: state-set producer prices declined almost continuously in real terms after 1967. Meanwhile, agricultural development policy did little to stimulate crop diversification and continued to concentrate on expanding peasant production of the traditional export crop. Senegal's *loi sur le domaine national* of 1964 reaffirmed communal prerogatives in allocating land and land use rights. Input distribution was handled by the cooperatives, and these institutions also shored up existing rural social relations of production. As the proponents of *animation rurale* had argued in the late 1950s and early 1960s, rural patronage relations that tied peasants to notables, and notables to the state, diverted potentially productive resources away from productivity-enhancing investment, crops other than groundnuts, and nonagricultural forms of production (such as artisanal activities) in the rural areas. The poverty of Senegal's peasants and stagnant productivity in the groundnut economy were decisive and enduring constraints on the expansion of the economy as a whole. Within these constraints, profits to be had in the agricultural sector lay in the marketing circuit, not production, and marketing was controlled by the state.

The postcolonial expansion of the Senegalese business sector was thus guided along commercial lines into niches defined by the state and according to terms set by the regime. Licenses, contracts, and credit were allocated through the political machine to civil servants, politicians, local-level government administrators, leading Senegalese merchants, and traders and transporters who had been linked to Senghoriste political factions since the 1950s. Over the course of the 1960s, an elite group of dynamic and wealthy Senegalese businessmen emerged. Majhemout Diop estimated in 1968 that about 250 of them had achieved *"une certaine importance"* on the national level.[22] A few amassed fortunes. Politics and politically mediated commercial opportunities were firmly established as the main avenues of private wealth accumulation. How would this wealth be deployed? The regime's responses to the political challenges that erupted at the end of the first decade of independence played a critical role in expanding and entrenching the political system that worked to canalize local accumulation along rentier lines.

The 1970s: Rentierism

At the end of the 1960s, the vulnerability of Senegal's clientelist system of political control was exposed. Economic recession, followed by government austerity measures affecting students, civil servants, and unionized workers, ignited smoldering frustration with the political status quo. Several simultaneous and mutually reinforcing currents of opposition erupted in 1968 and 1969 in a broad attack on the Senghor-UPS political monopoly and on the neocolonial economic strategy pursued by the regime. In the vanguard were two movements that the regime had failed to absorb or completely control in the 1960s: student groups and labor unions. Industry-level strikes expanded into general strikes that included civil servants. Criticism of excessive centralization of power in the hands of Senghor arose within the regime.

Meanwhile, the government confronted the first clear signs of trouble in the groundnut basin. France's groundnut subsidy was withdrawn in 1968, and producers bore the full brunt of a price decline of almost 20 percent. Many refused to reimburse debts owed to the cooperatives for seed and fertilizer or to contract new loans. State agents such as agricultural extension workers became targets of peasants' frustration. The government referred to the peasants' resistance to state exploitation as the *malaise paysan*. It signaled the depth of the political and economic crisis of 1968.

Islamic leaders issued calls for order, and the government used force to restore a semblance of urban peace. Yet the challenges of 1968 were profound enough to force the government to move on several fronts, making concessions to disaffected groups, creating new corporatist structures to coopt and divide the opposition, decentralizing power within the state apparatus, and accommodating restive elements within the regime. The

1968–1970 political crisis and the changes that followed in its wake represent a critical juncture in the development of a rentier class in Senegal.

In the midst of the broader crisis, 2,600 small-scale traders, transporters, and small business owners gathered to form the Union des Groupements Economiques du Sénégal (UNIGES).[23] Many of the transporters and traders had been pushed out of intermediary positions in the state-controlled groundnut economy when the government assumed direct control over the purchase of the crop in 1968. A militant tone dominated the opening congress of UNIGES, echoing the protests of the times. The organization denounced Senegal's neocolonial economic policies that forced the local private sector "to vegetate in marginal sectors of the economy."[24] Foreign monopolies in the import trade and French banks' stranglehold over private credit came under sharp attack. UNIGES blamed the government for economic stagnation, declared that the regime was "incapable of implementing a coherent policy promoting the national interest," and perhaps most significantly, called for the privatization of the groundnut and rice trades. It demanded that the government promote local private participation in the industrial sector and ban foreign capital from thirty branches of economic activity, including butcheries, bakeries, and the fishing, garment-making, and printing trades.

The government countered this current of protest by creating a second association to represent what the regime called "moderate and responsible" private sector interests: the Confédération des Groupements Economiques du Sénégal (COFEGES). Prominent defectors from UNIGES, including businessmen with ties to the ruling party and some of the wealthiest private traders, were among the 200 members of the new organization. One of COFEGES' two presidents was Ousmane Seydi, a member of the National Assembly, one of the largest OCA-authorized rice importers, and a shareholder in SONADIS, the distribution chain created by the state. The other was Ousmane Diagne of the Société Sénégalaise pour le Commerce et l'Industrie (SOSECI), whose rapid ascent in the Senegalese business world was "a sensation," propelled by "very favorable political patronage," bank credits, and the "remarkable business sense of its director."[25] Led by these successful and politically well-placed businessmen, COFEGES stressed its full support of Senghor, its loyalty to the UPS, and its favorable view of the role of French capital in the Senegalese economy. In a "progovernment fashion," members expressed interest in participating in joint-venture arrangements with foreign investors and in increased access to bank credit.[26]

The government then proclaimed that it would vigorously assist the local private sector. This commitment was backed up with the creation of two lending facilities that began to provide loans to Senegalese businessmen.[27] In the wake of these initiatives, UNIGES and COFEGES were fused in 1970 at Senghor's request. The fusion created a new, thoroughly domesticated local business organization, GES (Groupements Economiques du Sénégal), which affirmed its solidarity with the ruling party and vowed to work "within the framework of options defined by the government."[28]

Elimination of UNIGES as an independent political force put an end to attacks on foreign capital and on the regime. Yet the GES was pushed forward by the ambitions of its members and the momentum of the times. In 1970, it called for a restructuring of the agricultural cooperatives to allow the Senegalese traders to participate in the marketing of groundnuts. The regime, defending Senegal's "socialist option," proved inflexible on this front. In May 1971, the GES executive bureau was dissolved by the government. Soon the organization was fully domesticated and absorbed into the factional political structures of the regime.

Promotion of Senegalese businessmen "in domains that did not encroach upon legitimate vested interests" became one of the government's most prominent goals of the 1970s.[29] What the government called its "framework of options" for local businessmen expanded the regime's reservoir of patronage resources, enhancing its ability to deal with the broad *crise de confiance* of 1968–1970. These options offered new opportunities for the accumulation of wealth on the part of businessmen, important marabouts, politicians, and state agents. They did little to support or induce the movement of local wealth into productive activities, either alongside, in partnership with, or at the expense of French and Lebanese capital. The government did not create reserved sectors for local private capital. It did, however, create a series of new lending facilities that channeled funds into the hands of well-connected individuals, religious leaders, and local businessmen. At the same time, the government created opportunities for the deployment of these funds—in the commercial sector. The net result in the 1970s was the rise of a better-financed and wealthier Senegalese business sector, more intimately intertwined with the political class and entrenched in politically mediated rent-collecting activities.

State efforts to create space for Senegalese entrepreneurs within the trading circuit were far-reaching and touched virtually every aspect of state-regulated commerce. Most notably, the regime made a number of moves that allowed Senegalese with finance and connections to engage in lucrative import operations. Breaking with the practices of the 1960s, the government began to use the allocation of import licenses and quotas to "rapidly insert" Senegalese businessmen into a domain long dominated by French trading companies: the importation of consumer goods in heavily regulated product categories. Through this process, the most lucrative niches of the import trade had been Senegalized by 1980s. Officials also turned a blind eye to import fraud conducted through the Port of Dakar and to a growing current of contraband trade that flowed across the Senegal-Gambia border.

Transborder contraband assumed major proportions as the groundnut economy declined. Groundnuts that escaped the state monopoly were sold in Gambia, where returns were higher.[30] A counterpart flow of consumer goods imported under Gambia's liberal trade regime supplied a growing share of Senegal's rural market. Contraband flourished under the tacit protection of Senegal's main Islamic confrérie, the Mouride order. Peasants benefited from better terms of trade, and nonpayment of Senegalese import duties and taxes allowed merchants to collect commercial markups that would have gone to the state treasury. For the Mouride elite (marabouts and businessmen linked to the confrérie), contraband was a source of wealth that helped to offset declines in the income they derived directly from groundnuts. Touba, the religious capital of the Mourides, emerged as a de facto duty-free zone in Senegal's heartland. Mouride leaders protected the Senegal-Gambia contraband circuit from interference from Dakar; the regime accepted the losses as the price to be paid for shoring up the power of the confrérie and the alliance that constituted the bedrock of its own legitimacy.

Over the course of the 1970s, contraband trading circuits organized within the networks of the Mouride confrérie spread to Senegal's major urban areas, including Dakar. Expansion was propelled forward by drought and by the flight of the Mouride faithful away from rural decay and into an urban "informal economy" organized largely around commerce. Rural exodus enhanced the influence of Mouride marabouts in the urban areas, reinforcing the dependence of the Dakar-based political class on the ability of the Islamic elite to control their followers and to provide legitimacy for the regime. This dependence was reflected in the regime's commitment to ensuring that the confréries, the marabouts, and big businessmen linked to the marabouts were among the leading beneficiaries of efforts to promote the local private accumulation of wealth in the 1970s and 1980s.[31]

Official promotion of the local private sector in the 1970s created a stratum of Senegalese businessmen planted firmly in real estate and state-mediated commercial activities and tied to the political machine. The rentier character of local private accumulation was reinforced. Businessmen tended to confine their activities to nonproductive commercial transactions and financial transfers that were mediated by the government. Those who accumulated wealth in these ways tended to not invest in productive assets, and their continued success often depended upon the regime's willingness to turn a blind eye to import fraud, contraband, and nonreimbursement of state loans. Rentierism made private fortunes insecure and dependent upon the continual renewal of political privilege.

In the 1970s, the "local private sector" dissipated as a distinctive political force. What, then, did the 1968–1970 confrontation between Senegalese business interests and the government mean? Majhemout Diop offered a nuanced analysis of this period, stressing the ambivalent nature of the political project advanced by the business stratum.[32] Diop was struck by the fact that elements calling for "free enterprise" denounced the regime while demanding that it intervene more actively in the economy on their behalf. Both UNIGES and COFEGES zeroed in on the state groundnut monopoly, but what many wanted was the reinstatement of state-licensed private traders, rather than "free trade" per se. And attacks on foreign capital voiced in the language of nationalism were accompanied by demands that the government pressure foreign enterprises to take on Senegalese shareholders, suppliers, and managers. From the perspective of the 1980s, it is clear that "the local private sector" as such had no economic base from which to advance a specific vision of its role in productive sectors of the economy. Fatton put the matter starkly when he wrote that "after a decade of independence, [the Senegalese private sector] had not developed beyond the artisanal stage."[33]

The insecurity and shallowness of this economic base helps to explain why the most specific of the demands of UNIGES and COFEGES focused on access to trade and credit. It also helps explain why, in the final reading, the demands of these two groups differed more in tone than in substance. The 1968–1970 episodes cannot be read as the birth of "national capital" or of a "comprador bourgeoisie" (a *bourgeoisie liée*), or as a struggle between these two "factions of capital."[34] Senegalese private capital had not developed to the point where two discrete "factions," with different economic bases, different needs, and different visions of the future, could be discerned. Senegalese business wanted a better deal. What that deal would be was not determined by the needs of a national capitalist class.

A Context Not Conducive to Investment

While clientelism and rentierism enhanced the ability of the regime to remain in power, the limits and contradictions of this system became increasingly apparent by the late 1970s. Rent-seeking interests operating within the regime privatized state resources at an impressive rate and captured the bureaucratic levers of economic policy implementation. As a bureaucratic organization, the state became more responsive to the particularistic interests of its agents and their allies than to managerial directives aimed at promoting the regime's basic economic policies. One result was the growing incapacity of the regime to circumscribe the scope of rentier activity.

From the perspective of groundnut producers and the owners of local manufacturing industry, patterns of state intervention in the economy became less coherent, more unpredictable and contradictory, and (for peasants) more predatory in nature. The use of state power to promote rentierism began to undercut the coherence of legal structures, long-established market structures, and government programs designed to sustain industrial and agricultural production.

These changes were reflected in the acceleration and intractability of the process of decline of Senegal's agricultural and industrial sectors. Productivity, output, and new investment were already falling when the economy was hit by drought and a severe balance of payments disequilibrium in the 1970s. By the 1980s, Senegal was in the midst of profound economic crisis compounded by the financial bankruptcy of the state. Pervasive clientelism and rentierism compromised the ability of the government to respond to the recession with coherent initiatives aimed at stemming the decline of either the export-oriented agricultural sector or the industrial sector.

State institutions charged with encouraging groundnut production (such as the Ministry of Rural Development) and with appropriating agricultural surpluses on behalf of the state (the groundnut marketing board) ceased to do either in the mid-to-late 1970s. Corruption, fraud, and inefficiency diverted resources away from groundnut producers and from the state treasury, and into the hands of state agents and the regime's rural clients.[35] These informal mechanisms of surplus extraction compounded already high taxation rates imposed on groundnut producers. Peasants responded by withdrawing from official marketing circuits, declining to use inputs such as fertilizer that were sold by the state, and reducing their dependence on groundnut cultivation.[36] Meanwhile, the privatization of groundnut revenues sapped the state treasury.

Analogous processes were under way in the commercial and industrial sectors. Large-scale fraudulent importation and contraband were blatant in the 1980s. Long-established light industries (shoes, textiles, enamel cookware, and cosmetic products) faced competition for the first time from illegally imported goods that began to supply a large segment of the domestic market. Loss of captive markets was reflected in production cutbacks, falling rates of profit, layoffs, and wage compressions in the industrial sector.

The inability of the government to enforce protectionist trade measures set in motion a process of deindustrialization. French interests rapidly divested from light industry and the commercial sector, citing contraband, political turbulence, and secular economic decline as reasons for bailing out. Meanwhile, state banks holding large portfolios of bad loans went bankrupt. Several, including the national development bank, were liquidated. The judiciary hesitated to go after "borrowers of grand standing" who remained under the umbrella of political protection.

The flight of CFA francs into foreign bank accounts accelerated as talk of reforming Franc Zone monetary policies floated in the air. Businesses set up in the 1970s to fill government service and supply contracts folded because the state could not pay its debts. What observers described as "anarchy" prevailed in trading circuits. In the grip of a seemingly in-tractable fiscal crisis, the government adopted policies aimed at taxing the commercial circuit more heavily. Measures like new value-added taxes were for the most part futile: commerce was now essentially an informal sector business. The government seemed unable to adopt measures that would plug the holes that allowed imports to slip through the tax net. Meanwhile, it resisted external pressures to tax urban real estate, the other mainstay of Senegal's rentier class.

In Senegal in the 1980s, there appeared to be no social agent to pro-vide the impetus for reestablishing or creating the economic and legal con-ditions conducive to private investment in production. At a more funda-mental level, it seemed that state power did not exist in the form or measure needed to realize such a project.

Conclusion

In the late 1980s, the neocolonial era ended in Senegal. The groundnut economy, the state groundnut marketing board, the banking sector, the light industrial sector, and once hierarchical trading circuits had collapsed. Market structures created under the hegemony of colonial merchant capi-tal no longer existed to provide the regime with a financial base or to in-tegrate a disparate ruling alliance and political class into markets orga-nized from above by the state. The government had few resources to fuel the patronage machine: rentiers scrambled after rents to be had in the im-port trade and for resources provided by the IMF, the World Bank, and the French government. Abdou Diouf, Senghor's *dauphin*, retained a weaken-ing grip on power. Alliance with the Islamic elite was proving to be just as critical as it had been in the 1960s and 1970s; Diouf, however, appeared to hold less weight in this alliance than his predecessor.[37] The marabouts continued to direct their followers to vote for the ruling party. Their sup-port for the regime was decisive in its electoral victories of the late 1980s, even though it was clear that growing numbers of the faithful declined to follow the order. The marabouts' calls for order also proved to be largely ineffective in April 1989, when Mauritanian traders fled Senegal in the face of urban mobs who attacked the most proximate symbol of their de-clining purchasing power and material distress: the neighborhood shops and shopkeepers.[38] A shudder of fear ran through the Lebanese and French communities in Senegal.

What does this process imply for the possible rise of an indigenous capitalist class in Senegal—one that invests capital in the production of goods and services? The effects are, no doubt, contradictory. Rentierism proves to be unsustainable over time, both as a mode of private accumu-lation and as a mode of political domination. Several processes conspire to undermine its viability. Decay of the productive sectors of the economy makes the flow of cash through Senegalese commercial circuits largely dependent upon the supply of external grants and loans. This inflow cannot be sustained for long in the absence of the creation in Senegal of new wealth. Meanwhile, the demise of centralized and hierarchical trading structures gives rise to competition, which reduces rents. And competition in the commercial sector and the bankruptcy of the state erode the regime's ability to structure patterns of accumulation from above. The net result is pressure that obliges the holders of wealth and power to seek other ways of reproducing their gains.

In theory, then, pressures and incentives that might lead to wealth-generating investment in the domestic economy do exist. And investment opportunities exist, in spite of Senegal's poverty and the lack of the natural resources like lumber, gold deposits, or abundant rain-fed pastoral or farming land that have created possibilities in other parts of Africa. For Senegalese entrepreneurs and firm managers, decline of Dakar's old import-substitution industrial sector creates new openings. Senegalese owners of food-processing industries are appearing in the ranks of the business class. They are becoming more prominent representatives of industrial sector interests as their French counterparts sell out and leave the country, and as the Europeans who remain realize that their clout does not suffice to deliver the kind of government action needed to stem the decline of industry.[39]

Senegal has an offshore fishing industry that has been a site of local private investment and a target of state support since 1980.[40] There is good rice-farming land in the Casamance region, below Gambia. In the north, development of the Senegal River Basin may yet prove to be more than a boondoggle or fiasco (varying according to one's proximity to the state) for the Senegalese. Artisanal-scale groundnut processing is a growing business in the groundnut basin, as is market gardening on the periphery of Dakar. Among those with incentives to invest are the Mouride leaders, for in addition to pursuing private wealth, they are also interested in creating economic organizations that provide material support and institutional infrastructure for their followings. Their bases of privilege and power lie in Senegal; unlike most of the political class, they have reason to invest locally rather than in more secure overseas ventures.

At the same time, however, the very processes that have so weakened the state and the economy have created a context that does not favor the investment of capital. Economic decay and political instability favor speculation and discourage fixed investment. Industrialists argue that the country has become little more than a market for imported consumer goods. In an open economy such as Senegal's, competition can undercut the value of rents without forcing the wealthy to protect their gains by investing locally in productive activities. The weakening of centralized political authority reduces the elite's confidence in the future and opens the political arena to a free-for-all that heightens the unpredictability of outcomes. In a process that is evident in growing resistance to the "Mouridization" of social and economic life, an already parcelized state apparatus is becoming the site of conflicts articulated in terms of ethnic and regional interests.[41] Weakening, fragmentation, and bankruptcy of the state leaves Senegalese business interests without the infrastructural, financial, and political support that has proven to be critical in promoting private investment in other contexts.

Thus, the exhaustion of rentierism as a mode of domination and accumulation will not necessarily give way to capitalist transformation. What replaces it in the short or long term in any given context is a contingent question, and the case of Senegal underscores the fact that *political* contingencies can be decisive in shaping the outcome. In Senegal today, state power does not appear to exist in the measure or forms necessary to promote and support a capitalist project.

Notes

1. I would like to thank Deborah Brautigam, Peter Trubowitz, Robert Vitalis, and the editors of this book. The study is based on field research carried out in Senegal and France between 1984 and 1987, followed by a research trip to Dakar in December 1990 and January 1991. An earlier version of some of the material presented here first appeared in *Journal of Development Studies* 26, no. 3 (1990). A more detailed version of the argument can be found in Catherine Boone, *Merchant Capital and the Roots of State Power in Senegal, 1930–1985* (Cambridge and New York: Cambridge University Press, 1992).

2. See Mark Gallagher, *Rent-Seeking and Economic Growth in Africa* (Boulder: Westview Press, 1991), p. 32.

3. Productive investment is defined here as activity that generates relative surplus value through the combination of capital and wage labor. In the 1970s, some analysts of African class formation argued that productive investment would occur inevitably as local ruling elites accumulated wealth and confronted the inherent limits of neocolonialism and compradorism as ways of reproducing their privilege. Fawzy Mansour, for example, wrote that "a local bourgeoisie is bound to appear . . . and to present itself more and more insistently as a partner and/or a substitute for foreign capital, thus gradually transforming the regime" (as cited by Timothy Shaw, "Beyond Neo-Colonialism: Varieties of Corporatism in Africa," *Journal of Modern African Studies* 20, no. 2 [1982]).

4. Nicola Swainson, *The Development of Corporate Capitalism in Kenya: 1918–1977* (Los Angeles: University of California Press, 1980).

5. Robert Brenner, "The Origins of Capitalist Development: A Critique of Neo-Smithian Marxism," *New Left Review*, no. 104 (1977), p. 67.

6. Peter Flynn, "Class, Clientelism, and Dependency: Some Mechanisms of Internal Dependency and Control," *Journal of Commonwealth and Comparative Politics* 12, no. 2 (1974), pp. 133–156; Robert Fatton, *The Making of a Liberal Democracy: Senegal's Passive Revolution, 1975–1985* (Boulder: Lynne Rienner, 1987), pp. 92–107.

7. Flynn, "Class, Clientelism, and Dependency," p. 148.

8. Nicos Mouzelis, "Political Transitions in Greece and Argentina: Toward a Reorientation of Marxist Political Theory," *Comparative Political Studies* 21, no. 4 (January 1989), pp. 443–466.

9. Janet MacGaffey helps to illustrate this point by providing a contrary case. In Kisangani, Zaire, productive investment occurred when entrepreneurs did not have access to state-mediated rentier activities and when the near collapse of the Zairian state helped to "insulate" investors from the arbitrary predations of state agents. See Janet MacGaffey, *Entrepreneurs and Parasites: The Struggle for Indigenous Capitalism in Zaire* (Cambridge: Cambridge University Press, 1987).

10. Donal Cruise O'Brien, *Saints and Politicians: Essays on the Organization of a Senegalese Peasant Society* (Cambridge: Cambridge University Press, 1975).

11. See O'Brien, *Saints and Politicians;* Edward J. Schumacher, *Politics, Bureaucracy, and Rural Development in Senegal* (Los Angeles: University of California Press, 1975); and Momar Coumba Diop and Mamadou Diouf, *Le Sénégal sous Abdou Diouf* (Paris: Editions Karthala, 1990).

12. Between 40 and 44 percent of government fiscal receipts in the 1960s came from the import trade. The export tax on groundnuts generated another 20 percent. See International Monetary Fund, *Surveys of African Economies*, Vol. 3, *Dahomey, Ivory Coast, Mauritania, Niger, Senegal, Togo, and Upper Volta* (Washington, D.C.: IMF, 1970); and Monique Anson-Meyer, *Mécanismes de l'exploitation en Afrique: L'exemple du Sénégal* (Paris: Editions Cujas, 1974). Nonreimbursed loans from the cooperatives, cash siphoned off at various stages of the marketing process, sums absorbed by the marketing board, etc., represented additional resources extracted from the groundnut marketing circuit.

13. Majhemout Diop, *Histoire des classes sociales dans l'Afrique de l'Ouest*, Vol. 2, *Le Sénégal* (Paris: François Maspero, 1972); Samir Amin, *Le monde des affaires sénégalais* (Paris: Editions de Minuit, 1969).

14. I use the word "businessmen" rather than a gender-neutral term because the vast majority of those to whom I refer are men. In contrast to the situation prevailing in Ghana, Togo, and southern Nigeria, women merchants throughout most of Senegal are confined to the retail trade in foodstuffs. In the 1980s, Senegalese women—often wives of functionaries or other salaried workers—did carve out a prominent place in the contraband import business (in textile goods, jewelry, etc.) conducted via the Dakar-Yoff Airport.

15. *Marchés tropicaux* (September 30, 1961), p. 2385.

16. Schumacher, *Politics, Bureaucracy, and Rural Development*, pp. 136–137.

17. See Amin, *Le monde des affaires sénégalais*, pp. 60–63, and Diop, *Histoire des classes sociales*.

18. Amin, *Le monde des affaires sénégalais;* Diop, *Histoire des classes sociales*, p. 151.

19. Rita Cruise O'Brien, "Lebanese Entrepreneurs in Senegal: Economic Integration and the Politics of Protection," *Cahiers d'études africaines* 15, no. 57 (1975), p. 106.

20. Ibid., p. 112.

21. Amin, *Le monde des affaires sénégalais*, p. 53.

22. Diop, *Histoire des classes sociales*, p. 151.

23. On UNIGES, see Diop, *Histoire des classes sociales*, p. 167; Régine Nguyen Van Chi Bonnardel, *La vie de relations au Sénégal: La circulation des biens* (Dakar: IFAN, 1978); and Sheldon Gellar, *Senegal: An African Nation Between East and West* (Boulder: Westview Press, 1982).

24. UNIGES, "Rapport du Premier Congrès," Dakar, June 1, 1968.

25. Amin, *Le monde des affaires sénégalais*, p. 53.

26. Bonnardel, *La vie de relations au Sénégal*, pp. 823–826, 845–846.

27. The lending institutions were the Société Nationale de Garantie (SONAGA), which began to provide commercial loans, and the Société Nationale des Etudes et de Promotion Industrielle (SONEPI), which loaned to artisanal-scale businesses.

28. *Jeune Afrique*, no. 494 (June 23, 1970), p. 50; *Marchés tropicaux*, (February 7, 1970), p. 306; *Le bulletin de l'Afrique noire*, no. 595 (April 15, 1970), p. 12002.

29. Ibid.

30. Sales of Senegalese groundnuts in the Gambia were estimated at about 10,000 tons a year in 1963/64. Sales to the state marketing agency that year totaled nearly 800,000 tons. In 1979/80, total production was estimated at 780,000 tons. Almost half of this—359,000 tons—escaped state-controlled channels.

31. See Momar-Coumba Diop, "Les affaires mourides à Dakar," *Politique africaine* 1, no. 4 (November 1981), pp. 90–100.

32. Diop, *Histoire des classes sociales*, pp. 167–174.

33. Fatton, *The Making of a Liberal Democracy*, p. 60.

34. Thus, Fatton's reading ("the Senegalese bourgeoisie was calling for the necessary conditions conducive to its crystallization as a national and independent bourgeoisie") seems overdrawn. Anson-Meyer sees the 1968–1971 period as marking the creation of a bourgeoisie tied to foreign capital (*une bourgeoisie liée*). From the perspective of the 1980s, this conclusion also seems to have been premature. See Fatton, *The Making of a Liberal Democracy*, p. 60, and Anson-Meyer, *Mécanismes de l'exploitation*, pp. 92–95.

35. See Nim Casswell, "Autopsie de l'ONCAD: La politique arachidière du Sénégal, 1966–1980," *Politique africaine*, no. 14 (1984), pp. 38–73.

36. Total agricultural production (including food crops) fell below 1979 levels in 1983/84 and 1984/85. Fertilizer use fell from 62,000 tons countrywide in 1967, to 13,000 tons countrywide in 1970, and to 3,000 tons in the groundnut basin only in 1983/84. See World Bank, *Senegal: Tradition, Diversification, and Economic Development* (Washington, D.C.: World Bank, 1974), p. 63; and Eliot Berg Associates, "Adjustment Postponed: Economic Policy Reform in Senegal in the 1990s" (a report prepared under USAID/Dakar contract), Dakar, October 1990, p. 83.

37. See Diop and Diouf, *Le Sénégal sous Abdou Diouf*.

38. Financial losses of the events of April 1989 were estimated at somewhere between 4.5 and 12.5 billion CFA francs. Local food-processing industries (like SENLAIT and CODIPRAL-Nestlé) and the Banque Sénégalo-Koweitienne (BSK) were among the big losers.

39. The CNP (Conseil National du Patronat), formed in 1986, represents the fusion of what remained of UNISYNDI (Union Intersyndicale d'Entreprises et d'Industries), the grouping representing European industrialists in Senegal and the CNPS (Conseil National du Patronat Sénégalais). It seems that the CNPS developed as an offshoot of the GES when the mostly educated, salaried managers of formal sector enterprises broke with the COFIGES. The breakaways apparently saw the GES as a clientelistic arm of the ruling party embracing mostly old-style, unschooled *commerçants*. The fusion of UNISYNDI and the CNPS was provoked by the adoption of World Bank–sponsored structural adjustment measures targeting light industry in 1986. By 1990, the major achievement of the CNP appeared to be the rescinding of many of the new measures aimed at liberalizing the import trade. The president of the CNP in 1990 was Moctar Sow, the Senegalese head of SENLAIT (a firm producing canned milk, which is a food staple in Senegal).

40. The fishing industry has become the target of foreign takeover. See "La pêche industrielle victime de l'état," *Africa International*, no. 238 (May 1991), pp. 52–55.

41. Trouble in the Casamance in the 1980s and early 1990s is an indication of the problem. The activity of Dakar-based land speculators contributed to the rise of what the government defined as the Casamançais secessionist revolt.

9

State Deterioration and Capitalist Development: The Case of Zaire

Janet MacGaffey

Most postcolonial African states have practiced repressive personalistic government and excessive economic regulation. In addition, their administrative capacity and efficiency have declined drastically as newly independent governments have grappled with the problems resulting from the colonial economic legacy of a peripheral capitalist economy and lack of trained and experienced personnel, with Cold War politics and global recession, and with the systematic pillage and self-enrichment of the new governing class. In this context, rent-seeking activity interferes with market forces and the economic environment is unpredictable. The state thus fails almost everywhere to fill the role that it performed in the genesis of Western capitalism, giving rise to a peculiarly African context for the formation and functioning of capitalism, in which cooperation with the state is only rarely an effective tool to further capitalist interests. The Eurocentric preoccupation with the part played by the state in the literature on developing capitalism in Africa has tended to obscure this reality.

This chapter looks at the way people have organized for themselves a rational, dependable system that functions as an alternative to the collapsed official one. It shows that the fostering, creation, and maintenance of various kinds of personal ties, the means by which people organize this alternative system, is now a more useful strategy for any capitalist entrepreneur than cooperation with a corrupt and administratively ineffective state; and it examines the effect of this situation on the development and functioning of capitalism.[1]

Although I will deal with the case of Zaire in detail, I wish to emphasize that Zaire is not unique. What is going on in Zaire is occurring in much of Africa.

Capitalism and the State

Weber considered the notion of rationality to be central to the development of both the modern state and capitalism. He emphasized the impor-

189

tance of the expansion of knowledge and the depersonalization of power and authority in both the political and economic arenas. With the development of the modern state in Europe, political arbitrariness and uncertainty decreased predictability; the economy came to be regulated by economic rather than political decisions. In contrast, the arbitrariness of the state in the patrimonialist systems so prevalent in Africa is a key factor inhibiting the growth of capitalism. When the inherited colonial state was patrimonialized in the postcolonial era, it became the major avenue of upward mobility. As a result it did not serve either capitalist or socialist systems well.[2]

What this situation means in terms of the context in which African capitalists operate is neatly summarized by Thomas Callaghy:

> The calculability nexus is very weak; state arbitrariness, instability, corruption and inefficiency are very high; patrimonial, not bureaucratic, administration and adjudication are the norm; the personalization of power and authority structures, political and nonpolitical, is pervasive; entrepreneurs, both domestic and foreign, do not control all the means of production, especially in the rural areas, as important restrictions on the market use of these factors remain; liquidity preferences remain high and investment patterns lean heavily toward speculation and the short term; technologies remain rudimentary and not easily transferable; important restrictions on a free labor market continue to exist; markets are not well developed and economic, political and social impediments continue to exist, and in many cases formal markets are actually shrinking, while *magendo* economies grow into much of the gap; noncapitalist modes of production remain very important; only partial incorporation into the world economy is the norm; national financial, banking and monetary systems are quite unsophisticated; and transportation and communications infrastructures, already weak, are disintegrating in many areas of the continent.[3]

These conditions are general, even if there are (or may be) exceptions. In Nigeria, in the early years of independence, state support brought about what has been referred to as "nurture capitalism."[4] Opinions differ on the nature of capitalist development in Kenya.[5] But several observers conclude that although in most of Africa the conditions outlined by Callaghy are pervasive and rent-seeking prevails, indigenous capitalism of some sort is, nevertheless, in the process of development. One study concludes that "the emergence of capitalist social relations of production constitutes the central dynamic process in a wide range of African societies, despite important variations in the specific features of this process."[6] Another study points out that foreign capital did not seriously invest in manufacturing in most African colonies until the end of the 1950s, so that the lateness of African industrialization is not solely symptomatic of the weakness of local capitalism; and at least in some countries, the gains of indigenous capitalism, from such a recent and relatively small base, are an achievement that offers promise rather than cause for concern.[7]

Even in Zaire, a nascent indigenous bourgeoisie is emerging, despite a situation apparently inimical to any such process.[8] Faced with a predatory state and a politicized economy, how do potential capitalists gain access to resources and set up the financing and infrastructure they need? What strategies and skills must they develop, lacking state support and in the absence of calculability and rationality? In coping with this particularly African context, what specifically African solutions can we discern?

Zaire Since Independence

Belgium handed over political but not economic control upon Zaire's independence in 1960. The power of the new dominant class was based on control of the state, not of the economy, and on partnerships with foreign business interests that retained control of large-scale economic enterprise. Under President Mobutu, Zaire became a patrimonial state. Mobutu created a highly personalized and centralized government; the single-party MPR (Mouvement Populaire de la Révolution) was a mere propaganda arm of the state apparatus rather than a political machine. Mobutu granted power, privileges, and material goods in return for the support, loyalty, and obedience of officials and administrators. This pattern was replicated throughout all levels of government by means of a patronage system.

After Mobutu came to power in 1965, the strategy of the state-based class was to develop a public sector strong enough to serve its economic interests. The reasons for the failure of this strategy are complex. They include the colonial legacy of a low level of education and lack of experience in government or management for Zairians; economic policies carried over from the colonial period (which neglected food production and developed an economy to export primary raw materials); the economic disruption caused by a disastrous indigenization of the economy in the Zairianization decrees of 1973–1976; the seemingly unbounded greed of a powerful few in the governing class; falling commodity prices on the world market for Zaire's principal exports, along with the huge increase of petroleum prices; and a large national debt arising from extravagant investments during the economic boom of the early 1970s. Officials and administrators must thus squeeze wealth out of their position in the state apparatus through corrupt practices to maintain the patronage that is the basis for their power, weakening the state administration and decreasing its revenues. The state is unable to collect many of its taxes, provide social services, or maintain, let alone develop, transportation infrastructure; the official marketing system barely functions; justice is frequently corrupt, and regulations cannot be implemented nor laws enforced.[9]

These problems are compounded by the spiraling economic crisis that began in the mid-1970s and its accompanying high inflation and devastating decline in real wages. In 1990, in Kinshasa, they had fallen to a mere 6 percent of their real value on the eve of independence in 1960.[10] This means that anyone in the official wage and salary sector needed to find means to increase their income several times over in order to survive and support a family.

The failure of the public sector, the decline in the administrative capacity of the state, impossibly low wages at all levels of society, and rampant scarcities of goods have contributed to a rapid expansion in "second economy" activities[11] and to the increasingly predatory nature of the state.

In this situation, when the state is unable to implement laws and regulations and when the economic activity outside its control is on a huge scale, it is no longer the principal avenue of class formation. Holders of state office continue to use their positions to gain access to the more lucrative activities of the second economy, but cooperation with the state becomes decreasingly useful to capitalist entrepreneurs and officials alike. As Paul Kennedy comments, paradoxically, ·

> One of the major consequences of statism—in addition to economic stagnation and even decline—is that the state loses much of its control over the formal economy anyway, and therefore its ability to obtain revenue and direct resources, whether for productive or *essentially parasitic purposes.*[12]

We need then to investigate the strategies people use in Zaire to compensate for the absence of an effective state and a rational predictable economic environment. Despite the problems resulting from severe state decline, it is less detrimental to capitalist development than in some other countries—for example, Uganda. The development of capitalism is always historically specific, so we will now turn to a brief historical outline of the process of capitalist penetration, the relations of capitalism with the state, and the different forms of capitalism present in Zaire today.

Capitalism in Zaire

Zaire was almost unique in Africa in the colonial period in the power of its "Colonial Trinity": the state, the big companies, and the church.[13] The state provided a degree of support for the mining and plantation companies unequaled in other colonies, granting enormous land concessions and backing up the recruitment and control of labor with state force, as well as imposing a head tax that drove people to seek work to get the money to pay it. The Catholic church, which ran the schools, supported this endeavor with an education designed to produce a labor force that was literate but lacked the skills to advance beyond agricultural work or wage labor. On the eve of independence, the Congo was the most industrialized country in Africa south of the Sahara, except for South Africa: in 1959, 10 percent of salaried workers worked in the manufacturing industry, the highest rate for industrial workers on the continent.[14]

After independence, as the administrative efficacy of the state declined with patrimonialization, this degree of industrialization was not sustained. Since the onset of the economic crisis in the mid-1970s, it has drastically deteriorated. Industry is now functioning far below capacity because of the shortage of foreign exchange to buy essential materials and spare parts. Zaire is no longer the favorable environment it was for multinational capitalist enterprises; they, like everyone else, must confront Zaire's political and economic problems. Their size and power, however, give them significant advantages over businesses owned by nationals. They operate effectively by becoming completely self-sufficient in terms of transportation, communication, and the provision of supplies, services, and affordable goods for their workers. They do this by routinely having their own river barges, airplanes, road maintenance systems, generators, and radio telephones; by running company stores and dispensaries; by employing agents to deal with the bureaucracy; and by organizing for themselves imports of all they need. Politically they are sufficiently influential to evade or manipulate political constraints.

Like the multinationals, the "parasitic capitalists" of the state-based class also have the advantage of political power. This form of capitalism consists of the large-scale enterprises of this class. State power has been used to acquire private property and businesses, and the surplus is channeled into the pockets of "a parasitic bourgeoisie whose wealth and business interests derive from their political and administrative positions."[15] The term "parasitic" aptly reflects the way in which those in the top level of society have used their virtually unlimited power to pillage the natural riches of their country and amass vast fortunes. They squander profits in conspicuous consumption or deposit them in foreign bank accounts, rather than using them to expand their enterprises or to invest and help develop the local economy. Their position in the state has enabled them to manipulate legislation in their favor and gain access to scarce resources in order to suck the economic lifeblood of their country for their own benefit. In turn, their immense wealth, political power, and connections protect them from the consequences of bad management; they can afford to plunder unheedingly.[16] The neglect and mismanagement of their vast enterprises in Zaire have contributed to the decline in the national production of food and export crops.

Despite this unfavorable context, however, a nascent true bourgeoisie of local capitalists who do not hold political positions has also emerged. These entrepreneurs invest in productive enterprise for the local market and manage and expand their businesses in rational capitalist fashion. This incipient bourgeoisie is as yet small and its future uncertain. Along with its emergence, however, we should note the enormous expansion in the 1980s of small and medium-sized enterprises. Kennedy notes the "tendency to overlook the degree to which everywhere small and medium-sized firms constitute the numerical majority. Together their economic and political weight is also very formidable."[17] A few specifics indicate just how formidable this numerical majority is. An International Labour Organisation survey in the mid-1980s found 12,000 informal sector businesses in Kinshasa. In 1985, informal transport enterprises, operating outside the law, provided nearly half the city's transportation. Two-thirds of Zaire's expenditures on construction occur in the informal sector; in 1985, unplanned growth accounted for 70 percent of the residential urban area of Kinshasa and accommodated two-thirds of the population.[18] The economy could not function without these enterprises. They represent an economic base for the subordinated classes that did not exist in the 1960s and thus a power shift in society. This shift was manifested in the overt political protests of 1990, which resulted in the formation of multiple political parties and, by October 1991, in the wresting of power from Mobutu by the opposition.[19]

Such enterprises in retail trade and services, construction, and transport provide a starting point for the accumulation of capital and experience. Some of these entrepreneurs may be able to take advantage of political and economic circumstances to develop large-scale capitalistic businesses in the future, as did the entrepreneurs of the new indigenous bourgeoisie in the past. I have documented this process for Kisangani and North Kivu,[20] where I found the same progress—from transport, real estate, and trade, to the production of food and export crops, to manufacturing—that other chapters in this book document for other African countries.

We will now examine the ways in which business owners must operate to be successful in Zaire's current economic and political context.

Responses to the Decline of the Official System

As official economic organization and infrastructure have deteriorated until they barely function, a parallel unofficial system has arisen. Production and distribution for the second economy has expanded, and people have organized transportation, information systems, and means to finance their enterprises for themselves.

Since imported goods and materials are scarce because of the shortage of foreign exchange for official imports, entrepreneurs organize their own supply sources through smuggling networks and contacts in other countries and in the customs, who purchase and ship goods for them and help them evade border controls.

The enormous scale on which primary export commodities are smuggled out of the country and goods are imported in exchange indicates the importance of this illicit commerce in the economy. Diamond smuggling, for example, developed after independence in the early 1960s; by 1979, the equivalent of 68 percent of official production was being smuggled.[21] More gold is smuggled than is officially exported, according to a recent study.[22] From 30 to 60 percent of national coffee production is smuggled out of Zaire annually. Ivory poaching and illegal export have decimated Zaire's vast elephant herds to the verge of extinction. People solve the problem of the unavailability of foreign exchange and therefore their inability to import the goods they need for their businesses through this illegal trade. In return for smuggled exports come manufactured goods, foodstuffs, vehicles and spare parts, fuel, construction materials, and pharmaceuticals.[23] For those who do not themselves smuggle or have access to smugglers, personal connections to suppliers, such as the managers of the big import houses, can make the difference between being able to count on a supply of goods so that one's business can flourish and an often fruitless, time-consuming search and dissatisfied customers. Such personal ties organize not only Zaire's retail trade but the wholesale trade as well: one Asian wholesaler in Kisangani stated emphatically that "90 percent of wholesalers operate by means of personal connections."

Enterprises are financed as well as supplied outside the official system. Foreign exchange can be obtained through smuggling or on the parallel money market that functions at specific locations in cities. Smugglers to Congo Brazzaville take manufactured goods, foodstuffs, and gold to sell for CFA francs, which, on their return, they sell to the "Dames de Bronze" (illegal foreign exchange dealers) at "Le Beach" in Kinshasa.[24]

Credit is virtually unobtainable through the banks, except for large companies and the politically powerful. Banks favor foreigners over nationals, and members of the foreign business community have an advantage over nationals with regard to credit anyway, since they offer one another interest-free loans.[25] Savings cooperatives and credit unions exist but are obstructed by the big financial institutions.[26] The majority finance their enterprises by forming rotating credit associations, common throughout Africa, in which members of a small group each contribute monthly to the pot and take turns drawing out the whole amount. They are known in Zaire as *likelemba* and *musiki*.

The worst infrastructural problem is transportation. Shortage of foreign exchange for road repair machinery, rolling stock, ferries, spare parts, and fuel, and the embezzlement of tax revenues and aid money have resulted in appalling rural roads and a barely functioning parastatal river and rail system. Yet huge quantities of goods somehow move as they are smuggled and in other ways illicitly traded. How is this possible?

The trucks and other vehicles, spare parts, and fuel that are in such short supply are imported illegally, sometimes through direct barter for standardized quantities of export commodities.[27] Smugglers employ porters who headload their goods along forest paths, or organize convoys of bicycles loaded with goods. These transporters make better money than they can in the formal wage sector.[28] Some second economy trade simply depends parasitically on the official system: drivers for big companies illegally take on passengers and freight and pocket the fees; other transportation workers participate in a system of reciprocal favors to give those with whom they have personal connections reduced or free passage for persons and goods.

The information infrastructure is likewise nonfunctional. The telegraph, telephone, and mail systems are hopelessly slow and unreliable. Businesses of any consequence have their own radio telephones; otherwise, market information comes through personal networks.

The response to the decline of the official system, then, has been to utilize personal ties. The scarcity of goods is overcome by personal supply lines or by connections to persons in charge of allocation. Lack of foreign exchange is remedied by the parallel money market, which is supplied through smuggling networks. The credit that is denied to all but the powerful is organized on the basis of mutual trust and cooperation between individuals. In general, the reciprocal favors of personal relationships help to solve the problems of the breakdown of transportation and information infrastructure.

We will now examine the different kinds of personal ties that in these ways supply a degree of the rationality and predictability that are otherwise conspicuous by their absence.

The Nature of Personal Ties

Personal ties can be reciprocal, between persons of equal power and status, or they can be relations of inequality categorized as patron-client ties. James Scott warns against the indiscriminate use of this term to refer to any relationship of personal dependency, regardless of how exploitative it may be. He avoids the evaluative terms of patron and client by speaking of relations of personal dependency between members of different classes. The question of how equitable or exploitative particular ties are then becomes a matter for empirical analysis rather than an assumption.[29]

The political system, as mentioned above, functions through ties of political patronage. Members of the emergent indigenous bourgeoisie must have some such connections to those wielding political power and holding official positions to facilitate interactions with the bureaucracy. Other ties between fractions of capital consist of the business connections some of these local capitalists have to big companies and multinationals, acquired during their years as employees before they established their own enterprises.

Other examples of relations of personal dependency between individuals in different classes in Zaire are those between unlicensed traders and farmers. The unlicensed traders go out to the rural areas where the official marketing system is defunct and buy up food crops to supply the urban markets. They establish relations of dependency with the farmers to whom they pay an advance to purchase their harvest. They may pay in cash or in kind, bartering needed manufactured goods that are otherwise locally unobtainable or too costly for the farmer to buy. In the absence of competition, the trader can set the price or terms of exchange as he, or she, wishes; it is set low enough to transfer all risk to the farmer and does not reflect the market value at the time of harvest. The farmers may be entirely dependent on these traders to market their crops, so the power wielded by the latter in this monopoly situation makes this a very unequal relationship.

Traders will also have more reciprocal relations of personal dependency with truckers whose routes they regularly travel, who give them reduced rates. Once in the city, they have connections among the market women who buy the produce they supply, and whom they will allow to defer payment until after the goods are sold.[30] The traders thus finance both the farmer and the retailer through personal ties, providing to both a service they can count on and compensating for its unavailability in the official system.

Less often discussed in the literature than patronage relations, but widespread and highly significant for coping with the current situation in Zaire today, are reciprocal ties, which vary according to class level. John Waterbury refers to such ties as cronyism: links between coequals. He considers them too short-lived to provide the minimal durability that patronage requires.[31] The reciprocal ties I identify in Zaire, however, are based on durable relationships and are of as long-lasting significance as patronage. Particular to the dominant class is the use of personal ties for reciprocal favors based on membership in alumni groups of schools and universities, on connections in business organizations such as the Lions International and the Rotary Club, and on the ties deliberately created and carefully maintained between persons with differing areas of expertise known as *relations*. These latter ties are set up across ethnic boundaries. Referred to as "the new tribalism" by members of the dominant class, they are established and maintained between individuals who, for example, hold positions in the bureaucracy, education, transportation, the judiciary, etc., whose expertise can be useful in times of need to expedite personal or business affairs.[32] They constitute an inner organization for the dominant class that serves to maintain its boundaries by the exclusion of persons who do not have such connections.[33] John Rapley, in Chapter 3 of this book, also emphasizes the importance in the Côte d'Ivoire of intraclass personal relations.

Bonds of ethnicity, kinship, and locality are the basis for other kinds of personal relations involving reciprocal favors, mutual confidence, and trust. They constitute "social assets for the poor," since they create earning opportunities for them and are the counterpart of the more privileged income-generating opportunities of the powerful.[34] Cooperation depends on trust, which in turn depends on common values and a common ethic, the same ways of thinking and behaving, the same methods of working, and the same predictable reactions. All these can arise from common ethnicity, from the bonds of kinship, family, friendship, and neighborhood or village of origin. Such bonds enable individuals to tap into smuggling networks, make it possible to obtain and ship goods from other countries from a personal contact resident there, and help to minimize tariffs as the goods come into Zaire. Thus, those who need an airplane ticket when they are scarce, reduced freight charges, or information on erratic schedules can find them if they have a *"frère"* (someone who is a relative or a member of the same ethnic group) who works for Air Zaire; a trader with a kinsman who is a riverboat captain can reduce her operational costs because her goods come down the river for free; a market retailer can supply her stall with wax-print cloth if a family member works for a big wholesaler. Thus, for example, members of the Tetela ethnic group are dominant in the ownership of pharmacies in one zone of Kisangani because they are privileged in getting their supplies from a particular Tetela official in the Ministry of Health.

Life in Zaire operates through these personal ties. They provide cooperation and organization that can be counted on. The mutual trust and confidence on which they are founded substitute for the protection and sanctions that a functioning state should provide. For any capitalist entrepreneur, developing, maintaining, and activating such relationships is one of the most critical skills for the successful operation of a business; manipulating personal ties is a crucial strategy for coping with the exigencies of the current political and economic situation and the inadequacies of government and infrastructure.

Costs and Benefits

What are the costs and the possible benefits for the development of capitalism in this context? It is an important question how far capitalism can develop in a situation in which personal deals, connections, and ties of clientelism prevail over the market competition that, ideally, should foster such development by forcing entrepreneurs to compete through technological innovation or organizational superiority. My view is that, in Zaire's patrimonial state, the trust and mutual cooperation of the personal connections of the second economy presently supply a sufficient degree of predictability and rationality to allow local capitalism a measure of success. While this reliance on personal connections must constrain the full development of capitalism according to the ideal model, the degree to which it does so is not evident. It should also be remembered that the ideal of free market competition and freedom from personal ties has seldom, if ever, been realized in the history of global capitalist development. As the newspapers continually reveal, personal deals frequently prevail over market rationality in the developed West and other parts of the world besides Africa. Such dealing is simply more highly developed in Africa than it is in the West, as a response to drastic state decline and economic crisis.

Hernando DeSoto has pointed out some of the costs of such a situation in his study of the informal sector of Peru. Enterprises operating on the margins of the law must bear the costs of the bribes they pay to evade it. They also suffer from the absence of a legal system that promotes and supports economic efficiency.[35] Furthermore, the organization of credit, supplies, raw materials, transportation, etc., through personal connections and personal arrangements, though more efficacious than trying to operate in the official system in Zaire's current political and economic situation, is extremely time-consuming.

Operating costs are lowered for small and medium-sized enterprises when the state provides services for all. In Zaire, where the state does not do this, these enterprises, which are the ones least able to afford the costs of providing such services for themselves, suffer a disadvantage.

However, the costs of informality that DeSoto describes, and the costs of paying directly for services that the state is generally supposed to provide, are offset to some degree by the reduction of operating costs by entrepreneurs who rely on the reciprocal favors of personal ties or avoid taxes, licensing fees, and other regulations by operating in the second economy. In some cases also, small-scale entrepreneurs solve transportation problems by activating personal ties to operate parasitically on the large companies of the official system.

There are other ways besides tax evasion the second economy may reduce costs. For example, fuel stolen from a copper mining company in South Shaba is transported to North Shaba and sold to truckers who travel through the rural areas to buy up the food harvest. This illegal trade ensures sufficient fuel supplies to offset shortages in the official economy and enables the harvest to be marketed, thus keeping food prices in the towns lower than they would otherwise be.[36] In effect, the mining company is subsidizing the urban food supply. The cost to the mining company is doubtless passed on to the consumer, but since minerals are exported, this cost is not borne by Zairians.

Another negative effect for the economy as a whole that results from this system is that when people provide for their own services, they tend to stop putting pressure on the state to provide them, aggravating the problem for other producers who are unable to provide services for themselves. But it must be noted that in Zaire the state no longer has the capacity to finance and organize in any sustained and efficient way the public services that it should provide. Such pressure could not have any effect in the absence of very radical political change and reform of administrative capacity.

On the other side of the cost-benefit equation, the second economy offers opportunities for social mobility unavailable in the official economy. The rich and powerful have superior access to resources and to the more lucrative activities of the second economy. They consolidate their social position by participating in this economy, but they have no institutionalized means to monopolize its activities, many of which are accessible to ordinary people. Reliance on the relatively lucrative activities of the second economy for accumulation of venture and working capital helps, in some cases, to make possible the establishment and expansion of capitalist firms. People can trade without licenses, smuggle, grow crops for illegal trade, and produce goods and services in the informal sector to make more money than they can through the inadequate wages and salaries of formal-sector employment. They can also in this way evade the fees and taxes that raise the costs of legal commerce. They may by these means accumulate enough to invest in and expand businesses sufficiently to become capitalist entrepreneurs.[37]

Political accommodation of some sort is necessary as enterprises become large in scale, but some sort of arrangement is possible that avoids takeover by the state or ruin from its intervention. As businesses increase in size and become visible to the authorities, they start to become part of the official economy, and the state moves to regulate and tax them. This does not necessarily mean that they are absorbed by the state, which even if it wants to frequently lacks the capacity to do. Recent follow-up on some of the large indigenous capitalist enterprises I studied in 1980 showed that three were indeed in decline, but not because of state intervention. They had successfully survived such intervention in radicalization and demonetization.[38] In one case, decline was due to succession problems in the company's management and in two cases to the economic situation following the structural adjustment reforms of 1983 and the resulting difficulties of importing materials for manufacturing. Some sort of negotiated accommodation is needed with the state, but the entrepreneur can still function independently and outside state control. Tom Forrest has likewise emphasized the existence of private trajectories of accumulation in Nigeria that occur without access to state resources.

Conclusion

The organization of the economy through personal ties has provided some degree of predictability and rationality in the face of economic crisis and the drastic decline in the functioning of the official system caused by state decay. As Eva Bellin has pointed out, in the cronyism system prevailing in Tunisia, personal ties may abet and do not necessarily subvert the rational use of economic resources. In Tunisia, they constitute an economically rational and justifiable response to two problems: the overextended state and the lack of information.[39] In Zaire, they constitute a similar response to a decaying infrastructure, scarcity of goods and foreign exchange, and lack of credit. The enterprises of the emergent bourgeoisie constitute an advancement and expansion of productivity, despite the lack of state provision of infrastructure and protection.

Zairian capitalists have thus found their own unique solutions to some of their particular and specific problems and means other than state cooperation and support to promote expansion of their enterprises. How successfully they will continue to do so cannot be known in advance. As Paul Lubeck says:

> In fact, there is no correct or universally applicable model for predicting a successful transition to capitalism during a concrete historical conjuncture; rather, the particular combination of social forces depends upon the character of the precapitalist social formation, the conditions of the historical conjuncture, the nature of the world economy and state system, and the dialectical interplay of subjective and objective forces in a particular society.[40]

As this book goes to press, Zaire is again in the throes of political upheaval as the struggle to achieve multiparty democracy threatens to bring the country to the brink of civil war. I have argued that the second economy has enabled people to defy the state, to survive, and even to get wealthy. The new economic base thus created for the subordinated classes has changed the balance of power in Zairian society.[41] One can see this change as a contributory factor to the overt opposition to the president expressed in the present struggle. If these present political troubles provide opportunities for entrepreneurs, as has been the case in the past, the degree to which the new society that emerges provides a stable political system, a nurturing state, and supportive legislation will determine whether sustained expansion of the new capitalist enterprises that may arise can this time take place.

Notes

1. Earlier versions of this chapter were presented at the workshop on African bourgeoisies at Queen's University, Ontario, April 1991, and at the American Political Science Association meetings, August 1991, in Washington, D.C. I am grateful for comments and insights gained from participants at both, most especially those of Colin Leys.

2. Thomas M. Callaghy, "The State and the Development of Capitalism in Africa: Theoretical, Historical, and Comparative Reflections," in D. Rothchild and N. Chazan, *The Precarious Balance: State and Society in Africa* (Boulder: Westview Press, 1988).

3. Ibid., p. 78.

4. Sayre Schatz, *Nigerian Capitalism* (Berkeley: University of California Press, 1977), pp. 3–4.

5. The received view in Kenya has been that, in contrast to much of Africa, capitalist development and industrialization have been relatively successful, and that the relationship between capital and the state has been extremely important in this process. After independence the African merchant class was ready to move into large-scale capitalist production. The postcolonial state provided these indigenous capitalists with advantages that had been denied them during the colonial period; by the 1970s they were moving into industrial concerns with greater possibilities for profit and market domination. The state strongly supported these moves, mainly through credit institutions, and was crucial in mediating the relationship between foreign capital and the indigenous bourgeoisie (Nicola Swainson, *The Development of Corporate Capitalism in Kenya, 1918–1977* [Berkeley: University of California Press, 1988], Chapter 5, pp 284–286). Himbara's research, however, suggests that this view is mistaken.

6. John Sender and Sheila Smith, *The Development of Capitalism in Africa* (London: Methuen, 1986), p. 128.

7. Paul Kennedy, *African Capitalism: The Struggle for Ascendancy* (Cambridge: Cambridge University Press, 1988), p. 87.

8. Janet MacGaffey, *Entrepreneurs and Parasites: The Struggle for Indigenous Capitalism in Zaire* (Cambridge: Cambridge University Press, 1987).

9. For example, the law liberalizing prices of the structural adjustment reforms of 1983 is simply not implemented for local produce in rural areas. Local government, in several regions of the country, continues to impose price controls.

10. For details on the impossibility of making a living in the wage and salary sector at any level of Zairian society, see Janet MacGaffey with Vwakyanakazi Mukohya, Rukarangira wa Nkera, Brooke Grundfest Schoepf, Makwala ma Mavambu ye Beda, and Walu Engundu, *The Real Economy of Zaire* (London: James Currey; Philadelphia: University of Pennsylvania Press, 1991), Introduction.

11. Defined here as unmeasured and unrecorded economic activities that deprive the state of revenue or involve misuse of state position. Some of these activities are illegal; others are legal in themselves but made illegal because they are carried out to avoid taxation or to in some other way deprive the state of revenue.

12. Kennedy, *African Capitalism*, p. 77. Emphasis mine.

13. Crawford Young, *Politics in the Congo* (Princeton: Princeton University Press, 1965), p. 32.

14. Jean-Louis Lacroix, *Industrialisation au Congo: La transformation* (Paris: Mouton, 1967), pp. 25–27.

15. John Iliffe, *The Emergence of African Capitalism* (Minneapolis: University of Minnesota Press, 1982), p. 81.

16. These points are developed further in MacGaffey, *Entrepreneurs and Parasites*, pp. 62–64, 186–196. See also Crawford Young and Thomas Turner, *The Rise and Decline of the Zairian State* (Madison: University of Wisconsin Press, 1985), p. 180.

17. Kennedy, *African Capitalism*, p. 115.

18. Philippe Delis and Christian Girard, "L'immobilization privée du sol à Kinshasa," *Les annales de la recherche urbaine*, no. 25, January 1985, pp. 34–53.

19. I have developed these arguments in Janet MacGaffey "Initiatives from Below: Zaire's 'Other Path' to Social and Economic Restructuring," in Goran Hyden and Michael Bratton, eds., *Governance and Politics in Africa* (Boulder: Lynne Rienner, 1992).

20. MacGaffey, *Entrepreneurs and Parasites*.

21. Fernand Bezy, Jean-Philippe Peemans, and Jean-Marie Wautelet, *Accumulation et sous-developpement au Zaire, 1960–1980* (Louvain-la-Neuve: Presse Universitaire de Louvain, 1981), p. 172.

22. Vwakyanakazi Mukohya, "Import and Export in the Second Economy in North Kivu," in MacGaffey et al., *Real Economy of Zaire*.

23. Ibid.

24. Makwala ma Mavambu ye Beda, "The Trade in Food Crops, Manufactured Goods and Mineral Products in the Frontier Zone of Luozi, Lower Zaire," in MacGaffey et al., *Real Economy of Zaire*, p. 111.

25. MacGaffey, *Entrepreneurs and Parasites*, p. 77.

26. Ibid., p. 193.

27. Vwakyanakazi, "Import and Export," p. 61.

28. Makwala, "Trade in Food Crops," pp. 103–113; Rukarangira wa Nkera and Brooke Grundfest Schoepf, "Unrecorded Trade in Southeast Shaba and Across Zaire's Southern Border," in MacGaffey et al., *Real Economy of Zaire*, pp. 78–81.

29. James Scott, "Patronage or Exploitation?" in Ernest Gellner and John Waterbury, eds., *Patrons and Clients* (London: Duckworth, 1977), p. 36.

30. Makwala, "Trade in Food Crops," pp. 114–117.

31. John Waterbury, "An Attempt to Put Patrons and Clients in Their Place," in Gellner and Waterbury, *Patrons and Clients*, p. 336.

32. MacGaffey, *Entrepreneurs and Parasites*, pp. 207–208.

33. Studies of Brazil and Andalusia have detailed the personal networks that constitute the inner organization of classes. In Andalusia, highly developed institutions of sponsorship and introduction extend the personal influence of the members of the upper class well beyond the network of friends and relatives and make better instruments for getting things done than do the networks of the lower class. Anthony Leeds, "Brazilian Careers and Social Structures: A Case History and Model," in Dwight B. Heath, ed., *Contemporary Cultures and Societies of Latin America*, 2d ed. (New York: Random House, 1974), p. 292; John Corbin, "Social Class and Patron-Clientage in Andalusia: Some Problems of Comparing Ethnographies," *Anthropological Quarterly* 52, no. 2 (1979), pp. 108–109.

34. N. Vijay Jagannathan, *Informal Markets in Developing Countries* (Oxford: Oxford University Press, 1987), p. 29.

35. Hernando DeSoto, *The Other Path: The Invisible Revolution in the Third World* (New York: Harper and Row, 1989), p. 158.

36. Rukarangira and Schoepf, "Unrecorded Trade," pp. 87–88.

37. Following Kennedy, capitalist enterprises are defined as those employing a firm-type structure and operating in the modern sector. Their business activities are oriented toward profit and the achievement of expansion and capitalist accumulation (Kennedy, *African Capitalism*, p. 8).

38. The failure of Zairianization resulted in heavy pressure on the government to extend control over the economy. In the 1975 radicalization decree, the state took over large-scale commercial, agricultural, and industrial enterprises, except for ranches, plantations, and most multinationals. In the demonetization of 1980, when the currency was changed and all large-denomination bills had to be exchanged for new ones in the space of five days, many people lost huge sums of money and many businesses were bankrupted.

39. Eva Bellin, "The Rentier Paradigm in the Middle East: Comparative Lessons from Tunisia and Saudi Arabia," paper presented at the American Political Science convention, Washington, D.C., 1991.

40. Paul M. Lubeck, ed., *The African Bourgeoisie: Capitalist Development in Nigeria, Kenya, and the Ivory Coast* (Boulder: Lynne Rienner, 1987), p. 11.

41. MacGaffey et al., *Real Economy of Zaire*, Conclusion.

10

An Alliance of Oil and Maize?
The Response of Indigenous
and State Capital to
Structural Adjustment in Nigeria

Paul M. Lubeck & Michael J. Watts

> The solidarity bloc in Germany, then, rested upon two strong pillars of
> vested interests. Clearly, its successful functioning was contingent upon
> the ability of both groups to impose this policy on the rest of . . . [soci-
> ety]. . . . Thus the compromise between iron and rye had to be supple-
> mented by [other] compacts . . . [and] for these reasons the solidarity bloc
> could not offer a quiet refuge of eternal harmony of interest. It could be
> maintained only by continual hard bargaining and it was perpetually
> menaced by disruption and disintegration. (Alexander Gerschenkron,
> *Bread and Democracy in Germany* [Ithaca, N.Y.: Cornell University
> Press, 1989], pp. 47–48.)

Nigerian Indigenous
Accumulation in Comparative Perspective

What is to be made of contemporary Nigerian capitalism and the Nigerian
social structure of accumulation? In the debates over indigenous capitalist
development and the comparative political economy of "catching up,"
Nigeria occupies an ambiguous position. This ambiguity turns on whether
this big, brash, oil-rich economy is compared with other sub-Saharan
African states, or with a select club of newly industrializing countries
(NICs) that, according to Alain Lipietz at least, Nigeria appeared poised to
enter during the booming 1970s.[1] If one compares the Nigerian economy
to other African capitalisms—in terms of capital owned and/or controlled
by private and public sector accumulators—then the massive scale of indigenous capital accumulation in Nigeria surely has no African rival on
the continent except South Africa. However, it is Nigeria's fortuitous population base and its hydrocarbon resources that largely explain its preemi-
nence in African indigenous accumulation, rather than any intensive mode
of accumulation arising from advanced productive technologies, entrepreneurial innovation, or the organizational discipline of a dynamic, cohesive,
capitalist class. More specifically, the strength of indigenous accumulation

arises from Nigeria's large internal market (90 million inhabitants), the export revenues and manufactured products derived from its petroleum and natural gas reserves, the relative success of state-mandated indigenization of industry decrees for entry into all sectors, and not least its aggressive, if somewhat anarchic, entrepreneurial culture. But do African comparisons actually suggest that Nigeria is capable of moving beyond backwardness and sluggish import substitution toward "NICdom" at a moment of unprecedented globalization of production, finance, and consumption? The World Bank in its new *Global Economic Prospects* report (1993) clearly thinks not.

Alternatively, if Nigeria is compared to other newly industrializing states in Latin America, South Asia, and East Asia who have entered, or are now poised to enter, export-oriented industrialization, it is incontrovertibly a failed NIC. To return to the lexicon of Lipietz and the French regulationists, Nigeria represents a pathetically failed and hollowed-out peripheral fordism. Nigeria's petroleum-financed capitalist road and ambitious import-substitution industrialization strategy produced, in spite of the country's unquestioned regional hegemony during the 1970s and early 1980s, a striking lack of anything like systematic capitalist accumulation. As the *Economist* put it in 1986, what Nigerian oil-based accumulation produced was a sort of "organized chaos," a "massive foreign debt whose size nobody knows, a mountain of expensive equipment that mostly does not work and a military dictatorship."[2] It is not difficult to inventory the causes of failure: unregulated foreign borrowing; an absence of public sector accountability and record keeping; the mushrooming of parastatal agencies; intense regional, ethnic, and religious conflict that has rendered the society ungovernable except by military decree; and cleavages within the embryonic bourgeoisie so severe that any unified class project appears futile.

Historically, like so many OPEC states, the mismanagement of petroleum rents was so egregious that even foreign exchange earnings of $25 billion in 1980 were, by 1983, insufficient to stave off economic crisis and rising foreign debt. When the Babangida government accepted a World Bank–administered structural adjustment program (SAP) in 1986, greater fiscal discipline produced an unprecedented economic depression, widespread social misery, and the doubling of external debt from about $17.5 billion in 1983 to $36 billion in 1992.[3] Not only was Nigeria's highly protected manufacturing sector unable to replicate the problematic Latin American model of deep import-substitution industrialization—i.e., intermediate industries (steel, chemicals, paper, cement) and engineering industries (automobiles)—but the import-export boom had also bust, and in a dramatic fashion. In the wake of the deflationary policies of the SAP, Nigeria was reclassified as a low-income country when its GNP per capita income average crashed from $1,172 in 1982 to about $350 in 1989

(Figure 10.1). Nigeria's ambition and oil-driven euphoria had, to employ the current World Bank parlance, turned to economic regress.[4]

Comparisons with the East Asian NICs underscore the relative immaturity of Nigeria's indigenous capital and the chronic dearth of state capacity during the petroleum boom, what in Weberian terms is a total lack of calculability and bureaucratic-legal rationality. When compared with the ethnically diverse "second tier" NICs of Southeast Asia—Malaysia, Thailand, and Indonesia—Nigeria's performance continues to be singularly unimpressive, even though it shares many social and structural similarities with Indonesia and Malaysia. Central to any understanding of the disjuncture between Nigeria's failure and the Asian NICs' successes is a theorization of the relationships between economic and political elites articulated within a capitalist "developmentalist" state.[5] Such states support indigenous capital with financial and fiscal subsidies, technical assistance and marketing information, cheap inputs from intermediate (state) industries, and accumulation opportunities from the protected domestic market. State support for indigenous capital is contingent, however, upon the fulfillment by indigenous producers of targets set by the "plan rational" political elite. All successful Asian NICs have constructed varied alliances for national accumulation based upon what Alexander Gerschenkron refers to as a "solidarity bloc,"[6] an alliance between state economic elites and indigenous capitalists who accumulate in myriad ways in cooperation with, and in competition against, foreign capital. There are good reasons, rooted in the peculiarities of history and institutional character, why Korea and Taiwan cannot be used as the litmus test for Nigerian developmental rectitude, but Malaysia, conversely, is a comparable case, for it is ethnically divided and like much of British West Africa experienced indirect rule between Malay Muslim sultans and the British colonial state. Even though there is a complex and unstable ethnic division of labor in which the Muslim Malays control the state apparatus and the Chinese dominate the domestic industrial and commercial sectors (a division not unlike Nigeria), the two competing fractions of the indigenous bourgeoisie have created an accumulating alliance in tandem with foreign capital, especially since the race riots of 1969. Despite ethnic tensions and its own version of bureaucratic authoritarianism, Malaysia posted a 10 percent growth rate in 1990, experienced rising living standards (GDP/capita = $2,182) even for the poorest rural dwellers, and attracted a substantial foreign-owned manufacturing base in electrical and electronics industries increasingly linked to domestic and regional capitalist enterprises.[7] Malaysian success throws the Nigerian failure into vivid relief and draws particular attention to the costs and benefits of state sector involvement for indigenous accumulation, the technical and organizational competence of the managerial bourgeoisie, the relation of the state bourgeoisie to indigenous private capitalists, and intracapitalist relations among distinct fractions of private capital.

Figure 10.1 The Boom and Bust Cycle: Nigeria 1970–1990

Values of Exports and Imports

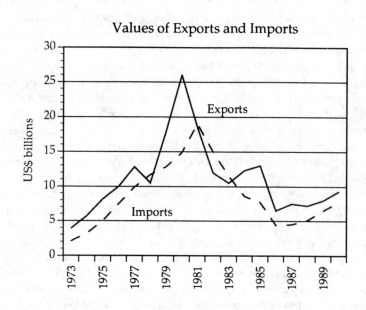

Per Capita Income

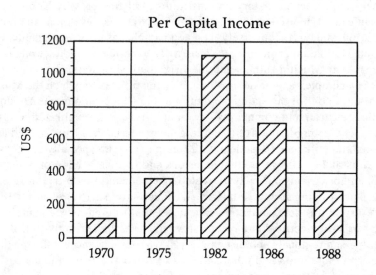

Sources: African Recovery, Vol. 4, No. 1, 1990, p. 7; Henry Bienen and Mark Gersovitz, *Nigeria: Absorbing the Oil Wealth* (London: Euromoney Publications, 1982), pp. 47–48.

In this chapter, we seek to link the contemporary debate over developmental and embedded states with ideas of an older vintage drawn from Gerschenkron and Weber.[8] We will examine the contours of Nigerian accumulation in general as a precondition for grasping the specific role of indigenous capitalist classes located in the private and public sectors under the SAP (1986–1992). State economic intervention certainly has been, and continues to be, a crucial factor in the formation, consolidation, and expansion of the Nigerian bourgeoisie. But how this intervention can be disciplined and directed toward productive accumulation is perhaps *the* paramount problem of Nigerian development. Like Chalmers Johnson, we accept the centrality of the relationship between the state's managerial bourgeoisie and the domestic private sector bourgeoisie as a tension that requires resolution before indigenous accumulation can advance rapidly in Nigeria. But in view of the abysmal record of Nigeria's state enterprises, a business-as-usual position with respect to the state is totally untenable. The trenchant arguments put forward by neoliberals on the right and Warrenites on the left that point out that accumulation, both indigenous and in general, requires real prices, market forces, and, above all, the advancement of productive forces—both technical and social—in industry and agriculture must, therefore, be given due weight. Yet, however powerful is the argument for allowing the "market" and/or the "forces of production" to reign undistorted by state intervention, the pressing weight of Nigeria's historical structures dictates, almost certainly, that the Nigerian state will remain central to both the general process of capital accumulation as well as to indigenous capital accumulation. In this sense, our position stands in contradistinction to the neoliberal orthodoxy of the World Bank, both positively and normatively. We believe that a developmental state is key and furthermore that state capacity is inseparable from particular class alliances; and prescriptively we reject the idea that orthodox trade-led growth—a "back to the future" idea in which primary commodity export-led growth can somehow be made to work "right"—represents a viable medium- or long-term growth strategy.

Our argument is that indigenous accumulation must be rooted in both a specific class alliance—that is to say, domestic sources of accumulation in specific sectors—and a disciplined state capable of laying the basis for calculated and systematic accumulation. In what follows we begin with an analysis of why the Nigerian state and the managerial bourgeoisie will be involved in indigenous accumulation, and trace how the impact of the SAP has in some way refashioned both the state and the opportunities for domestic accumulation. Second, we detail the record of state industry and infrastructure during the 1980s. Third, we outline the sources, character, and trajectories of accumulation in the agricultural and industrial sectors as a prerequisite for theorizing the role of the state in Nigeria in the 1990s. And we conclude with a discussion of the possibilities of a class alliance—what we, in recasting Gerschenkron's notion of a compromise between "iron and rye," refer to as an alliance between "oil and maize"—which promises both new sorts of intersectoral linkages and forms of accumulation that presuppose a state capacity more in keeping with the complexities of regional and identity politics in contemporary Nigeria.

The State and Indigenous Accumulation

First and foremost, Nigeria is, and will be for future decades, an energy exporter—one highly dependent on oil and, probably, liquid natural gas exports. Between 95 and 97 percent of the foreign exchange earnings needed for importing the "forces of production" are earned from oil. Hence, given this structural relationship to the world economy, and thus to OPEC political allegiances, it follows that the revenues from export sales of crude oil, natural gas, and other downstream manufactured products will be controlled by the Nigerian state via joint ventures between transnational energy firms and the Nigerian National Petroleum Corporation (NNPC). As in Mexico, the total privatization of the hydrocarbon sector has never been seriously considered by the most ardent neoliberal advisers, but in the face of industrial stagnation the federal government has recently announced a package of tax, pricing, and financial incentives designed to encourage private capital to invest in fertilizer plants, oil refineries, and petrochemical operations.[9]

Aside from the hydrocarbon link to the world economy, a second institutional factor—the relationship between the private and state sector bourgeoisie—literally overdetermines the predominance of the Nigerian state in indigenous accumulation. Historically, the division between the Muslim north and the Christian south arises from regional political and religious structures that have overlapped with historical patterns of economic and educational opportunity to create distinct regional fractions of the bourgeoisie that are hegemonic in their respective sectors: the Muslim northerners dominate the political apparatus and thus key ministries of the state sector, and the Christian southerners dominate the technical and internationalized fractions of the private sector.[10] Reinforced by these multiple, overlapping features of region, religion, and educational advantage, the cleavage between the state and private bourgeoisie blocks the informal functioning of the "developmentalist" state alliance because of the intense competition between the regional fractions, and also because of a Hobbesian competition among all players for rentier opportunities, i.e., primitive accumulation. Structurally, however, the comparatively backward northern bourgeoisie must have a strong state sector in order to create a comparable bourgeoisie, to ensure regional parity, and to reproduce their hegemony over the state.[11]

In the northern states, aristocrat-origin Muslim civil servants and generals, whose cohesion and power arises from their "status-honor," have formed a bourgeois alliance (a complex configuration of merchants, industrialists, and commercial farmers). As a power bloc, it has consistently exercised dominance over the state apparatus, be it a civilian or military regime, since independence.[12] But because of their technical and educational backwardness relative to their better-educated and economically more advantaged Christian, southern Nigerian rivals, the northern bourgeoisie cannot compete effectively in an open market. Among the southerners' advantages are a long-term historical involvement in the international economy; the predominantly southern location of transnational import-substitution industries; immediate proximity to hydrocarbon reserves and downstream industries; greater integration into Western, scientific, technocratic culture and international business practices; and a much higher level of educational achievement among all social strata. The global and market-related advantages enjoyed by the southerners do not displace the northerners, who are hegemonic in the political sphere, as indicated by their skill in forming reliable ruling coalitions with Middle Belt Christians and opportunistic southerners. Contrast this outcome with that of the highly educated Yorubas who have never been able to form an electoral coalition and who are divided by complex urban affiliations and identities. The mutually reinforcing effect of these divisions institutionalizes northern domination of the state sector as well as the distribution of petroleum revenues.

Structural adjustment, therefore, has had an immediate effect on the structure of the Nigerian bourgeoisie. Reduction in state economic involvement and the institutionalization of market forces obviously threatens northern hegemony and the competitive advantage of the northern bourgeoisie on the one hand, and privileges the more competitive cultural capital and industrial location of the southern bourgeoisie on the other. Obviously, the dominant class coalition controlling the Nigerian state is at a disadvantage under neoliberal policies like the SAP, for this fraction of the Nigerian bourgeoisie requires an active, interventionist state in order to ensure northern regional economic parity with their southern competitors and, equally important, to provide rentier accumulation opportunities for the rapidly commercializing aristocracy and their commoner allies. Of course, state involvement has receded from the high tide of economic nationalism during the 1970s, but the state sector remains institutionally central to indigenous accumulation and the class structure of indigenous accumulation (Figure 10.2).

Recent events confirm the structural dominance of the northern fraction over the state apparatus. In 1985, when General Babangida seized power from General Buhari, a representative of the northern, Muslim bourgeoisie (i.e., the Kaduna mafia) and opted for an alliance with the

Figure 10.2   The Growth of the Nigerian Public Sector (at current factor cost): 1970–1985

Source: Central Bank of Nigeria, *Economic and Financial Review* (various issues).

World Bank and structural adjustment, most of his key appointments were from southern technocratic groups who favored greater deregulation and more market forces. For example, Samuel Oluyemi Falae was appointed secretary to the federal government; a former World Bank official, Kalu I. Kalu, was his first finance minister; and Chu Okongwu has served Babangida from the finance and budget ministries from the early phases of the SAP. As opposition mounted against the decline in living standards and the restructuring of an economy addicted to the cheap foreign exchange generated by an overvalued currency, Babangida's need for a stable and dependable power bloc—within the dominant region and within the state—drove him increasingly into an alliance with central political figures from the north who command loyal followings and possess greater cohesion as a regionally based class, despite his initial alliance with southerners against Buhari. A key figure in this alliance was a Sokoto royal, Abubaker Alhaji, a former minister of finance and later ambassador to Britain. In turn, this allowed him to appoint one of his allies (Ibrahim Dasuki) as sultan of Sokoto—Nigeria's highest Muslim office—although it incurred the wrath of Christian officers who attempted an anti-Muslim coup in April 1990. Similarly, Babangida's alliance with the Muslim aristocracy enabled the northern-dominated political party (the National

Republican Convention) to dominate the recent highly "managed" elections for state governors, even winning the southern urban center of Lagos State. Since state governors will exert great influence in the presidential election within their jurisdictions, it is a safe wager that the northern elite will provide the next president, slated to take office in January 1994. If successful, once again the northern fraction of the bourgeoisie will control the state and thus guarantee state involvement in indigenous accumulation.

Crisis, Rationalization, and Appropriate State Intervention

Whatever the constraints imposed by the SAP, it is readily apparent that the structural features of dependence on oil exports and of northern hegemony over the state apparatuses will ensure the state bourgeoisie's intimate involvement in the regime of accumulation. But in view of its disastrous record of waste, mismanagement, and sheer looting, can the Nigerian state bourgeoisie sustain accumulation, either indigenous or foreign, without assistance from agencies like the World Bank? A shift away from the industrial policies of the petroleum boom (i.e., overvalued currency, imported food and manufacturing inputs, and an overextended state industrial sector) was inevitable with or without Babangida's SAP once the foreign exchange earnings from oil exports dried up (they fell from $25 billion in 1980 to $6.14 billion in 1986). Windfalls like the petroleum boom may be consumed like manna from heaven, but they do not establish a disciplined social structure of accumulation among a class of indigenous producers directly involved in competitive production for a market. Only greater competition, market forces, real prices, and learning from the more productive practices of foreign capital can create the social structure of accumulation to sustain indigenous capital and thus wean them from rentier distributive politics. Alternatively, a disciplined "developmentalist" state might have been able to rationally invest petrodollar revenues, but it would require a powerful, autonomous, and technocratic bureaucracy insulated from rentier opportunities. Accordingly, Babangida's decision to go for the World Bank's SAP implicitly recognized that the weakness of the state and indigenous capital required the resources of international finance capital (World Bank and IMF) in order to supply the discipline, calculability, and rationality necessary to rekindle the embers of accumulation. Thus, however painful for the weak, Babangida's SAP is best conceived as an alliance among unequal capitalist partners (international and local, state and private)—an alliance whose members are simultaneously engaged in both cooperation and competition, in order to institutionalize conditions that will enable them to "grow" their way out of the present crisis. Foreign capitalist involvement is, in other words, a necessary means to rationalize and discipline the restructuring of comparatively backward indigenous private and state capitalist accumulation, which is simultaneously strengthened and undermined by its dependence on petroleum rents.

Before analyzing indigenous accumulation sector by sector, the broad contours of the SAP need to be outlined. In order to obtain World Bank loans to finance internal restructuring and to roll over external debt from private lenders, Babangida accepted the SAP package. The main features were: an erratic devaluation of the naira from $1.50 in 1983 to about $.05 in 1993; the liberalization of trade by eliminating import licenses; the privatization and commercialization of nonfinancial public enterprises (NFPEs); the reduction of subsidies, especially petrol; and the general encouragement of foreign investment and market forces. Predictably, the SAP has shattered living standards among the wage and salaried groups, reducing the real minimum wage from about $201 to $16 per month by 1991, and reducing educational, social, and health expenditures so far that universities have collapsed, cholera is widespread (the highest reported globally), and malnutrition, destitution, and unemployment are common. In turn, each tightening of the screw has stimulated widespread rioting led by students, unemployed workers, market women, and a burgeoning urban lumpenproletariat. And state repression of dissidents and authoritarian management of a transition to civilian rule have virtually eliminated the legitimacy of Babangida's government.

The Record of State Industry and Infrastructure

Petroleum dependency coupled with the peculiarities of Nigeria's regional political economy produce a set of structural forces that, in our opinion, will ensure state-centered development. But if the state is central to indigenous accumulation, what, in view of its unenviable record, is an appropriate and feasible role likely to be? In other words, what interventions will enhance intensive accumulation, and is the state capable of such disciplined intervention in the areas of finance, infrastructure, and intermediate industrialization? Nationalist theorists, such as Adebayo Adediji, who rightly attack neoliberal orthodoxy must address the question of state capacity if their alternative strategies are to have any political credibility. If the Nigerian state lacks the organizational capacity to provide elementary inputs such as electricity, then it is unlikely to be able to manage fordist industrial strategies focused on steel or petrochemicals. Nigeria faces a crisis of production, investment, and confidence so severe that the nationalist strategies of the 1970s can be credible only if the state can be shown to be capable of coping with the exigencies of the global economy in the 1990s.

There is little evidence that the state is capable of fulfilling its basic infrastructural responsibilities and ensuring systematic capital accumulation. Rent-seeking and corruption have not ended as a result of state retrenchment in the 1980s; the crisis has only altered the means and intensified the search for rents. When the central bank instituted both an official rate and a market rate for dollars, dozens of indigenous banks sprouted (from twenty-six in 1980 to 120 in 1991)—many with no branches except near the central bank—in order to buy foreign exchange at the official rate and sell it at the market rate. Pressure from the IMF has forced the central bank to institute a single, unified rate, thus forcing the failure of many banks. Yet the naira continued to fall, approaching the unprecedented exchange rate of 50:1 against the dollar. A state is often defined as an institution exercising legitimate authority over a territory, but the discipline of state officials is so feeble that economic policy cannot be enforced within Nigeria's territory. Transportation of subsidized gasoline into neighboring states is so extensive that it has caused a fuel shortage and rioting in Nigerian cities. In general, the Nigerian state is incapable of policing its borders and thus protecting its internal market from imports of cheaper or banned commodities. What is a realistic expectation from Nigeria's state sector in the current neoliberal moment of the world economy? If new technologies and new investments are needed—and this is now the global pattern—the problem is not how to expand state economic responsibility, but rather whether it can manage infrastructural and strategic intermediate industries at a minimum level of efficiency to avoid undermining private capital accumulation.

The choices confronting Nigeria are difficult and in some respects cruel. The state must withdraw from areas of demonstrated incompetence, refocus its energies on more limited organizational goals, explore innovative sources of discipline outside of colonial-type bureaucracies, exert territorial sovereignty over its national market, and, above all, facilitate intensive private accumulation. A recent World Bank study of 179 firms in 1988 suggests that the state cannot provide a basic industrial infrastructure. Ninety-two percent of firms surveyed (165 of 179) required their own electricity generators at an average cost of $130,000 because the Nigerian Electrical Power Authority's power supply (NEPA) was unreliable. This limitation actually destroys capital investment. At the Jos steel mill, which lacks an independent source of power, interruptions of the power supply damaged equipment worth 75 million naira.[13] Similarly, more than two-thirds of all the companies surveyed had invested in private water boreholes. The additional cost represented from 10 to 25 percent of the total value of machines and equipment.[14] Elsewhere the Bank reports that up to 50 percent of NEPA's capacity is idle and that only 400–500 of its fleet of 3,000 vehicles were operable, thus reducing proper repair and maintenance of investments.[15] Lack of capital investment in its generators is not the central problem, however; rather, it is "huge overcapacity in generation, inadequate operational practice, poor maintenance, a grossly oversized 30,000–strong staff starved of competent middle management, and a nonperforming centralized utility bureaucracy that has little autonomy and is subject to instructive overcontrol by the government."[16] Frustrated consumers riot and attack NEPA installations and employees; companies such as Dunlop and Berger Paints generate their own electricity (at great cost) after huge losses incurred by power surges, equipment losses, and excessive downtime.[17] One could say that this self-provision of power is a kind of privatization, but it is inefficient, irrational, and expensive. NEPA's nightmarish performance is unfortunately replicated in many sectors, including transportation and telecommunications, as any traveler with experience with Nigerian Airways or with Nigerian telephones can readily testify.

Notwithstanding reasonable nationalist sentiments favoring indigenous control over strategic industries and industrial infrastructure, the opportunity cost of capital allocated to most of Nigeria's state industries is prohibitive if compared to the returns from alternatives such as small- and intermediate-scale industries or downstream uses of Nigeria's abundant oil and natural gas resources. The Ajaokuta steel complex, with a final price tag of at least $6 billion, is a stellar example. Already eight years behind schedule in 1993 and still not projected to produce until 1995, over $4 billion had been spent despite "gross mismanagement. . . . and theft of equipment and machinery."[18] Not surprisingly, the Nigerian steel industry is popularly referred to as the "steal sector."[19] More alarmingly, it is designed with antiquated Soviet blast furnace technology to produce 1 million tons per year for a market estimated at 300,000 tons per year and at a price six times the world market price. The World Bank has refused to commit funds, arguing that Ajaokuta will become a permanent foreign exchange guzzler requiring at least $200,000 a year just to import high-quality coal.[20] It will be a net loser of foreign exchange even after capital costs are written off.[21] Instead, they recommend that the direct gas reduction steel plant at Aladja be expanded from 400,000 to 1 million tons per year. The Bank made similar arguments against a proposed aluminum smelter ($1.4 billion), the largest in Africa, noting in its review that the necessary alumina, petroleum coke, and pitch will have to be imported, that the largely borrowed capital cost is 60 to 100 percent higher than similar projects, and that the end product will have to be heavily subsidized to be competitive on the world market. As one might expect, given the role of northerners in the state capitalist sector, Finance Minister Abubaker Alhaji was chairman of the aluminum parastatal.[22]

Privatizing the deficit-ridden public enterprises offers opportunities for Nigerian private capital. Prior to the SAP, the federal and state governments established over 850 parastatals, so pruning, privatizing, and commercializing state enterprises was an enormous task for the privatization agency, the Technical Committee on Privatization and Commercialization. By March 1992, seventy-eight enterprises had been privatized, but after the more profitable ones are sold, dim prospects are forecast for obtaining buyers for the three steel rolling mills,[23] the paper companies, the Nigerian National Shipping Line, the vehicle assembly plants, and Nigerian Airways. Deregulation of parastatal monopolies over air travel and telecommunications promises profitable ventures for Nigerian private capital.[24]

Thus, international financial capital, i.e., the World Bank, performs a progressive role by rationalizing productive capital investment and by restraining the appetite of rentier capitalists in the interest of the majority of Nigerians. By refusing to fund projects like Ajaokuta or the aluminum smelter, and by forcing the privatization of parastatals that consume revenue, the World Bank injects a rationality and discipline that the country's indigenous and bureaucratic bourgeoisie have so far proven incapable of exercising on their own. While the state sector is still a drag on accumulation, the SAP has had a significant impact on restructuring the economy toward productive accumulation, especially in the hydrocarbon sector. Bearing in mind the tensions between rational state intervention to provide necessary infrastructure and grandiose state industrial expansion beyond the state's technical and fiscal capacities, we now turn to the place of indigenous capital within the general process of accumulation within each sector.

Accumulation in Agriculture:
Peasants, High-Profile Farmers, and Agroindustrial Linkages

There is a widespread sentiment that the oil boom, or more properly the period of state-led investment between 1973 and the collapse of oil prices in the early 1980s, was associated with widespread stagnation and crisis in Nigerian agriculture.[25] Yet notwithstanding the enormous problems of interpreting the highly contradictory and unreliable aggregate sources of data on output and productivity,[26] the picture is, as Tom Forrest has recently argued, rather more complex.[27] It is certainly unwise to assume, on the basis of the unprecedented growth of food imports (which peaked in 1982, accounting for roughly 18 percent of total imports) and the poor performance of the agricultural export sector, that agrarian accumulation had taken a leave of absence from the Nigerian political economy after the first oil boom. If urban employment opportunities spawned by state-led construction projects drew labor out of agriculture—creating, as P. Collier believes, a crisis of profitability in labor-intensive crops such as cocoa and palm oil[28]—some regions and some commodities experienced growing commercialization and buoyancy. The World Bank, in what is probably the most reliable of statistical reconstructions, estimates that agricultural output exceeded population growth over the period 1970–1982.[29] Some sectors—for example, poultry, wheat, and maize—proved to be the sites of substantial investment and accumulation (and also periods of bust and depression).[30] Moreover, the combination of relatively high real food prices, 80–90 percent fertilizer subsidies, and substantial infrastructural investments (especially in irrigation through the River Basin Development Authorities, and more generally through jointly financed World Bank Agricultural Development Projects[31]) lends some credence to Forrest's assessment that dubious aggregate figures hide a great deal of variability over time and space and dynamism in production.[32]

Nevertheless, by the mid-1980s there was a sense in Nigeria that the battle for agriculture was being lost.[33] President Buhari's minister of agriculture, Bukar Shuaib, conceded in late 1985 that all the agricultural parastatals were taking "heavy losses" (by 1984 the marketing boards had posted cumulative losses of more than half a billion naira), that the Green Revolution of President Shagari had come to nought, and that the proliferation of state bureaucracies—gigantic and overambitious for the most part—had proved to be a Tolstoyan encumbrance on systematic accumulation in agriculture. As one farmer near Ibadan put it: "In government agricultural projects there are more vehicles than crops."[34]

Nevertheless, under the close technical guidance and financial backing of the World Bank, since 1985, the SAP has reversed many of the price distortions and some of the rigidities and biases against agriculture, most particularly through the abolition of the state-administered marketing boards in 1986; import bans on grain, rice, poultry, and meat promulgated between 1985 and 1987; the deregulation of food prices; the privatization of many parastatals, including the fertilizer procurement system; and, most critically, priority for Agricultural Development Projects (ADPs) over the River Basin Development Authorities. These bold initiatives were the building blocks of the government's agricultural blueprint under the SAP, entitled "Agricultural Policy for Nigeria" (1988), which focused on food and industrial raw material self-sufficiency complemented by an expanded export capability. The centrality of agriculture under the SAP was reflected in the 1989 budget, which made the largest allocation of funds to agriculture to date.[35]

In aggregate terms, the impact of structural adjustment on agricultural output is difficult to determine with any confidence. According to a recently released study by the Central Bank of Nigeria (CBN) and the Nigerian Institute of Social and Economic Research (NISER), comparisons of pre-SAP (1982–1985) and post-SAP (1986–1989) output reveals an average increase of over 50 percent for eleven crops (including export commodities and staple foodstuffs).[36] A World Bank report[37] estimates that agriculture grew by 6 percent per annum over the period 1986–1990; the contribution of agriculture to GDP rose from 25.2 billion naira in 1988 to 28.7 billion naira in 1990.[38] Cocoa and palm kernels appear to have been the success stories in the export sector, but it is unclear whether the food production has responded as well.[39] What does seem clear and incontrovertible, however, is that producer prices have increased dramatically: real food prices for the seven major staple foodstuffs increased by 40 percent per year on average between 1986 and 1989, while cocoa producer prices leaped from 1,600 naira per tonne in 1986 to 11,000 per tonne in 1988. It must be said, of course, that there have been, to use the language of the central bank, "phenomenal increases in the prices of farm inputs such as fertilizers, pesticides and tractors"[40] and that the performance of the Directorate for Foods, Roads, and Rural Infrastructure has been singularly unimpressive.[41] Nonetheless, with Nigeria's population growing at an estimated annual rate of 3.5 percent, the internal market for food, oils, and fibers provides an enormous market and opportunity for indigenous accumulation. The unreliability of state statistics on imports and exports arising from illegal (subsidized) fertilizer exports and imports of banned grains and flour to and from neighboring states undercuts any confident prognostications, but the structural reforms coupled with the expanded ADP drive have restructured the conditions for indigenous agricultural accumulation. As Jane Guyer noted upon her return to Ibarapa District in Oyo State in 1987–1988, the regular refrain from politician to mechanic was "everybody's farming now."[42]

In these relatively new conditions, we can identify four distinct "structures of accumulation" through which accumulation is taking place in agriculture, although in practice there are complex linkages between them, and in some cases specific individuals may "straddle" different agrarian strategies. In short, the four structures of accumulation are: farmer-trader accumulation, land speculation, "high-profile farming," and agroindustrial corporate linkages (both indigenous and foreign). Underlying all of these is the 1978 Land Use Act, which, in spite of its bureaucratic impediments, has unquestionably laid the basis for both wider state acquisition of land and for capitalist farmers and speculators to register and acquire large-scale holdings.[43] None of these changes, which tend to emphasize new actors in agriculture or expanded operations by long-standing actors (e.g., farmer-traders), should imply, of course, that there are not other important shifts in the production patterns of categories of people already farming and a shift in the proportions of people in those categories who are actively engaged in farming (e.g., new or expanded roles for women, returned sons, migrants, and so on). All of these activities were proceeding simultaneously in the early 1990s,[44] though we have chosen to emphasize these salient accumulation strategies rather than the complexities of shifting forms of peasant production.

In the northern states (and to a lesser extent in the south), structural adjustment strengthened and expanded the accumulating activity of a distinct stratum, if not a separate class, of farmer-traders who owned and farmed hundreds and sometimes thousands of hectares. In a country where 90 percent of the farms are under 5 hectares and whose average farm size is 2 hectares in the south and 3 hectares in the north, it is noteworthy that the growth of 10- to 100-hectare farms is now recognizable and that 500 plus–hectare farms are common in the northern states.[45] By the early 1980s, it was clear on the basis of the first generation of ADP projects in Gombe and Funtua that while the output figures were unimpressive, they had contributed to the proliferation of a class of prosperous farmer-traders (typically with connections to local government and aristocratic families) who had come to represent the most significant class of agrarian accumulators.[46] Since the peasant farmer route to capitalist agriculture is notoriously slow and is accompanied by the continual reproduction of a transformed peasant community, the instantaneous formation of an agrarian bourgeoisie under the stimulus of the SAP is unlikely. Like most studies of peasant differentiation in ADPs, Mustapha's recent work on Kano State does, however, provide hard evidence that the SAP has been beneficial to rich peasant farmers in rural Kano. Between 1986 and 1990, rich peasants expanded their holdings by 20 percent, and 50 percent claimed some improvement had occurred in their farming operations; and some had doubled their plough teams and fertilizer use.[47] A similar picture emerges from the Sokoto area, where work by A. Labaran[48] and A. Mamman[49] shows two processes of land accumulation at work: one focuses on the acquisition of low-lying swampland (*fadama*), which is converted into intensively irrigated market gardening, and the other on upland farms outside the closely settled area (high population, fragmented holdings), which can be acquired in larger lots for grain production, much of which enters regional circuits of exchange (especially into Niger). While the rich farmer-traders are differentiating themselves from their neighbors, they are still dependent on local labor and forms of cooperation in order to produce a marketable surplus.[50] On the other hand, the northern large-scale farmer-traders are expanding their holdings, branching out into sales of machinery, inputs, and fertilizer and obtaining the political clout needed to evolve into a class of commercial farmers.[51]

A second type of agrarian accumulator originating from urban centers is the civil servant, retired military officer, or urban merchant who invests in commercial agricultural enterprises such as poultry or grain production (typically in irrigated production on a project managed by the River Basin Development Authority). We refer to this class as "high-profile farmers," and it is to be distinguished from the land speculators who are not "real farmers," as *West Africa* put it, because "they are more noise-makers than real farmers in the large-scale class."[52] These high-profile capitalist farmers have been touted as the "Millionaire Farmers Club" and include a number of well-publicized large-scale landlords and growers.[53] Some examples are:

> *Ahmed Joda,* former federal permanent secretary, who owns Benue Valley Farms, a 639-hectare maize, soy, and integrated livestock complex twenty miles east of Yola

- *Ayo Ogunlade,* former federal commissioner of information and chair of Adegbemile Food Industries, which owns 17,000 hectares in Gongola, Akwa Ibom, and Lagos states and an unreported amount of land in three other states
- *General Obasanjo,* former head of state, and CEO of Temperance Farms in Oyo and Ogun states; engaged in maize production for brewery supply, poultry production, gari-processing, and integrated livestock[54]
- *Bamanga Tukur,* former civilian governor of Gongola State, who acquired land in 1983 (1,000 hectares) that expanded in 1987 because of opportunities created by SAP;[55] engaged in food production, integrated poultry production, and a joint venture with Upper Benue River Basin Development Authority to produce maize on a large scale

There are others who have been drawn into agriculture as "overnight farmers" on a less grandiose and less capitalized scale, of course. The case of the so-called wheat frenzy in northern Nigeria provides a compelling case in point.[56] In May 1986, Babangida announced a total ban on wheat imports, effective in January 1987, followed by a staggering 650 percent increase in producer prices between 1986 and 1988. By 1989, it was estimated that 200,000 hectares were under wheat cultivation in five northern states, the center of which was Kano. Many military officers, merchants, politicians, and bureaucrats were drawn into irrigated wheat production, often acquiring or renting large acreages through political connections, fraudulent land transactions, or outright force.[57] But while Babangida hoped that Nigeria would be self-sufficient in wheat by 1992, the wheat ban was actually lifted in October 1992.

The wheat boom reveals the fragile and contradictory quality of agrarian accumulation. The productivity and quality of indigenous production is uniformly low, and much of the soft wheat is in any case inappropriate for flour milling. Hence, in spite of the (often exaggerated) growth of Nigerian wheat production,[58] the twenty-two Nigerian mills that required 12,000 tonnes per day could only acquire 60,000 tonnes per year locally! As a consequence, all of the flour mills have been producing at best at 7.5 percent of capacity, and at least 300,000 tons of wheat are smuggled into Nigeria annually. In other words, import substitution produced an accumulation crisis in the agroindustrial milling and bread industries and created enormous rent-seeking and smuggling opportunities.[59] Renewal of wheat imports in 1992 due to the pressures of the milling lobby will certainly undercut the wheat growers in exactly the same way that the commercial poultry sector, which was booming between 1970 and 1986,[60] collapsed because of the increase in maize prices (due to competition with local breweries) and the disappearance of imported feeds and pharmaceuticals.[61]

Since large-scale farms typically depend on the Nigerian state or an uncertain agricultural service system, research has found that few of the large farms of between 5,000 and 40,000 hectares ever operate at full capacity.[62] Guyer noted the volatile production among large maize farms in Oyo State, some of which lay fallow due to the absence of contracts from breweries and feedmills.[63] Furthermore, in spite of all the subsidies and corrupt transfers garnered by this self-conscious class of agrarian capitalists, their impact on aggregate food and raw material production remains negligible. Since the peasantry produces more cheaply because of superior flexibilities, especially labor, and less dependence on unreliable technologies (spare parts and repair costs), it is difficult for commercial farmers to obtain labor at critical moments in the production cycle and thus surpass peasant production. Insofar as more speculative ventures, like banking or political investments in rent-seeking opportunities, remain open to urban capital, it is difficult to perceive how a significant class of commercial farmers will transform agrarian production, especially when an unstable and mercurial state policy determines the availability and prices of so many essential inputs (machinery, irrigation investments, etc.). The continuing corruption and fraud associated with the National Fertilizer Company (NAFCON) and its "missing fertilizer"[64] and the abandonment of the wheat import ban are both cases in point.

A third category, related to but distinct from the high-profile farmers, are the land speculators. A great deal of evidence concerning land speculation and fraudulent land acquisition was brought to light by the Land Commission convened by the People's Redemption Party in the early 1980s in Kano State. Military officers, high-ranking civil servants, and persons charged with administering land policy gained access to land illicitly,[65] typically in advance of state development. Udo noted that many army officers from the Gowon and Obasanjo administrations acquired land for speculative purposes in periurban areas and the trend has clearly continued.[66] The recent land rush on the Mambilla Plateau in Taraba State illustrates how peasants were forcibly dispossessed in the wake of a report that ranked the plateau as having enormous untapped agricultural potential.[67] The corrupt land allocation system produced a situation in which "new landlords emerged daily, but the parcels of land acquired from peasants were merely fenced and left unutilized."[68]

A fourth type of agrarian accumulation associated with the SAP centers on agroindustrial linkages, and especially on investment by Nigerian and foreign capital in input supply (i.e., forms of vertical integration and coordination). State policy has been designed to force local sourcing by manufacturers, and the Raw Material Research and Development Council, established in 1987, has been charged with replacing imported inputs and raw materials. In general, the import ban has dramatically stimulated local sourcing; according to the World Bank the proportion of local raw materials in the total used by a sample of firms increased from 30 to 40 percent between 1986 and 1988, while capacity utilization rose by almost 10 percent over the same period.[69] The Manufacturers Association of Nigeria (MAN) reported recently that 52 percent of raw materials were sourced in Nigeria by 1989, a marked improvement from the 30 percent prior to the SAP. Subsectors for which local inputs accounted for over 50 percent included textiles (57 percent), food and beverages (58 percent), and leather (54 percent); capacity utilization in these three sectors was on average in excess of 65 percent. A more recent MAN study estimates that in 1990, 78 percent of raw materials in the food and beverage sector were being locally sourced. Before the implementation of the SAP, Nigerian manufacturers imported well over 75 percent of their raw materials.

The Nigerian state has actively facilitated corporate investment in agriculture by modifying the Nigerian Enterprises Promotion Decree of 1972 to permit foreign equity participation up to 80 percent in agriculture and through privatizing forty-four agricultural projects (mills, farmland, machinery, poultry facilities), which were sold in open bidding through the Technical Committee on Privatization and Commercialization in 1990. In addition, in the first round of debt-equity conversions in 1988, 35 percent of the applications received were for agricultural investment representing 65 percent of the value of the promissory notes converted.[70] And not least, through the de facto privatization and decentralization of the state-run capital-intensive irrigation schemes,[71] the River Basin Authorities are attempting to link "contract peasants" to industrial enterprises in order to produce industrial raw material inputs that were formerly imported.[72] Nigeria's thirty-four breweries, for example, are required to use locally produced, high-yielding maize (and secondarily sorghum) to displace imported barley, a switch that constitutes an agrarian revolution in the grain areas of the north, although livestock, industrial, and food consumers also compete for the limited supply of maize, whose price has increased by 300 percent since 1987.[73] Millers, food processors, soap and detergent manufacturers, and soft drink enterprises are all developing local sources either by organizing plantations (for example, Unilever's palm estates, the UAC/Marquis farm, Cadbury's sorghum estates) or by subcontracting to local producers (Afprint and Texlon's cotton outgrowers in Gongola, fruit and vegetable contractors on the Mambilla Plateau).

Two sectors in which backward linkages have generated new sources of agrarian accumulation are textiles and brewing, both of which confirm that it is the large enterprises (50–500 employees) that most aggressively pursue local sourcing.[74] Nowhere has the shift to local sourcing been more successful than in textiles. In the early 1980s, Nigeria boasted Africa's third-largest textile industry after South Africa and Egypt, employing over 100,000 workers in some 100 firms.[75] Cotton production has been organized by manufacturers through outgrower schemes, capital-intensive plantations, and licensed buying agents who have replaced the marketing boards. A survey by MAN in the first half of 1989 showed that average capacity utilization in textiles was 40 percent as opposed to 31 percent for manufacturing as a whole, and that 62 percent of raw materials were obtained from domestic sources.[76] Interviews with World Bank staff confirm that enormous amounts of Nigerian textiles are smuggled to neighboring states, due in part to overpriced currencies in the neighboring francophone states whose currency is backed by the French franc. Thus, the backing of African currencies by the French central bank provides an unintended export subsidy for Nigerian manufacturers. The same officials believe that Nigeria could export textiles to Europe and North America if it joined the Multifiber Agreement.[77]

The ban on malted barley from January 1988 had a similar effect in the brewing sector, which employs 30,000 people (and another 400,000 in ancillary activities).[78] The impact was quite dramatic. In July 1988, Nigerian Breweries took out a full-page advertisement in the *Guardian*[79] to announce its acquisition of 8,000 hectares of farmland in Niger State for maize and sorghum production. Premier Breweries acquired estates in Anamabra, and North Breweries, among others, was especially active in major land purchases in Plateau State. By 1989, Guinness Nigeria, Pabod Breweries, and Nigerian Breweries all announced beer made from 100 percent local content.

The role of new foreign corporate capital in the post-SAP period has, on balance, been quite limited, in spite of the efforts by the Nigerian state to attract investors. In some instances, existing foreign industrial capital acquired land for expanded local production, and in others it took over established Nigerian companies (for example, UAC bought Marquis Herds in Oyo, and Leventis bought Bendel farms).[80] UAC Marquis is an interesting case because the Nigerian owner, Chief Bola Marquis, retained a portion of his assets for his own agribusiness ventures, while the UAC farm is part of a vertically integrated business for producing sausages for their snack food outlets (Kingsway Rendezvous). The collapse of the Oyo-based Texaco gari project in 1988—a 2,600-acre estate and outgrower scheme—shows, however, that large-scale corporate investment remains a risky and volatile undertaking. Problems in labor recruitment, market development in relation to highly competitive local alternatives, and escalating import costs finally demolished what was from its inception a dubious enterprise.[81] Indeed, corporate farming still accounts for only a relatively small proportion of total agricultural output, and as Forrest properly notes, it was often undertaken under state pressure with the result that little more than land clearance was accomplished.[82] Indeed, all of the new forms of agrarian accumulation remain quite weak and underdeveloped. The scale and heterogeneity of farm output and the as yet undeveloped state of farm lobbies suggest that agriculture will remain at the periphery of the political landscape in Nigeria, at least for the immediate future. But the emergence of millers, brewers, and other agroindustrial interest groups, coupled with slow and uneven differentiation within the peasant sector, portends new sorts of alliances between and within sectors—such as what we have metaphorically called an alliance of oil and maize—and may hold some potential for more systematic forms of agrarian and agroindustrial accumulation in the post-SAP period.

The Problem of Indigenous Investment in Manufacturing

During the petroleum boom, manufacturing grew not by increasing efficiency but by the extensive injection of petroleum-driven capital. Capital-intensive sectors grew at the expense of small-scale industries in which Nigeria possessed a comparative advantage. The World Bank describes the industrial sector as insular, technically backward, and lacking incentives to improve their quality or efficiency. Currently, manufacturing accounts for only 8.5 percent of GDP and is declining on a per capita basis. Infrastructural problems and indigenization laws, moreover, represent further obstacles to new manufacturing investment. The bias of the World Bank–administered program favors agriculture and agroindustrial linkages and opposes highly protected, import-dependent industries such as automobiles, consumer electronics, semidurables, and intermediate metal processing. Together with the decline in economic activity, internal demand, and the removal of import licenses, the steep devaluation of the naira eliminated most of the simple assembly manufacturing that relied on imported inputs, many of which were really vehicles for foreign exchange repatriation from the commercial activities of international firms operating in Nigeria. MAN believes that structural adjustment has led to the deindustrialization of Nigeria, estimating that 20 to 30 percent of manufacturers have failed and that industrial capacity currently hovers around 35 percent, a figure still in excess of the pre-SAP level of 25 percent. In response, the World Bank has approved a loan of $240 million for a fund to finance the foreign exchange needs of small and intermediate industries that have suffered disproportionately from restructuring and foreign exchange shortage.

Hardest hit are the private sector industries producing intermediate goods: metals, paper, cement, and chemicals. The automobile industry, which once assembled over 100,000 vehicles a year, is operating below 10 percent capacity. Yet there is evidence that restructuring is forcing innovations, though few innovators in manufacturing appear to be Nigerian. One exception is the auto parts producers studied by Forrest at Nnewi, a small city of 100,000 near Onitsha.[83] With Taiwanese technical assistance and machinery imports, indigenous industrialists have followed a classical pattern from importing auto parts from overseas to local production of batteries, filters, cables, brake pads, fan belts, etc. Here careful firm histories illustrate the dynamic potential of small to medium-sized capitalist enterprises using indigenous organization and cultures of discipline. Funding for small- to medium-scale enterprises for Nigerian entrepreneurs with high local sourcing is being organized with funding from the World Bank, the Ecobank, and the African Development Bank.[84]

Of course, import-dependent manufacturers such as automobile assemblers have not prospered during the SAP. Of the six remaining firms, two are in receivership, and the remainder are operating at a fraction of capacity. Peugeot, for example, produced 5,900 vehicles in 1990 but has the capacity to produce 59,000. It has announced a plan to invest 83 million naira in a plan involving forty local manufacturers of components; by April 1991, Peugeot claimed that its vehicles contained 35 percent local content, up from 10 percent in 1987.[85] Volkswagen has announced a similar project.[86] Hence, given the scale of the internal market and support for backward linkages, restructuring has forced firms to deepen the industrialization process and to integrate local capital as component producers.

The question one must pose, given the Latin American experience, is whether deepening import substitution will ever produce goods at prices competitive for export to the world market. On the other hand, Nigeria's internal market is large enough and its hydrocarbon resources are rich enough to allow the country to postpone dealing with international competition for another decade. Simply crawling out of the recession on the basis of supplying the domestic market would be a triumph for the manufacturing sector. While it is interesting to note that Calabar has been designated the first site for the construction of an Export Free Trade Zone to attract foreign investment, the medium-term future of manufacturing growth lies in agroindustrial linkages, spin-offs from the oil and gas sector, and modest investments in selected durable goods industries.[87]

Hydrocarbons, Energy, and Petrochemical Linkages

If local manufacturing is most negatively affected by the SAP, Nigeria's oil and natural gas industries are actually undergoing a revival and expansion. Nationalist intervention during the 1970s institutionalized state sector participation in the flagship industries of Nigerian accumulation, both indigenous and foreign. While the import-dependent manufacturing sector is dying for want of local sources or foreign exchange, the hydrocarbon sector has experienced something of a boom, marked by increased foreign investment from BP, Mobil, Chevron, and others; the expansion of downstream manufacturing plants; greater use of natural gas; and near completion of the Liquified Natural Gas (LNG) project for export. Under an agreement signed in July 1991, the Nigerian government has provided fiscal incentives and profit guarantees in exchange for training Nigerian nationals, increased investment and exploration, and the right of the NNPC to become the operator when it chooses.[88] Here joint state and foreign capital appear to have advanced the scale of indigenous activity as well as the technical capacity of Nigerian firms, both state and private.

Not only is the hydrocarbon sector Nigeria's most profitable indigenous industry, but it also represents the most promising engine of economic growth since 60 percent of all equity in local subsidiaries is owned by the NNPC. Potentially, it can feed downstream industries and enable Nigeria to develop export capacity, a shipping industry, and export refineries for the West African region, possibly through the potential market offered by ECOWAS, the Economic Community of West African States. At the height of its expansion, Nigeria's oil sector produced 2.3 million b/d of petroleum; in 1989, production averaged 1.64 mbd. Recoverable reserves are estimated to be 16 billion barrels, but the government is pushing oil companies to increase exploration to reach 20 billion barrels, because demand for Nigeria's low-polluting petroleum is expected to rise in the next decade. Shell, which produces about half of Nigeria's oil, expects to increase its annual investment from $700 million to $1.2 billion by 1992. Production is expected to reach 2.5 mbd. Additional output (100,000 b/d) from pressure-induced condensate production—which is not counted as part of Nigeria's OPEC quota—will be a joint venture between Mobil and the NNPC, funded by the World Bank.[89]

Initially, the Gulf crisis created a mini–petroleum boom that raised output by 250,000 b/d; production for 1991 averaged nearly 1.9 mbd even though prices have declined since the end of the war. From a longer-term perspective, the Gulf crisis underscores how Nigeria's fortune may shift due to international conflicts over oil resources. From August 1990, the mini–petroleum boom increased Nigeria's estimated foreign exchange earnings from $6.90 billion (1988) and $8.14 billion (1989), to $13.30 billion (1990), and finally to $16.55 billion (1991).[90]

The NNPC, Nigeria's most important parastatal, has always been the subject of political squabbling and rumors of leaking revenue. Recently it was reorganized into eleven subsidiaries, which will eventually be organized as commercial enterprises. Unlike steel, the NNPC is a parastatal worthy of investment and attention, for it has control over petrochemicals, refining, pipelines, liquified natural gas, and technical services. It has aggressively attempted to gain control of the West African market by selling crude and refined products in NNPC tankers to neighboring states at attractive prices. Their strategy is to build export refineries, but technical breakdowns, fires, and other obstacles have forced the NNPC to attempt to buy equity in overseas refineries, e.g., a 49 percent equity agreement with a refinery in Kansas. It has set up the most advanced electronic monitoring system for its pipelines in Africa. In this regard, the NNPC is comparable to the more successful Latin American parastatals in that it can produce products and generate income in a market environment and in joint ventures.

Nigeria's four refineries are designed to process 445,000 b/d and to serve as the anchor of an ambitious petrochemical industry. Downstream plants produce ingredients for soaps, detergents, plastics, solvents, carbon black, and asphalt materials for buildings and highways. Liquified petroleum gas and other fuels are produced for the domestic market. A second phase of the petrochemical industry will produce benzene, ethylene, propylene, and polyethylene.[91] More significantly, due to pressure from the World Bank, which is financing part of the second phase, the NNPC is open to private equity participation in downstream production. Joint ventures are also planned to substitute inputs presently imported from oil service companies: pumps, valves, shallow drilling equipment, and pipelaying equipment.[92] All of this has important potential for regional and African economic integration. Finally, carbon black produced by the petrochemical industry will be used in local tire production. Firestone will combine local natural rubber and carbon black to produce over a million tires annually.[93] Despite the general crisis in manufacturing, state investment in petrochemicals is an outstanding example of successful linkage formation between a former enclave and the Nigerian economy.

Nigeria possesses vast reserves of natural gas as well as associated gas produced from lifting oil. In fact, proven reserves of natural gas amount to 2.8 million cubic meters, surpassing the estimated value of petroleum reserves. Currently, about 77 percent of associated gas is flared (burned off), 12 percent marketed, and 11 percent used in the field; but several projects are committed to marketing this valuable resource. While international energy companies complain that the price for marketing is too low, Mobil and Chevron are planning to invest in gas collection; Chevron, for example, is planning to build a methanol plant from gas feedstocks. A fertilizer plant, built and managed by Kellogg, already uses gas to produce about 700,000 tons annually. Potential industrial users are projected to consume 1.1 billion cubic feet per day, about four times current consumption.[94] Several more fertilizer plants have been commissioned to reduce imports and to use the 77 percent of the natural gas that is now flared. By 1989, a joint venture between the Nigerian Gas Corporation (NNPC) and Shell had commissioned a $65 million processing plant, which, via the 380-kilometer ($310 million) Lagos-Escravos pipeline, in turn delivers gas to NEPA power stations and industrial consumers in the Lagos area, where about 60 percent of Nigeria's industries are located. Additional collection and processing plants are being commissioned, so that linkage to natural gas has been modestly successful.

In 1989, the NNPC formed a joint venture with Shell (20 percent), Agip (10 percent), and Elf (10 percent) to form a company, Nigeria LNG, to build a $2.5 billion LNG processing plant at Bonny. The project includes extensive pipelines to eastern Nigerian oil fields as well as tankers to transport LNG. It is scheduled to export 4 million tons of LNG to Europe and the United States by 1995.[95] Financing appears secure as the project has the support of the World Bank and support from European consumers, but final approval has yet to be completed. Again, if successful, LNG exports will enhance Nigeria's foreign exchange resources and economic recovery. On balance, it is clear that the Nigerian state has made progress in the energy sector. Accordingly, rather than investing in steel, state investment should focus on downstream petrochemical industries that could supply local industries with raw material. This is an ideal linkage.

Recently, an indigenous oil firm, Consolidated Oil, rented a rig from Gabon owned by Schlumberger and struck oil at 4,800 feet offshore, Nigeria's first indigenous oil discovery. Currently, between fourteen and seventeen indigenous firms have licenses, and they include the names of some of Nigeria's leading industrial capitalists: Ibru, Abiola, and Henry Stevens (Fajemirokun and Dantata).[96] Though the oil sector is usually seen as an enclave, where only Nigerian state capital is involved, and only as a passive partner, this breakthrough for indigenous capital indicates that linkages to and learning from the international energy industry are possible.

Conclusions: Regional Hegemony and Industrial Strategy

Nigeria's urban industrial sector has suffered enormously during the last decade, but a partial recovery has been rebuilt on strong linkages to indigenous resources. The size of its internal market, the dynamism and potential of its agriculture, and its hydrocarbon resources make Nigeria an exception to the image of Africa as an international welfare case, or a model of economic regress. Notwithstanding its potential, however, there are major political and organizational obstacles confronting the Nigerian political economy in the last half of the 1990s. Without a stable class alliance to discipline state activities, one cannot be sanguine about a state-centered strategy of industrialization. Privatization pressures are pruning many unproductive state investments, but the urban industrial sector will not recover until the economy is reflated by a combination of the agrarian sector and the hydrocarbon sector. Perhaps an alliance of "oil and maize" can provide the foundation for a revival and expansion of indigenous capitalism for the twenty-first century.

Economic crisis has, meantime, not only begun to change the structure and character of Nigeria's fragmented, indigenous accumulating classes, but it also promises to restructure the relationships among states within the region of West Africa. In this case, economic, political, and strategic factors combine to offer an opportunity for Nigeria to strengthen its hegemony in ECOWAS. Possessing an economy and population twice as large as the remainder of the ECOWAS states combined, Nigerian political elites have long made claims to lead the region and to dominate the long-touted West African common market. Nigeria already supplies electricity to Niger and is now embarking on a $110 million project to construct a 400-kilometer line to Benin, Togo, and Ghana.[97] Petroleum products and a variety of manufactures (including textiles and plastics) are supplied to neighboring states. In the last year, faced with a collapse of the government of Benin, Nigeria supplied financing to maintain the national administration in place.[98]

Since the formation of ECOWAS under Nigerian sponsorship, the main obstacle to economic integration has been French political and economic interests and their client elites led by Houphouët-Boigny of Côte d'Ivoire. Recently, the long-standing French "special relationship" with Africa has been questioned by forces favoring greater integration into Europe and greater democracy in the former colonies of sub-Saharan Africa. The economic collapse of the region coupled with the strength of French investments in Nigeria offers the material basis for a new alliance in which both France and Nigeria stand to gain by cooperating to form a viable regional economic unit. Because the overvalued African franc (CFA) is backed by the French franc, Nigerian-produced goods easily undercut the price of French manufactures throughout the region. After a successful visit by Babangida to Paris, one solution being discussed calls for CFA devaluation in order to coordinate it with the Nigerian naira and thereby facilitate regional commerce and investment. France would, of course, retain its role as the region's technical and investment leader, while Nigeria would become the political leader and producer of lower-value industrial and agricultural commodities.[99] Most of the remaining states of West Africa are characterized by porous frontiers, fragile elite coalitions, and weak administrations—not to mention financial dependence on France in the case of the francophone states. Should Nigeria and France strike a bargain, the postcolonial era could give way to a new phase of regional political and economic development.

Whether Nigeria's role as the regional "hegemon," and indeed whether it will prove capable of harnessing its own internal energies and capacities, remains an open question. The 1993 budget delivered by Ernest Shonekan starkly reveals the nature of the problem.[100] On the one hand, the nation was basically broke (a 46 billion naira deficit was run in 1992 and 58 percent of the country's 1993 foreign exchange earnings would be absorbed into servicing the debt); on the other hand, the budget process itself was a fiasco since the senate refused to participate (on the grounds that their role had been seriously compromised by the military government's efforts to tightly regulate the return to civilian rule in 1994). It is precisely the legacy of politicized accumulation and state indiscipline under conditions of fiscal austerity that Nigeria must confront if it is to avoid the catastrophic failures of the 1970s and capture the potential that resides in its enormous domestic market, its indigenous energies, and its natural resource wealth.

Notes

1. Alain Lipietz, *Mirages and Miracles* (London: Verso, 1988).
2. *Economist*, May 3, 1986, p. 3.
3. *Economist*, Economist Intelligence Unit (EIU), nos. 1–4, 1992.
4. World Bank, *Global Economic Prospects* (Washington, D.C.: World Bank, 1993).
5. Chalmers Johnson, *MITI and the Japanese Miracle* (Stanford: Stanford University Press, 1982).
6. Alexander Gerschenkron, *Bread and Democracy in Germany* (Ithaca: Cornell University Press, 1946).
7. Paul Lubeck, "Malaysian Industrialization, Ethnic Divisions and the NIC Model," in J. Henderson and R. Applebaum, eds., *States and Development in the Pacific Rim* (Newbury Park, Calif.: Sage Publications, 1992).
8. Alice Amsden, *Asia's Next Giant* (London: Oxford University Press, 1989); Robert Wade, *Governing the Market: Economic Theory and the Role of Government in East Asian Industrialization* (Princeton, N.J.: Princeton University Press, 1990).
9. *Newswatch*, April 26, 1993, p. 29.
10. There are, of course, exceptions to this broad pattern. A large-scale industrial, financial, and commercial bourgeoisie exists in the Muslim north, centered along the Kano-Kaduna axis; southerners like General Obasanjo have been head of state, while the technocracy of the federal government recruits primarily from southern states.
11. P. Lewis, "The Political Economy of Public Enterprise in Nigeria," Ph.D. diss., Princeton University, 1992.
12. The continued strength of the Muslim northerners was revealed in the recent presidential primaries in which the southern candidate was a Muslim Yoruba allied with a former general from Katsina with connections to the ruling northern aristocracy.
13. EIU, 4, 1990, p. 20.
14. Kyu Sik Lee and A. Anas, eds., *Manufacturers' Response to Infrastructure Deficiencies in Nigeria*, Infrastructure and Urban Development Department, Discussion Paper (Washington, D.C.: World Bank, 1989), p. 28.
15. Ibid., p. 93.
16. *Newswatch*, April 5, 1993, p. 47.
17. Ibid., December 21, 1992, p. 17.
18. EIU, 1, 1990, p. 20.
19. Ibid. In the latest iteration of corruption, the Delta Steel Company management has been accused of profligate behavior while the workers live in Aladja in pitch darkness due to electricity problems. This is in spite of the fact that the company's daily electricity consumption (mostly unpaid) was estimated to be equivalent to total monthly consumption of Lagos State (*Newswatch*, August 10, 1992, p. 52).
20. EIU, 3, 1989, p. 17.
21. In a world-class myopic gesture, the Nigeria government attempted in 1989 to privatize the Ajaokuta Steel Company, but according to R. Synge (R.

Synge, *Nigeria to 1993: Will Liberalization Work?*, London: Economist Intelligence Unit, 1989, p. 72), these are not the most attractive assets on the disposals list!

22. *West Africa*, July 1–7, 1991, p. 1089.

23. Synge, *Nigeria to 1993*, p. 72.

24. *Financial Times*, March 16, 1992.

25. P. Collier, "Oil Shocks and Food Security in Nigeria," *International Labour Review* 127, no. 6 (1988); M. Watts, ed., *State, Oil and Agriculture in Nigeria* (Berkeley: IIS/University of California Press, 1987).

26. See P. Mosley, "Policy Making Without Facts: A Note on the Assessment of Structural Adjustment in Nigeria 1985–1990," *African Affairs*, 91 (1992).

27. Tom Forrest, *Politics and Economic Development in Nigeria* (Boulder: Westview Press, 1993), pp. 184–185.

28. Collier, "Oil Shocks and Food Security."

29. World Bank, "Nigeria and Agriculture," Sector Memorandum 4723-UNI, Washington, D.C., 1985.

30. See P. Clough, "Grain Marketing in Northern Nigeria," *Review of African Political Economy*, no. 34 (1985); K. Swindell and A. Mamman, "Land Expropriation and Accumulation in the Sokoto Periphery, Northwest Nigeria, 1976–1986," *Africa* 60, no. 2 (1990).

31. ADPs began as pilot projects in the mid-1970s and were designed to transform peasant agriculture by providing rural infrastructure (roads) and extension services, tractor services, small-scale irrigation, improved seed varieties, agricultural chemicals, and subsidized fertilizer.

32. Forest, *Politics and Economic Development*, p. 186.

33. *Newswatch*, November 25, 1985.

34. *Newswatch*, November 25, 1992, p. 21.

35. *African Business*, April 1989, p. 49.

36. Central Bank of Nigeria, quarterly reports 1–4, Lagos, 1992; Nigerian Institute of Social and Economic Research, "Survey of Nigeria, *Economist,* August 21–27, 1993, p. 7.

37. Cited in Mosley, "Policy Making Without Facts," p. 234.

38. *African Business*, March 1992, p. 40.

39. There is a large discrepancy between annual food output figures for the period 1986–1989 from the CBN (9.2 percent) and the Nigerian Federal Office of statistics (-1.2 percent).

40. Central Bank of Nigeria (CBN), *Annual Report and Statement of Accounts (For the Year Ended December 30, 1990)* (Lagos: CBN, 1991), p. 68.

41. Fertilizer quadrupled in price between 1985 and 1989 (*Newswatch*, July 27, 1992, p. 35), while the DFRRI has little to show for itself after spending 2 billion naira in six years (*Newswatch*, October 5, 1992, p. 10).

42. Jane Guyer, "Everybody's Farming Now: The Example of Ibarapa District, Oyo State," paper delivered to the annual meeting of the African Studies Association, Chicago, 1988.

43. G. Myers, "This Is Not Your Land: An Analysis of the Impact of the Land Use Act in South West Nigeria," Ph.D. diss., University of Wisconsin, Madison, 1990. Myers found that not all commercial farmers and new elites wished to register their property (largely for political or bureaucratic reasons), but the act has provided opportunities for elites and speculators to gain access to land and to legitimize their acquisitions (p. 356).

44. See Guyer, "Everybody's Farming Now."

45. Synge, *Nigeria to 1993*, p. 45.

46. R. Mustapha, "Structural Adjustment and Multiple Modes of Livelihood in Nigeria," UN Research Institute for Social Development Discussion Paper No. 26,

Geneva, 1991; G. Williams, "The World Bank in Rural Nigeria Revisited," *Review of African Political Economy*, no. 43 (1988); D. Eyoh, "Reforming Peasant Production in Africa," *Development and Change* 23, no. 2 (1992).

47. Mustapha, "Structural Adjustment," p. 16.

48. A. Labaran, "Land Appropriation and Capitalized Farming in the Sokoto Region," in M. Mortimore, et al., eds., *Perspectives on Land Administration in Northern Nigeria* (Kano: Bayero University, 1987).

49. Cited in Swindell and Mamman, "Land Expropriation."

50. P. Clough, "Grain Marketing in Northern Nigeria," *Review of African Political Economy*, no. 34 (1985).

51. See *Newswatch*, August 14, 1989.

52. July 4, 1988, p. 687.

53. Myers, "This Is Not Your Land," p. 360; *Newswatch*, August 14, 1989, pp. 13–18.

54. Guyer, "Everybody's Farming Now," p. 12.

55. Myers, "This Is Not Your Land," p. 360.

56. K. Kimmage, "The Evolution of the Wheat Trap," Department of Geography, Cambridge University, 1989; G. Andrae and B. Beckman, *Industry Goes Farming*, Report No. 80 (Uppsala: Scandinavian Institute of African Studies, 1987).

57. *Newswatch*, November 30, 1992, pp. 35–37.

58. The Nigerian flour millers claimed in 1990 that only 6,000 tons of wheat were produced in Nigeria, while Kano State claimed that it alone accounted for an annual output of 400,000 tons (*African Business*, October 1990, p. 26).

59. A local bag of flour sold for 420 naira in 1990, while an imported (i.e., smuggled) bag sold for 600 naira (*African Business*, October 1990, p. 26).

60. Commercial poultry production grew from 51,000 to 74,000 tons between 1970 and 1986. Since SAP, it has fallen by 22,000 tons (*Newswatch*, August 3, 1992, p. 38).

61. *Newswatch*, August 3, 1992, p. 38.

62. Synge, *Nigeria to 1993*.

63. Guyer, "Everybody's Farming Now," p. 15.

64. *Newswatch*, September 14, 1992, p. 18. According to the *Financial Times* (April 1, 1993, p. ix), half of NAFCON's fertilizer production cannot be accounted for.

65. See P. Koehn, "Government Land Allocation in Bauchi and Kano States, Nigeria." Paper delivered to the African Studies Association, Washington, December 1982.

66. R. Udo, "The Land Use Decree and Its Antecedents," unpublished manuscript, Department of Geography, Nsukka University, 1985; *Newswatch*, August 14, 1989; *Daily Times*, February 20, 1988.

67. *Newswatch*, July 13, 1992, p. 22.

68. Eyoh, "Reforming Peasant Production," p. 23.

69. World Bank, *Nigeria: Industrial Sector Report*, Vol. 2, Main Report (Washington, D.C.: World Bank, 1991).

70. EIU, 1, 1989, p. 21.

71. The Sokoto River Basin Development Authority and the Upper Benue River Basin Development Authority both leased land to private companies (in excess of 35,000 hectares in both cases) during the 1980s (Forrest, *Politics and Economic Development*, p. 198).

72. Andrae and Beckman, *Industry Goes Farming*.

73. *Newswatch*, February 19, 1990, p. 16.

74. World Bank, *Nigeria: Industrial Sector Report*, p. 37.

75. Andrae and Beckman, *Industry Goes Farming*, p. 1.

76. EIU, 4, 1989, p. 15.

77. Anthony Hawkins, *Making Profits in Nigeria: Opportunities and Operating Conditions to 1995* (London: Business International Limited, 1991), p. 98.

78. *African Business*, May 1988, p. 48.

79. July 19, 1988, p. 15.

80. Forrest, *Politics and Economic Development*, p. 199.

81. Guyer, "Everybody's Farming Now."

82. Forrest, *Politics and Economic Development*, p. 199.

83. Tom Forrest, "The Advance of African Capital," Queen Elizabeth House, Oxford, Working Paper No. 24, April 1990.

84. *West Africa*, March 11–17, 1991, p. 361.

85. *West Africa*, April 15–21, 1991, p. 556.

86. EIU, 2, 1990, p. 21.

87. *Newswatch*, February 12, 1990, p. 33.

88. The growth of foreign investments has not been without its problems, however; an article in *Newswatch* (August 17, 1992, p. 49) noted the rising tensions in the Bonny area associated with nonemployment of indigenes by oil companies.

89. EIU, 2, 1990.

90. EIU, 4, 1990, p. 6.

91. EIU, 2, 1988, p. 16.

92. EIU, 3, 1988, p. 14.

93. EIU, 1, 1988, pp. 21–22.

94. EIU, 3, 1987, p. 20.

95. EIU, 3, 1989, p. 15; EIU, 4, 1989, p. 13.

96. *Newswatch*, February 17, 1992, pp. 22–27.

97. *West Africa*, 1990, p. 3014.

98. On the military front, Nigeria is the main force commanding ECOWAS peacekeeping forces in Liberia, which is caught in a vicious civil war. Here Liberia's rich supply of high-grade iron ore is said to provide the economic incentive. And Nigerian businessmen are active throughout the region.

99. *Africa Confidential*, April 1990, pp. 1–2.

100. *Newswatch*, February 8, 1993, p. 27.

11

African Capitalism and the Paradigm of Modernity: Culture, Technology, and the State

Bruce J. Berman

The Bourgeoisie and Capitalist Development

Western theories of social development, liberal or Marxist, are themselves the product of the process they have sought to analyze. They share the same underlying premises of the hegemonic culture of modernity; in this sense Marxism represents only a critical variant that remains part of the same cultural universe as the liberal theories it attacks. In particular, development theories have assumed the inevitable universal spread of the modern industrial nation-state.[1] Mass production, the dominance of science-based technology, bureaucratization, secularization, and the cultural movement described by the Parsonian "pattern variables" are the accepted components of the development process and comprise collectively what we can call the paradigm of modernity. Some societies may move faster on the path of development, while others may lag behind, but the ultimate outcome of a world of institutionally similar nation-states and a global culture with declining local variations is taken for granted. The major point of contention between liberals and Marxists has been the necessary end of the process of development: capitalism or socialism.[2]

The collapse of the Soviet Union and the end of the systems of state socialism in its former East European satellites led to what is likely to be an unexpectedly brief period of Western triumphalism. The very phrase used by Francis Fukuyama and others to describe the West's victory, "the end of history," reveals the underlying assumption that the capitalist nation-state is the culminating moment, the inevitable telos of the whole story of human development. Despite some misgivings that development and modernization actually mean "Westernization" and the efforts of some theorists to be sensitive to the effects of indigenous cultures on the process, the Eurocentrism of development theory generally recognizes only one history and one culture that are assumed to interrupt and redirect the history and culture of all other societies.

Development theory has thus treated Western experience as "history," making it difficult to see it as a particular historical conjuncture, one of several potential trajectories of human development. The unilinear evolutionary assumptions contained in these theories have universalized Western experience and abstracted it into structural models, at their most extreme and elegant in the theorems of economics, that effectively decontextualize the components of the paradigm of modernity. Mainstream modernization theory and orthodox Marxism are committed to constructing a formal and positivist social science in which invariant "laws" of development are linked to reality through "objective" factual (preferably, quantitative) indicators. They lead to a conception of the development process as a massive exercise in social engineering to move the backward societies of the non-Western world as quickly as possible along the inevitable road to the industrial nation-state.

Moreover, both modernizers and their critics have generally seen "culture" as primarily, if not exclusively, an issue of technology (and hence as a problem of "technology transfer"), thanks to the hegemony of the U.S. model of development in the discourse of development after World War II. For Americans, who were the primary authors of liberal development theory, the superiority of the U.S. model lay in its combination of advanced science, technology, and managerial efficiency. It is worth remembering, too, that in the African studies of the 1960s, dominated by U.S. political scientists and development theorists, any recognition of the differences of African cultures, or any suggestion that Western models of industrial development were not necessarily possible or desirable in Africa, was apt to be dismissed as racist and reactionary.

While Africans have been treated in development theory as equal in their ability to participate in the universal path of historical development, African societies and cultures, however, have not been seen in the same way. The Western paradigm of development has implicitly (and sometimes explicitly) assumed the inherent inferiority of "backward" non-Western societies and their inability to survive in competition with the rationality and efficiency of the technologically, scientifically, and organizationally superior societies of the West. Underlying the treatment of African societies in development theories is a concept of "primitive society," developed by evolutionary anthropologists of the late nineteenth and early twentieth centuries. According to this idea, the societies of Africa, Oceania, and the Americas were living fossils, stable but stagnant relics of earlier stages of social evolution.[3] The "high civilizations" of Asia, meanwhile, were treated by such concepts as Marx's Asiatic mode of production as consisting essentially of cyclical dynastic struggles over an unchanging peasant base. Both liberal and Marxist approaches to development were equally dismissive of "backward" indigenous peasant agriculture and artisan craft production; neither could be either a source of innovation or a base for development. This understanding was implicit in the shared assumption in liberal and Marxist concepts of dual economies in Third World societies, consisting of a dynamic modern sector that would eventually absorb and transform a technologically stagnant and backward "traditional" sector.[4]

Consistent with this way of seeing things has been a general tendency among both modernizers and their critics to treat all non-Western societies, including those of Africa, as peoples without history, whose only significant story is that of their subjugation by and response to the West, the process through which they finally joined the stream of real world history. The diverse forms of indigenous subjectivity and historical experience are, in this perspective, treated as essentially irrelevant. If they are dealt with at all, it is as obstacles to development posed by "traditional values." In fact, although the language used frequently belies it, the underlying idea of much of the literature is that the indigenous societies of Africa will be not so much transformed as replaced by modern, secular societies; and the key agents of this process will be indigenous elites, including business elites or capitalists, conceived of as bearers of the necessary universal values of global modernity.

The basis of Western power and the necessary and inevitable form of a developed society, economy, culture, and polity was the nation-state. All "multinational" sociopolitical forms, including the antique empires of Europe itself, would collapse into a number of smaller, but more dynamic and powerful, nation-states; the localized ethnicities of small-scale peasant and tribal communities would be absorbed into the larger society of the modern nation—the movement from empire to nation or from tribe to nation. Development meant national development only; any suggestion that units smaller or larger than the nation should be the basis of development was rejected as reactionary or utopian.

For many development theorists, nation-building was therefore the central component of the modernization project.[5] Arguments within the paradigm focused on the overarching strategy and goal of development, capitalism, or socialism; the primary institutional locus of development, state, or market; and the principal agents of development, the political and bureaucratic elites of the state, or a "national" capitalist class. Many of the debates in development theory in the 1970s and 1980s revolved around the actual or potential role of this national bourgeoisie, the conditions fostering or inhibiting its existence, its relationship to the state and to international capital, and its capacity to produce real or "authentic" capitalist development.

The matter was particularly contentious with regard to Africa, where the presence and role of a national bourgeoisie was questioned and denigrated more than in other regions of the Third World. Liberals questioned the economic and technological capabilities of indigenous capitalists in Africa. The Keynesian development economics that was dominant through the 1970s, with its focus on an interventionist state shaping macroeconomic policy, expected little from indigenous capitalists and gave the key role to the Western-educated elites in the state.[6] Marxists and *dependentistas*, meanwhile, argued over whether African capital could ever be anything but a cockleboat towed behind the battleship of international capital.[7] Many on the left also preferred a more state-controlled and centrally planned development process, with greater reliance on large-scale public enterprise, and advocated a development directly to socialism, without a stop at capitalism on the way.

From the perspective of the sociology of knowledge, political and economic forces have shaped a dramatic narrowing of the scope of theoretical discourse and empirical analysis in studies of development during the past fifteen years. During the 1980s, the growing African economic crisis, the virtual disappearance of foreign corporate investment, the imposition of structural adjustment programs (SAPs), the decline and death of state socialism in the USSR and Eastern Europe, and the rapid development of the new industrial powers of Asia have produced a renewed emphasis on the presence and developmental role of indigenous capital in African development. This has been powerfully reinforced by the reassertion of neoclassical orthodoxy in economics and the support given to it as the basis of policy toward the Third World by neoconservative governments in the United States and Britain, and by the primary international agencies of control over national economies: the World Bank and the International Monetary Fund. In the face of triumphant capitalism and its insistence on the supremacy of the market as the engine of development, the only viable or, indeed, acceptable agent of that development was a capitalist class. Students of African development, regardless of theoretical persuasion, were pressed to find such a class, analyze its activities and potential, and identify the conditions that would promote its growth.

The chapters in this book are part of the process of identification and assessment of African capital. The authors, regardless of their particular theoretical orientation, have not, however, stepped outside the paradigm of modernity: African capitalists are analyzed in relation to their ability to contribute to "development" only as the paradigm has hitherto conceived of it.

The African crisis has continued unabated, however. In the face of mounting negative evidence, the World Bank has recently conceded the failure of structural adjustment programs,[8] the sacrifice of the poorest and most vulnerable sectors of African societies on the altar of "the market" having failed to produce the expected growth and development. In the face of such persistent failure, the African crisis must also be regarded as a crisis of the paradigm of modernity itself and the various projects of national development that have been its concrete expression in the Third World. In this last chapter, therefore, I would like to push the analysis a step further to a critique of the dominant paradigm itself. The role of the capitalist class in Africa will be considered as part of an essential and much broader process of revising development theory so that it is less abstract and Eurocentric, can deal effectively with the varieties of historical and cultural experience, and can confront again the fundamental meaning of "development." The remainder of this chapter focuses on an agenda for theoretical reconstruction.

Capitalism in General Versus Historical Capitalisms

The search for a universal theory of development has difficulty, not surprisingly, in dealing with the great variety of patterns actually found in the real world, which tend to be all too easily dismissed as deviant cases. There is a profound difference, however, between the theoretical constructions of an abstract market or of capitalism in general and the actual historical capitalisms in which human beings have found themselves. As Philip Corrigan and Derek Sayre point out in *The Great Arch*, their important study of the relationship between the state and culture in capitalist development,

> Empirically we are only ever talking about historically particular capitalisms. . . . They are actively constructed through the transformation of pre-existing social forms. This historical legacy both constrains and provides the (only) resources for capitalist construction, "in-forming" it, giving it its particular shape and weight. . . .
> This dialectic of constraint and construction is central to historical understanding; it is also, in many ways the most difficult thing to grasp. . . . The "logical incongruities," in short, must serve as the starting point for reconstructing the history of capitalist civilization in England—or anywhere else, since in the real world all cases are in their own ways "peculiar." They should not be dismissed as a set of irritating disturbances to be put on one side.[9]

The reconstruction of development theory must likewise aim to explain the idiosyncrasies of real historical cases and not be content with abstract generalizations isolated from the diverse contexts of experience. Theory cannot be the end and purpose of analysis, as it has so often become, but should be treated as the conceptual toolbox of historical understanding. And that box needs to be expanded. In Chapter 2 of this book, Colin Leys notes the importance of considering again the Weberian problematic for the study of capitalist development. This would bring back concern with the subjectivity both of culture and of the individual comprehension and rationality (*verstehen*) of historical actors. In particular, it would focus attention on the relationship between rationality and accumulation and on the relationship of legal-rational authority and the bureaucratic institutions of the state and capital. As Leys also points out, however, the Weberian approach lacks a causal theory of what drives capitalist development that can compare with the Marxist understanding of the internal contradictions and struggles of capitalist social relations that provide the system with its relentless dynamic.

Bringing Marx and Weber together spotlights two crucial subjects. First is the problem of hegemony—the development of a mutually intelligible and widely accepted universe of discourse between the state and capital, which provides both the criteria for rational analysis and action, and authoritative accounts of social and physical reality. This means that capitalism involves the transformation not only of the material forces of production, but of culture and social identity as well. Second is the related issue of the essential role of the state in the development of all historical capitalisms, a role that, as Corrigan and Sayre have shown, is as much cultural as political and economic. The problem is that hegemony and, in particular, the state tend to be treated in the prevalent instrumental or structural approaches in Marxist theory in mechanical and deterministic ways. The state always acts to "meet the needs of capital," either through the deliberate instrumental interventions of the authorities, or, more mysteriously, "because of the system itself."[10] The first attributes to historical actors an omniscience and omnipotence they cannot possibly possess; the second eliminates conscious human agency from history. For both, the study of culture and historical subjectivity is impossible as well as irrelevant.

In her recent review of the process of industrialization in Africa, Lynn Mytelka concludes that we must recognize "the non-linearity of the process itself" and the essential contingency of the outcomes: "Models that stress linear forms of causality fail to grasp this reality. They also cannot deal adequately with what is a dynamic process of interaction, different in each historical conjuncture and political-economic setting."[11] Development theory needs to deal with the prevailing phenomenon of contingent and heterogeneous historical outcomes. We cannot do so, however, if we remain wedded to the aping of the forms and methods of the physical sciences that emphasize controlled experiment, theoretical construction of universal laws, and prediction as the necessary criteria of scientific knowledge. This not only betrays the continuing sense of inferiority of social scientists vis-à-vis the "hard" sciences, but also denies the essentially historical character of the social sciences, which they actually share with several of the natural sciences such as geology, paleontology, evolutionary biology, and astronomy.

Historical sciences—and the study of human socioeconomic development is surely one of the most important—deal with unique sequences of events that will never recur in quite the same form. The explanatory task of historical science is not prediction but the construction of narratives of the contingent processes of change. Recognizing the essential historicity of

the subject of development and that contingency is its essential characteristic allows us both to recognize that minute changes in events can produce
"cascades of accumulating difference" and to make a place in history for
human agency.[12] If contingency tells us that human agency makes a difference in history, then the theories that structure our narratives explain
the choices of human agents and the consequences of their activity.

Historical contingency also means that there are no guarantees and no
sure bets about development, especially of a system so deeply ridden with
contradictions and conflicts as capitalism. We cannot rely on a rational, innovative, and skilled bourgeoisie appearing as needed; on the creation of a
skilled and productive working class; or on the emergence of an efficient
state that fosters capitalist accumulation and technological change, while
simultaneously containing the fires of class conflict. Moreover, the ability
of these internal social forces to achieve their goals and act as effective
agents of development is also dependent upon an international political
and economic context over which even the most powerful of nation-states
have only limited control. For African nation-states, the international environment defines conjunctural opportunities and constraints that can undermine and destroy their best-laid plans as readily as aiding their success.

There is also no guarantee of effective bourgeois cultural hegemony.
In the cultures of existing capitalisms, hegemony has been a continuing
struggle, not a stable condition once achieved. Most have also generated
not only the modernist and secular challenges of the left, but also repeated
antimodernist and antisecular reactions on the right. For the most part, the
latter have been relatively marginal in their impact and easily contained or
supressed. Others, like that of Iran's Islamic revolution, have sent an entire society careening down a path that was scarcely conceivable in the
West before it actually happened. Industrial modernity and a secular nation-state can no longer even be considered a one-way trip.

While such analysis makes clear that African experience cannot and
will not replicate that of the West, it also shows that Africa's past and
present do not necessarily rigidly determine its future. There are choices
that can make that future different, and that possibility is what lends the
study of development a particular urgency. Equally important, contrary to
the expectations of Eurocentric theories of a single universal history, the
"traditional" cultures of the non-Western world show a striking persistence
and resilience. Instead of disappearing, they are changing and transforming themselves into new variations of cultural difference instead of suc-
cumbing to a universal culture of secular rationalism. Such diverse and
idiosyncratic trajectories of change fatally undermine our notions of
modernity and development and force us to acknowledge, as James Clifford has pointed out, "that Westerners are not the only ones going places
in the modern world."[13] And where they seek to go challenges the alleged
superiority of Western culture and even the desirability of its project of

modernization. Third World intellectuals critical of Western forms of development have seen it instead as the source of increasing poverty, violence, social decay, and environmental destruction. This disenchantment has been reinforced by the visible growth of similar problems of social and environmental dysfunction in the West itself, as well as the failure of the Soviet alternative model of modernity and the increasing poverty, disorder, and violence of the transition of former socialist societies to "free market" economies.[14]

This Third World critique of modernity joins a growing chorus of critics in the West itself who recognize that globalization of the Western model of industrial society is, on environmental grounds alone, suicidal and seek alternative values and paths development.[15] The urgency of the critique is reinforced by the development of new social movements in the West as well as the Third World that are antimodernist but not necessarily antidevelopment. Are there no other environmentally sustainable ways to develop the forces of production, relieve the desperate poverty in which an increasing proportion of the human family live, and ensure essential human rights, dignity, and freedom from oppression? And can achieving these goals be compatible with the continuity of a multiplicity of different cultures within an international system that is increasingly tightly integrated economically, socially, and politically?

The issue of Africa's bourgeoisies and their role in development must, then, finally be considered in the context of the issues outlined above. In order to do this in a more concrete way, I will examine in the next section three historically specific aspects of Western capitalist development: culture, technology, and the nation-state. This provides a theoretical baseline for a discussion in the following section of African difference and the conditions that do not exist and probably cannot and should not be created in African societies. The final sections will examine specifically the issues of appropriate technology, culture, and political choice in development, and how these can shape our understanding of the role of African capitalists.

Culture, Technology, and the State in Western Capitalism

For each Western nation-state there are distinct variations in each aspect of culture, technological development, and the state; and for the history of any particular society, the cumulative contingent impact of idiosyncratic details is not only important but often decisive. It should be understood, therefore, that what I discuss here are only some broad common denominators in Western experience.

What set capitalism in Western Europe and North America apart from all that came before was the pursuit of profit through the systematic reorganization and control of the production process. This development proceeded unevenly, with repeated, often spectacular, failures; and it provoked furious and desperate resistance from both the traditional artisans it displaced and the new industrial proletariat it called into being. What emerged by the end of the last century was the mass production of uniform goods in large factory units that were components of even larger corporations combining capital and labor, production, and distribution in a single complex system.[16]

This system and the process that led to it provided the implicit model of industrial modernity that was universalized in liberal and Marxist development theories. It was accompanied and facilitated by a profound cultural transformation that reoriented Western experience of time, space, labor, bodily life, and the production of knowledge. The elements of this hegemonic culture are so deeply and widely rooted in the diverse forms of academic and professional knowledge of Western societies that they are virtually invisible to us, a part of the taken-as-given fabric of reality itself. It is these elements of Western culture, and the objective knowledge of and control over the world they claim to supply, that promote the effort to universalize Western experience and the rejection of non-Western cultures as backward and irrational.

The central component of the hegemonic culture of capitalist society is, as Leys points out in Chapter 2, instrumental rationality—the objectification and systematic calculation of the causal relation of means and ends. The identification of rationality with the production of intended effects links with the development of an understanding of the physical universe as a mechanical system, following universal and invariant laws, rather than as a living organism. The understanding of this system permits the rational and predictable control of nature, in both the laboratory and the factory.[17] The mechanical system model was applied as well to the social world, to the labor process in particular, with the same focus on achieving rational and predictable control. In the mid–eighteenth century, Josiah Wedgewood wrote to his partner that he was "preparing to make such *Machines* of the *Men* as cannot Err."[18]

The basis of the culture of instrumental rationality is an epistemic order of "development in time":

> Development was a new connection which posited dynamics (as opposed to stasis); transformation (as opposed to unrelated, specific change); structure (as opposed to taxonomy); and totality (as a spatio-temporal whole). Anything and everything in bourgeois society had to be comprehended and explained as an order of development-in-time. And that development was necessarily dynamic, transformative, structural and whole.[19]

On a macrosocial level, such an epistemic order is clearly expressed in the diverse theories of social, economic, and political development produced in the West during the past two centuries. It also provided, at a

microsocial level, the metaphysical basis for the "Babbage principle" and
the later development of scientific management, which minutely analyzed
the capitalist labor process into a sequence of simple steps that could be
rationalized, routinized, and, eventually, mechanized.[20] Objective knowledge of causal sequences of events in space and time made possible rational
intervention to produce stable, orderly, and predictable outcomes. The ultimate goal, pursued in every sphere of nature and society, was the reduction of knowledge to a rational calculus that would banish or at least minimize uncertainty.[21]

The principal practical and institutional expressions of this new rationality are technology and bureaucracy, and the diverse disciplines of specialized knowledge intimately associated with them. Michel Foucault revealed the significance of these "disciplines" in the double meaning of the
word: as a particular branch of knowledge and as a mode of ensuring the
control, orderliness, and efficiency of human conduct.[22] Disciplines function in both senses simultaneously as they make individuals into objects of
study and define human activity as in need of organization, regulation, and
control.[23] The successful application of instrumental rationality toward
concrete, but often distant, goals requires the coordination of extended sequences of activity and the use of humans as uniformly effective and predictable instruments. Herein lies the basis for the Western conception of
discipline and for the pervasive resort to the mechanical metaphor for the
bureaucratic machine.[24]

In no sense, then, is technology, both as knowledge and as artifacts,
socially and politically neutral, or the product of an autonomous process of
invention. Recent studies in the history and sociology of technology have
revealed the degree to which it is a construct of particular historical con-
junctures, shaped by sociocultural, economic, and political factors.[25] The
transfer of technology from one cultural context to another is never either
an automatic consequence of industrial investment or a simple technical
matter of introducing improved methods. It is always fraught with potential social consequences and conflicts that will affect its acceptance and
use. The technology developed in the West is an explicit bureaucratic
and, indeed, capitalist technology. It is a "prescriptive technology" that
both requires and is shaped to fit the "culture of compliance," i.e., the dis-
ciplinary order of the bureaucratized workplace.[26] The subordination of
Western workers to the factory labor and technology-based control was facilitated by the negative moral connotations of work in Western culture
and by the increasing denigration of craft knowledge in comparison with
"objective" organizational and technological knowledge of managers and
engineers.[27]

The hegemonic culture of instrumental rationality and its technological and bureaucratic forms are intimately connected to the development
and character of the Western nation-state. It is necessary to insist on this

because both liberal and Marxist theories tend to reduce the state to functional but largely epiphenomenal roles. The state, however, is not simply an externality that sometimes provides support for, but mostly simply disrupts, the free market; nor is it a determined superstructure that obediently meets the needs of capital. The nation-state is as important a component of the historical development of capitalist society as the sphere of capitalist production itself. State intervention has been essential for capitalist development, particularly in the administration of a uniform and consistent law, the formation and protection of national markets, and the control of labor through the replication in juridical and political forms of capitalist social relations.[28] The role of the state goes even deeper, however. Through the turmoil and struggle of capitalist development, the state emerged as the principal agent of major cultural transformations "integral to the making of a bourgeois social order, a civilization. Capitalism is not just an economy, it is a regulated set of social forms of life."[29]

The state is the most powerful agent of the hegemonic culture of instrumental rationality. It is because it is also a system of knowledge, the "massively authoritative organization of what is to count as reality": 'How things are' (allowed to be) is not simply a matter of ideological assertion . . . it is concretized in laws, judicial decisions (and their compilation as case law), registers, census returns, licenses, charters, tax forms, and all the other myriad ways in which the state states [sic] and individualities are regulated."[30] It does so through diverse practices of social surveillance and the reflexive monitoring of its own activities.[31] The state's expertise is expressed in the disciplines of instrumental rationality, whose development it directly fosters and which constitute the professional ideologies of the bureaucratic apparatus.[32]

The state has also played a crucial role in the development of the technology of industrial capitalism. It has supported research institutes and schools for scientific and technical training. It has also provided testing facilities, profitable contracts, and, most crucially, direct financial support, outside the constraints of the market, for the development by private capital of complex technical systems that firms could not and would not have been able to sustain from their own resources. State support has been instrumental in technological development, from the development of interchangeable parts for mass production (the so-called American system) during the nineteenth century to the development of automated machine tools and computers in the second half of the twentieth century.[33]

The single most important factor shaping the state's influence on the development of industrial technology has been its preparations for and involvement in war. The professional armed forces of Western nation-states have provided a major influence on the structure, methods of discipline and labor control, and organizational management of the civilian state bureaucracy and private enterprise.[34] Industrialization in Europe was substantially imitative and driven by the politico-military imperatives of a highly competitive and violent state system. As Björn Hettne points out, "Contrary to conventional modernization theory and orthodox Marxism, similarities in the pattern of economic growth did not reveal any inherent tendencies towards 'modernity' but political imperatives that made industrialization necessary for security reasons."[35]

The pattern of development outlined in the last few pages—of a hegemonic bourgeois culture of instrumental rationality, its expression in bureaucratic administration and technology, the active role in both of an increasingly complex and effective state, the effect of vigorous interstate competition and warfare in a relatively stable international system of similar states, and the linkage of these factors to private accumulation and the systematic transformation of the forces of production—constitutes a distinctively Western experience that cannot and will not be reproduced anywhere else. Even in the West, these general processes were subject to distinctive national and even intranational regional variation; and, as noted earlier, it is these idiosyncratic details, the contingencies of history, that are often of greatest importance in the history of any particular country. Outside Western Europe and North America, and this would include Eastern Europe as well as Asia, Africa, and South America, the possibility of finding similar antecedents, trajectories, and outcomes of development is small.

First, nowhere else, except for Japan,[36] can we find development emerging out of the contradictions and crises of a feudal economy and polity. Nowhere else do we find the particular combination of the cultural and institutional power of the Catholic church and the profound sociocultural upheavals of the Renaissance and Reformation. Nowhere else do we find the scientific-technological revolution that began in the seventeenth century. Nowhere else do we find the extended 400-year process of developing centralized national states in a state system largely unchallenged by, and gradually extending imperial hegemony over, all non-Western polities. Second, non-Western societies are not only different from the precapitalist social order of the West, but they all had distinctive internal trajectories of change that were moving in different directions from that of Europe. Third, non-Western societies also had universal but widely differing experiences of Western hegemony, conquest, and imperial control that were a part of the development of the West itself and a disruptive intrusion into their own processes of change. Fourth, the possibilities of development in all non-Western societies will remain subject in the future to a global system increasingly dominated by a handful of advanced capitalist states, the international political and economic institutions they control, and a few hundred transnational corporations controlled by their citizens.

Culture and Technology in Contemporary Africa

The improbability of any indigenous replication of Western experience becomes clear from even a cursory examination of the issues of culture, technology, and the state in Africa. With regard to culture, there is no evidence that a hegemonic bourgeois culture of instrumental rationality has developed within any society or state in Africa. Elements of it exist through the presence of expatriate business people and aid officials, the influence of Western governments, the wide spread of Western popular culture, and especially the thousands of African engineers, teachers and professors, entrepreneurs, and government officials who have imbibed substantial parts of it through their training both at home and in Western universities. The influence of the latter, socially and politically as well as economically, and how they have interpreted Western bourgeois culture and adapted it to their specific sociocultural context, are matters about which we need to know a great deal more. As Leys points out in Chapter 2, we need to study these elements in African societies as classes, not simply as individuals, firms, and institutions, and to examine if a common intellectual and cultural orientation exists, as well as any collective social and political projects. John Rapley's analysis in Chapter 3 of some social dimensions of the Ivoirien bourgeoisie is an important contribution in this area.

There is also little evidence of the development in Africa of national cultures and societies coterminus with the existing state structures or extending much beyond the interethnic elite coalitions of the preindependence "nationalist" movements.[37] African culture and identity continue to find the most vital level of their development and expression in the diverse ethnic communities that are continuous with precolonial societies. We are beginning to understand that the precolonial societies of Africa were dynamic, not the static living fossils Europeans believed them to be, and that the specific social forms Europeans encountered in their conquest of Africa were often of quite recent origin.[38] Moreover, the African response to the powerful political and economic forces unleashed by colonialism was not to abandon their traditional cultures and identities, as modernization theory posited, but instead to react to those forces from within their cultures and attempt to adapt both to the new circumstances.

For example, John Lonsdale has recently shown the richness and complexity of the intellectual and cultural response of the Kikuyu to the changes brought by colonialism, including the introduction of capitalist forms of production and the beginning of class formation, and how this response both redefined the nature of Kikuyuness, sought to control the impact of European culture on the Kikuyu, and shaped the internal conflicts that found expression in Mau Mau.[39] In developmental terms, this reveals the continuing dialectic of cultural continuity and change, even in a people

widely understood to have been among the most deeply affected by Western values and capitalism and to have produced one of Africa's most notable capitalist classes.[40]

Unfortunately, the expectation of Eurocentric development theories
that traditional cultures would disappear during modernization, has led to
a hostile response in the West to expressions of their continued viability
and dynamism and to denunciations of atavistic "tribalism."[41] It has been
difficult for us in the West and for Western-trained African elites to accept
that indigenous societies can be a viable basis for development, partly because to recognize this would open up the possibility of a multiplicity of
paths to development, and partly because the denigration of Africans'
stock of knowledge and techniques is an intrinsic part of the mythology
of their "primitiveness." Nowhere is this more pronounced than in the
treatment of the role of technology in African development.

Africa today is a scene of technological chaos. In the Western experience, the major technological innovations developed out of existing indigenous knowledge and practice, at first ad hoc and then increasingly systematically. The major technological changes were shaped by and
influenced in turn the cultures and social relations within which they were
created, and interacted with each other to produce yet further changes.
This has rarely been the experience in Africa since the continent came
under European domination during the last century.

The technology introduced during the colonial period was of European
origin and design and intended to serve the needs of the imperial powers
for administrative control, communications, and the production and export
of cash crops and raw materials. The manufacturing technology that was
introduced later was also wholly European in origin and design, the production machinery often being the castoffs of some metropolitan parent
company. After independence, African dependence on foreign, mostly
Western, technology has continued, and in some areas, such as the military, it is virtually complete. And from the perspective of the paradigm of
modernity, any adaptation of technology to African circumstances is inconceivable. African governments themselves largely accept the view that
development involves the adoption of the most advanced technology available in the industrial world; anything less would be backward and retro-
grade, an admission of failure.[42]

However, the attempt by African states, spurred by international and
bilateral aid donors, international corporations, and development experts,
to replicate aspects of the historically and culturally specific experience
of Western industrialization, is a major component of the social upheaval
and economic decline that has overtaken much of Africa in the past
decade. Western plants and equipment, and the instrumental rationality
and models of reality underlying them, have little connection with indigenous culture and social conditions in Africa and rarely operate in the

same way or meet the same standards of efficiency as in their place of origin.

Africa has been the scene of some of the most spectacular failures of industrial planning of our time—the Nigerian steel industry immediately comes to mind (see Lubeck and Watts, Chapter 10), but there are many other examples.[43] More generally, there is little impetus to assimilate foreign technology and operate it efficiently, and both foreign and local firms in Africa "frequently failed to attain nominal capacity levels, while overall performance fell well below that of best practice plants in the advanced industrial countries."[44] Inefficiency and underutilization of capacity are only part of the problem. In addition, adherence to the Western mass production model, which introduced technology inappropriate to African conditions and failed to produce adequate gains in employment, has been a source of environmental deterioration; it has produced increased dependence on imported raw materials and intermediate inputs, thus expanding the need for foreign exchange and placing growing pressure on agriculture to deal with a deteriorating balance of trade.[45] The products of such industrialization themselves are criticized for being reproductions of Western consumer goods for a narrow urban market, beyond the reach of the African worker or peasant and often pushing out more desirable and/or less expensive indigenous products.[46]

Various NGOs have, of course, introduced many examples of "intermediate" or "appropriate" technology, largely in rural areas or the urban informal sector. This technology is intended to serve directly African needs and to offer alternative trajectories of development more open to the mass of the population marginalized or victimized by advanced Western technology. However, even appropriate technology is rarely designed in Africa but is largely produced for Africans by expatriate experts.[47] Little research and development of any kind takes place in Africa, and even that is largely defined by the issues and standards of advanced technology in the West.

The net result is the uneasy coexistence of every possible form of technology, from the most basic to the most sophisticated high technology, almost all of them with limited or no sociocultural links to the societies they so deeply affect. Technological innovation in Africa is thus largely a matter of the push from African governments, international corporations, and aid agencies, with very little resulting from indigenous demand or initiative.[48] African scientists and engineers primarily train in and pursue careers defined by the practices and standards of the West, with little if any connection to indigenous societies or their forms of knowledge and technique.[49] In such a context of technological anarchy, what then is the appropriate role of an African bourgeoisie in the transformation of the forces of production? Such a question is, as we shall see below, unanswerable unless some broader questions are dealt with first.

Modernization and the Crisis of the Nation-State in Africa

The inadequacies and failures of the state in Africa have been a matter of growing concern for years, particularly its increasingly predatory relationship with civil society and its decline into a decrepit apparatus of tyranny and piracy. Basil Davidson has recently concluded that the imposition of the nation-state in Africa has been a profound mistake, although he does point out that both ideological and political pressure from the imperial powers made it impossible for the "nationalist" leaders of the 1950s and 1960s to achieve independence through any other political form or with anything less than full acceptance of the modernity paradigm.[50] The problems have their root in the origins of the modern state in Africa in European colonialism. What Europe transferred to Africa was a partial replica of its own bureaucratic state apparatus.[51] At first the metropoles focused on the extension and maintenance of effective politico-administrative control over African peasants and pastoralists, usually through a small garrison and a civil apparatus of prefectoral field administrators. Later, the colonial state acquired an increasingly complex bureaucratic structure of social and economic management in line departments of agriculture, health, education, etc., and a parastatal sector of marketing boards, cooperative societies, and public corporations. Even this pattern was uneven, however, and in smaller and poorer colonies, especially in the French empire, the development of the state beyond the control apparatus was often rudimentary right up to independence. Moreover, Africans had very limited access to the upper levels of the colonial bureaucracy until the end of the 1950s, when hasty "Africanization" began. The political institutions of the liberal democratic nation-state were equally hurriedly tacked on to the state in elaborate independence constitutions.

The most crucial characteristic of the African colonial state was that it was, at its core, a guardian bureaucracy based on an ideology of authoritarian paternalism. Colonial states were there to guide to a higher level of civilization, forcefully if necessary, an indigenous population generally regarded as primitive, backward, and ignorant; as well as to serve the economic and strategic interests of the metropole. Despite attempts to rationalize it, this dual mandate was often contradictory. Colonial authorities were often ambivalent about the value of capitalist development and torn between the demands of metropolitan interests and those of emergent indigenous accumulators. The latter, especially at the beginning, tended to be drawn from their own African subordinates, upon whom they depended for stability and control. While development rewarded their collaborators, it also disrupted indigenous societies and encouraged an African elite to make increasing political and economic demands.

The crisis of the colonial state reached a culmination in the twenty years after World War II. Africans replaced the European officials right to the top of the bureaucracy, but the central control apparatus retained its paramount importance. With the rapid decay of the tacked-on institutions of political democracy, the growing threat of military interventions, and the withering of political party organizations, African rulers continued to rely on the continuity of the guardian state to sustain their control. The power of senior administrators remained one element of stability in an increasingly disorderly political environment. At the same time, the relationship between the state apparatus and indigenous capital remained as ambivalent as in the colonial era. State cadres, whether in ostensibly socialist or capitalist regimes, were deeply suspicious of development occurring outside state control.[52] They were also caught between the demands of international aid donors and investors, whose importance to development they largely accepted without question, and those of an indigenous bourgeoisie of questionable competence that was also divided by regional and ethnic cleavages. Furthermore, with the lack of public political processes for influencing policy and the concentration of power and wealth in the state, the relationship between the state apparatus and indigenous capital was open to outrageous abuse and corruption on both sides, as the chapters by Himbara, Boone, MacGaffey, and Lubeck and Watts in this book richly document. Whether the state elites abuse their power by grabbing wealth in the private sector, or indigenous business people seek rents by milking the state, the result is unlikely to be significant development of the forces of production.

The state elites in Africa are also avatars of the West's history of industrial mass production based on large production units and employing the most advanced Western technology. Their devotion to the modernization model conditioned their openness to foreign donors and investors who have, as Mytelka has pointed out, more influence in Africa than anywhere else in the Third World. It also shaped the urban bias of investments and markets and the strong focus on parastatal industries, including joint ventures with international capital.[53] Moreover, the management deficiencies and limited expertise in technology evaluation and choice in African states actually increase reliance on Western technocratic models, devotion to brandname technology ("no one has ever been fired for buying IBM"), and belief in technological breakthroughs and quick fixes.[54]

African governments, not surprisingly, have a strong bias in favor of large-scale, capital-intensive enterprises, whether parastatals, foreign private investments, or indigenous capitalist firms. Where the state supports private industrial capital, it favors enterprises that replicate the scale and technology of the MNCs. There is a strong bias against the informal sector and small-scale enterprise, urban and rural, and governments have shown little interest in providing infrastructure and support for them.[55]

The structural and ideological heritage of the African state makes it difficult for it to be consistently supportive of indigenous capitalist development

even under the best of circumstances. In the conjuncture of the crisis of the
past decade, the distinctive characteristics of the African state are accentuated and its relationship to indigenous capital and ability to supply it
with essential support and services rendered yet more equivocal.

First, with the imposition of structural adjustment programs, cuts in
public expenditure have led to serious deterioration in the basic administrative capabilities of many states. At the same time public discontent and
disorder following declines in real wages and steeply rising food prices
have forced increased reliance on the coercion and political control. Second, the reimposition of neocolonial forms of indirect rule through increasing supervision of parts of the state apparatus by representatives of
external aid agencies has reinforced the dominance of the modernization
model in African states. Moreover, the coupling of the supposed reform of
African administrative capabilities with the introduction of advanced computer technology has accentuated techno-idolatry and dependence on
Western knowledge in the state apparatus.[56] The result is a state that has
withdrawn from a substantial part of its direct involvement in economic
management and development in favor of privatization of state enterprises
and the "freeing of markets," but is increasingly dependent on Western-
controlled finance, policies, and technology and more distanced from its
own social context.

Conclusion:
African Capitalists in an Alternative Development

In this chapter I have explored some of the theoretical and methodologi-
cal grounds for believing that the dominant Western paradigm of modernity and its linear, deterministic, and evolutionary understanding of development are a source of problems rather than solutions for the multiple
crises of contemporary African societies. Both modernization and Marxist
theories have misconstrued an inherently contingent historical process by
universalizing the idiosyncratic historical, cultural, and political characteristics of Western experience, as well as tending to ignore the historical,
cultural, and political differences of African societies that make the reproduction in Africa of Western development strictly impossible. Instead, the
efforts to reproduce a secular, industrial, and capitalist nation-state within
the contemporary world economy may be the principal source of the socioeconomic dysfunction and decay that has been the dark shadow of
African "development" since the colonial period. In these circumstances,
even if African capitalists emerge and act according to their paradigmatic
role in modernization, the result is more likely to be the recurrence and in-
tensification of crises than the production of development, regardless of
the criteria employed for measuring it. The real utopianism of our age may

be the continued faith in and attempts to reproduce and sustain the paradigm of modernity throughout the world (including in the West itself).

We must consider, therefore, the possibility of alternative concepts and constructions of development in both theory and practice. In a contingent world where individual and collective choices do make a difference in the shaping of social change, alternatives are always possible, although all alternatives are not equally feasible, and many are simply not available at all. Development theory is ultimately about the making of social choices, a normative application of political and social theory; and the issues involved are essentially political in the broadest possible sense. For Africans this means confronting the great issues of human values and human agency in diverse cultural contexts, and being willing and able to find their own idiosyncratic paths toward a more humane and equitable future.

We should not expect uniform outcomes. Indeed, the preservation and enrichment of human diversity must be a central underlying premise of global development. This does not mean that all elements of modern industrial society are to be rejected out of hand, but rather that they must be subject to critical scrutiny as to their suitability in a specific context and to whether and how they should be adapted to local circumstances. Borrowing, adaptation, and rejection of features of other societies have been aspects of human development from its beginning, along with autonomous innovation and social construction. They should continue to be so in the future, but in an environment of free and unconstrained choice that constitutes the essential political condition of an alternative development. At present, the continued effort by African governments, aid agencies, and international capital to impose the paradigm of modernity constitutes for the vast majority of the people of the continent an act of coercion that is as violent in its methods as in its consequences.

The maintenance of social diversity must be matched with ecological sustainability as the underlying premises of global development. Environmental constraints define the real parameters within which development can take place, but they are neither fixed nor unchanging, varying among local ecosystems and according to the current state of human knowledge and technology. Ecodevelopment "consists of specific elements: a certain group of people, with certain cultural values, living in a certain region with a certain set of natural resources. . . . [It] means that the local community and local ecosystem develop together towards a highter productivity and a higher degree of needs satisfaction, but above all that this is sustainable in both ecological and social terms."[57]

I can only outline here in the most cursory way aspects of the kind of development theory and practice that would be based on the above premises. Focusing once more on the three areas dealt with earlier—technology, culture, and the state—I would like to suggest how the role of the bourgeoisie in African development should be approached within the

context of broader questions relating to the development and choice of appropriate technology, the qualitative understanding of the meaning of development in different cultural settings, and the role of the state and character of the political process within which such issues are decided.

A bourgeoisie that pursues an industrialization based upon imported
technology and forms of production organization might produce some
wealthy industrialists but is unlikely to produce a transformation of the
forces of production that will relieve the poverty of the mass of the population. The crux of the issue is finding a path toward a flexible, decentralized,
and indigenously grounded industrial system. According to Mytelka, this involves a shift in development theory and practice in at least four ways:

> First, from quantitative to qualitative goals, that is, from an emphasis on
> level to one of structure and form; second, from a view of the rural sec-
> tor in terms of its extractive potential to one which stresses its importance
> as a market for domestic manufacturers and a source of inputs for indus-
> try; third, . . . the conceptualization of more flexible, geographically de-
> centralized and confederal forms of manufacturing systems which inter-
> face the mass production and the informal sectors while linking
> knowledge and goods production activities; and fourth, from reliance on
> imported technology in all its forms to the building of indigenous tech-
> nological capabilities throughout the economy and society.[58]

A bourgeoisie meeting these criteria would likely be far more numerous, smaller in its scale of operations, and more geographically dispersed
than the mass production model allows for. It would also be tied much
more closely to local sourcing and markets. Indeed, it may ultimately be
found precisely in the informal sector or second economy and among the
"surplus population." When we step away from the perceptual constraints
of the modernization model, this sector and its people can be more clearly
seen as actually the "real" economy and society of contemporary Africa.
Here is where the great mass of ordinary people increasingly survive, with
resilience and ingenuity, under the trying circumstances of economic crisis and political disorder visited upon them by the staggering dysfunctions
of the formal economy and the state of the modern sector. It is here, too,
that indigenous cultures survive and adapt.

The source of an indigenous, technically innovative, and developmental bourgeoisie may then be the microenterprises of rural communities and
the periurban settlements of African cities. Where is this possible and what
kind of supportive services—financial, transportation, communications, research, etc.—are needed to its development? There is evidence that such
contingent possibilities do exist both in Africa and elsewhere. In Africa
and Asia where government policy, support services, and structural conditions have favored small enterprise, local entrepreneurs have been able
to succeed and to develop indigenous technological capability, as in the

cases analyzed by Deborah Brautigam (see Chapter 7) or in the remarkable instance, documented by Ian Smillie, of the 40,000 workshops of the Suame Magazine in Kumasi, Ghana, and the emergence there of an indigenous light engineering and machine tool industry.[59]

What then is appropriate technology for alternative development? What constitutes appropriate technology must be understood first as a matter of contextually relative judgment, and second as referring more to the process by which technology is developed than to its specific form. Appropriate technology is neither "low" nor underdeveloped nor second best, nor even always small-scale. If we accept the contingency and multiplicity of historical trajectories of development, appropriate technology is what emerges from indigenous processes of learning and innovation and meets qualitative criteria of evaluation, and not solely quantitative criteria of increasing productivity. The alternatives to the mass production model can be based on Western scientific knowledge and technical expertise as well as develop through incremental changes and adaptations from indigenous knowledge and technique to meet needs defined in the local sociocultural context. The question of the social construction of appropriate technology is thus inseparable from fundamental questions of social choice and the meaning of development in a particular society. It is not merely a technical question, but also, and most critically, a political issue.

An alternative development would also include ethnodevelopment, "a most radical concept since it turns the tables on the conventional conception of ethnicity as an obstacle to modernization. . . . It is development within a framework of cultural pluralism, based on the premise that different communities in the same society have distinctive codes of behaviour and different value systems."[60] This involves recognizing the stubborn persistence and continued change of African cultures and the ethnic identities connected to them, and the importance of their having room for continued development and noncoercive adaptation to Western modernity. From this perspective, African capitalists must be seen as members of cultures as well as of a class; and as agents of change, not as bearers of an alien "modern" culture of instrumental rationality that supersedes and destroys indigenous cultures, but as potential mediators and innovators in the process of adaptation. Their role in the process of developing appropriate technology can be an important component in such cultural change and can contribute to the empowerment of Africans by decreasing the deference to "advanced" knowledge and technical expertise that is a major component of Western hegemony.[61]

Finally, consideration of the possible role of African capitalists in indigenous technological development and cultural pluralism as integral parts of development reveals that the existing states in Africa constitute a major obstacle to the conception and pursuit of an alternative development, as well as to industrial modernity. At the same time, however,

appropriate technology and a vigorously developmental indigenous bourgeoisie cannot result from acting on neoclassical fantasies of virtually re-
moving the state from the economy. Both local technological innovation
and its linkage with small entrepreneurial enterprise, including provision
of research, technological advice, and credit schemes, require strategic
state support.

Unfortunately, "most policy interventions that are likely to have a significant impact upon the development and diffusion of AT [appropriate
technology] do directly impinge on underlying political power. Consequently it is probably the social and political basis of the AT-enabling
state rather than the intelligence of policy design which is the single most
important factor determining the effectiveness of policy."[62] The ideological biases and vested interests within the African state, plus those of the
state's local allies and foreign aid donors and investors, constitute the
major social forces blocking the exploration of alternative forms of development. And these also constitute the major obstacles to the democratization of African politics.

To this must also be added the increasing limits on the capacity of all
nation-states, even in advanced capitalist societies, to control effectively
their domestic economies within the world system. Under these circumstances, political reform is an essential condition for an alternative development in which indigenous African capitalists can play an effective role,
but it is reform that must focus on institutional levels both above and
below the nation-state: decentralization and devolution to local areas
within African states as well as the development of transnational regional
and global institutions.[63] The possibility of alternative development in
Africa is ultimately inseparable from institutional reform and the replacement of the modernity paradigm in the West itself.

Notes

1. Lynn Mytelka, "The Unfulfilled Promise of African Industrialization,"
African Studies Review 32, no. 3 (1989), pp. 77–78. For an account of the spread
of the industrial mass production model in both Western and Soviet society, see
Thomas Hughes, *American Genesis: A Century of Invention and Technological Enthusiasm, 1870–1970* (New York: Penguin Books, 1989), especially Chapters 6–7.
2. A good example is the influential Marxist text by Bill Warren, *Imperialism: Pioneer of Capitalism* (London: New Left Books, 1980). I am asked repeat-
edly by students why so much of Warren sounds exactly like liberal development
economics.
3. Adam Kuper, *The Invention of Primitive Society: Transformations of an Illusion* (London and New York: Routledge, 1988).
4. Mytelka, "Unfulfilled Promise," pp. 86–87.
5. Björn Hettne, *Development Theory and the Three Worlds* (London: Longman, 1990), pp. 28–29.
6. Ibid., pp. 49–50.

7. The classic example of the clash between Marxists and dependency theorists over these issues is found in the "Kenya debate," circa 1978–1983. See the summary and analysis in Gavin Kitching, "Politics, Methods and Evidence in the 'Kenya Debate,'" in H. Bernstein and B. Campbell, eds., *Contradictions of Accumulation in Africa* (London and Beverly Hills: Sage Publications, 1985). Dependency theory is not explicitly treated here for a number of reasons. First, as I have written elsewhere (*Control and Crisis in Colonial Kenya: The Dialectic of Domination* [London: James Currey; Athens: Ohio University Press, 1990], Introduction and Chapters 1 and 10 passim), insofar as dependency theory posits a self-reproducing process of "underdevelopment" that is the mirror image of capitalist development in the West, it is simply an inaccurate depiction of the complex and contradictory impact of capitalism and imperialism on the non-Western world, an image that is dictated by the logic of theory construction rather than historical reality. Second, insofar as dependency theorists have recognized diverse patterns of local class formation, relations with international capital, and state activities that make for the possibility of various forms of "dependent development," they tend to merge and enter into direct dialogue with various Marxist approaches.

8. As explained by Gerald Helleiner at the meeting of the Canadian Association of African Studies on May 14, 1993. For some of the evidence and analysis of the consequences of structural adjustment programs in Africa, see Bonnie Campbell and John Loxley, eds., *Structural Adjustment in Africa* (London: Macmillan, 1989); Efrong Essien, *Nigeria Under Structural Adjustment* (Ibadan: Fountain Publishing, 1990); J. Barry Riddell, "Things Fall Apart Again: Structural Adjustment Programs in Sub-Saharan Africa," *Journal of Modern African Studies* 30, no. 1 (1992); Judith Marshall, *War, Debt and Structural Adjustment in Mozambique* (Ottawa: North-South Institute, 1992).

9. Philip Corrigan and Derek Sayre, *The Great Arch: English State Formation as Cultural Revolution* (Oxford: Basil Blackwell, 1985), pp. 189–190.

10. For a fuller discussion, see Berman, *Control and Crisis*, pp. 11–34.

11. Mytelka, "Unfulfilled Promise," p. 109.

12. The phrase is Stephen Jay Gould's in his incisive analysis of the impact of contingency on theory and method in historical science in *Wonderful Life: The Burgess Shale and the Nature of History* (New York: Norton, 1989), pp. 277–291.

13. James Clifford, *The Predicament of Culture: Twentieth-Century Ethnography, Literature and Art* (Cambridge: Harvard University Press, 1988), p. 17.

14. See the interesting discussion in Tariq Banuri, "Development and the Politics of Knowledge: A Critical Interpretation of the Social Role of Modernization Theories in the Development of the Third World," in Frederique Apffel Marglin and Stephen A. Marglin, eds., *Dominating Knowledge: Development, Culture and Resistance* (Oxford: Clarendon Press, 1990), pp. 58–67.

15. This search for an alternative or "another development" has a long history in the West, from the reactionary romanticism and peasant populism of the nineteenth century to the green movements and countercultures of the twentieth. For a succinct account of such alternate theories see Hettne, *Development Theory*, pp. 152–194.

16. The early stages of this process and the conflicts that shaped it, in what became the industrial heartland of Britain, are analyzed in John Foster, *Class Struggle and the Industrial Revolution: Early Industrial Capitalism in Three English Towns* (London: Methuen, 1974). The sequence of development of industries and changes in the labor process in one English city (Coventry) are analyzed in Andrew Friedman, *Industry and Labour: Class Struggle at Work and Monopoly Capitalism* (London: Macmillan, 1977). For accounts of the American experience, which focus more on the development of organization and technology than

relations between labor and capital, see Alfred Chandler, *The Visible Hand: The Managerial Revolution in American Business* (Cambridge: Harvard University Press, 1977); David Hounshell, *From the American System to Mass Production, 1800–1932* (Baltimore: Johns Hopkins University Press, 1984); and Hughes, *American Genesis*.

17. For the religious, political, and economic dimensions of the concept of a mechanistic universe during the scientific revolution of the seventeenth century, see James R. Jacob and Margaret C. Jacob, "The Anglican Origins of Modern Science: The Metaphysical Foundations of the Whig Constitution," *Isis* 71, no. 257 (1980).

18. Quoted in Adrian Forty, *Objects of Desire: Design and Society from Wedgewood to IBM* (New York: Pantheon, 1986), p. 33. Wedgewood, in his combination of experimental method and rational analysis of the physical characteristics of pottery and the labor process, and in his innovative business acumen in the design and marketing of his product, is a notable example of the development of "practical reason" in early industrial capitalism (pp. 16–41).

19. Donald M. Lowe, *History of Bourgeois Perception* (Chicago: University of Chicago Press, 1982), p. 11.

20. Harry Braverman, *Labor and Monopoly Capital* (New York: Monthly Review, 1974), Chapters 3–6; Bruce Berman, "The Computer Metaphor: Bureaucratizing the Mind," *Science as Culture*, no. 7 (1989).

21. Philip Davis and Reuben Hersh, *Descartes' Dream: The World According to Mathematics* (Boston: Houghton-Mifflin, 1986).

22. Michel Foucault, *Discipline and Punish: The Birth of the Prison* (New York: Pantheon, 1977), Part 3.

23. Cathy Ferguson, *The Feminist Case Against Bureaucracy* (Philadelphia: Temple University Press, 1984), p. 31.

24. Max Weber echoed these elements in his definition of discipline:

> The content of discipline is nothing but the consistently rationalized, methodically trained and exact execution of the received order in which all personal criticism is unconditionally suspended and the actor is unswervingly and exclusively set for carrying out the command. In addition the conduct under orders is uniform. . . . What is decisive for discipline is that the obedience of a plurality of men is rationally uniform. (Max Weber, *From Max Weber: Essays in Sociology* [London: Routledge, 1948], p. 253.)

25. For examples of recent research see Donald Mackenzie and Judith Wajcman, eds., *The Social Shaping of Technology* (Milton Keynes, UK: Open University Press, 1985); and Wiebe Bijker, Thomas Hughes, and Trevor Pinch, eds., *The Social Construction of Technological Systems* (Cambridge: MIT Press, 1987).

26. Ursula Franklin, *The Real World of Technology* (the 1989 Massey lectures) (Montreal and Toronto: CBC Enterprises, 1990), pp. 23–24.

27. Stephen Marglin, "Towards the Decolonization of the Mind," in Marglin and Marglin, *Dominating Knowledge*, pp. 19–20; and his seminal paper, "What Do Bosses Do? The Origins and Function of Hierarchy in Capitalist Production," Part 1, *Review of Radical Political Economics*, no. 6 (1974).

28. Ellen Meiksins Wood, "The Separation of the Economic and the Political in Capitalism," *New Left Review*, no. 127 (1981).

29. Corrigan and Sayre, *The Great Arch*, pp. 187–188.

30. Ibid., p. 197.

31. Anthony Giddens, *The Nation-State and Violence* (Cambridge: Polity Press, 1985), especially Chapters 2–3.

32. Bruce Berman, "Perfecting the Machine: The Bureaucratic Ideologies of the State," *World Futures*, no. 28 (1990).

33. Merritt R. Smith, ed., *Military Enterprise and Technological Change* (Cambridge: MIT Press, 1985); David Noble, *Forces of Production: A Social History of Industrial Automation* (New York: Alfred Knopf, 1984); Kenneth Flamm, *Creating the Computer: Government, Industry and High Technology* (Washington, D.C.: Brookings Institution, 1988).

34. William McNeill, *The Pursuit of Power: Technology, Armed Force and Society Since 1000 AD* (Chicago: University of Chicago Press, 1982), Chapters 7–10; Samuel Finer, "State and Nation-Building in Europe: The Role of the Military," in Charles Tilly, ed., *The Formation of National States in Western Europe* (Princeton: Princeton University Press, 1975). See also the essays by O'Connell, Misa, Allison, and Noble in Smith, *Military Enterprise*.

35. Hettne, *Development Theory*, pp. 37–38. It should be added that there were as many failures as successes in the war-driven process of industrialization and nation-building in Europe. Historical maps of the continent are littered with polities that did not survive the competition. (See Tilly, *Formation of National States*, and McNeill, *Pursuit of Power.*)

36. On the distinctiveness of the feudalism of Western Europe and its influence on capitalist development, and the similarities, unique among non-Western societies, of feudalism, merchant capitalism, and state-building in Japan, see Perry Anderson, *Lineages of the Absolutist State* (London: New Left Books, 1975), especially pp. 435–461.

37. The contrast between the development of nationalism and national cultures in Western Europe and the elite nationalism of Africa is succinctly analyzed in Ben Anderson, *Imagined Communities: Reflections on the Origins and Spread of Nationalism* (London: New Left Books, 1983), especially Chapters 1–3 and 7.

38. See, for example, Charles Ambler, *Kenyan Communities in the Age of Imperialism* (New Haven: Yale University Press, 1988); and, on colonialism and the construction of ethnic identities, Anderson, *Imagined Communities*, Chapter 10.

39. John Lonsdale, "The Moral Economy of Mau Mau: Wealth, Poverty and Civic Virtue in Kikuyu Political Thought," in Bruce Berman and John Lonsdale, *Unhappy Valley: Conflict in Kenya and Africa* (London: James Currey; Athens: Ohio University Press, 1992).

40. However, as David Himbara shows in Chapter 4 of this book, the passion for accumulation of Kikuyu entrepreneurs is not in itself sufficient to ensure their effective managerial and technical capabilities.

41. Thus, a major element in the intense hostility of the British to what they called "Mau Mau" was their perception of it as an irrational and atavistic rejection of modernity and development. See Bruce Berman, "Nationalism, Ethnicity and Modernity: The Paradox of Mau Mau," *Canadian Journal of African Studies* 25, no. 2 (1991).

42. See, for example, CASTAFRICA II, *Science, Technology and Endogenous Development in Africa* (Paris: UNESCO, 1988). The growing gap between the use of computers and application of information technology in developed and developing societies has become an index of backwardness. Juan Rada, "Information Technology and the Third World," in Tom Forester, ed., *The Information Technology Revolution* (Cambridge: MIT Press, 1985).

43. Ian Smillie, *Mastering the Machine: Poverty, Aid and Technology* (Peterborough, Ont.: Broadview Press, 1991), pp. 166–168; see also Andrew Coulson,

"The Automated Bread Factory" and "Tanzania's Fertilizer Factory," in Andrew Coulson, ed., *African Socialism in Practice: The Tanzanian Experience* (Nottingham: Spokesman Books, 1979), pp. 175–190.

44. Mytelka, "Unfulfilled Promise," p. 88.

45. Raphael Kaplinsky, *The Economies of Small: Appropriate Technology in a Changing World* (London: IT Publications and Appropriate Technology International, 1990), pp. 145–147; Mytelka, ibid., pp. 83–84.

46. See the study by Steven Langdon of the impact of Western breakfast cereals in Kenya, "Multinational Corporations, Taste Transfer and Underdevelopment: A Case Study from Kenya," *Review of African Political Economy*, no. 2 (1975).

47. Kaplinsky, *Economies of Small*; Smillie, *Mastering the Machine*.

48. Charles Davis, Scott Tiffin, and Fola Osotimehin, "Developing Capacity in Management of Science, Technology and Innovation in Africa," paper presented at the conference of the Canadian Association of African Studies, Montreal, May 1992.

49. Susantha Goonatilake, *Aborted Discovery: Science and Creativity in the Third World* (London: Zed Books, 1984).

50. Basil Davidson, *The Black Man's Burden: Africa and the Curse of the Nation-State* (London: James Currey, 1992), pp. 99, 113–117, 162–165. See also Jean-François Bayart, *L'état en Afrique: La politique du ventre* (Paris: Fayart, 1989); and Robert Fatton, Jr., *Predatory Rule: State and Civil Society in Africa* (Boulder and London: Lynne Rienner, 1992).

51. The account of the colonial state in the following paragraphs is based on William Cohen, *Rulers of Empire: The French Colonial Service in Africa* (Stanford: Hoover Institution Press, 1971); Geoffrey Kay, *The Political Economy of Colonialism in Africa* (Cambridge: Cambridge University Press, 1972); Bruce Berman, "Structure and Process in the Bureaucratic States of Colonial Africa," *Development and Change* 15, no. 2 (1984); Anne Phillips, *The Enigma of Colonialism: British Policy in West Africa* (London: James Currey, 1989); and Berman, *Control and Crisis*.

52. The Tanzanian experience illustrates how state cadres equated socialist development with bureaucratic control, even in programs of "decentralization," their deep hostility toward popular initiatives, and their ability to turn the ostensible ruling party into another agency of state control. See Andrew Coulson, *Tanzania: A Political Economy* (Oxford: Clarendon Press, 1982), especially Chapters 21–23.

53. Mytelka, "Unfulfilled Promise," pp. 89–93, 104–105.

54. Kaplinsky, *Economies of Small*, pp. 204–205; Smillie, *Mastering the Machine*, pp. 230–232. The lack of expertise of African politicians and bureaucrats makes them easy prey for the high-pressure tactics of corporate vendors of technology. Not wishing to appear backward or willing to settle for second best, they are all too amenable to paying through the nose for what they are told is the very latest and best of Western technology. A particularly egregious example is the Tanzania Housing Bank, which was persuaded in 1984 to purchase four microcomputers at approximately US$32,439 each "on the incorrect understanding that the machines were compatible, cheaper, and more powerful than the auditing machines they were to replace" (Suzanne Grant Lewis and Joel Samoff, "Introduction," in Grant Lewis and Samoff, eds., *Microcomputers in African Development: Critical Perspectives* [Boulder: Westview Press, 1992], p. 14).

55. Smillie, *Mastering the Machine*, pp. 216–220; Kaplinsky, *Economies of Small*, pp. 171–173.

56. Grant Lewis and Samoff, "Introduction"; Bruce Berman, "The State, Computers and African Development: The Information Non-Revolution," in Grant

Lewis and Samoff, eds., *Microcomputers in African Development;* Per Lind, *Computerization in Developing Countries: Model and Reality* (London and New York: Routledge, 1991), pp. 7–8, 19–21.

57. Hettne, *Development Theory*, pp. 188–189.

58. Mytelka, "Unfulfilled Promise," p. 110.

59. Smillie, *Mastering the Machine*, pp. 171–176.

60. Hettne, *Development Theory*, pp. 193–194. See also Rudolfo Stavenhagen, "Ethnodevelopment: A Neglected Dimension in Development Thinking," in R. Apthorpe and A. Krahl, *Development Studies: Critique and Renewal* (Leiden: E. J. Brill, 1986).

61. Marglin, *Dominating Knowledge,* pp. 26–27.

62. Kaplinsky, *Economies of Small,* p. 221.

63. Hettne, *Development Theory*, pp. 249–251.

Contributors

Bruce J. Berman is professor of political studies at Queen's University in Kingston, Ontario. He is the author of *Control and Crisis in Colonial Kenya* (1990) and, with John Lonsdale, *Unhappy Valley: Conflict in Kenya and Africa* (1992). His current research focuses on the politics of knowledge in Africa and the role of technology in African development.

Deborah Brautigam is associate professor of political science at Columbia University, where she also directs the Economic and Political Development Program in the School of International and Public Affairs. She is the author of articles and chapters on the governance and economic performance, and on the comparative politics of industrialization in Africa and Asia.

Catherine Boone received her Ph.D. from MIT and is assistant professor of government at the University of Texas, Austin. She was a visiting scholar at the Harvard Academy of International and Areas Studies in 1991–1992 and has recently published *Merchant Capital and the Roots of State Power in Senegal, 1930–1985* (1992).

David Himbara was born in Rwanda and lived in Uganda and Kenya before coming to Canada. He received his Ph.D. from Queen's University and is preparing to take up a teaching post. He is the author of *Kenyan Capitalists, the State, and Development* (1994).

Colin Leys is professor of political studies at Queen's University. His publications include *Politicians and Policies in Acholi* (1965) and *Underdevelopment in Kenya* (1974). His most recent book is *Namibia's Liberation Struggle: The Two-Edged Sword* (1994), co-edited and co-authored with John Saul.

Paul M. Lubeck is professor of sociology and history at the University of California, Santa Cruz. He is the editor of *The African Bourgeoisie: Capitalist Development in Nigeria, Kenya and the Ivory Coast* (1987). His book, *Islam and Urban Labor in Northern Nigeria,* received the Herskovits prize in 1987. His current work assesses the impact of the electronics industry in the multi-ethnic state of Malaysia.

Janet MacGaffey is associate professor of anthropology at Bucknell University in Pennsylvania. She is the author of *Entrepreneurs and Parasites: The Struggle for Indigenous Capitalism in Zaire* (1987) and, most recently, *The Real Economy of Zaire,* with V. Mukohya, et al. (1992).

Sheila M. Nicholas recently finished her Ph.D. in the Department of Political Studies at Queen's University and is continuing her research on capitalist development in Africa.

Tom Ostergaard is with the Ministry of Foreign Affairs at Denmark. He received his Ph.D. in political studies at the University of Copenhagen, and was formerly a researcher at the Centre for Development Research in Copenhagen.

John Rapley received his Ph.D. from Queen's University and is currently a post-doctoral fellow and research associate at Queen Elizabeth House, Oxford. He is the author of *Ivoirien Capitalism: African Entrepreneurs in Côte d'Ivoire* (1993).

Michael J. Watts is professor of geography and development studies at the University of California, Berkeley. He is the author of several books including, most recently, *Reworking Modernity* (1992), with Alan Pred. He is working on a comparative study of the politics of agriculture in West Africa.

Index

265

About the Book

Recent debates have focused on the relative merits of state-led vs. market-oriented development strategies in Africa. Yet neither the state nor the market can accomplish anything independently of the caliber and distinctive trajectory of the indigenous entrepreneur class. This book breaks new ground in the study of this key dimension of African development, looking at the variations in the technical and political capabilities of Africa's diverse capitalist classes.

The authors discuss the specific functions that indigenous capitalists must perform to initiate and sustain a successful process of capital accumulation. Combining case studies based on recent fieldwork in East, West, and Central Africa with theoretical and comparative discussions, they point the way to a new research agenda in this field.